# Understanding Literary Theory
## SECOND EDITION

# UNDERSTANDING LITERARY THEORY
## SECOND EDITION

Sherman Sutherland
*Ohio University*

Sabino Falls
Tucson

*Senior Acquisitions Editor:* Paul Hasui
*Editorial Development:* George Daguaito
*Editorial Assistant:* Jennifer Andrews
*Production Manager:* Elizabeth Bradley
*Associate Production/Design Coordinator:* Christina Watkins
*Senior Cover Design Coordinator:* Renee Kelly-Leonard
*Senior Marketing Manager:* Calista Marcotte
*Marketing Assistant:* Jeremy Marcotte

*Cover design:* Teal Richardson/OhQue
*Cover image:* detail of *Natureza morta com livros e vela* Henri Matisse (1890)

---

Copyright © 2016 by Sabino Falls Publishing. All rights reserved.

No part of this work covered by the copyright herein may be reproduced, transmitted, stored or used in any form or by any means graphic, electronic, or mechanical, including but not limited to photocopying, recording, scanning, digitizing, taping, Web distribution, information networks, or information storage and retrieval systems, except as permitted under Sections 107 or 108 of the 1976 United States Copyright Act, without the prior written permission of the publisher.

Library of Congress Control Number: 2016954433
Cataloging-in-Publication Data
Sutherland, Sherman.
    Understanding literary theory / Sherman Sutherland.—2nd ed.
       p. cm.
    Includes bibliographical references and index.
    ISBN-13: 978-1-939-37507-0 (pbk. : alk. paper)
    ISBN-10: 1-939-37507-X (pbk. : alk. paper)
    1. Criticism.   2. Literature—History and criticism—Theory, etc.   I. Title
PN81.S88 2016
801—dc22                                                         2016954433

The policy of Sabino Falls Publishing is to use only paper from mills that operate under strict sustainable forestry guidelines, including Chain of Custody certification from the Forest Stewardship Council, the Sustainable Forestry Initiative and the Programme for the Endorsement of Forest Certification.

Find our books at your favorite retailer or visit us online at www.SabinoFalls.com

Printed in the United States of America

10 9 8 7 6 5 4 3 2

# Contents

| | |
|---|---|
| Preface | vii |
| Introduction | 1 |

## 1 Formalism — 8
### New Criticism — 8
- Summary — 8
- The Intentional Fallacy — 10
- The Timeless Nature of Literature — 12
- The Affective Fallacy — 13
- Close Reading — 14

### Russian Formalism — 15
- Summary — 15
- Symbolists vs. Futurists — 16
- The Moscow Linguistic Circle and *Opajaz* — 17
- Defamiliarization — 18
- The Bakhtin Circle — 21
- Dialogism — 22
- Heteroglossia — 23
- After Formalism — 24
- Implementation — 25
- Important Moments in Formalism — 26
- Important Terms — 27
- Study Questions — 28

## 2 Psychoanalysis — 30
- Summary — 30
- Sigmund Freud — 31
- The Text as Dream — 33
- After Freud — 35
- Jacques Lacan — 36
- Archetypal Criticism — 38
- Northrup Frye — 39

| | |
|---|---|
| Implementation | 41 |
| Important Moments in Psychoanalysis | 43 |
| Important Terms | 44 |
| Study Questions | 44 |

## 3 Marxism — 47

| | |
|---|---|
| Summary | 47 |
| The Roots of Marxism | 48 |
| Marx's Ideas | 49 |
| Marxism in Russia | 52 |
| Reflection Theory | 53 |
| The Frankfurt School | 54 |
| Cultural Hegemony | 56 |
| Ideological State Apparatuses | 58 |
| The Political Unconscious | 61 |
| Implementation | 63 |
| Important Moments in Marxism | 65 |
| Important Terms | 66 |
| Study Questions | 66 |

## 4 Feminism — 70

| | |
|---|---|
| Summary | 70 |
| Feminist Pioneers | 71 |
| Revolution | 72 |
| The First Wave | 74 |
| The Other Sex | 75 |
| The Second Wave | 76 |
| Reading from a Feminist Perspective | 78 |
| The Third Wave | 81 |
| Implementation | 82 |
| Important Moments in Feminism | 84 |
| Important Terms | 85 |
| Study Questions | 85 |

## 5 Structuralism — 90

### Structuralism — 90

| | |
|---|---|
| Summary | 90 |
| The Rules of Language | 91 |
| The Sign, the Signifier and the Signified | 92 |
| The Nature of Words | 93 |
| Barthes, Jakobson and Lévi-Strauss | 94 |

### Narratology — 96

| | |
|---|---|
| Summary | 96 |
| Vladimir Propp | 97 |
| Tzvetan Todorov | 99 |
| Modern Narratology | 100 |
| Implementation | 103 |

| | |
|---|---|
| Important Moments in Structuralism | 105 |
| Important Terms | 106 |
| Study Questions | 107 |

# 6 Post-Structuralism — 111
| | |
|---|---|
| Summary | 111 |
| The Death of the Author | 115 |
| Michel Foucault | 116 |
| Deconstruction | 117 |
| Deconstructing the Center | 121 |
| Implementation | 122 |
| Important Moments in Post-Structuralism | 124 |
| Important Terms | 124 |
| Study Questions | 125 |

# 7 Postmodernism — 128
| | |
|---|---|
| Summary | 128 |
| The Postmodern Period | 129 |
| Defining Postmodernism | 130 |
| Metanarratives | 130 |
| The Incredulity toward Metanarratives | 131 |
| The Rise of *le petit récit* | 133 |
| Deleuze and Guattari | 134 |
| Postmodern Hyperreality | 136 |
| Fredric Jameson | 138 |
| Modernism vs. Postmodernism | 140 |
| Implementation | 141 |
| Important Moments in Postmodernism | 142 |
| Important Terms | 143 |
| Study Questions | 143 |

# 8 Reader-Response Criticism — 147
| | |
|---|---|
| Summary | 147 |
| Why Worry about the Reader? | 148 |
| Before Reader-Response | 149 |
| Stanley Fish v. the Affective Fallacy | 150 |
| The Source of Meaning | 151 |
| Interpretive Communities | 152 |
| Reception Aesthetics | 153 |
| Filling the Gaps | 154 |
| Reception and History | 155 |
| The Horizon of Expectations | 155 |
| Reading Psychologically | 157 |
| Authorial Reading | 159 |
| Implementation | 161 |
| Important Moments in Reader-Response | 164 |
| Important Terms | 165 |

Study Questions ........................................... 165

## 9 New Historicism ................................... 167
Summary .................................................. 167
New Historicism: Defined? ............................. 169
Old vs. New Historicism ................................ 169
Foucault and Power ..................................... 171
Foucault and Discourse ................................. 172
Clifford Geertz: Culture as Text ....................... 173
Geertz's Thick Description ............................. 174
Implementation .......................................... 174
Important Moments in New Historicism ............. 177
Important Terms ......................................... 178
Study Questions ......................................... 178

## 10 Postcolonialism ................................. 182
Summary .................................................. 182
The Beginnings of Postcolonialism .................... 183
Voices from the Heart of Darkness ................... 185
Edward Said and Orientalism .......................... 186
The Silent Subaltern .................................... 188
Homi K. Bhabha and Hybridity ........................ 190
The Postcolonial West .................................. 191
Decoloniality ............................................. 192
Implementation .......................................... 193
Important Moments in Postcolonialism .............. 195
Important Terms ......................................... 196
Study Questions ......................................... 196

## 11 Ethnic Studies ................................... 200
### African American Criticism ....................... 201
Summary .................................................. 201
W.E.B. Du Bois .......................................... 203
The Role of African American Literature ............ 204
The Stages of African American Literature ......... 204
Signifyin(g) .............................................. 205
Reconsidering the Canon ............................... 207
Contemporary African American Criticism .......... 208
### Asian American Criticism ......................... 210
Summary .................................................. 210
Anti-Asian Bias .......................................... 212
Yellow Peril .............................................. 213
Yellowface ................................................ 214
The Problem with the "Model Minority" ............. 214
Frank Chin and Authenticity ........................... 215
### Latina/o Criticism .................................. 217
Summary .................................................. 217
Organizing the Latina/o Community ................. 218

|  |  |
|---|---|
| Latina/o Students Strike | 220 |
| Contemporary Latina/o Criticism | 220 |
| **Native American Criticism** | **222** |
| Summary | 222 |
| The Origins of Native American Criticism | 224 |
| Native American Literary Traditions | 225 |
| The Native American Literary Renaissance | 226 |
| Contemporary Native American Theory | 226 |
| Implementation | 230 |
| Important Terms | 231 |
| Study Questions | 231 |

## 12 Queer Theory — 242
- Summary — 242
- The History of Sexuality — 244
- Compulsory Heterosexuality — 246
- The Homosocial Continuum — 247
- Sexual Identity as a Performative Act — 248
- Implementation — 250
- Important Moments in Queer Theory — 252
- Important Terms — 253
- Study Questions — 253

## 13 Ecocriticism — 256
- Summary — 256
- The Beginnings of Ecocriticism — 257
- The Problem of Anthropocentrism — 258
- Ecofeminism — 259
- Ecosocialism — 261
- Deep Ecology — 261
- Social Ecology — 262
- Implementation — 263
- Important Moments in Ecocriticism — 264
- Important Terms — 266
- Study Questions — 266

## Stories
- Anton Chekhov: "Gooseberries" — 270
- Kate Chopin: "The Story of an Hour" — 279
- Edgar Allan Poe: "The Cask of Amontillado" — 283

## Glossary — 288
## Index — 298

# Preface

This book was conceived during a talk given by Anne Lamott. At one point, she mentioned an oft-repeated suggestion: Write the book that you wish was already available. I'd heard other writers offer various forms of the same advice but, for some reason, it resonated with me this time. As I considered my next book project, it occurred to me that the book I wished for most was a new introduction to literary theory.

Anybody who has taught a beginning theory course knows that students need clarification of many theoretical texts. In an ideal world, we would have enough class time for both a thorough lecture on each theoretical concept and a lengthy discussion on how those concepts work in practice. For over a decade, I searched for an introductory text to supplement the theoretical works I assigned. I wanted something that could clearly and accurately explain what the important ideas meant, why they mattered, and how they fit into the bigger picture. Every book I found fell short of my needs. Some were frustrating for my students to read, no clearer than the texts they tried to explain. Others offered explanations that were incomplete or completely inaccurate. All of them omitted at least one school of literary criticism that I felt was important. For example, while most of the more recent texts discuss African American criticism and postcolonialism, none of them include more than a passing mention of any other ethnic approach.

This book, then, grew out of the handouts I'd made for my students to supplement their supplementary readings. Each chapter begins with basic information about the theoretical approach it discusses: when it originated, what it focuses on and why, it's advantages and disadvantages, and its definition. The chapters end with a list of terms relevant to the theory, a timeline of important events in that approach's development, and a list of study questions that are intended to enhance one's understanding of each approach. There is also an implementation section in each chapter which demonstrates how the theory might be used. The appendices feature a few of the literary selections discussed in these implementation sections. The other works discussed are included in volume one of the Sabino Falls *Anthology of Short Fiction*.

My goal was to put together a book that explains the theoretical approaches that I discuss in my courses. It is my hope that others will find it helpful as well.

## Acknowledgements

A book like this is not possible without the help and support of numerous people.

I have enjoyed the fellowship of numerous friends and colleagues throughout the years who have assisted me by reading drafts, helping me to clarify my thoughts, or simply inspiring me in ways they can't imagine. These people come from an array of academic fields and they include Dee Anderson (Ohio University), Rami Arav (University of Nebraska), Iver Arnegard (Colorado State University), Lawrence Beemer (Hesser College), Becky Brooks (Ohio University), David Bruzina (University of South Carolina), David Burton (Ohio University), Michael Carroll (University of Nebraska), Thom Conroy (Massey University), Markos D'Quead (Mid-Plains College), Richard Duggin (University of Nebraska), Andrew Escobedo (Ohio University), Ellen Fangman (Creighton University), Carolyn Gascoigne (University of Nebraska), Barbara Grueser (Ohio University), Harland Hoffman (University of Nebraska), Doug Huston, (M.I.T.), Erin Joy (Metropolitan Community College), Daniel Kline (Ohio University), Steven Lovett (Creighton University), Dennis Lupher (Ohio University), Patrick Madden (Brigham Young University), Patrick Marton (Ohio University), Andrew McGreevy (Ohio University), John J. McKenna (University of Nebraska), Joseph McLaughlin (Ohio University), Zakes Mda (Ohio University), Robert Miklitsch (Ohio University), Scott Minar (Ohio University), Patrick Munhall (Ohio University), James Phelan (Ohio State University), John Price (University of Nebraska), Gerald Prince (University of Pennsylvania), David Raabe (University of Nebraska), Michael Ryan (Ohio State University), Thomas Scanlon (Ohio University), Ashley Seitz-Kramer (Westminster College), Robert Smith (University of Nebraska), Darrell Spencer (Southern Utah University), John Tapia (Missouri Western State University), James Taylor (University of Colorado), Candice Thomas-Maddox (Ohio University), Brian Tichota (University of Missouri), Tony Viola (Marshall University), Brian Vodehnal (University of Nevada), Karen Walker-Sparks (Ohio University), Matthew Wanat (Ohio University), Don Welch (University of Nebraska), Leon Widhalm (Oxford University), Eleanor

Williams (Johns Hopkins University), Sara Woods (University of Nebraska), and Rich Wyatt (University of Nebraska).

I would also like to thank all of my students over the years who served as willing test subjects as I completed this book. I am forever grateful to the teachers Aitken, Irene and Tom, who showed me how to read literature. Thank you to Ohio University for providing me the opportunity (and the libraries) to complete a work such as this.

I am particularly indebted to my first editor, Helen Chase, whose tireless efforts and meticulous work brought this book to life. Special thanks also to Paul Hasui and Jennifer Andrews for their continued support and unending patience throughout the editorial process.

Finally, I want to thank my family for their endless encouragement, and I wish to express my sincerest thanks to my daughters, Tara and Veda, who teach me every day about the importance of literature.

Thank you. I feel that this book is yours as much as it is mine.

# Introduction

Most of us, at one time or another, have probably uttered some variation of the following: "This book is good"; "That movie was bad"; or "That has to be the most stupid song I've ever heard in my entire life."

Our friends usually respond to these comments with a simple question: "Why?" Why is this book good? Why was that movie bad? Why is that song stupid? To answer, we offer our praises or complaints, proving our point with examples from the text (whether the text is a book, a movie or a song). This, in its simplest terms, is literary criticism: the evaluation and interpretation of literary works.

When we want to develop this criticism into a more sophisticated analysis, we use literary theory. Literary theory provides us with the frameworks to guide our understanding of a text. It is, in essence, a more refined way of answering that simple question: *Why?* Literary theory is the collection of concepts and strategies that guide our reading of literature. It comprises the various approaches to literary criticism and the ideologies that shape those approaches. It might help, then, to think of the branches of literary theory as tools we can use to delve more deeply into a text. Much like a paleontologist uses shovels, picks and trowels to uncover mysteries underground, a reader can use different theoretical approaches to uncover secrets within a text.

There are several branches of literary theory, each with its own unique body of thought. But these branches are not autonomous. Each theoretical approach either influences, evolves from, or reacts to one or another branch. Russian formalism, for example, developed into structuralism, which inspired post-structuralism, which helped shaped many of the theoretical approaches that followed. In this sense, the corpus of literary theory is like a large family. And, as in many families, there are occasional differences of opinion within its ranks.

While modern literary theory began around the turn of the twentieth century, literary criticism has been practiced in one form or another since at least the time of the ancient Greeks. We don't know exactly when it began because the earliest literary analysis is likely lost to time. Still, we have examples of criticism from Plato and Aristotle that survive today. When we consider that Greek drama likely has its roots in the Dionysian dithyrambs that predate even Thespis—and that biblical texts and Chinese poetry preceded these by centuries more—it would be reasonable to assume that some form of literary analysis took place well before our earliest existing texts.

Plato's literary interests were primarily in rhetoric. This is reflected in his body of work, especially *Republic* (c. 380 BCE) and dialogues such as *Gorgias* (c. 390 BCE) *Ion* (c. 390 BCE) and *Phaedrus* (c. 360 BCE). He spent little time with poetry and drama because he saw them as frivolous amusements that distracted one from the important search for truth. Aristotle had a different view. He saw the characters in a play as amalgamations of several different real people. For Aristotle, this meant that drama could serve as a distilled version of truth. A play could be, in other words, more true than actual truth. In *Poetics* (c. 335 BCE), Aristotle details his ideas on structure, characterization, and the essential elements of a dramatic performance. The work is considered one of the most important contributions to Western literary thought. Writers still utilize many of his ideas today.

Analysis of literature wasn't limited to Greece, however. In India, Bharata Muni, explored and explained drama. His book, *Nātya-śāstra* (c. 200 BCE-400 CE; trans. *A Compendium of Dramatic Arts*) outlines the ideal specifications of every aspect of a play, including the writing, the actors, the action, and even the stage dimensions. Rome's Horace offers his criteria for both poetry and drama in *Ars Poetica* (c. 15 BCE; trans. "The Art of Poetry"). Longinus, from either Rome or Greece (scholars aren't sure) wrote *On the Sublime* (c. 100-300 CE), in which he analyzes a thousand years' worth of literature and thought, including Homer, Plato and the book of *Genesis*. In Asia, Lu Ji presents the principles of Chinese poetics in *Wenfu* (c. 300 CE; trans. "On Literature").

And so it went for the next two millennia. Most of our surviving literary analyses written before the Common Era focus on either rhetoric or drama. From the dawn of the Common Era until the twentieth century, however, more emphasis is placed on poetry. Scholars see a number of reasons for this: advancements in the poetic form, the relative ease with which poetry could be reproduced (both orally and in print), etc. Much of the early Common Era analysis of poetry was produced in the non-Western world. Liu Xie's *The Literary Mind and the Carving of Dragons* (c. 520 CE) is still regarded as one of China's greatest works of literary aesthetics. al-Jāḥiẓ wrote over two hundred books, several of them on grammar, rhetoric and poetry. His *Kitab al-Bayan wa al-Tabyin* (c. 860; trans. *The Book of Eloquence and Exposition*) is seen as the beginning of literary criticism from the Islamic world. Rājaśekhara, from India, wrote *Kāvyamīmāṃsa* (c. 890) as a guide for poets to understand what constitutes good poetry.

Analysis of literature continued in the West in the Medieval Era and throughout the Renaissance and the Enlightenment. Dante's *Letter to Can Grande della Scala* (c. 1307), Sir Philip Sidney's *An Apology for Poetry* (c. 1579), Nicolas Boileau-Despréaux's *L'Art poétique* (1674; trans. *The Art of Poetry*), and Alexander Pope's *An Essay on Criticism* (1709)—written in rhyming heroic couplets—are all devoted to poetry. There are, of course, texts from these eras that discuss other genres as well. After the publication of Michel de Montaigne's *Essais* (1580; trans. *Essays*), some critics, such as Francis Bacon and Joseph Addison, turned their attention to the familiar essay. The Elizabethan plays of Shakespeare and his contemporaries reinvigorated the critical interest in dramatic works. Six decades later, John Dryden's *An Essay of Dramatic Poesy* (1668) argued that Shakespeare's oeuvre proves that the play is the artistic equivalent of the epic poem.

By the nineteenth century, literary analysis seemed to be more popular than ever. During this time, renowned works of criticism were produced by such literary luminaries as William Wordsworth, Samuel Taylor Coleridge, Percy Bysshe Shelley, John Keats, Ralph Waldo Emerson, Edgar Allan Poe, Matthew Arnold and Oscar Wilde, among others. Conspicuously absent from their discussions, though, was any prolonged discourse on fictional prose. Fiction had been established since at least the publication of Murasaki Shikibu's *The Tale of Genji* (c. 1010). Still, fiction was considered a lesser form of literature than other genres. While most intellectuals viewed poetry and drama as insightful artistic endeavors, they saw fictional works as mere entertainments, unworthy of critical inquiry. This began to change in the latter half of the nineteenth century. As fiction writers began to capture the serious issues of life and death with a more realistic lens, they gradually gained the attention of literary critics. A leading figure among these was Henry James, who would go on to write over one hundred reviews and critiques of fiction as well as dozens of his own acclaimed stories and novels. By the time James published his preeminent essay, "The Art of Fiction" (1884), he had already helped make fiction an acceptable subject of scholarly analysis.

As literary criticism moved into the twentieth century, it developed into the field of study that we have today. It is that study that this book focuses on. *Understanding Literary Theory* introduces you to a variety of modern theoretical approaches to literature. It is designed to show you how literary theorists analyze and interpret texts. We begin with the fundamentals set forth by formalist thinkers and end with the most recent advances in ecocriticism. In between, we examine the more popular approaches including feminism, new historicism, and post-structuralism, as well as less common approaches like narratology. Simply put, this book will introduce you to a diverse range of critical theories to help you refine your understanding of *why* you have the opinions that you do about a text.

As you progress through the chapters, you'll begin to notice that one theoretical approach might provide a more fruitful interpretation of one text, while a different school of theory might work best with another piece. You should keep in mind, though, that you can use any theoretical approach (or any combination of approaches) on any work of literature that you choose. Some theorists prefer to approach all works of literature from the same theoretical perspective—whether that perspective is new criticism, feminism, post-colonialism, psychoanalysis, etc. A Marxist, for example, might see signs of the struggle between rich and poor in every text he or she encounters, while a feminist might notice the subtle patriarchal influences permeating those same texts. One thing that keeps theoretical readings continually interesting is that each reader approaches a text from his or her own unique point of view. Still, these unique readings all share a common purpose: to uncover what's hidden within a text. When used skillfully, literary theory can provide new insight to a text and to the world around us.

This book is not meant to replace the primary works of theoretical scholarship that it describes. Rather, its intention is to introduce you to the various approaches that theorists use. In time, you will be able to apply these approaches to all types of texts (whether those texts are stories, advertisements, or jokes you hear at work). This book aims to be the first step toward a deeper understanding of any text you encounter.

## Great Moments in Literary Criticism from Plato to Henry James

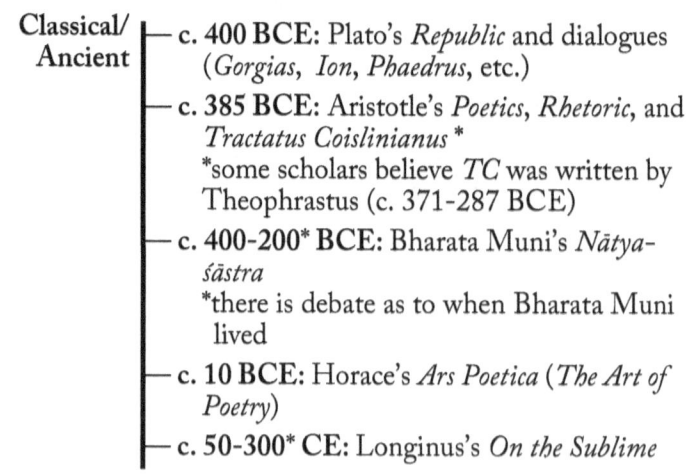

Classical/Ancient
- c. 400 BCE: Plato's *Republic* and dialogues (*Gorgias*, *Ion*, *Phaedrus*, etc.)
- c. 385 BCE: Aristotle's *Poetics*, *Rhetoric*, and *Tractatus Coislinianus* *
  *some scholars believe *TC* was written by Theophrastus (c. 371-287 BCE)
- c. 400-200* BCE: Bharata Muni's *Nātyaśāstra*
  *there is debate as to when Bharata Muni lived
- c. 10 BCE: Horace's *Ars Poetica* (*The Art of Poetry*)
- c. 50-300* CE: Longinus's *On the Sublime*

|  |  |
|---|---|
|  | *not much is known about Longinus, including his date of birth |
|  | — c. 300 CE: Lu Ji's *Wenfu* (*On Literature*) |
|  | — c. 500 CE: Liu Xie's *The Literary Mind and the Carving of Dragons* |
|  | — c. 860: Al-Jāḥiẓ's *Kitab al-Bayan wa al-Tabyin* (*The Book of Eloquence and Exposition*) |
|  | — c. 890: Rajashekhara's *Kavyamimamsa*a |
|  | — c. 1040: Bi Sheng (990–1051) develops moveable type for printing in China |
| Medieval |  |
|  | — c. 1320: Dante Alighieri's *Letter to Can Grande della Scala* (introduction to *Paradiso*) |
|  | — 1374: Giovanni Boccaccio's *Genealogia Deorum Gentilium* |
| Renaissance |  |
|  | — c. 1440: Johannes Gutenberg develops his moveable type printing press |
|  | — c. 1579: Sir Philip Sidney's *An Apology for Poetry* |
|  | — 1580: Michel de Montaigne's *Essais* |
|  | —1668: John Dryden's *An Essay of Dramatic Poesy* |
| Enlightenment |  |
|  | — 1711: Alexander Pope's *An Essay on Criticism* |
|  | — 1779-81: Samuel Johnson's *Lives of the Poets* |
|  | — 1790: Catharine Macaulay's *Letters on Education* |
|  | — 1791: Olympe de Gouges' *Déclaration des droits de la femme et de la citoyenne* |
|  | — 1792: Mary Wollstonecraft's *A Vindication of the Rights of Woman* |
| 19th Century |  |
|  | — 1808-1819: Coleridge's lectures on literature |
|  | — 1846: Edgar Allan Poe's "The Philosophy of Composition" |
|  | — 1850: William Wordsworth's *The Prelude* |
|  | — 1848: Karl Marx and Friedrich Engels' *Das Kommunistische Manifest* (*The Communist Manifesto*) |

├─ 1865: Matthew Arnold's *Essays in Criticism*
├─ 1884: Henry James' "The Art of Fiction"

## Selected Bibliography

Alighieri, Dante. *The Divine Comedy*. Trans. John Ciardi. New York: Norton, 2007.
Aristotle. *The Rhetoric and the Poetics of Aristotle*. New York: Modern Library, 1984.
—. *Poetics I with the Tractatus Coislinianus: A Hypothetical Reconstruction of Poetics II*. Indianapolis: Hackett, 1988.
Arnold, Matthew. *Essays in Criticism*. New York: Dent, 1966.
Boccaccio, Giovanni. *Boccaccio on Poetry: Being the Preface and the Fourteenth and Fifteenth Books of Boccaccio's Genealogia Deorum Gentilium*. Trans. Charles Grosvenor Osgood. Whitefish, MT: Literary Licensing, 2011.
Chi, Lu (Lu Ji). *The Art of Writing: Lu Chi's Wen Fu*. Minneapolis: Milkweed, 2000.
Cooper, Lane. *An Aristotelian Theory of Comedy: with an Adaptation of the* Poetics, *and a Translation of the* Tractatus Coislinianus. Ithaca: Cornell UP, 2009.
Dryden, John. *An Essay of Dramatic Poesy*. Charleston: BiblioLife, 2009.
Eagleton, Terry. *The Function of Criticism*. New York: Verso, 2006.
—. *The Significance of Theory*. New York: Blackwell, 1991.
—. *After Theory*. New York: Basic, 2004.
Foltz, Richard. *Religions of the Silk Road: Overland Trade and Cultural Exchange from Antiquity to the Fifteenth Century*. New York: Palgrave, 2000.
Gass, William H. *Fiction and the Figures of Life*. Boston: Goodine, 1989.
Gouges, Olympe de. *Déclaration des droits de la femme et de la citoyenne*. Paris: Mille et Une Nuits, 2003.
Griswold, Rufus Wilmot. *Passages from the Correspondence and Other Papers of Rufus W. Griswold [1898]*. Ithaca: Cornell UP, 2009.
Horace. *Epistles Book II and Ars Poetica*. Cambridge: Cambridge UP, 1990.
Hsieh, Liu (Liu Xie). *The Literary Mind and the Carving of Dragons: A Study Of Thought And Pattern In Chinese Literature*. Whitefish, MT: Literary Licensing, 2011.
James, Henry. *Theory of Fiction*. Lincoln: Nebraska UP, 1971.
Karl, Frederick R. *American Fictions 1940-1980: A comprehensive History and Critical Evaluation*. New York: Harper, 1983.

—. *American Fictions 1980-2000: Whose America is it Anyway?* New York: Xlibris, 2001.
Longinus, Dionysius Cassius. *On the Sublime.* Charleston: Nabu, 2010.
Macaulay, Catharine. *Letters on Education, With Observations on Religious and Metaphysical Subjects.* New York: Gale, 2002.
Montaigne, Michel de. *The Complete Essays.* New York: Penguin, 1993.
Muni, Bharata. *Natyashastra.* New Delhi: Munshiram, 1999.
Plato. *Early Socratic Dialogues.* New York: Penguin, 2005.
—. *Gorgias.* Indianapolis: Hackett, 1988.
—. *Phaedrus.* New York: Penguin, 2005.
—. *Plato's Ion and Meno.* Millis, MA: Agora, 1998.
—. *The Republic.* New York: Simon, 2011.
Poe, Edgar Allan. "The Philosophy of Composition." *Graham's American Monthly Magazine of Literature and Art*, 28.4 (April 1846). 163-67.
Pope, Alexander. *An Essay on Criticism.* Lenox, MA: Hardpress, 2010.
Prashar, Sadhana. *Kavyamimamsa of Rajasekhara.* New Delhi: DK Print World, 2000.
Sidney, Sir Philip. *An Apology for Poetry and Astrophil and Stella: Texts and Contexts.* Kimball, MI: College Publishing, 2001.
Wollstonecraft, Mary. *A Vindication of the Rights of Woman.* New York: Penguin, 1992.
Wordsworth, William. *The Prelude: Or, Growth of a Poet's Mind.* Oxford: Oxford UP, 1970.
Zhang, Xiumin. *The History of Chinese Printing.* Paramus: Homa and Sekey, 2009.

# 1

# Formalism

## NEW CRITICISM

**FOCUSES ON:** a close reading of all aspects of the text—but only the text—noting any poetic devices and all possible definitions of individual words.

**BECAUSE:** New Critics believe that a quality literary work has an organic wholeness and unity, and that its parts all work together to serve the text's one true meaning.

**DEVELOPED IN:** 1920s.

**NOTABLE PRACTITIONERS:**
- John Crowe Ransom (1888-1974)
- F.R. [Frank Raymond] Leavis (1895-1978)
- Robert Penn Warren (1905-89)
- Cleanth Brooks (1906-94)
- Monroe Beardsley (1915-85)
- I.A. [Ivor Armstrong] Richards (1893-1979)
- Allen Tate (1899-1979)
- Sir William Empson (1906-1984)
- W.K. [William Kurtz] Wimsatt, Jr. (1907-75)

**IMPORTANT PREDECESSORS:**
- Sir Philip Sidney (1554-86)
- Matthew Arnold (1822-88)
- Oscar Wilde (1854-1900)
- Samuel Taylor Coleridge (1772-1834)
- T.S. [Thomas Stearnes] Eliot (1888-1965)

**ADVANTAGES:** provides a systematic method for analyzing a literary text as a timeless work of art.

**DISADVANTAGES:** by ignoring extra-textual elements such as historical and biographical information, a new critical approach will often overlook the work's context and allusions to non-literary subject matter.

**DEFINITION:** the practice of interpreting a literary work through thorough analysis of the text itself, disregarding outside elements (such as historical and biographical information) in an effort to find the text's one correct meaning.

---

New criticism was, in America and Britain, the foremost school of literary analysis for the first half of the twentieth century. While other theoretical approaches had begun to take shape by this time—and many can trace their roots to before new criticism's development—new criticism enjoyed its leading status well into the 1950s.

The term, *new criticism*, was coined by John Crowe Ransom in his book, *The New Criticism* (1941). New criticism as an approach to literature, though, had been in use well before this. Some would argue that I.A. Richards' *Principles of Literary Criticism* (1925) heralded the beginning of new criticism. Others suggest that new criticism began several years earlier, with T.S. Eliot's essay, "Hamlet and His Problems" (1919). Eliot, however, wasn't a proponent of new criticism, calling it "the lemon-squeezer school of criticism." While some might dispute when it began, we can't deny that new criticism brought about an overwhelming change to the study of literature.

The first New Critics advocated an objective, rather than subjective, form of criticism. They were in search of a systematic (and, they would argue, scientific) method with which to analyze literature. Before new criticism, literary analysis in the English-speaking world was an undisciplined—and sometimes haphazard—practice. There were literary scholars, of course (people have been analyzing literature since before Plato), but there was no organized "school" of literary theory like we have today. Before new criticism, a literary critique might focus on any number of things: the author's biographical information, the time of the text's composition, the state of the author's world when the text was written, etc. All manner of outside influences could factor into the critique of a literary work. Common, too, before the rise of new criticism, was what some would call an "appreciative criticism" that functioned mainly to extol the virtues of a worthy work of literature. The early New Critics sought to change this and to standardize the study of literature.

If good literature has artistic value, the New Critics reasoned, then we should be able to develop a set of criteria with which to measure that value. Some of the early new criticism scholarship, then, is focused on identifying these criteria and applying them to a variety of literary works. An early text in this vein is Sir William Empson's *Seven Types of Ambiguity* (1930; first published in the U.S. in 1947). As the title implies, Empson identified seven different types of ambiguity that can operate within a literary text:

1) "when a detail is effective in several ways at once" (a metaphor, for example)
2) when "two or more alternative meanings are fully resolved into one" (often the use of two different metaphors to describe the same thing)
3) "two apparently unconnected meanings are given simultaneously" (puns, allegory, etc.)
4) "alternative meanings combine to make [an idea] clear"
5) "a fortunate confusion, as when the author is discovering his idea in the act of writing" (often takes the form of a simile connecting two different statements).
6) when "what is said is contradictory or irrelevant and the reader is forced to invent interpretations."
7) a "full contradiction, marking a division in the author's mind" (similar to the fourth ambiguity, except the contradiction is never resolved in the text).

*Seven Types of Ambiguity* was groundbreaking in several respects, most notably, perhaps, in that it initiated the close reading of literary texts, a hallmark of new criticism that is still practiced today. Almost immediately, the book made Empson a leading figure of the new criticism movement. (Though, later in his career, Empson found himself at odds with some aspects of new criticism—particularly with regard to authorial intent).

The primary focus of Empson's book is poetry, as was the case with many early new criticism texts. The original New Critics were a diverse group of intellectuals with no formally established doctrine to unite them, but they all shared a common belief in the superiority of poetry. Many of these early New Critics were either poetry scholars or poets themselves—or both—and this interest guided the early new criticism. Poetry enjoyed a privileged position among the early New Critics because, to them, poetry is the purest expression of literary art. Fiction, though, had been steadily gaining legitimacy since Henry James' "The Art of Fiction," and early modern writers like Chekhov, Joyce and Woolf helped solidify fiction's status as a literary form worthy of thoughtful study. As new criticism developed into a unified, if amorphous, body of study, the same methods that were used to analyze poetry were also applied to other literary genres. Eventually, the word *poetry* was used by the New Critics to describe quality literature in any form.

## The Intentional Fallacy

The guiding principles of new criticism are, for the most part, the result of one prevailing belief: a literary text, according to the New Critics, is an autonomous work of art, existing by itself and independent from its history and its author. As W.K. Wimsatt and Monroe Beardsley put it, the literary work, once written, is not the author's (it is detached from the author at birth and goes about the world beyond his power to intend about it or control it). The poem belongs to the public.

Inherent in this belief are a number of conclusions. If good literature is timeless, as the New Critics suggest, then it's unnecessary to learn anything about when the text was written. If good literature is autonomous, then any information about the author becomes irrelevant. All meaning, then, must be contained within the text and, if this is true, the text must have one "correct" meaning and it is the job of the intelligent critic to interpret that meaning for everyone else.

Of these conclusions, primary importance was ascribed to the independent nature of the text itself. Most New Critics believed, to varying degrees, that the only thing necessary for literary analysis (besides a thorough understanding of literature) is the literary text itself. This idea was given voice by Wimsatt and Beardsley "The Intentional Fallacy" (1946). In the first paragraph, they summarize the New Critics' credo:

> the design or intention of the author is neither available nor desirable as a standard for judging the success of a work of literary art.

To expand on this, "The Intentional Fallacy" identifies three types of evidence available for interpreting a work of literature:

1) internal evidence, which is the text itself and includes its form and any artistic and poetic devices, as well as the various definitions of each individual word.
2) external evidence, which, as Beardsley and Wimsatt describe it, "consists of revelations (in journals, for example, or letters or reported conversations) about how or why the poet wrote the poem—to what lady, while sitting on what lawn, or at the death of what friend or brother)"
3) contextual evidence (often details about the author's other work or about the author's life which would, supposedly, contextualize the piece in question)

Wimsatt and Beardsley argue that the first type of evidence (internal evidence) is always an acceptable source for critical analysis. The second type (external evidence) is never acceptable, and belongs in the category of literary biography. The third type (contextual evidence) is acceptable, but it's easy to confuse contextual evidence with external evidence. The type of contextual evidence that Beardsley and Wimsatt are interested in mainly involves "meanings attached to words or topics by an author or by a coterie of which he is a member." To put it simply, again, what they are concerned with are the words on the page.

(As we'll see later in this text, the post-structuralists also maintained a singular focus on only the text, but for very different reasons. While the New Critics believed that a discussion of the author's intention might interfere with our ability to discover the text's one true meaning, the post-structuralists worried that such a discussion would *limit* the text to only one interpretation. The post-structuralists hoped to uncover as many equally-valid interpretations as possible; the New Critics, by contrast, were always in search of a text's one correct meaning.)

Wimsatt and Beardsley knew that their ideas regarding the intentional fallacy would be met with resistance (particularly from scholars like Empson). After all, while it makes sense to ignore the author when considering a writer like Homer—a person (or persons) we know very little about—we also have many authors about whom we know a great deal. Can't we consider their intentions? What if, for example, we found an essay the author wrote, titled, "This is what this poem means"? Mightn't that change our understanding of the work? Wimsatt and Beardsley would say No. Even if we had such an essay, we would have no way of knowing if the author—consciously or not—was lying. And, even so, such an essay wouldn't change the words on the page. Remember, according to the New Critics, once the text is written, it no longer belongs to the author; it becomes, in a sense, public property left for everyone else to interpret. Many of the New Critics viewed literary genius as less a product of a human author than of divine inspiration. How can a simple author, then, be trusted to explicate his or her own work? True literary analysis was a job for experts who were well-versed in the art of literature. Besides, the New Critics argued, if the poem is successful, then the intention is clear; if the author needs to explain his intention, then the poem is ineffective.

## The Timeless Nature of Literature

Good literature, the New Critics believed, speaks to universal truths—truths that are relevant to people from any culture and any time. For Wimsatt and Beardsley, this belief shaped another characteristic of a new criticism reading. In a footnote to "The Intentional Fallacy," they claim:

> the history of words *after* a poem is written may contribute meanings which if relevant to the original pattern should not be ruled out by a scruple about intention

If literature is truly timeless, Wimsatt and Beardsley are saying, then we must consider all connotations of the words in a text, even when we know, philologically speaking, that the author couldn't have possibly had certain definitions in mind. These new definitions, in fact, could add a depth to our understanding of a poem that we wouldn't have otherwise considered.

The implication here is that, when Polonius says in *Hamlet*, "This is the very ecstasy of love," we should read the word, "ecstasy," to mean not just "madness," which is what ecstasy meant in Shakespeare's time, but we should also read ecstasy in the context of our current meaning. After all, If we hope to decipher the one correct meaning from a text, then we must consider all the possible definitions of the words within that text. And, if great literature is timeless, Wimsatt and Beardsley argue, then what a word means today should be just as relevant to a thorough interpretation as what the word meant hundreds of years ago. Most New Critics would suggest that we simply ignore those definitions that don't contribute to the organic unity of the work. But they would also argue that, if we thoughtfully consider these more recent definitions, it's much more likely that we will see how these new connotations can enhance our understanding of the work.

For some scholars, though, Wimsatt and Beardsley's assertion is problematic. Another look at Shakespeare can illustrate their reservations. As one example, when Lady Capulet wants to know if Juliet is busy, she asks, "What, are you busy, ho?" This last word, while a mere exclamation in Elizabethan England, has an entirely different meaning today. Still, is it irrelevant? The New Critic might point out that, at this point in the play, Juliet has already secretly married Romeo while she has another suitor, Paris, who expects to be her husband. For many New Critics, then, our modern contextual understanding of Lady Capulet's question could be a relevant source for analysis.

Beardsley revisits this idea in his later book, *The Possibility of Criticism* (1970). To prove his point, Beardsley uses a line from Mark Akenside's 1744 poem, *The Pleasures of Imagination*:

> Which fill'd himself, he rais'd his plastic arm

Even though plastic, as we know it, was still centuries away when Akenside wrote his poem, Beardsley argues that our contemporary understanding of the word, *plastic*, is still relevant as we read this poem today. His argument, in essence, is, since it would be impossible to ascribe our contemporary understanding of the word, *plastic*, to the category of external evidence that Wimsatt and Beardsley describe in "The Intentional Fallacy," then *plastic* (as we understand it today) must be considered internal evidence, making it a worthy subject for analysis.

While not all new Critics fully shared Beardsley's view, this was nevertheless a key idea in new criticism.

## The Affective Fallacy

The scholars associated with new criticism occasionally had minor disagreements involving the intricacies of new criticism philosophy (frequently these disagreements presented themselves in back and forth exchanges in scholarly journals). One such disagreement involved the role of the reader in the interpretation of a text. I.A. Richards' background in psychology colored his approach to literary analysis and, while at Cambridge, he began to consider that the reader actually had an active role in shaping the meaning of the text. Richards gave his students a variety of poems to read—some written by recognized masters, others from beginning and novice poets—and then he analyzed the students' reactions. Richards identified several difficulties that students have while reading a text and these findings would go on to influence his analysis of literature. (These preliminary studies would eventually take shape, in the 1970s, as reader-response criticism.)

Wimsatt and Beardsley, however, disagreed with this type of approach. They voiced this disagreement in the form of their essay, "The Affective Fallacy" (1949). In it, they argued again for a critical approach that focuses on only the literary text and against, in this case, an approach that examines the affect the text has upon the reader. The epigraph to their essay, a quote from Eduard Hanslick, sums up their feelings on an affective reading of a literary text: "We might as well study the properties of wine by getting drunk." An affective reading, they argued, pulled the conversation away from an objective discussion and left it to the whims of the varied emotional responses of individual readers.

This essay didn't enjoy the same success as their earlier effort, "The Intentional Fallacy," but this may have been due more to the fact that relatively few scholars, at this time, had any interest in utilizing a reader-centered approach to analysis.

## Close Reading

While new criticism doesn't enjoy the prominence it did in the early half of the twentieth century, one development from new criticism that has been used by nearly every subsequent literary theory is the close reading of a text. A close reading provides a step-by step method for analyzing a work of literature. It is an in-depth analysis of a short work or of several short passages from a longer work.

At its most basic, a close reading is a three-step process of observation, interpretation and communication. It begins with reading the work from beginning to end and highlighting, in the process, any words, images or ideas that stand out for any reason. Perhaps an unknown word is used, or a common word is used in an uncommon way; maybe an image is particularly effective—or maybe it's confusing. In this step, we also take note of the overall tone of the piece, as well as any literary elements used, including, but not limited to:

images, figurative language (symbols, similes, metaphors), tone, repetition, rhythm, word order, style, characterization, diction, paradoxes, omissions, sensory details, viewpoint, audience, word order, punctuation.

The next part of observation involves further analysis of everything that was highlighted earlier. Here, we should have a good dictionary at hand as we note every definition of our highlighted words. This is also the step where we scrutinize our highlighted images, ideas and poetic devices, making notes within the text. At the end of this step, well over half of the text should be annotated in some way.

The second step is to interpret what we uncovered in our first step. What have we learned from our observations, in other words? Have we seen this image before? If so, where? What does this idea remind us of? Is there a dominant metaphor? Do the poetic devices reinforce or contradict the content of the piece? How might different definitions of individual words enhance our understanding of the piece? How might the poetic devices contribute to the organic unity of the whole work?

Finally, after thorough observation and interpretation, the third step of a close reading is communication. Here, we are sharing our findings with like-minded peers. This step may take the form of a student's critical essay, an explication in a scholarly journal, or a book-length analysis from a literary scholar. As this communication is part of an ongoing conversation, it is our responsibility to see what has already been said (in the form of scholarly articles and analysis) before we join that conversation.

## RUSSIAN FORMALISM

**FOCUSES ON:** the text itself, primarily with regard to its literary devices.
**BECAUSE:** Russian Formalists were primarily interested in the fundamental components of a literary piece and how they work together.
**DEVELOPED IN:** 1915.
**NOTABLE PRACTITIONERS:**
    Boris Tomashevsky (1890-1957)  Pavel Medvedev (1892-1938)
    Viktor Shklovsky (1893-1984)  Yury Tynyanov (1894-1943)
    Valentin Voloshinov (1895-1936)  Vladimir Propp (1895-1970)
    Mikhail Bakhtin (1895-1975)  Boris Eikhenbaum (1896-1959)
    Roman Jakobson (1896-1982)  Grigory Gukovsky (1902-50)
**IMPORTANT PREDECESSORS:**
    Edmund Husserl (1859-1938)    Vladimir Mayakovsky (1893-1930)
**ADVANTAGES:** reveals the poetic devices in a piece of literature and how they work.

**DISADVANTAGES:** the focus on literary devices can come at the expense of the work's content and its historical and biographical context.

**DEFINITION:** a literary theory developed in Russia that aimed to apply an objective and scientific approach to the study of literature, focusing primarily on artistic and technical devices within the text itself and ignoring, for the most part, outside elements such as biographical, political and historical information.

---

While new criticism was changing the study of literature in the United States and Britain, Russian formalism was shifting the theoretical conversation in Russia. Russian formalism took shape about a decade before new criticism and, through its practitioners, helped spawn structuralism and narratology. It began as two separate but related groups: the Moscow Linguistic Circle and a group in Petrograd (today's Saint Petersburg) called the Society for the Study of Poetic Language (often referred to by its Russian acronym *Opojaz*). A third group we commonly associate with the formalists, the Bakhtin Circle, formed a few years later and arrived, in 1924, in Petrograd (by then named Leningrad).

Russian formalism arose in an environment of literary change in Russia. Throughout the late nineteenth century and into the twentieth, the Symbolist movement dominated the literary conversation. Russia's Symbolists followed a similar path as their European Symbolist counterparts, adhering to the same tenets outlined in Jean Moréas' "Symbolist Manifesto" published in Paris:

> In this art, scenes from nature, human activities, and all other real world phenomena will not be described for their own sake; here, they are perceptible surfaces created to represent their esoteric affinities with the primordial Ideals.

The Symbolists, in other words (as their name suggests) saw in words and images their poetic potential to represent something else. A work of literature, to the Symbolists, spoke to universal truths through imagery and symbolic thought. True literary genius, to the Symbolists and many of Russia's academics, was less the result of a writer's hard work than a product of divine inspiration.

## Symbolists vs. Futurists

By 1910, the poets and writers from two avant-garde groups of artists, the Acmeists and the Futurists, had begun to express dissatisfaction with the views of the Symbolist movement. They found the Symbolists' preference for vagueness and ambiguity to be outdated and stifling, and their understanding of the creative process to be misguided. Vladimir Mayakovsky would later sum up the Futurists' argument in his essay, "How Verses are Made" (1926; trans. 1970). To Mayakovsky, poetry was a "production" and the poet was a "craftsman" rather than, as the Symbolists seemed to believe, a "guardian of mystery."

The Futurists, much more than the Acmeists, hoped for a complete break from Russia's literary past, issuing their own manifesto titled, "A Slap in the Face of Public Taste" (1912). In it, they called for throwing "Pushkin, Dostoevsky, Tolstoy, etc., etc. overboard from the Ship of Modernity" and demanded the right to modernize poetry and the poet's vocabulary, as well as the right to "feel an insurmountable hatred for the language" preferred by the Symbolists. They also expressed an uncompromising distaste for Symbolist authors, denouncing by name many of Russia's most popular contemporary writers, including Andreyev, Blok, Gorky and Sologub. It was in this environment, still two years before the 1917 Revolution, that Russian formalism came to be.

## The Moscow Linguistic Circle and *Opajaz*

Russian formalism had modest beginnings. It started, in 1915, with a group of students from Moscow University meeting to discuss issues of linguistics. These meetings, organized by Filip Fortunatov and inspired by the work of scholars like Edmund Husserl and Ferdinand de Saussure, soon became regular. Today, we might describe this early incarnation of the Moscow Linguistic Circle as an intense study group comprised of enthusiastic students who would eventually become leading scholars in their chosen fields. Other students in this group included Petr Bogatyrev Grigory Vinokur and Roman Jakobson. Jakobson was close friends with two leaders of the Futurist movement, Mayakovsky and Velimir Khlebnikov, and he attended many meetings of their group. Mayakovsky, in turn, went to numerous Moscow Linguistic Circle meetings. These friendships had a profound effect on the direction of the Moscow Linguistic Circle, reinforcing the Circle's interest in literary issues and shaping much of the group's research and scholarship (and acerbic tone).

A year later, in Petrograd, a similar society formed. This group, the *Opajaz*, was composed of literary theorists (Boris Eikhenbaum, Viktor Shklovsky) as well as students from Petrograd University (Leo Jakubinsky, Yevgeny Polivanov) who studied under the famed linguist Jan Baudouin de Courtenay. Owing to the literary theorists in their group, the *Opojaz* had a literary interest from the start. It wasn't long before both groups (the Moscow Linguistic Circle and the *Opojaz*) shared some of the same members (Boris Eikhenbaum and Boris

Tomashevsky) and the two groups came to complement each other and grow in a similar direction.

This direction was in opposition to the principles of the established Symbolist movement and it was this opposition that led to a growing rivalry between the Symbolists and the Formalists. Like the Futurists, the Formalists disagreed with the Symbolists' views of both poets and poetry. The Formalists expanded on Mayakovsky's belief that poetry was crafted by human beings rather than divinely inspired. Following this line of reasoning, it was logical, then, to be able to study the tools of this craft—words—with the same rigor and scrutiny as any scientific study. The Futurists, being mainly poets and artists with little background in formal linguistics, weren't interested in engaging in such comprehensive study. The Formalists, though, with their intensive training in linguistics and literary theory, were eager (and capable) to take on the task.

In "The Theory of the Formal Method" (1926), Boris Eikhenbaum outlines seven tenets of the formalist movement:

1) that literature is autonomous, and should be viewed as independent from its history and its author
2) that literature can—and should—be studied as a science
3) that this scientific method should focus on linguistics
4) that poetic language differs from practical language
5) that this difference is due to the use of literary devices
6) that structure and method are critical components of a literary text
7) that the arrangement of a literary text's parts is a fundamental feature of that text.

The Formalists shared with the New Critics the belief in the autonomous nature of a literary text. The New Critics, though, used this belief to discern a text's singular meaning. The Formalists, on the other hand, were less concerned with meaning than with how a text was constructed to create that meaning. In "Art as Technique" (1917), Shklovsky sums up the Formalist approach to meaning: "Art is a means of experiencing the process of creativity. The artifact itself is quite unimportant."

## Defamiliarization

Working from a linguistic perspective, the Formalists began by breaking literary works down to their constituent parts. (They worked primarily with poetry in their early years but expanded into prose later.) Shklovsky is given credit for recognizing a clear difference between poetic language and practical language. Practical language is what we use to convey information:

"The house is on fire."
"Turn left at the next light."
"I love you."

Practical language is (ideally) clear and direct. Its purpose, again, is to provide information. Poetic language, on the other hand, is indirect. While it may also convey information, the primary purpose of poetic language is to obscure its topic. Shklovsky called this process "defamiliarization." By taking the familiar and making it unfamiliar (or "making it strange"), poetic language, in effect, rouses the reader to take notice. Instead of simply saying, "I love you," for example, Elizabeth Barrett Browning says,

> How do I love thee? Let me count the ways.
> I love thee to the depth and breadth and height
> My soul can reach, when feeling out of sight
> For the ends of Being and ideal Grace.
> I love thee to the level of everyday's
> Most quiet need, by sun and candlelight.

Or we could imagine a war correspondent reporting on the events of the Crimean War and then compare that to Tennyson's poetic description:

> Flash'd all their sabres bare,
> Flash'd as they turn'd in air
> Sabring the gunners there,
> Charging an army while
> All the world wonder'd:
> Plunged in the battery-smoke
> Right thro' the line they broke;
> Cossack & Russian
> Reel'd from the sabre-stroke,
> Shatter'd & sunder'd.
> Then they rode back, but not,
> Not the six hundred.

A literary text, according to Shklovsky, also defamiliarized its subject through the rearrangement of its story elements. In life, events progress one after another, chronologically. In literature, though, these events are not always presented in the same chronological order (common examples from popular cinema are *Pulp Fiction* and *Memento*). In recognition of this fact, Shklovsky conceptualized *fabula* and *syuzhet*. *Fabula* is usually translated simply as "story," but it more accurately describes all of the events in a literary text; *syuzhet* (translated as "discourse" by narratologists) refers to how those events are organized and presented in the text. While the difference between the two might seem like common sense to students today, this wasn't the case a century ago.

Identifying *fabula* and *syuzhet* led to the Formalist realization that the constructed form of a work was inseparable from its content; both were intricately intertwined in the process of defamiliarizing the artistic subject.

According to Shklovsky and Jakobson, this defamiliarization is necessary—and therefore art is necessary—because we are inclined to become too familiar with our surroundings. If, on our daily walk, we encounter the same thing every day, eventually we will no longer *see* it. We become automatized to our surroundings. Literature, Shklovsky says, is "created to remove the automatism of perception." It forces us to look at things more closely—and thus see them anew—by presenting them in a way that makes them unfamiliar. It accomplishes this through the use of its poetic language.

The Formalists saw that what made poetic language poetic—what gave it its "literariness," as Jakobson described it—was the use of poetic devices like rhyme, rhythm, metaphor, etc. (They distinctively included the *sound* of words in this category as well.) It was therefore these devices (as well as their linguistic elements) that the Formalists focused on. They argued, too, that these poetic devices were what every literary theorist should focus on (in contrast to the approach of the Symbolists and many of their contemporary academic scholars). In *Modern Russian Poetry* (1921), Jakobson makes his case with typical Formalist flair:

> The object of the science of literature is not literature, but literariness—that is, that which makes a given work a work of literature. Until now. literary historians have preferred to act like the policeman who, intending to arrest a certain person, would, at any opportunity, seize any and all persons who chanced into the apartment, as well as those who passed along the street. The literary historians used everything—anthropology, psychology, politics, philosophy.

To the Formalists, literary history wasn't the study of how a literary work fits into a categorical segment of human history, but how the accumulation of literary devices has shaped literature throughout time. How has stream-of-consciousness writing developed over the years, for example, and how has it led to other narrative effects? By focusing on only the text and examining these devices of literature, we are able to understand how literature works, and this, to the Formalists, was what's important. What they found was that literary devices interrupt our perception, thereby slowing down our experience and forcing us to understand commonplace items in a new way. Literariness, in other words, generates defamiliarization, and defamiliarization is a product of art.

Unfortunately, in the decades after the Revolution, it became increasingly unacceptable to ignore historical, political and social issues. In *Literature and Revolution* (1924), Leon Trotsky devotes an entire chapter to outlining the deficiencies of the "extremely arrogant and immature" Formalist school. His primary complaint stems from the Formalist belief in the autonomy of art. As Trotsky sees it, Formalism is "the only theory which has opposed Marxism in Soviet Russia [. . .] Formalism opposed Marxism with all its might theoretically." The adversarial tone that the Formalists adopted to gain followers in their earlier years earned them many "enemies" (Eikhenbaum's term) among Russia's established (and respected) writers and intellectuals. As Russia grew into Stalin's Soviet Union, these adversaries had little sympathy for the Formalists as they faced increasing censure from the government.

## The Bakhtin Circle

The changes in the literary climate, though, didn't happen until several years after the transfer of power was complete. In the years immediately following the Revolution, the Formalists and the Futurists enjoyed a privileged status because Lenin's minister of education had close ties with Mayakovsky's Futurist group. The Russian arts community was as vibrant as ever. Though long prose works were less common in this period (due to shortages of paper on which to print them), poets and theorists alike found receptive live audiences throughout Russia's cities.

It was during this time, in 1918, that the Bakhtin Circle was formed in Nevel, a Russian town about three hundred miles west of Moscow and three hundred miles south of Petrograd. Early members of the group included Pavel Medvedev, Valentin Voloshinov, and the group's namesake, Mikhail Bakhtin. While there is some debate now whether Bakhtin actually graduated from Petrograd University as he claimed, we do know that, in 1918, he was teaching at a school in Nevel. Soon, he began to meet regularly with his circle to discuss literature, politics and philosophy. In its early years, the Bakhtin Circle was more of a philosophical group than a literary one. This began to change after 1924 when Bakhtin moved to Petrograd (by then named Leningrad). In Leningrad, Bakhtin became familiar with the ideas of the Formalists. It wasn't long before Bakhtin's interests veered more specifically toward language and literature.

Much of Bakhtin's major work wasn't published until several decades after it was written, for a variety of reasons. "Towards a Philosophy of the Act," completed in 1919, wasn't published until 1986. *Rabelais and his World*, written to be Bakhtin's doctoral thesis, was deemed unacceptable by his committee and wasn't published until 1965. And, what we now consider Bakhtin's most groundbreaking work, *The Dialogic Imagination*, wasn't published in full until 1975 (though the four essays that comprise the book were each published earlier). Medvedev and Voloshinov, however, enjoyed a good deal of publishing success in the 1920s. At least, we think they did. A few scholars argue that the works by Medvedev and Voloshinov were actually written by Bakhtin and attributed to his colleagues so the texts would get published (unlike Bakhtin, Medvedev and Voloshinov were members of the Communist party and—at least until Stalin's purges—benefitted in various ways from their membership). Besides several academic essays attributed to him, Medvedev is also listed as the author of *The Formal Method in Literary Scholarship* (1928). Voloshinov published *Freudianism: A Marxist Critique* (1926) and *Marxism and the Philosophy of Language* (1929). The only major work attributed to Bakhtin during this time was his *Problems of Dostoyevsky's Art* (1929). Unfortunately, Bakhtin was accused of anti-communist activities later that year and exiled for six years in Kazakhstan.

## Dialogism

While Bakhtin is most often categorized as a Formalist, he disagreed with some of formalism's fundamental concepts. Like Trotsky and the Symbolists, Bakhtin believed that a work's content and context shouldn't be ignored. But Bakhtin had very different reasons for this view. As he explains in "Discourse in the Novel," Bakhtin believes that all language—including the language in a literary text—is dialogic. What he means is, language results from a dialogue between a speaker and a listener. Bakhtin notes that previous theorists have always postulated a monologic language; in a monologic language, a singular voice works to constrain each word in the language to only one specific meaning: a word is spoken by a speaker and it is comprehended by a listener. According to Bakhtin, language is much more complex than that.

Since language is dialogic, or reliant upon dialogue, language is "alive and developing," growing and changing with each new utterance. Each time a word is spoken, it has a meaning that is unique from every other time that same word has been used. While the difference may be imperceptible, it is still there. According to Bakhtin, a word's specific meaning depends upon where we utter it, when we utter it, how we utter it, to whom we utter it, who we are when we utter it and, of course, how that word is used in a sentence. In other words, the meaning of a word depends upon its context and its content. When somebody says, "This is awesome" after receiving the birthday present they always wanted, for example, it has a very different meaning than when somebody sardonically says the same thing after their football team gives up the winning touchdown. This idea extends to the words in a literary work, as well. Bakhtin knew that the Formalists were wrong to separate words from their context; to understand what words truly mean, we need to know the specific context in which they are spoken.

In "Discourse in the Novel," Bakhtin identifies two opposing forces—the centripetal and the centrifugal—constantly at work in the development of language. The centripetal force pulls each word inward toward one specific meaning. A dictionary, with definitions to tell us what a word means and how that word should be used, is the most common type of centripetal force. At the same time, though, people are constantly using words in ways that don't conform to their dictionary definitions. Bakhtin describes this as a type of centrifugal force, pushing each word outward from a singular meaning. The continual opposition between these two forces is another factor that contributes to the unstable nature of language.

## Heteroglossia

Bakhtin also recognized the many layers within a language: "languages of social groups, 'professional' and 'genetic' languages, languages of generations and so forth." In other words, we have one language for our best friends, one for our coworkers, one for our employer, another for our teachers, another for our parents, still another for our grandparents, etc. As Bakhtin says,

> All words have the "taste" of a profession, a genre, a tendency, a party, a particular work, a particular person, a generation, an age group, the day and hour.

Bakhtin coined the term, heteroglossia, to describe this simultaneous existence of these various levels, or strata, of languages operating within each of us.

Each utterance of a word carries with it the residual effects of everything that the word has ever meant for the speaker in the past. At the same time, it also resonates with everything the word has ever meant for the listener. This was conspicuously exemplified in recent U.S. political discourse. Members of the "Tea Party" movement gained national attention when they urged Americans to "tea bag the fools in D.C." Tea Party members saw the phrase as a reference to the Boston Tea Party of 1773. It had a second layer of meaning, though, for those who understood the term "teabag" as a sexual euphemism. According to Bakhtin, all communication through language operates in a similar way.

Just as we are constantly being shaped by everything we see, feel and experience, the heteroglossic levels of language are constantly being shaped in the same way. And, since language is the result of a dialogue between speaker and listener, and since the speaker and listener are always changing (even if ever so slightly), then our language is always changing. Because of this, we will never get to a point where that change is complete, with our language or ourselves. Language, then, as

Bakhtin says in *Problems of Dostoyevsky's Art*, is characterized by its unfinalizability.

Unlike his predecessors, Bakhtin saw prose—especially the novel—as superior to other literary forms. The novel is superior, Bakhtin argued, because it encourages heteroglossic activity. Unlike poetry, which works to limit language, the novel contains many voices, each with several heteroglossic levels of language. Even in a story with just two characters, we have the voice of the author, the voice of the narrator and the voices of both of the characters, all of which gradually transform as they interact with each other throughout the course of the story. The many voices in a novel, each operating on many levels, results in what Bakhtin calls a dialogized heteroglossia. The epic poem, on the other hand, according to Bakhtin, has one unifying voice that remains constant throughout the course of the work. The novel, furthermore, is the only literary form that is able to integrate aspects from other genres into its own structure. If we were to incorporate prose into an epic poem, for example, the poem would no longer be a poem. This, too, Bakhtin argues, gives us reason to privilege the novel over other literary forms.

Two other characteristics that distinguish the novel involve Bakhtin's idea of the chronotope and the carnivalesque. Chronotope translates literally from the Greek as "time-space"; Bakhtin created the term to "[express] the inseparability of space and time" in literary prose, particularly the novel. Bakhtin wants to remind us that, as a novel's characters move about in their (fictional) space, they also move forward in time, following the same rules that govern reality in our nonfictional world. Bakhtin first gave us the idea of the carnivalesque in his book, *Rabelais and His World*. As the term suggests, carnivalesque refers to a jovial atmosphere in which the conventional rules of society (temporarily) do not apply; social hierarchies are ignored, erased or even inverted, and traditionally undervalued items briefly enjoy preeminent status. During a carnival, individuals become part of a larger whole and, in so doing, come away with a renewed sense of self. Bakhtin saw in the novel not only its conventionally lower status, but also its unique ability to embrace this adventurous carnivalesque spirit. And, unlike the poem, the novel is able to provide its reader with a sense of community.

The work of the Bakhtin Circle, and Mikhail Bakhtin in particular, shaped the way we read and understand literature today. Whether we argue that Bakhtin was ahead of his time or, as Vitalii Makhlin does, that the West was simply far behind the times, it would be hard to overestimate the profound effect that Bakhtin has had.

## After Formalism

Disenchantment with formalism—particularly new criticism—began to gain momentum in the late 1940s. During this time, the Chicago School of criticism argued (with some success) for a more Aristotelian approach. Marxism, feminism and psychoanalysis were gradually gaining credibility during this time as well. Still, it wasn't until the fifties and sixties that another theoretical approach (structuralism) was able to challenge new criticism as an equally-valid approach to literature.

Many literary scholars today argue that formalism is ineffective because it provides an overly narrow approach to a literary work. Proponents of new historicism and psychoanalysis, in particular, find formalism's dismissive attitude toward the author and his or her history to be problematic. Still, it would be difficult to overstate the effect formalism had on literary analysis. From providing a systematic approach to the study of literature to suggesting a close reading of a literary text, formalism forever changed the nature of literary study.

## Implementation

When analyzing any work of literature from a formalist perspective, we always begin with a close reading of the text: observation, interpretation, communication. For longer prose pieces, after reading the text, we might decide to focus on a few specific incidents that are representative of the whole. Or, we could focus on one aspect of the text that permeates the entire work—an underlying theme or an overarching metaphor, perhaps, or the narrative technique.

In Chekhov's "Gooseberries," for example, the New Critic might focus on the framed narration and try to determine what effects the framed narration has on the story as a whole. Does the meaning change, for example, when we consider that the bulk of the story is actually Ivan's dialogue, telling the story of his brother? How long ago, within the context of the story, did Ivan's visit to his brother take place? And why does Ivan tell the story in the first place? Should we trust Ivan's account of the story events? Are there other elements in the story, in other words, that suggest Ivan's story either is or isn't true? (Perhaps we see something in the text that suggests a fabrication.) A New Critic, in other words, will look carefully at all aspects of the narration, particularly if the narration is unconventional in any way. (This is the case even if the narrative technique isn't the focus of the New Critic's analysis.)

Reading the story through the lens of new criticism, we might also investigate why Ivan, after his story, makes the following appeal to Alyohin:

> do not cease to do good! There is no happiness and there should be none, and if life has a meaning and a purpose, that meaning and purpose is not our happiness but something greater and more rational. Do good!

What does this quote mean? It seems to suggest that not only is Ivan *not* happy, but also that he doesn't see his brother as happy, either (or, rather, that he sees his brother's happiness as illusory). Is Nikolay actually rich and powerful, or are his wealth and power false? If so, how might that contribute to the organic wholeness of the piece?

The New Critic, regardless of his or her focus, would also pay particular attention to the story's title. A gooseberry is defined as a fruit, but it could also describe the thorny shrub on which gooseberries are found. In British slang, a gooseberry is equivalent to what Americans might colloquially call a "third wheel." The New Critic, remember, would look to all definitions of significant words, whether or not they were part of the author's vocabulary or supposed "intent." Might these other definitions enhance our understanding of the piece or contribute to the work's meaning? If we consider the gooseberry to be a thorny bushes (or a friend who tags along on a date), how might that change the meaning of the piece?

Aside from the various definitions of *gooseberry*, what about the gooseberries themselves? Nikolay thinks they're delicious, but Ivan recognizes them as "hard and sour." What does this tell us? In the story, the gooseberries are tied inextricably to Nikolay's dream estate, but this estate was less than dreamy, with its coffee-colored stream and nearby brickyard and glue factory. How does this detail affect the story's meaning?

There are any number of ways a New Critic might approach this story—or any literary work. What the conventional New Critic will avoid, though, is any information about the author or the history surrounding the text's composition. Most New Critics, for example, don't care that Chekhov wrote this story when he was thirty-eight years old, or that he was still one of Russia's most desired bachelors at this time, or that he grew up in a large family with an abusive father. The New Critic is also unconcerned with historical information regarding Russia in the late nineteenth century. The fact that Chekhov's story was written two years after the coronation of Nicholas II—and the subsequent Khodynka Tragedy—is of no concern to the New Critic. The key, in a conventional new critical reading, is to keep our attention focused on the details of the text itself as we move toward our one "correct" meaning.

## Important Moments in Formalism

**1912:** Russian Futurists' manifesto, "A Slap in the Face of Public Taste"
**1915:** first meeting of Moscow Linguistic Circle
**1916:** *Opajaz* formed in St. Petersburg, Russia

**1917:** Viktor Shklovsky's "Art as Technique"
**1917:** Russian Revolution
**1918:** Bakhtin Circle formed in Nevel, Russia
**1919:** T.S. Eliot's "Hamlet and His Problems"
**1921:** Roman Jakobson's *Modern Russian Poetry*,
**1924:** Leon Trotsky's *Literature and Revolution*
**1924:** Bakhtin moves to St. Petersburg
**1925:** I.A. Richards' *Principles of Literary Criticism*
**1925:** Shklovsky's *Theory of Prose*
**1926:** Boris Eikhenbaum's "The Theory of the Formal Method"
**1926:** Valentin Voloshinov's *Freudianism: A Marxist Critique*
**1926:** Vladimir Mayakovsky's "How Verses are Made"
**1928:** P.N. Medvedev's *The Formal Method in Literary Scholarship*
**1929:** *Marxism and the Philosophy of Language*
**1929:** Bakhtin's *Problems of Dostoyevsky's Art*
**1930:** Sir William Empson's *Seven Types of Ambiguity*
**1941:** John Crowe Ransom *The New Criticism*
**1946:** W.K. Wimsatt and Monroe Beardsley's "The Intentional Fallacy"
**1947:** Empson's *Seven Types of Ambiguity* published in U.S.
**1949:** Wimsatt and Beardsley's "The Affective Fallacy."
**1965:** Bakhtin's *Rabelais and his World*
**1970:** Beardsley's *The Possibility of Criticism*
**1975:** Bakhtin's *The Dialogic Imagination*
**1986:** Bakhtin's "Towards a Philosophy of the Act"

## Important Terms

point of view
   first-person narrator
   third-person narrator
   central consciousness
   second-person narrator
characters
   protagonist / hero
   antagonist
   sympathetic character
   unsympathetic character
   dynamic character
   static character
affective fallacy
intentional fallacy

theme
rhyme
meter
plot
characterization
setting
conflict
   complication
   crisis
   climax
   epiphany
   resolution (falling action)
authorial intent
metaphor

simile
defamiliarization
dialogism
*fabula*

tension
literariness
heteroglossia
*syuzhet*

## Study Questions

1. Identify all the poetic devices you can find in Chopin's "The Story of an Hour," Poe's "The Cask of Amontillado," and Sui Sin Far's "In the Land of the Free."
2. Identify the point of view used by Bierce in "An Occurrence at Owl Creek Bridge," by Gilman in "The Yellow Wallpaper," and by King in "The Little Convent Girl." How are these points of view different? How would our understanding of the stories change if they utilized a different point of view?
3. Write about your favorite short story. What is the title? Who is the author? What is it you like about it? What new insights can you gain from the story when looking at it through the lens of new criticism? Specifically, who are the characters? What happens in the story? What poetic devices are at work in the story?
4. Perform a close reading on King's "The Little Convent Girl." What does the story "tell" us through a close reading that we wouldn't have noticed otherwise? How does this close reading enhance our understanding of the text?
5. Identify all of the plot devices used in Bierce's "An Occurrence at Owl Creek Bridge." What effects do these devices have on the meaning of the story?

## Selected Bibliography

Brooks, Cleanth. *The Well-Wrought Urn: Studies in the Structure of Poetry*. New York: Mariner, 1956.
—. *William Faulkner: First Encounters*. New Haven: Yale UP, 1985.
Brooks, Cleanth, and Robert Penn Warren. *Understanding Fiction*. New York: Prentice, 1979.
—. *Understanding Poetry*. New York: Holt, 1976.
Eliot, T. S. *Notes Towards the Definition of Culture*. New York: Faber, 1972.
—. *Selected Essays*. New York: Faber, 1999.
Empson, Sir William. *Seven Types of Ambiguity*. New York: Seabrook, 2008.
Elton, William. *A Glossary of the New Criticism*. Chicago: Modern Poetry, 1949.
Frye, Northrup. *Anatomy of Criticism*. Toronto: Toronto UP, 2007.

Jancovich, Mark. *The Cultural Politics of the New Criticism*. Cambridge: Cambridge UP, 2006.
Leavis, F. R. *The Critic as Anti-Philosopher*. Lanham: Ivan R. Dee, 1998.
—. *The Great Tradition*. New York: Penguin, 1983.
—. *Revaluation: Tradition and Development in English Poetry*. Lanham: Ivan R. Dee, 1998.
Lentricchia, Frank. *After the New Criticism*. Chicago: Chicago UP, 1981.
Lewis, C. S. *An Experiment in Criticism*. Cambridge: Cambridge UP, 1992.
Patnaik, J.N. *The Aesthetics of the New Criticism*. Atlantic Highlands: Humanities Press, 1983.
Ransom, John Crowe. *The New Criticism*. Santa Barbara: Praeger, 1979.
Richards, I. A. *The Principles of Literary Criticism*. New York: Routledge, 2001.
—. *Practical Criticism: A Study of Literary Judgment*. New York: Harcourt, 1963.
Wimsatt, W.K., Jr., and Monroe C. Beardley. *The Verbal Icon: Studies in the Meanng of Poery*. Lexington: Kentucky UP, 1954.

# 2

# Psychoanalysis

FOCUSES ON: the covert (unwritten) text and biographical information, as well as historical information that relates to the life of the author or characters.
BECAUSE: Psychoanalysts believe that literary texts, much like dreams, express unconscious feelings and emotions of the author and, through a close study of a literary work, the critic can uncover hidden information about the author or the characters.
DEVELOPED IN: 1900s.
NOTABLE PRACTITIONERS:
    Sigmund Freud (1856-1939)    Maud Bodkin (1875–1967)
    Viktor Tausk (1879-1919)    Jacques Lacan (1901-81)
    Carl Jung (1875-1961)    Charles Mauron (1899-1966)
    Northrop Frye (1912-91)    Harold Bloom (1930- )
    Julia Kristeva (1941- )    Slavoj Žižek (1949- )
IMPORTANT PREDECESSORS:
    Theodor Meynert (1833- 92)    Franz Brentano (1838-1917)
    Eduard von Hartmann (1842-1906)    William James (1842-1910)
    Theodor Lipps (1851-1914)
ADVANTAGES: can provide a unique understanding of a character's or an author's motivations.
DISADVANTAGES: psychoanalytic interpretations tend to overlook a text's historical, political, and socioeconomic context, as well as any artistic aspects of the text that may be worthy of study.
DEFINITION: the practice of examining a literary work through the lens of psychoanalysis, with particular interest in the unconscious of the work's author or characters.

---

    Psychoanalysis is, in layman's terms, the process of understanding one's mind by examining how the conscious and the unconscious aspects of that mind interact. As first developed by the Austrian neurologist, Sigmund Freud, the psychoanalytic therapy process involved a patient, usually reclined in a relaxed position, verbally expressing whatever thoughts came to mind. Through this practice, the psychoanalytic therapist would eventually be able to uncover and discern the inner workings of the patient's unconscious mind and determine the most effective course of therapeutic treatment. Through a similar method, albeit without the treatment, psychoanalytic literary theory seeks to understand more thoroughly either a character (or characters) in a literary work or the author of that work.

It's important to note that psychoanalysis is just one of numerous approaches to the study of psychology. Others include behaviorism, as practiced by John B. Watson and B.F. Skinner, and cognitivism as popularized by Noam Chomsky. There is also biological psychology, clinical psychology, developmental psychology, differential psychology, evolutionary psychology, and so on. While some therapists still practice psychoanalysis, those who do often combine psychoanalysis with additional forms of treatment. Most psychology experts today find other methods more effective in the treatment of patients. Psychoanalysis, though, remains the primary psychological approach to literature. Unlike other schools of psychology, psychoanalysis is uniquely conducive to the analysis of literary works. While other psychological methods require convenient access to the patient (or author or characters), a psychoanalytic reading can be performed when only the text is available. And, since the goal of a psychoanalytic literary approach is the analysis of a text, rather than the treatment of a patient, the ineffectiveness of psychoanalysis is not a concern.

Psychoanalysis is structured around a few fundamental beliefs. First, psychoanalysts believe that a person's childhood plays a significant role in shaping one's adult personality. Psychoanalysts also believe that we are guided by irrational, unconscious motivations. When these unconscious motivations conflict with our conscious needs, any number of mental problems may present themselves. As we try to understand these unconscious motivations, our mind deploys defense mechanisms to protect us. Psychoanalysts believe that we can only have mental balance when our conscious mind becomes aware of and understands the reason for our unconscious motivations.

## Sigmund Freud

Unlike with some other literary theories (new criticism and feminism, for example) we know who brought us psychoanalytic literary criticism: Sigmund Freud, with his book, *The Interpretation of Dreams* (1899) and his essay, "Delusion and Dream in Jensen's *Gradiva*" (1907).

Freud wasn't the first person to study the human mind (scholars and thinkers have been at it since the beginning of recorded time) but he was the first to apply his tools of psychoanalysis to the study of literature.

*The Interpretation of Dreams*, as the title suggests, details all aspects of Freud's theoretical study of dreams, including their origins, their meanings and how they relate to waking life. Freud saw the book as the key to unlocking the secret of dreams. The focus of the book is Freud's dream work and the role played by the unconscious, an aspect of the human mind that hadn't been given significant scientific attention. Consequently, *The Interpretation of Dreams* spends relatively little time discussing Freud's theories with regard to literature. His essay on Wilhelm Jensen's novel, *Gradiva*, though, applies his theories specifically to Jensen's literary text.

*Gradiva* is a 1903 novel that tells the story of an archaeologist who becomes so obsessed with the woman in a sculpture that he begins to dream about her. His dreams become so lifelike that he starts to think they may be real. As such, the novel was perfectly suited to Freud's new psychoanalytic analysis. After his essay on *Gradiva*, Freud would go on to write about other works of literature, most notably Shakespeare's *Hamlet* and Sophocles' *Oedipus Rex*.

Freud's beliefs were based upon the idea that the unconscious mind controls a significant portion of human behavior. While the idea of the unconscious wasn't new—Friedrich Schelling coined the term in the eighteenth century and Samuel Taylor Coleridge popularized it soon after—Freud is credited with making the unconscious a subject of scientific study. Within the unconscious mind are habits, phobias, hidden desires, and repressed emotions and memories. Freud believed that these inner workings of the unconscious found expression in dreams and in literature. As such, Freud saw in literary works the opportunity to peer into the author's unconscious mind.

What Freud believed he found were deep-seated desires and repressed memories, often from the patient's childhood. These memories and desires frequently had a sexual component which arose, according to Freud, from one of five stages of psychosexual development: the oral, the anal, the phallic, the latent and the genital. If any sort of problem occurred during one of these stages, it would present itself as a neurosis in adulthood. If a child was weaned too soon during the oral stage, for example, Freud believed that this child would grow into an adult with some type of oral fixation (smoking, overeating, alcoholism, etc.). The phallic stage (between ages three and six) often gave rise to Freud's Oedipus complex, where a child develops a sexual desire for his mother and, consequently, a jealousy of and hatred toward his father. When these feelings are not resolved, the result is a phallic fixation in adulthood, usually in the form of extreme aggression or ambition. Like many of Freud's theories, the Oedipus complex evolved from Freud's personal experience; he noted that, "I found in myself a constant love for my mother, and jealousy of my father. I now consider this to be a universal event in childhood."

Later in Freud's career, he developed a model for the human psyche that consists of three components: "das Es," "das Ich," and "das Über-Ich," translated from the German as "the It," "the I," and the "the Over-I," but more commonly known by their Latinized translations, "the id," "the ego" and "the superego. According to Freud, the id is the unorganized, instinctual aspect of our personality; it is where our libido is contained. The id is guided by the pleasure principle, constantly seeking to avoid pain and to satisfy our instinctual needs, desires and momentary whims without regard for any moral, ethical or emotional consequences. To Freud, a newborn baby is an example of a human who is "id-ridden," or dominated by their id. The superego, by contrast, is often compared to our conscience. It is where our feelings of guilt and remorse come from, as well as our desire to become an ideal member of society. The ego is the organized aspect of our psyche, guided by the reality principle. It works to balance the id's need for instant satisfaction with the superego's understanding of right and wrong and the individual's long-term aspirations. Freud believed that the majority of our defense mechanisms are active in the ego. The ego is often identified with the part of our psyche that we present to the world.

Freud published over a dozen books and scores of articles in his lifetime. He worked out explanations to nearly every conceivable type of human behavior. His ideas were so omnipresent during the first half of the twentieth century that the majority of us know about his more popular theories. Many students are probably familiar with defense mechanisms like projection (ascribing our own objectionable behaviors to others, rather than ourselves), displacement (the redirection of our emotions or impulses toward a nonthreatening person or object), rationalization (the attempt to justify controversial or unacceptable behaviors) and repression (pushing undesirable thoughts and needs into our unconscious). The same is true of some of his other concepts like penis envy (the desire of girls to have male genitalia and the power it represents), castration anxiety (fear of losing one's sexual function) and the Freudian slip (a mistake in speech or thought that reveals repressed thoughts or emotions). When we think about it, in fact, we realize that we are exposed—in literature, popular culture or conversation—to a variety of Freud's ideas on an almost daily basis.

## The Text as Dream

To Freud, a literary text is akin to a verbalized dream of the author. When looked at this way, a literary text could be read as if it was the transcript from a series of psychoanalytic sessions. To perform a psychoanalytic analysis of a text, then, the reader acts as a sort of psychoanalytic therapist, the author (or character) takes the place of the patient, and the story represents a series of repressed dreams or fantasies of the author or the character(s). In psychoanalytic literary criticism, we explore and evaluate the text for clues to understand the subject's unconscious.

In a traditional psychotherapy session, the skilled psychoanalyst listens carefully to what the patient says and to what the patient omits. What the patient *doesn't* say can be as informative as what he or she actually *does* say. If a patient talks freely and happily about his childhood, for example, but then unknowingly skips over any detail regarding his mother or his childhood pet, the therapist might take note of that omission and explore it further. A literary theorist working from a psychoanalytic perspective approaches a text in a similar fashion. Literary theorists see what is written on the page—the text itself—as the overt text. What is unwritten, whether it is consciously implied or unconsciously set down in the story, is the covert text. To a psychoanalytic literary critic, the overt (written) content of the text represents the author's conscious mind while the covert (unwritten) content represents the author's unconscious. The text, then, becomes a means through which we can psychoanalyze the author. Conversely, we can utilize these same analytic tools on the story's characters by closely considering the characters' words and actions. For psychoanalysts, a literary text, like a dream, does not make explicit statements. Both communicate indirectly and therefore they require detailed analysis in order to find their true meaning.

Freud was one of the most influential people in the twentieth century, and his efforts represented a giant leap forward in the study of human cognition. However, his theories have fallen out of favor in the last several decades. Any student who has taken an introductory course in psychology knows that the majority of Freud's work is viewed dismissively by nearly everyone in the psychology community. Intellectuals such as Simone de Beauvoir and Betty Friedan took issue with the patriarchal slant to his findings. A female subject's abusive past, for example, might have been seen by Freud as a fantasy rather than reality. Criticism of Freud, though, has been most pronounced among experts in the field of psychology. One of Freud's early critics was his erstwhile colleague, Carl Jung, who found Freud's emphasis on sexuality to be misguided. Later psychologists noted Freud's complete lack of real experimentation; his theories were based upon personal opinion and observation and his statistical sample—if we could call it that—consisted almost entirely of wealthy housewives from Vienna, Austria. Even if he had employed sound scientific methodology, any findings based upon such a small and specific group of subjects could hardly be used to explain human behavior. Other psychologists found that Freud's conclusions didn't stand up when exposed to exacting scientific scrutiny. While some therapists still use psychoanalysis, few do so according to Freud's methods. In literary studies, though, many of Freud's ideas and methods are still in use.

## After Freud

Freud was not only responsible for advancing the study of the human mind, he also influenced scores of other scholars in his own lifetime and beyond. Feminists such as Julia Kristeva and Luce Irigaray, Marxists like Herbert Marcuse, and psychologists including Alfred Adler, Erik Erikson, Erich Fromm, Carl Jung, Jacques Lacan, and Otto Rank were all influenced, in one way or another, by Freud. But not everyone followed in Freud's footsteps, so to speak.

Scholars who based their work on many of Freud's fundamental concepts, but disagreed with (and modified) a variety of Freud's specifics, came to be known as neo-Freudians. The scholars most often associated with neo-Freudianism were Alfred Adler, Erik Erikson, Karen Horney and Carl Jung. There was no neo-Freudian *school*, as it were, and most of the neo-Freudians didn't collaborate with each other; we refer to them today as neo-Freudians because they all distanced themselves from Freud in various ways, not because they shared a common dogma. The neo-Freudians did tend to focus less on sex than Freud and more on the conscious mind and social interaction, but this was more the result of coincidence than a shared interest. Adler focused on the individual and one's feeling of inferiority, developing the idea of the inferiority complex; Erikson formulated his theory of eight stages of psychosocial development; Horney's primary interest was neuroses, identifying three categories of neurotic needs (compliance, aggression and detachment); and Jung turned his attention toward the archetypes of the collective unconscious (which would eventually lead to archetypal literary criticism).

While the majority of neo-Freudians before the 1960's focused on therapy and treatment, rather than literature, this wasn't the case for all psychoanalysts after Freud. One of these was Charles Mauron. Mauron is most often remembered now as an astute translator of English literature into French but, during his life, he was also a respected literary scholar and an early proponent of the psychoanalytic approach to literature. Mauron's *Aesthetics and Psychology* (1935) helped keep psychoanalytic literary theory alive before it was embraced by the academic community. In *Des Métaphores Obsédantes au Mythe Personnel* (1962, *The Obsessive Metaphors of Personal Myth*), Mauron outlines a formulaic method of psychoanalytic literary analysis. Mauron's method began with the realization, agreeing with Freud, that the creative process is a form of sublimation in which undesirable impulses (often of a sexual nature) are redirected toward creative avenues. As an outlet of sublimated desires, the unconscious expresses itself through symbolic language and metaphor. When we examine an author's entire oeuvre, then, we should be able to find recurring symbols, metaphors and themes (the second phase). In the third phase, we can use these recurring ideas to develop an understanding of the author's unconscious. Finally, we can take what we've learned about the author's unconscious to analyze more thoroughly an author's individual text in relation to the author's life.

While Mauron's work is clearly based upon fundamental Freudian principles, it also diverges from Freud in many of the same areas that other neo-Freudian scholarship does. Still, with regard to method, Mauron's process could be applied with equal success to Freudian or to contemporary psychoanalysis.

## Jacques Lacan

Not all psychoanalysts sought to distance themselves from Freud. One theorist who maintained his identification as a Freudian was Jacques Lacan.

Lacan was a French philosopher, psychiatrist and psychoanalyst. As with Freud, Lacan's privileged status in the literary community did not equate to respect among psychology experts. Lacan has been referred to as a "fake" (Richard Dawkins) and an "amusing and perfectly self-conscious charlatan" (Noam Chomsky) whose "superficial erudition" (Alan Sokol) made him an "attractive psychopath" and "the shrink from hell" (Raymond Tallis). Still, Lacan advanced the psychoanalytic study of literature by incorporating a linguistic slant to his psychoanalytic approach to literature.

Lacan famously saw the unconscious as "structured like a language" and governed by the same type of sophisticated rules as a language system. For Lacan, this hypothesis is proven when we consider Freudian slips, our understanding of symbols and metaphors, and the process of dream interpretation. While Lacan referred to himself as a Freudian, the belief in a language-structured unconscious was a significant break from Freud. For Freud, the unconscious was an unstructured morass that could only communicate with the conscious through the use of symbols and metaphors. The consequence of Lacan's understanding of the unconscious was that, if the unconscious is structured like a language, then (following the structuralist understanding of language) that structure has to be there before the unconscious (before we are born to have an unconscious, in other words). But, if that is true, then our unconscious would have to be indistinguishable from everyone else's, which means that none of us are the distinctive, autonomous individuals that we always assumed we were. Not only that, but if our unconscious is structured as a mere replication of everyone else's, then we are—and will always be—fragmented selves. Put another way, according to Lacan's theory of the unconscious, we can never become a cohesive whole when part of our being (our unconscious) exists separate from us.

Language, for Lacan, also plays an important role as we mature through the stages of life. Lacan saw the psyche as composed of three parts; Lacan called them "orders": the Real, the Imaginary, and the Symbolic. While these orders do not specifically refer to periods of our lives, they do correspond to various phases of the maturation process. For example, Lacan posits the Real as taking place in our earliest moments of life (zero to six months). This is when we have a very limited perception of our world. We know when we feel something that we'll later understand to be hunger or various forms of discomfort, but we perceive very little beyond these basic biological needs. It is during this time, according to Lacan, that we are as close as we'll ever be to a whole, unfragmented self.

From six to eighteen months, corresponding with the Imaginary Order, we begin to focus on what Lacan calls our demands. Demands, unlike our needs, cannot be satisfied. This is illustrated by one aspect of the Imaginary Order, Lacan's mirror stage of human development. During the mirror stage, we are finally able to recognize ourselves in a mirror. This recognition brings with it a host of other issues. One is that we now become, in our minds, an object that can be viewed by others. Before this point, we naturally assumed that we were, so to speak, the center of a universe that revolved around us. Once we come to realize that we are an object, similar in nature to those (parental) objects that feed, bathe and clothe us, we develop this preternatural "demand" to return to that reality in which the world revolved around us and we were one with our mother. Since this narcissistic need is impossible to achieve, the mirror stage represents our first and most basic insatiable longing, or lack. According to Lacan, this sense of unquenchable want stays with us throughout our lives.

Lacan's Symbolic Order, on the other hand, is distinctive for its use of language. During this time, from about eighteen months to four years, language helps us name the things we desire, it helps us socialize by making us aware of societal expectations, and language helps us to differentiate other people and objects. This differentiation becomes important as we develop a fuller understanding of ourselves as separate individuals—similar to, but different from, other humans. Lacan's structuralist leanings are perhaps most evident in this Symbolic Order as we see structuralism's model of language applied to Lacan's theory of human development.

This focus on language made Lacan's work an attractive choice for literary theorists. His use of linguistic terminology also made psychoanalysis accessible to those studying literature. While Lacan's ideas have never held much sway among psychology experts, psychoanalytic literary critics see in his work a different understanding of human behavior that they can apply to works of literature. For this reason he remains (counterintuitively to psychologists) a popular figure in literary criticism.

## Archetypal Criticism

Archetypal criticism is most often grouped with psychoanalysis even though the two eventually grew into distinctly different approaches. As its name implies, archetypal criticism is primarily concerned with the representation of ubiquitous myths and archetypes in a literary text.

*The Golden Bough* (1890) by the Scottish anthropologist James Frazer represents one of our earliest modern studies of archetypes. In it, Frazer examines the development of cultures by examining their past and present religious practices and the myths and symbols associated with that development. *The Golden Bough* was a groundbreaking text in the field of historical anthropology and, as such, it became a significant influence on the work of the structuralist Claude Lévi-Strauss.

In contrast to Frazer's anthropological approach, Carl Jung studied archetypes from a psychological perspective. Jung saw archetypes as innate patterns of thought existing deep in our collective unconscious, shared by all of us and built up by the experiences of all our ancestors. By definition, an archetype is a prototype upon which all subsequent copies are modeled. Archetypes for Jung (what we refer to as Jungian archetypes) are unconscious ideas, patterns or beliefs that reside in all of us. A Jungian archetype could describe a figure (mother, father, God, devil), an event (birth, death, marriage), a motif (the Creation, the Fall, the journey), or a number or numerical order. Jung identified five primary archetypes:

> The self, which Jung characterized as the idealized version of ourselves that we aspire to; it is the combination of the conscious and unconscious in a person, and it represents the psyche as a whole.
> The shadow, which is the unconscious part of us that our conscious mind doesn't see in ourselves. It is usually understood to be dark and negative, but it can have light and positive aspects, especially for those individuals with a low sense of self-worth.
> The anima, the hidden feminine aspects of a man's unconscious
> The animus, the hidden masculine aspects of a woman's unconscious
> The persona, which Jung described as a kind of mask that we wear when we present ourselves to society.

Other common archetypes that we're all familiar with are figures like the hero, the villain, the trickster, and the wise old man; events such as an initiation or a marriage; and the motifs of the quest or the Ascension.

Unlike Freud, Jung had little interest in literary theory and he didn't develop his ideas into an approach to literature. His work, though, influenced experts in a number of different fields. One such person was the literary scholar Maud Bodkin, whose book, *Archetypal Patterns in Poetry: Psychological Studies of Imagination* (1934), is our earliest example of archetypal literary criticism. *Archetypal Patterns in Poetry* is based on Jung's research, examining literature through Jung's ideas of archetypes and the collective unconscious. Bodkin not only studied the responses of readers as they encountered archetypal patterns within a text, she also examined various manifestations of certain archetypes within a variety of literary works. While Bodkin's book was well received, relatively few people read it. *Archetypal Patterns in Poetry* was published when new criticism was reaching the height of its popularity and so the book did little to change the direction of literary criticism. It would be another twenty-three years before archetypal criticism would be accepted as a valid scholarly approach to literature.

## Northrup Frye

Northrup Frye's *Anatomy of Criticism* (1957) not only gave archetypal criticism credibility, but it made archetypal criticism the preferred approach for a great number of academics well into the 1970s. Frye's book expanded upon Bodkin's ideas while separating itself from the work of Frazer and Jung. While Frazer was interested in myths and archetypes from an anthropological perspective, and Jung focused on the manifestation of archetypes in the collective unconscious, Frye was only concerned with how archetypes work in a literary text and how they affect the reader. It was this new focus that steered the direction of archetypal criticism away from psychoanalysis.

*Anatomy of Criticism* is considered one of the most significant works of literary theory in the English language. It is comprised of four essays—"Historical Criticism: Theory of Modes," "Ethical Criticism: Theory of Symbols," "Archetypal Criticism: Theory of Myths," and "Rhetorical Criticism: Theory of Genres"—as well as a "Polemical Introduction" and a "Tentative Conclusion." Taken together, the essays present a comprehensive and systematic process through which one can thoughtfully approach a text from an archetypal perspective. As such, the majority of the book is devoted to categorizing symbols and archetypes and the stories in which they appear.

After explaining the need for criticism in his introduction, Frye begins by classifying literature according to Aristotle's three aspects: plot-driven (what Frye referred to as tragic fiction), character-driven (comic fiction) and idea-driven (essays and poetry). For Frye, tragic fiction is characterized, in part, by the protagonist's expulsion (either real or metaphoric) from society, while comedic fiction ends with society's acceptance of the hero.

Frye then further categorizes those three types as belonging to one of five "modes": the mythic, the romantic, the high mimetic, the low mimetic and the ironic. The mythic mode encompasses stories about gods, and the romantic mode includes those stories about heroic human beings (Odysseus). The high mimetic mode deals with noble human beings (Jean Valjean), the low mimetic with ordinary humans (Nick Carraway), and the ironic with weak humans who are below average in any number of ways (Humbert Humbert). Shakespeare's play, *Hamlet*, for example, would be categorized as a high mimetic tragedy since Hamlet is a noble human who, through the course of the play, is separated from society.

*Anatomy of Criticism* also classifies the five groups, or "phases," of literary symbols (literal, descriptive, formal, mythical and anagogic), the three types of imagery (apocalyptic, demonic and analogical), the five worlds in the Great Chain of Being (divine, human, animal, vegetable and mineral), and the four mythos, or genres, of literature (comedy, which corresponds to spring; romance, corresponding to summer; tragedy, for autumn; and irony or satire, paralleling winter). Frye goes on to not only describe various symbols and how they function, he also describes how symbols function in their respective aspects (comic fiction or tragic fiction). Thus, the forest is a safe haven for Robin Hood while being a dark representation of hell for Goodman Brown. Water is a gently flowing source of life in Frye's category of comic fiction but a raging portent of doom in tragic fiction. Animals in comic fiction are gentle and helpful creatures but, in tragic fiction they serve as fearsome vicious beasts.

Frye's book is all-encompassing and can provide students with a way to understand literature as much more than mere words on a page. *Anatomy of Criticism* represented a momentous leap forward in the study of literary criticism. Frye's archetypal criticism, along with the contemporaneous advance of structuralism as practiced by Barthes and Lévi-Strauss, finally proved that new criticism wasn't the only viable, academic approach to literary studies.

The popularity of archetypal criticism, however, began to wane in the 1970s. A number of new approaches to literature had taken shape by this time (including post-structuralism, feminism and reader-response) and the political climate during this period left many people looking toward the future in all manner of human endeavors. Some saw archetypal criticism's focus on symbols, rather on than the unique literary qualities of a work, as a significant drawback. Others argued that archetypal criticism was ill-equipped to deal with the diverse strategies of the emerging postmodern period. Proponents of archetypal criticism suggest its decline was due to the success of Frye's book, implying that the comprehensive nature of *Anatomy of Criticism* left no need for follow-up scholarship, allowing archetypal criticism to fade quietly from discussion. Whatever the reason, archetypal criticism is now seen most often as a thing of the past.

## Implementation

Significant advances in both psychology and neuroscience have made the ideas of Freud and his devotees seem quaint today. While we could argue that the modern practice of psychoanalysis bears some resemblance to Freud's method, today's psychoanalysis is based upon a very different understanding of how the brain works. A contemporary psychoanalytic literary critic, then, will approach a text in a similar manner as his or her Freudian predecessors while disregarding Freud's outdated ideas on such things as the Oedipus complex, penis envy, the id, ego and superego, and so on.

Reading a story like "The Cask of Amontillado" from a psychoanalytic perspective then, we might focus on the narrator, Montresor. He begins his story by telling us, "The thousand injuries of Fortunato I had borne as best I could, but when he ventured upon insult, I vowed revenge." As a reader, we have two questions after this opening line: What was this insult? and What kind of revenge has he planned? The second question, as we know, is answered throughout the course of the story. The answer to the first question, though, is conspicuously absent from the entire text.

If we utilize some of the tools of narratology while taking a psychoanalytic view of the story, we notice, first, a narrative distance of approximately fifty years ("For the half of a century no mortal has disturbed them."). But we also notice that the narrator employs mimesis (scene) to tell much of his story. In these scenes, the sensory details are often quite specific (the jingling of the bells, the smell of the nitre, the dampness of the catacomb walls). Thinking from a purely logical perspective, we might ask ourselves how it is possible for someone to recall such specific details some fifty years later. Even without formal psychological training, experience tells us that most people don't remember such exacting details after so long a period. (While most of us have an older relative who can remember details of an incident from their childhood, these memories rarely take the form of sustained narratives such as Montresor's and they rarely include specific memories of all five senses.) A psychoanalytic literary critic would consider how it is that Montresor remembers his story so vividly.

We might then conclude that Poe's narrator must have replayed these events over and over in his mind countless times over those fifty years. We would then ask, Why? Has he replayed them because he's been overcome with guilt all these years? Or, does he consider this episode with Fortunato to be one of his finest moments, and he relives that event with pride? We could also consider other motivations—perhaps Fortunato is but one of many victims who suffered the same fate, for example.

Our next step in a psychoanalytic approach is to reexamine the text for hints that one or another of these possibilities is the most likely. Is there anything in the text to suggest one conclusion over another? We might consider a passage like,

> "My friend, no. It is not the engagement, but the severe cold with which I perceive you are afflicted. The vaults are insufferably damp. They are encrusted with nitre."
> "Let us go, nevertheless. The cold is merely nothing. Amontillado! You have been imposed upon; and as for Luchesi, he cannot distinguish Sherry from Amontillado."
> Thus speaking, Fortunato possessed himself of my arm. Putting on a mask of black silk and drawing a *roquelaire* closely about my person, I suffered him to hurry me to my palazzo.

Does this quote suggest remorse, or pride? Montresor doesn't overtly say that he is proud of the way he manipulated Fortunato into the catacombs; this is a detail that we have to extract by paying close attention to what is unwritten in the story. A psychoanalytic critic will examine the entire text (or representative passages from a longer work) in much the same way.

When we "read" the covert text, we are essentially doing something we've done most of our lives. When we meet a stranger at a bus stop, on a train or in a bar, and he tells us about his career as a professional football player or as an astronaut, or his clandestine work for the CIA, we pay attention to the things this stranger doesn't tell us: does he have the physical build of a former athlete? Does he use the vocabulary of a trained astronaut? Does he display the mannerisms of someone who worked for the CIA?

Studying the covert text can reveal a number of details that we might otherwise neglect. If we look for what Montresor leaves out of his narration, we notice, in particular, one significant detail: the nature of Fortunato's "insult" that puts the story in motion. Montresor also doesn't overtly mention how much time and effort he spent in plotting his vengeance, but we know it was obviously a significant amount. While it's possible that the shackles were already in place, he still had to prepare the stones and mortar. He had to conjure up and rehearse the subterfuge that would convince Fortunato to willingly follow him into the catacombs, and he had to anticipate the occasion when Fortunato would be inebriated enough to be an easy victim, all while continuing to befriend Fortunato as if no "insult" had taken place.

We could also revisit that second-to-last sentence: "For the half of a century no mortal has disturbed them." How could Montresor know that Fortunato's bones haven't been disturbed unless he had checked them recently? And, if that is the case, what was the occasion of his visit? How long after this recent visit is he narrating his tale? And to whom is he telling the story? And why? Is Montresor confessing to someone—a priest or a policeman, perhaps? Is he talking to a stranger at a bar on the fiftieth anniversary of Fortunato's death? Maybe we think that Montresor's narratee is his grandson who has been having trouble with a classmate. Or perhaps Montresor is talking to his next victim.

From here, we could make any number of conclusions. Perhaps we think Montresor is a psychopath, or a sociopath. Or maybe he is hiding his guilt under a mask of false bravado. With a psychoanalytic reading, there are numerous paths toward which we can direct our approach, focusing on any aspect of the characters or the author that we deem worthwhile.

Another psychoanalytic approach that we can use with Poe's story is similar to the one suggested by Mauron. If we apply Mauron's process to Poe's body of work, we might notice a recurring theme of death or loss, or we may recognize a theme of unrequited love. It's also common for Poe to give us an unexpected ending, often resulting in some type of retribution. Mauron, remember, is looking for common thmes symbols and metaphors that appear throughout an author's entire oeuvre with the hope that these literary devices will give us some understanding into the author's unconscious. We can then apply this new understanding to a specific text. What conclusions can we make, then, about Poe and his work and how do these conclusions color our understanding of "The Cask of Amontillado"? Our goal in a psychoanalytic reading of a text is to find some truth about the author or one (or more) of the characters that we wouldn't be able to see through a different critical lens.

## Important Moments in Psychoanalysis

1890: James Frazer's *The Golden Bough*
1899: Sigmund Freud's *The Interpretation of Dreams*
1907: Freud's "Delusion and Dream in Jensen's *Gradiva*"
1908: Freud's "Creative Writing and Day-Dreaming"
1912: Carl Jung's *Psychology of the Unconscious*
1913: Freud's *Totem and Taboo*
1921: Jung's *Psychological Types*
1923: Freud's *The Ego and the Id*

**1924:** Freud's "The Dissolution of the Oedipus Complex"
**1925:** Freud's "A Note upon the 'Mystic Writing-Pad'"
**1928:** Freud's *Dostoevsky and Parricide*
**1933:** Jung's *Modern Man in Search of a Soul*
**1934:** Maud Bodkin's *Archetypal Patterns in Poetry*
**1934:** Jung's *The Archetypes and the Collective Unconscious*
**1935:** Charles Mauron's *Aesthetics and Psychology*
**1947:** Jung's *On the Nature of the Psyche*
**1949:** Jacques Lacan's "The Mirror Stage as Formative of the I"
**1949:** Lacan's "The Mirror Stage, Source of the I-Function"
**1951:** Lacan's "Some Reflections on the Ego"
**1953:** Lacan's "The Function and Field of Speech and Language in Psychoanalysis"
**1955:** Lacan's "The Freudian Thing"
**1956:** Lacan's "Fetishism: The Symbolic, the Real and the Imaginary"
**1957:** Northrup Frye's *Anatomy of Criticism*
**1958:** Lacan's "The Signification of the Phallus"
**1959:** Lacan's "Desire and Interpretation of Desire in *Hamlet*"
**1960:** Lacan's "The Subversion of the Subject and the Dialectic of Desire in the Freudian Unconscious"
**1962:** Mauron's *Des Métaphores Obsédantes au Mythe Personnel*
**1974:** Julia Kristeva's *Revolution in Poetic Language*
**1995:** Kristeva's *New Maladies Of The Soul*

## Important Terms

Archetype
Conscious
Displacement
Ego
Overt text
Sublimation
Symbol
Unconscious

Condensation
Covert text
Dream work
Id
Projection
Superego
Transference

## Study Questions

1. Using psychoanalysis, explain the behavior of one of the characters in Chekhov's "Gooseberries."
2. Identify all the archetypes you can find in Sui Sin Far's "In the Land of the Free" and Ambrose Bierce's "An Occurrence at Owl Creek Bridge."

3. From a psychoanalytic perspective, perform a close reading of Chopin's "The Story of an Hour."
   What does the story tell us, covertly, that we wouldn't have noticed without doing a psychoanalytic reading? How does psychoanalysis enhance our understanding of the text?
4. Using both narratology and psychoanalysis, describe what is happening in Gogol's "Diary of a Madman" when Poprishchin describes taking the letters that the two dogs, Meggy and Fidel, have written to each other. In other words, imagine that you are in the world of the story, watching these events take place. What do you see?
5. Using both narratology and psychoanalysis, describe what is happening at the end of Charlotte Perkins Gilman's "The Yellow Wallpaper."

## Selected Bibliography

Bodkin, Maud. *Archetypal Patterns in Poetry: Psychological Studies of Imagination.* New York: AMS, 1978.
Freud, Sigmund. *Delusion and Dream: an interpretation in the light of psychoanalysis of* Gradiva, *a novel, by Wilhelm Jensen.* Charleston: Nabu Press, 2007.
—. *The Ego and the Id.* Eastford: Martino, 2011.
—. *The Interpretation of Dreams.* New York: Basic, 2010.
—. *Totem and Taboo.* New York: Norton, 1950.
Frye, Northrup. *Anatomy of Criticism.* Toronto: Toronto UP, 2007.
Holland, Norman. *The Dynamics of Literary Response.* New York: Norton, 1975.
Jones, Ernest. *Hamlet and Oedipus.* New York: Norton, 1976.
Jung, Carl. *Psychological Types.* Princeton: Princeton UP, 1976.
Knapp, Bettina Liebowitz. *A Jungian Approach to Literature.* Carbondale: Southern Illinois UP, 1984.
Lacan, Jacques. "Desire and Interpretation of Desire in Hamlet." *Literature and Psychoanalysis: The Question of Reading: Otherwise.* Ed. Shoshana Felman. Baltimore: Johns Hopkins UP, 1982. 11-52.
—. *Ecrits: A Selection.* New York: Norton, 2004.
—. *My Teaching.* New York: Verso, 2009.
—. *The Language of the Self: The Function of Language in Psychoanalysis.* Baltimore: Johns Hopkins UP, 1997.
—. *The Four Fundamental Concepts of Psychoanalysis.* New York: Norton, 1998.
—. *The Seminar of Jacques Lacan: The Ethics of Psychoanalysis.* New York: Norton, 1997.
—. *The Seminar of Jacques Lacan: The Psychoses.* New York: Norton, 1997.

Paris, Bernard J. *A Psychological Approach to Fiction: Studies in Thackeray, Stendhal, George Eliot, Dostoevsky, and Conrad.* Piscataway: Transactions, 2010.

Ragland-Sullivan, Ellie. *Jacques Lacan and the Philosophy of Psychoanalysis.* Urbana: Illinois UP, 1987.

Skura, Meredith Anne. *The Literary Use of Psychoanalytic Process.* New Haven: Yale UP, 1983.

Tennenhouse, Leonard, ed. *The Practice of Psychoanalytic Criticism.* Detroit: Wayne State UP, 1976.

Wright, Elizabeth. *Psychoanalytic Criticism: A Reappraisal.* New York: Routledge, 1998.

Wyatt, Jean. *Reconstructuring Desire: The Role of the Unconscious in Women's Reading and Writing.* Chapel Hill: North Carolina UP, 1990.

# 3

# Marxism

FOCUSES ON: the overt (written) and covert (unwritten) text, as well as historical and biographical information, especially with regard to themes of economic power.

BECAUSE: Marxist critics believe that the dominant ideology of the ruling economic class is so pervasive that it affects everything we do and everything we create (including literary works) and their goal is to make us aware of this pervasive belief system in the hopes that this knowledge will begin the process of change.

DEVELOPED IN: 1910s.

NOTABLE PRACTITIONERS:

György Lukács (1885-1971)     Antonio Gramsci (1891-1937)
Walter Benjamin (1892-1940)   Max Horkheimer (1895-1973)
Bertolt Brecht (1898-1956)    Herbert Marcuse (1898-1979)
Theodor Adorno (1903-69)      Louis Althusser (1918-90)
Augusto Boal (1931-2009)      Fredric Jameson (1934- )
Terry Eagleton (1943- )

IMPORTANT PREDECESSORS:

Karl Marx (1818-83)           Friedrich Engels (1820-95)

ADVANTAGES: highlights the role that socioeconomic factors play in the creation of artistic works and the impact that they have on all aspects of our lives.

DISADVANTAGES: can ignore the unique literary and artistic value of a text.

DEFINITION: any of several branches of literary theory that examine a text through the lens of the political and socioeconomic theories of Karl Marx and Friedrich Engels.

---

Marxism, with respect to literary theory, refers to a group of related approaches to literature based upon the social, economic and political ideals put forth by Karl Marx and Friedrich Engels in the middle to late nineteenth century. Marx and Engels didn't consider themselves literary scholars. In fact, it wasn't until decades after their deaths (Marx's in 1883 and Engels' in 1895) that Marxism developed into a systematized method with which to approach literature. Marx and Engels were mainly interested in philosophy, sociology and history, especially as they relate to economics.

Today, the term, Marxism, is often maligned and misunderstood; it is commonly associated, in the West, with the repressive regimes of twentieth-century Russia, China and elsewhere. While the leaders of such governments may have claimed to base their philosophies on Marx's ideas, the societies that they created bore little resemblance to the ultimate society that Marx and Engels envisioned. While Marx understood that the ideal social structure would likely follow some sort of social class conflict, it's hard to imagine that he foresaw the senseless violence and suppression of thought that accompanied the "communism" of Stalin. Marx spent the majority of his adult life, after all, as the victim of the types of repressive governments that post-Revolution Russia became known for.

## The Roots of Marxism

Marx was born in 1818 in Trier, a town in the Lower Rhine Province of the Kingdom of Prussia (what is now Germany). During this time, Europe was in the midst of constant change geographically, politically and socially. Until 1806, the numerous small states that comprised modern-day Germany had been part of the Holy Roman Empire. Areas of Germany then changed hands several times during the Napoleonic Wars that finally ended in 1815 with Napoleon's defeat at Waterloo.

Aside from paving the way for Napoleon's rule (and the Napoleonic Wars that followed), the French Revolution of 1789 had another effect: it made other monarchies more cautious about possible uprisings in their own countries. The rulers of Austria, Britain, Prussia and Russia all worked quickly to quash even the slightest hint of rebellion in their own countries. In the newly-formed German Confederation, these efforts resulted in the 1819 Carlsbad Decrees, a set of rules that placed restrictions on student organizations, removed liberal professors from universities, and regularly monitored and censored every printed publication.

These censorship efforts didn't affect Marx for many of his early years. When Marx was in high school, though, his school was raided by the police after the government learned that "liberal" literature was being assigned to the students. Marx's empathy for the underprivileged developed during the years following this raid. Later, through his interaction with the Young Hegelians at the University of Berlin, this empathy began to develop into a more cogent system of philosophic beliefs. Marx's liberal leanings affected his graduate work as well. He knew that his dissertation wouldn't be approved by the conservative faculty at the University of Berlin; he submitted his work instead to the University of Jena, where he received his PhD in 1841.

The next year, in 1842, Marx moved to Cologne and began writing for a new, small newspaper, the *Rheinische Zeitung* (the *Rhine Newspaper*). Engels often wrote for this paper as well. Marx ultimately became editor of the *Rhine Newspaper*, but the paper was soon suppressed by the Prussian King Frederick William IV and then it was shut down completely in 1843.

Marx then moved to Paris and contributed to the only issue of the new radical newspaper, the *Deutsch-Französische Jahrbücher* (the *German-French Annals*). In 1844, in Paris, Marx then wrote for the last uncensored German-language newspaper still left in Europe, *Vorwärts!* (*Forward!*). By the end of the year, King Frederick William IV of Prussia convinced the French King, Louis Philippe I, to shut down the paper and to expel Marx from France.

From France, Marx moved to Belgium, but he was expelled two years later, in 1847, on charges that he supported a worker's revolution. He moved briefly back to France before returning to Germany in hopes of supporting the short-lived German Revolution of 1848. After this failed revolution, Marx remained in Germany and founded another reactionary newspaper, the *Neue Rheinische Zeitung* (the *New Rhenish Newspaper*). In 1849, the government closed down this new newspaper and expelled Marx again. He moved briefly with his wife and children to Paris, but he was soon expelled. He finally settled in London.

Friedrich Engels, like Marx, was a native of Prussia. Like Marx, Engels came from a well-to-do family; Engels' father owned and held shares in textile factories throughout Germany and Britain. Engels and Marx were familiar with each other's work, both contributing to many of the same radical newspapers, and they had met each other a few times in Germany, but it wasn't until they met at a café in Paris in 1844 that they befriended each other and began a lifetime of collaboration. Eventually, Engels would come to work in the office of one of his father's textile mills in Manchester, England, in order to serve as a financial benefactor for Marx. Engels and Marx worked together on numerous socialist writings, most notably *The Communist Manifesto* (published in 1848) and *Capital* (Part One published in 1867; Parts Two and Three published by Engels after Marx's death).

## Marx's Ideas

Marx developed a set of theories to describe the inevitable economic evolution of societies. Unlike other political and socioeconomic theories, Marxism offers us an analysis of our fundamental social structure. As Terry Eagleton points out, Marxism remains relevant because it is "the most searching, rigorous, comprehensive critique" of capitalism that we have ever had. As such, Marxism provides us with a means to question aspects of our social existence that we might otherwise fail to notice.

Marx categorized a society's development by its mode of production, or the way that the society is set up to manufacture and distribute goods and services. The mode of production includes the means of production (factories, tools, raw materials) and the relations of production (the relationship between the workers and the factory or business owner). Marx recognized that, as societies mature, they undergo four progressive stages involving their mode of production:

> the tribal, a primitive form of a communal classless society in which "products" like food and shelter are shared among the members.
> the ancient, characterized by a small ruling class (often believed to be gods or descendents of gods), ownership of property, and forced (slave) labor of outsiders.
> the feudal, typified by Europe in the Middle Ages, in which the primary form of property is land and the serfs of the lowest class have some rights (unlike slaves) but virtually no chance to improve their social position.
> the capitalist (or bourgeois), in which private individuals or entities own the primary means of production and members of the working class survive by selling their labor.

While it may be difficult to imagine today, capitalism was a recent development in the nineteenth century, owing to the industrial revolution that was taking root throughout the world. Marx believed that, as a society continued to evolve, capitalism would eventually give way to socialism, which would then be replaced by an advanced communal mode of production that he and Engels called communism. To Marx, the communist mode of production was as much an inevitable result of a society's progress as it was a goal to aspire to.

As capitalist societies develop, they advance toward maximum efficiency and productivity. This increased productivity, though, will inevitably be accompanied by an increased animosity between the wealthy owners (the bourgeoisie) and the working class (the proletariat). (Later Marxists developed dialectical materialism to conceptualize this interdependent conflict of opposites.) The natural tendency of the factory owner to produce products as inexpensively as possible is constantly at odds with the worker's desire to earn the highest possible wage for his efforts. According to Marx, these competing interests will eventually lead to conflict between the owner and the worker. This conflict will ultimately help to usher in the next successive mode of production.

Marx believed that capitalism also led inevitably to the alienation of the worker. He identified four types of worker alienation: alienation from the product of his or her work, alienation from the actual work, alienation from himself, and alienation from other workers. While Marx saw this alienation in all capitalist employment, it is most clearly evident in a factory assembly line. We could imagine, for example, a worker in a computer factory whose sole job is to attach specific components to the motherboards of computer after computer after computer. Because that worker has no sense of the finished computer, he becomes detached and alienated from the product of his work.

The worker on the end of the assembly line, though, who sees the computers in their completed state, is also alienated from the product because he has no concept of the work that was involved in building the computer. Even a worker who knows every position on the assembly line is alienated because he wasn't involved in the construction of the computer's individual parts—the processors, the wires, the screws, the plastic shell—nor was he involved in the design, engineering or programming of the computer. Likewise, the designers and engineers are detached from the construction and assembly of the product. Because of this division of labor, there is no one worker involved in the making of that computer, in other words, who could make an identical one completely from scratch. Each worker becomes, in essence, an automaton—a replaceable cog in the larger factory "machine"—whose only purpose is to contribute to the creation of a product. (Marx uses the term reification to describe this process.)

Rather than creating a product from its very beginning to its very end, our assembly line worker becomes alienated from his work through the endless repetition of his simple task. The worker has no control over how the final product will be constructed, how it will be used, how much it will cost or how much he will earn for his efforts. According to Marx, this creates a psychological void in the worker; he is unable to satisfy his innate need for productive labor. The worker's alienation from his work leads to his alienation from himself. Since his work life makes up a significant portion of his waking life, it becomes a significant factor in shaping his self-image. As he grows more into the role of his reified worker self, he becomes alienated from the individualized, unique human being that he was before he entered the workforce.

Finally, in a capitalist economy, the worker becomes alienated from other workers. The goal of the factory owner is to get as much work as possible out of his workers for the lowest possible cost. To do this, the owner pays the lowest wages possible (determined by laws, need and the number of available workers). The factory owner could pay more, but he doesn't have to, knowing that any worker who is unsatisfied with his or her wages could easily be replaced. This leaves workers in constant competition with each other for their jobs. As a result, the bourgeoisie (owners) have a more compliant workforce; workers are more willing to conform to the rules and whims of the employer when they know they could be easily replaced. Marx would argue that these same concepts apply to every worker in a capitalist society.

If we were to pay someone a small amount to build a product—a broom, for example—and then sell that broom back to them for twenty times what we paid them to make it, they would most likely think that was unfair. But, Marx says, this is the exact thing that happens to every worker every day in a capitalist society. While the product might be different (hamburgers, furniture, data entered into a computer, etc.) and the method of exchange is more advanced, Marx argues that all labor in a capitalist system follows these same fundamental principles. The reason workers don't revolt, according to Marx, is because the prevailing ideology, or fundamental belief system, of a capitalist society is shaped by the privileged class and it has conditioned us to accept this unfair situation as normal. The primary focus of Marxism, then, is the capitalist society's economic system and the ideology that enables it. Marxism's ultimate goal is to apply our understanding of this system to change the world for the better. As Marx notes in his "Theses on Feuerbach" (1845), "The philosophers have only interpreted the world, in various ways; the point is to change it."

## Marxism in Russia

Marxist ideas began to be incorporated into literary analysis in Russia after the 1917 Revolution. This wasn't an immediate change. For the first few years after the Revolution, in fact, literary discussion was more vibrant than ever. The Commissar of Education was friendly with members of both the Futurist and Formalist groups and so the government maintained an open-minded and supportive approach to the arts. Though publications were limited during this time (due to shortages of paper), it was common in Moscow and Petrograd to see impromptu literary debates taking place in shops and on street corners almost every afternoon and evening. These discussions were often lively and they often drew large crowds of passersby.

Eventually, the idea of a Marxist reading of a text was debated. These early Marxist arguments were usually proposed by one of the Symbolists in a debate with one or another of the Formalists (often Eikhenbaum or Shklovsky). The Symbolists, at first, had little success. Gradually, a Marxist approach became more popular in scholarly discussions. Even Shklovsky, one of the founding members of the Formalist group *Opajaz* (The Society for the Study of Poetic Language) later began to include Marxist thought in his analyses.

After Lenin's death in 1924, the move toward a Marxist approach became more insistent. Anatoly Lunacharsky became less influential as the Commissar of Education and Formalist thought no longer dominated the conversation. Leon Trotsky's *Literature and Revolution* (1924), reflected this more pronounced emphasis on Marxism. While *Literature and Revolution* doesn't provide a Marxist literary critique in the conventional sense, it does explain the need for such an approach and it outlines Trotsky's ideas on how a Marxist analysis should be undertaken. Because of this, Trotsky's book is sometimes considered the first example of Marxist literary criticism.

By 1932, when Stalin created the Soviet Writer's Union (and made himself president of the group), all literary scholars in Russia were expected to utilize a Marxist approach; those who didn't were either exiled, imprisoned, or executed. Consequently, because of these purges and the resultant suppression of thought, there were few advances in Marxist literary analysis in Russia after 1932.

## Reflection Theory

In the rest of the world, Marxism was just beginning to develop into a multifaceted method of literary analysis. Because the body of Marx's work was so extensive, twentieth-century literary scholars had a huge selection of Marx's ideas to study and to expand upon as they utilized Marxism in their own critical analyses. Much of this early study focused on the relationship between a society's economic base and its cultural superstructure. Marxist scholars most often equate the base with the means and the relations of production and the superstructure with a society's ideologies of culture, including the arts, law, politics and religion. In his preface to *A Contribution to the Critique of Political Economy* (1859), Marx outlines his ideas regarding the base and superstructure:

> In the social production which men carry on they enter into definite relations that are indispensable and independent of their will; these relations of production correspond to a definite stage of development of their material powers of production. The sum total of these relations of production constitutes the economic structure of society—the real foundation, on which rise legal and political superstructures and to which correspond definite forms of social consciousness. The mode of production in material life determines the general character of the social, political and spiritual processes of life. It is not the consciousness of men that determines their existence, but, on the contrary, their social existence determines their consciousness.

In other words, according to Marx, our laws, our politics, our arts and our fundamental beliefs are all shaped by the way we produce and distribute goods and services.

The exact nature of this relationship between the base and the superstructure, though, would become a point of debate among Marxist scholars throughout the twentieth century. The first Marxist literary theorist to address this issue was György Lukács from Hungary. Lukács saw this relationship as purely non-reciprocal. He believed that the base shapes the superstructure but the superstructure has no effect upon the base. This understanding formed the basis for Lukács' reflection theory: if the base shapes the superstructure, then the superstructure will reflect that base. Because of this belief, Lukács and his adherents came to be known as reflectionists (later referred to as vulgar Marxists).

Since literature is one aspect of the superstructure, each literary work, according to Lukács, will reflect the author's relationship to the economic base. Every author is a member of one or another social class. While a writer may try to conceal his social standing, Lukács believed that his choice of poetic devices would reveal his true worldview or *weltanschauung*. A bourgeois writer, for example, will use different metaphors, similes, images, etc. than a writer from the proletariat. Analyzing such textual elements would reveal the author's relationship to the economic base. He saw this as an important avenue of analysis because, like Engels and Marx, Lukács believed a society's ideology was a false consciousness, disseminated by the bourgeoisie. Lukács, therefore, advocated a close reading of a text, based upon the Formalist method, to examine a text's poetic devices. Thus began modern Marxist literary criticism.

## The Frankfurt School

Marxist theory expanded into a more sophisticated body of thought in Germany with the Frankfurt School. The Frankfurt School wasn't an actual *school*; the term refers instead to the group of theorists associated with the University of Frankfurt's Institute for Social Research. In that sense, the Frankfurt School is more akin to the "Circles" that formed in Russia in the early twentieth century (the Moscow Linguistic Circle and the Bakhtin Circle, for example). Unlike those Russian literary circles, though, the Institute for Social Research and the Frankfurt School were formally affiliated with a government-supported university (until 1933, when the Institute was disbanded during the rise of the Nazis; it then moved to Geneva and then the U.S. before returning to Frankfurt in 1951).

The Frankfurt School consisted of a diverse group of intellectuals from a variety of academic disciplines. The scholars most often associated with its pre-1933 incarnation included Theodor Adorno, Walter Benjamin, Erich Fromm, Max Horkheimer, and Herbert Marcuse. The common thread that united them all was an abiding interest in the work of Marx and Engels. The Frankfurt School was particularly intrigued by how Marxism, as it was then understood, failed to account for the developments in Europe following World War I. While the Revolution in Russia was an initial success—at least from the Bolshevik viewpoint—a similar revolution had failed in Germany in 1919. Italy, too, saw the seemingly inevitable move toward socialism overtaken by the fascism of Benito Mussolini.

One area of concern for the Frankfurt School was the direction that some Marxist study had taken. Most Marxist scholarship up to this point had a political agenda. Since Marx had written so extensively on such a broad range of issues, it was easy for anyone to use Marx's work to justify their own aspirations. As a (primarily) non-political entity, the Frankfurt School sought to study the work of Marx impartially, free from the influence of a political purpose. Still, the Frankfurt School did have an objective. Through the practice of critical theory—a term coined by Horkheimer—the Frankfurt School hoped to enlighten people to their ideological oppression in an effort to bring about social change. Or, as Horkheimer described it in his essay, "Traditional and Critical Theory" (1937), they wanted "to liberate human beings from the circumstances that enslave them."

The Frankfurt School members were like-minded enough that today they are often seen as part of a homogeneous whole. Still, because of their varied interests and scholarly backgrounds, members had diverging opinions on a number of topics. The most notable disagreement, with regard to literary studies, concerned the nature of twentieth-century art. In "The Work of Art in the Age of Mechanical Reproduction" (1936), Walter Benjamin sees in popular, mass-produced art the potential to bring about positive social change through action. Such mass-produced art, he believed, was stripped of the "aura" that accompanied, for example, an original painting. When the aura is thus stripped, the result is self-alienation, or a disconnect between the viewer / reader / consumer and the characters on the screen, in the photograph or on the page.

Benjamin argued that, when we recognize fictionalized characters as characters, and not as real people, we are less inclined to empathize with them. When this happens, we see the work of art objectively, making us unable to experience the cathartic release that Aristotle described. When we can't *feel* that catharsis, we are forced to *think* about the work, which will make us more inclined to fight for social change after our consumption of the artwork is complete. Similar ideas were expressed by the Marxist playwright, Bertolt Brecht, whose "estrangement effect" in his epic theater reminded his plays' audiences that what they were watching was not reality, but instead a constructed representation of reality. The goal was to help the audience understand that their own reality—the reality of their real lives—was constructed in a similar fashion and, upon this realization, they would be impelled to take action for change.

Mass-produced art also gave us the opportunity to see things we wouldn't otherwise notice. As Benjamin says,

> By close-ups of the things around us, by focusing on hidden details of familiar objects, by exploring common place milieus under the ingenious guidance of the camera, [. . .] the camera introduces us to unconscious optics as does psychoanalysis to unconscious impulses.

A photograph can capture, for example, split-second movements that would pass too quickly for us to see in real time. By the same token, a camera can zoom in on details that we can't perceive with the naked eye. Benjamin's expectation is that, through the recognition of these "unconscious optics," we will eventually come to question other aspects of our reality that have thus far been hidden from us (namely, our subjugation at the hands of the ruling-class ideology). Then we will be more inclined to change our situation.

Adorno, on the other hand, expressed a very different opinion on such artistic endeavors. His view was shaped partly by the developments he witnessed in Germany leading up to World War II, and partly by his subsequent experiences with what he described as the repressive conformity of America's culture industry. Except for some work of the modern period, which he believed expressed the true, unpleasant nature of reality, Adorno saw mass-produced art as an instrument of oppression. He believed the industries that provided such art (book publishers, movie studios) were capitalistic by nature. They served the bourgeoisie by turning books and movies into simple commodities. These commodities were produced for the sole purpose of generating a profit for the privileged-class owners of those publishing houses and movie studios. And, as a commodity of the ruling class, published books and movies will invariably promote and maintain the ideology of the ruling class. (It is, after all, the bourgeois owners of the movie studios and publishing houses who decide what movies get made and what books get published).

Despite uncharacteristic disagreements like these, the Frankfurt School maintained, on the whole, a unified approach to Marxist cultural studies. Though their goal of enlightening the populace to ignite social change was unsuccessful, they nevertheless guided Marxist theory toward a future as a serious approach to literature.

## Cultural Hegemony

Another early Marxist scholar was Antonio Gramsci from Italy. Gramsci wasn't a literary theorist; in fact, he saw literature as a tool of the bourgeoisie to maintain their control over the proletariat. (He argued that if, as Marxists believe, literature is a part of the superstructure, and the superstructure is shaped by the economic base—which is controlled by the ruling class—then literature can only represent the interests of the bourgeoisie.) Nevertheless, Gramsci's ideas greatly influenced Marxist literary criticism and shaped the future of Marxist literary scholarship.

Gramsci believed the relationship between the base and the superstructure was more complex than earlier theorists like Lukács understood it to be. The bourgeois maintain their control over the proletariat by preserving their bourgeoisie ideology. According to Gramsci, it is the proletariat themselves who give their consent to be controlled by the bourgeoisie and it is the proletariat who adopt bourgeois values and beliefs.

Gramsci grew up on the small Italian island of Sardinia. When he was twelve, he had to work sixty hours a week to support his family. At nineteen, he began attending the University of Turin on a small scholarship. In 1913, the twenty-two-year-old Gramsci became an avowed socialist. He argued for better pay and better working conditions for factory workers as part of Italy's popular socialist movement. When the 1917 Russian Revolution began, Gramsci reasonably assumed that a similar socialist revolution would soon take place in Italy.

Instead, though, the Fascist movement of Mussolini gained momentum and eventually took control of Italy. Gramsci was elected to the Italian Parliament on the Communist ticket in 1924, but Mussolini's regime soon had him under surveillance and, in 1926, Gramsci and the other Communist party leaders were arrested. During his incarceration, he wrote *The Prison Notebooks* (1935), the work for which he is most renowned today.

Gramsci hoped to understand, in Marxist terms, how the fascist regime of Mussolini could rise to power in a society that seemed so ripe for a socialist revolution. The interests of the fascist leadership, after all, were clearly—to Gramsci, at least—contrary to the best interests of the Italian working class. Gramsci found that a traditional reading of Marx was inadequate to explain these developments. In *The Prison Notebooks*, Gramsci advances his theory of cultural hegemony. Cultural hegemony, in simple terms, refers to the control of a society's cultural superstructure by one dominant group (usually the upper class). Since the small ruling class would be unable to control the masses through simple force, and since they can't gain total control through economic means, they must maintain control another way. The theory of cultural hegemony argues that the ruling class bourgeoisie of a society controls the masses by manipulating them into accepting the ruling-class worldview as their own. When the working class accepts the bourgeoisie ideology as normal and correct, the ruling class is easily able to impose their will politically, economically and socially. Once this is accomplished, the working class will fight to preserve the unfair status quo, even though it is contrary to its own best interests.

To effect societal change, Gramsci argues, it is necessary to make the masses aware of the cultural manipulation that they are exposed to and then to replace the dominant ideology of the privileged class with their own ideology. Unlike Lenin, who saw cultural concerns of secondary importance to political goals, Gramsci believed that the working class couldn't obtain economic and political power unless they first gained control of the cultural ideology. This, of course, is no easy task. The dominant ideology of the ruling class is intertwined not only with a society's worldview, but also its myths, religion and popular culture. As such, the dominant ideology is perpetually reinforced by all aspects of culture. It is reinforced, too, from generation to generation. Furthermore, as the ruling class gains more economic control, the individual members of the working class become more focused on the specific needs of their own family (feeding the children, paying the bills, fixing the leaky roof). This results in less time or energy to worry about economic unfairness, further strengthening the cultural control of the ruling class.

While Gramsci's interests weren't literary, he would become one of the most influential Marxists of the twentieth century.

## Ideological State Apparatuses

Gramsci's writings would go on to influence the Marxist thought of Louis Althusser in France. Much of Althusser's work on ideology is, in a way, a continuation of Gramsci's, but Althusser had a more hopeful attitude with regard to literature and the arts. This is because Althusser's understanding of the relationship between the base and the superstructure was different than Gramsci's. Whereas Gramsci saw this relationship as non-reciprocal (the base shapes the superstructure but the superstructure doesn't affect the base), Althusser recognized it as interdependent. As such, they can each inform and influence the other.

This means that, for Althusser, the superstructure can shape and influence the base just as the base shapes and influences the superstructure. In this view, literature can become more than simply a tool used by the privileged class to maintain control on the working class. The working class can also use literature and the arts to foment revolution and to bring about change.

Althusser's work coincides with a period that saw Marxism more widely accepted as a viable literary theory. Much of the Marxist thought before 1960 was social or philosophic in nature. We see this expressed in France with Jean-Paul Sartre's *Critique of Dialectical Reason* (1960) and the work of Maurice Merleau-Ponty. With regard to Marxist literary theory, most of it before 1960 had a limited audience (which consisted mostly of like-minded Marxists). There were a number of reasons for this, one of them being politics. After the end of World War II, the Cold War made words like communism (and, by extension, Marxism) synonymous with evil. In the United States, this belief took the form of McCarthyism, the Hollywood blacklist and the infamous behavior of the House Un-American Activities Committee. While the anti-communist fervor in other parts of the Western world was not as virulent as in the U.S., it still guided the direction of academic study and made Marxist literary analysis impractical for most Western scholars. Furthermore, because of the perceived superiority of new criticism during this time, there was little reason for theorists to pursue any other avenue of literary analysis, let alone a politically unpopular one like Marxism.

This began to change after the death of Stalin (in 1953) and the rise of the American and European countercultures. The advent of structuralism and archetypal criticism also paved the way for other theoretical perspectives besides new criticism. Consequently, a variety of social, political and academic factors provided a much more receptive audience for Marxist literary criticism in the 1960s. This more tolerant attitude toward Marxism began in France with Althusser's first major publications, *For Marx* (1965) and *Reading Capital* (1965), and his most famous essay, "Ideology and Ideological State Apparatuses" (1970). Thus began the renewed acceptance of Marxism in France.

Earlier Marxist thought argues that our economic system and, in particular, the ideology created by that system, effectively turn us into machines—Marx's idea of reification—but this is usually understood in a figurative sense. While the system treats us as if we are mere cogs in the huge economic engine, earlier Marxist approaches still recognize us as unique individuals with free will (though the system makes it nearly impossible to exercise that free will). Althusser sees this reification in a more literal sense. In "Ideology and Ideological State Apparatuses," he uses the term interpellation to describe how our ideology defines, shapes and *creates* us as ideological "subjects" while, at the same time, convincing us that we are unique, self-determined individuals with free will. As Althusser says, "those who are in ideology believe themselves by definition outside ideology [. . .] the accusation of being in ideology only applies to others, never to oneself." Furthermore, according to Althusser, this process begins even before we are born. While we may have brief moments of recognition of our situation, we are never fully aware of the true nature of our place in the capitalist society.

In the same essay, Althusser also discusses the role that Ideological State Apparatuses play in reinforcing the dominant ideology. Ideological State Apparatuses (abbreviated by Althusser as ISAs) are those institutions that maintain and perpetuate the ideology of the privileged class.

In doing so, these ISAs help the ruling class control the workers and keep them from revolting. Althusser identifies eight institutions as ISAs:

> the religious ISA (the system of the different churches),
> the educational ISA (the system of the different public and private 'schools'),
> the family ISA,
> the legal ISA,
> the political ISA (the political system, including the different parties),
> the trade-union ISA,
> the communications ISA (press, radio and television, etc.),
> the cultural ISA (literature, the arts, sports, etc.).

These are in contrast to the Repressive State Apparatuses (RSAs), which include "the Government, the Administration, the Army, the Police, the Courts, the Prisons, etc." While the RSAs maintain control overtly, through force (or the implied threat of force), the ISAs are more pernicious, working covertly to convince us that the unfairness inherent in a capitalist society is simply "the way it is" (and the way it should be). Since it would be impossible for the small ruling class to control the working class purely through force, the ISAs are necessary to maintain the system of class structure in the capitalist society.

We should note, if it isn't already obvious, that these ISAs don't consciously set out to perpetuate the capitalist system. Public school teachers don't go into work each morning hoping to shape their students into compliant members of the working class. What these ISAs do instead, according to Althusser, is repeatedly reinforce the need for control. Students are expected to come to class on time, to sit quietly at their desks, to do the work they are asked to do, and to speak or to use the restroom only after they are given permission to do so. The educational ISA, Althusser argues, teaches us "submission to the rules of the established order [or] the ruling ideology." Students are groomed, in other words, to become ideal reified workers.

The ISAs also maintain and perpetuate the dominant ideology by reinforcing our expected relationship with authority figures. The religious ISA expects us to respect the authority of our church and our God; the educational ISA expects respect for the authority of our teachers; the family ISA expects respect for the authority of our parents; and so on. These expectations, again, then unconsciously extend to respect for all authority, which leads, in our adult lives, to respect for the authority of our employer and our work supervisors.

While Althusser believed that RSAs and ISAs determined nearly every aspect of our lives, he saw hope for change in our art and our literature.

## The Political Unconscious

Contemporary Marxist criticism is guided primarily by the work of Terry Eagleton, from Britain, and the American Fredric Jameson.

While Althusser popularized Marxism in France, Jameson and Eagleton made Marxism relevant in the U.S. and England. This new interest was facilitated by Jameson's book, *Marxism and Form* (1971). In it, Jameson discusses the work of the major theorists of twentieth-century Marxist thought, namely Lukács, Adorno, Benjamin, Marcuse, Schiller, Bloch and Sartre. *Marxism and Form* describes the work of these scholars in order to differentiate their philosophies from the "communism" of Stalin that Marxism was most often associated with. This paved the way for Marxism to become accepted in the American and British academic communities.

Jameson's *The Political Unconscious* (1981) argues for a Marxist analysis of every literary text, seeing the Marxist approach "not as some supplementary method, not as an optional auxiliary to other interpretive methods [. . .] but rather as the absolute horizon of all reading and all interpretation." In much the same way that psychoanalytic theory examines the mental unconscious, Jameson proposes that a Marxist critique should focus on the political unconscious. He based this on the belief that everything we do, whether we consciously realize it or not, is influenced by our political milieu.

Jameson offers a procedure for a modern Marxist analysis that involves three steps or phases (he calls them "semantic horizons"): the political, the social and the historical. In the first phase, the political horizon, we view the text as if it is a "symbolic act" or a symbolic commentary on the ideology of the ruling class. In what ways, in other words, does the text symbolically reinforce, perpetuate or undermine the dominant ideology?

In contrast to the political horizon, which treats the text as if it emanates from one voice, the social horizon approaches the text as if it is (to use Bakhtin's term) dialogic. In this second phase, we read the text as an ideological dialogue between the dominant and the oppressed social classes. The text communicates this conversation through what Jameson calls ideologemes, the most fundamental components of an ideology's expression. Just as Ferdinand de Saussure identified phonemes as the smallest units of a language, and Claude Lévi-Strauss identified mythemes as the smallest units of myth, Jameson's ideologemes are the smallest articulated units of an ideology. These ideologemes take the form of individual statements or opinions that are shaped by one or another ideology. When we express an opinion about a topic, for example, and that opinion—unbeknownst to us—has been shaped by our ideology, that opinion is an ideologeme. In a literary text, ideologemes can take the form of character actions, dialogue or narrative statements that serve as the voice of an ideology.

Ideologemes operate as individual utterances in a conversation between contrasting socioeconomic belief systems. According to Jameson, the idea of a single voice within a text is an illusion. All texts are dialogic, even those that seem to put forth only one side in this ideological conversation. While the literary masterpieces of history survive because they perpetuated only the voice of their dominant social class, they nevertheless had, originally, another voice to which they were opposed. If this other voice doesn't appear in the text, Jameson's social horizon would have us restore or artificially reconstruct it. Doing this allows us to see more clearly where the text stands in this ideological debate. Then we realize, for example, that the entire genre of the fairy tale works to undermine the "hegemonic aristocratic form of the epic, with its somber ideology of heroism and baleful destiny."

The historical horizon examines the text from the perspective of a society's successive modes of production. To Jameson, the mode of production is reflected in the form of the literary text; he uses the term "ideology of form." Thus, the terza rima that Dante utilizes in *The Divine Comedy* is different from the modernist prose of Joyce because their respective societies had different modes of production. Jameson identified different forms of literature with each mode of production. (While Marx later revised his paradigm to recognize just four historical stages of development—the tribal, the ancient, the feudal and the capitalist—some scholars, Jameson included, prefer Marx's earlier model.) Jameson, therefore, found that myth and magical narratives corresponded with the tribal mode, kinship narratives with the Neolithic, religious and sacred narratives with the Asiatic, political narratives with the ancient, quest narratives with the feudal, and "commodity reification" narratives with capitalism. The text's form, then, provides an unconscious commentary on one or another societal mode of production.

Moving outward from these three successive interpretive horizons, Jameson argued, was the most complete and accurate way to conduct an analysis on any piece of literature.

Like Jameson, Eagleton believes that any text can—and should—be read from a Marxist perspective. While Eagleton doesn't provide the same type of systematized approach on the level of Jameson's three horizons, he does offer in his books a number of thoughtful historical explications of theory in general and Marxism in particular which underscore the need for Marxist analysis. Such analysis is important, Eagleton believes, because he sees in literature not only the power to reinforce the dominant class' ideology, but the power to shape that ideology as well. While he has taken a more inclusive approach to theory in the last few decades, arguing against what he calls the "fetishism of method," he remains an avowed Marxist, imbuing nearly everything he writes with his Marxist viewpoint.

Most people consider Eagleton's writing style much more accessible than Jameson's, giving him a much wider popular appeal among nonacademics. He is also one of the most overtly political and outspoken Marxist scholars working today. He often writes on nonacademic and political topics, often with humor and biting sarcasm. When discussing modern capitalism he sardonically suggests it is "in impeccable working order"; and he describes America's answer to unemployment as "an ingenious solution [. . .] over a million more people would be seeking work if they were not in prison." Such an approach likely leads him to be taken less seriously by those who still cling to the disproven notion that Marxism equates with Stalinist communism.

Still, because of Eagleton's thorough knowledge of theoretical history and his clear explanations, he is rightly considered the most important Marxist critic today. Any student interested in Marxism would do well to begin with him.

## Implementation

Marxist critics are interested in a capitalist society's economic disparity between the wealthy ruling class and the underprivileged working class. A Marxist reading, therefore, will focus on how a text speaks to those issues—whether it does so overtly or covertly, intentionally or inadvertently.

Marxist literary criticism begins with the premise that a capitalist society's dominant ideology permeates and shapes every aspect of our conscious and unconscious being. As a result, this ideology shapes all of our art and literature. Marxist critics disagree, though, exactly how much and in what way it is shaped. This diversity of opinion results in a variety of Marxist approaches to a text. Some prefer a structured method similar to Jameson's three-horizon process while others find that a less structured approach is better suited to an individual text. Whatever method one prefers, all Marxist approaches work toward a goal of making readers aware of the insidious nature of a society's dominant ideology.

Jameson's approach begins in the political horizon. In Gilman's "The Yellow Wallpaper," for example, a Marxist might see the story's plot as a politically symbolic act, representative of the oppression that the working class is subjected to by the wealthy ruling class. The dominant ideology is represented by the narrator's husband, John. He spends the story, after all, subtly imposing his will upon his wife. He decides where and how she spends her time, when she eats, and what medication she takes. The narrator, on the other hand, expresses the ideology of the oppressed. In much the way that the oppressed working class is described by Gramsci, Gilman's narrator willingly accepts her oppression, even as she disagrees with it.

As we move into the social horizon, our focus moves from the overarching "symbolic act" of the story to the dialogic interaction between the story's ideologemes, the individual story elements that engage in this ideological dialogue. The discourse of their respective ideologemes begins early in the narrative: she thinks there is something strange about the mansion they rent, he laughs at her; she believes she has a real illness, he "assures friends and relatives" that she is fine; he forbids her from doing any creative activity, she slyly writes in her diary. These competing ideologies push back and forth throughout the story.

In the historical horizon, we would note that the story, written at the end of the nineteenth century, was a product of a period of capitalist development that saw some of the greatest discrepancies between the wealthy ruling class and the oppressed working class. The dreadful conditions that most workers endured were overshadowed by the ideological pride for the "achievements" of America's most well-known industrialists like Andrew Carnegie, John D. Rockefeller, and so on. "The Yellow Wallpaper," then, in the form of the short story, is an ideological product of this period. Unlike early novels, which were often read by members of the privileged classes who didn't have to work sixty hours a week, the short story enjoyed a wider audience. It is, to Marxists, a commodity that was designed and produced with the primary goal of making money. In this view, the writer takes the role of the bourgeois factory owner who designs and produces that commodity to attract the largest possible purchasing audience. In Jameson's historical horizon, then, we would want to consider how the historical mode of production shapes our understanding of the story we are analyzing.

Those who prefer a less structured Marxist approach might focus on any number of aspects of Gilman's story. Some use as a guide Ira Shor's 1972 essay, "Questions Marxists Ask About Literature." Others prefer to concentrate on the author's life, socioeconomic status or place in history. How might Gilman's ideological milieu, for example, have shaped her story? Is there anything in the story—or in her life—that might suggest a political or philosophical position? A Marxist reading could also center on the story's characters, themes or literary devices, or on the values that the text seems to favor. Or, it might have a more general focus on the story's plot. We could note, for example, that the entire premise of "The Yellow Wallpaper" is based upon a situation that would be alien to a working-class family. While postpartum depression can affect women of all social classes, only a member of the privileged classes would have the luxury of a wet nurse and a three-month stay in a country estate while being treated with a "rest cure."

Alternately, a Marxist reading might equate the narrator's husband with a bourgeois factory owner who controls every aspect of his workers' lives. The narrator, too, is reminiscent of the reified factory worker who remains nameless (or, at least, nameless until the end; some readers argue that the delusional narrator's single mention of "Jane" in the second-to-last paragraph is a reference to herself). In a reading such as this, we might note other story elements that reinforce this understanding of the narrator as factory worker: her husband reinforces her subordinate role by addressing her with appellations such as "blessed little goose" and "little girl"; she has little control over her own life; she is confined to the same room day after day; she is required to focus on a singular task (to "rest"); any deviation from this task (such as writing in her diary) must be done in secret; and her only means of mental escape is to stare at the walls. A Marxist might further argue that the way she is transfixed by the wallpaper mirrors the reification process of the subjugated factory worker who becomes inured to her life of oppression.

There are any number of story elements that a Marxist critic might focus on as he or she draws his own conclusions. In contrast to the New Critics (and the Symbolists before them) who viewed literature as a product of inspiration, or the psychoanalysts who saw literature as a product of the author's unconscious, Marxists see literature as a product of an ideology. Whatever Marxist approach one chooses, the goal is to make us aware of the pervasive nature of the dominant ideology so that we might take that first step toward change.

## Important Moments in Marxist Criticism

**1844:** Engels' *The Condition of the Working Class in England*
**1845:** Marx's "Theses on Feuerbach"
**1848:** Marx's and Engels' *The Communist Manifesto*
**1849:** Marx's "Wage Labor and Capital"
**1852:** Marx's "The Eighteenth Brumaire of Louis Napoleon"
**1859:** Marx's *A Contribution to the Critique of Political Economy*
**1867:** Part One of *Capital*
**1885:** Part Two of *Capital*
**1894:** Part Three of *Capital*
**1917:** Russian Revolution
**1918:** Ernst Bloch's *The Spirit of Utopia*
**1923:** Lukács' *History and Class Consciousness*
**1923:** Institute for Social Research (the Frankfurt School) founded
**1924:** Leon Trotsky's *Literature and Revolution*
**1927:** Marx's *Economic and Philosophic Manuscripts of 1844* first published (in Russia)
**1930:** Bertolt Brecht's "The Modern Theater is the Epic Theater"
**1932:** Marx's and Engels' *The German Ideology* first published (in Russia)
**1933:** Frankfurt School relocates to Switzerland and then the U.S.
**1935:** Antonio Gramsci's *Prison Notebooks*

**1936:** Walter Benjamin's "The Work of Art in the Age of Mechanical Reproduction"
**1937:** Max Horkheimer's "Traditional and Critical Theory"
**1944:** Theodor Adorno and Max Horkheimer's *Dialectic of Enlightenment*
**1951:** Theodor Adorno's *Minima Moralia*
**1960:** Jean-Paul Sartre's *Critique of Dialectical Reason*
**1964:** Herbert Marcuse's *One-Dimensional Man*
**1965:** Louis Althusser's *For Marx*
**1965:** Althusser's *Reading Capital* (written with Étienne Balibar, Roger Establet, Jacques Rancière, and Pierre Macherey)
**1968:** Benjamin's *Illuminations* (a collection of his essays) translated into English
**1968:** Althusser's *Lenin and Philosophy and Other Essays*
**1970:** Althusser's "Ideology and Ideological State Apparatuses"
**1971:** Fredric Jameson's *Marxism and Form*
**1976:** Terry Eagleton's *Criticism and Ideology*
**1976:** Eagleton's *Marxism and Literary Criticism*
**1979:** Augusto Boal's *Theatre of the Oppressed*
**1981:** Fredric Jameson's *The Political Unconscious*
**1990:** Eagleton's *The Ideology of the Aesthetic*
**1991:** Jameson's *Postmodernism: The Cultural Logic of Late Capitalism*
**2011:** Eagleton's *Why Marx Was Right*

## Important Terms

alienation
bourgeoisie
commodity
communism
Ideological State Apparatus
means of production
proletariat
reification
Repressive State Apparatus
superstructure

base
capitalism
commodity fetishism
dialectical materialism
ideology
mode of production
reflection theory
relations of production
socialism

## Study Questions

1. Consider your own life and describe how the Marxist ideas of alienation, reification or interpellation might apply to you.
2. Marx's idea of commodification describes how a capitalist society turns our actual labor into a commodity like a pair of shoes or a computer. Detail three examples where you have experienced this yourself.

3. Reread your favorite short story with a conscious eye toward uncovering examples of how the dominant ideology influenced and shaped the text.
4. Consider a story of your choice through the lenses of both psychoanalysis and Marxism. How would these two readings compare? What can you gain from a Marxist reading of the story that you couldn't get from a psychoanalytic reading, and vice-versa? Use specific scenes from the story as you develop your position.
4. How would a Marxist critic compare Grace King's "The Little Convent Girl" to Sui Sin Far's "In the Land of the Free."?
5. From a Marxist perspective, write a brief essay about a story of your choice that uncovers some truth about the story that isn't explicitly stated in the text. Examine all aspects of the story to find at least one significant truth that is implied but not actually written in the text. Perhaps you'd like to focus on the story's plot or its theme. Maybe a character's motivations become more clear when viewed from a Marxist point of view.

## Selected Bibliography

Althusser, Louis. *For Marx*. New York: Vintage, 1969.
—. *Lenin and Philosophy and Other Essays*. New York: Monthly Review, 2001.
—. *On Ideology*. New York: Verso, 2008.
—. Politics and History: Montesquieu, Rousseau, Marx. New York: Verso, 2007.
—. *Reading Capital*. New York: Verso, 2009.
Adorno, Theodor. *Minima Moralia: Reflections on a Damaged Life*. New York: Verso, 2006.
—. and Max Horkheimer. *Dialectic of Enlightenment*. Palo Alto: Stanford UP, 2007.
Benjamin, Walter. *Illuminations*. New York: Pimlico, 1999.
Boal, Augusto. *Theatre of the Oppressed*. London: Pluto, 2008.
Brecht, Bertolt. *Brecht on Theatre: The Development of an Aesthetic*. New York: Hill and Wang, 1977.
—. "The Modern Theatre is the Epic Theatre: Notes to the Opera Aufstieg und Fall der Stadt Mahagonny." *Brecht on Theatre: The Development of an Aesthetic.* Ed. John Willett. London: Methuen, 1964. 33-42.
Eagleton, Terry. "Base and Superstructure Revisited." *New Literary History*, 31.2, Economics and Culture: Production, Consumption, and Value (Spring 2000). 231-40.
—. *Criticism and Ideology: A Study in Marxist Literary Theory*. New York: Verso, 2006.

—. "Estrangement and Irony." *Salmagundi*, 73, Milan Kundera: Fictive Lightness, Fictive Weight (Winter 1987). 25-32.
—. "God, the Universe, Art, and Communism." *New Literary History*, 32.1, Views and Interviews (Winter 2001). 23-32.
—. *The Ideology of the Aesthetic*. New York: Wiley, 1991.
—. *Literary Theory: An Introduction*. Minneapolis: Minnesota UP, 2008.
—. "Marxism and Deconstruction." *Contemporary Literature*, 22.4, Marxism and the Crisis of the World (Autumn 1981). 477-88.
—. *Marxism and Literary Criticism*. Berkeley: California UP, 1976.
—. *Why Marx was Right*. New Haven: Yale UP, 2011.
Gramsci, Antonio. *Prison Notebooks*. New York: Columbia, 2010.
Habermas, Jürgen. *The Structural Transformation of the Public Sphere: An Inquiry into a Category of Bourgeois Society*. Boston: MIT, 1991.
Jameson, Fredric. *The Political Unconscious: Narrative as a Socially Symbolic Act*. Ithaca: Cornell UP, 1981.
—. *Marxism and Form: Twentieth-Century Dialectical Theories of Literature*. Princeton: Princeton UP, 1974.
—. "The Politics of Theory: Ideological Positions in the Postmodernism Debate." *New German Critique* 33, Modernity and Postmodernity (Autumn, 1984). 53-65.
Lukács, György. *A Defence of History and Class Consciousness: Tailism and the Dialectic*. New York: Verso, 2002.
—. *History and Class Consciousness: Studies in Marxist Dialectics*. Boston: MIT Press, 1972.
—. *The Historical Novel*. Lincoln: Nebraska UP, 1983.
—. *Lenin: A Study on the Unity of His Thought*. New York: Verso, 2009.
—. *The Theory of the Novel*. Boston: MIT Press, 1974.
Marcuse, Herbert. *One-Dimensional Man: Studies in the Ideology of Advanced Industrial Society*. Boston: Beacon, 1991.
Marx, Karl. *A Contribution to the Critique of Political Economy*. Trans. N.I. Stone. Chicago: Kerr, 1904.
—. *Capital*. New York: Penguin, 1992.
Marx, Karl, and Friedrich Engels. *The Communist Manifesto*. New York: Signet, 2011.
Sartre, Jean-Paul. *Critique of Dialectical Reason*. New York: Verso, 2006.
Shor, Ira. "Questions Marxists Ask About Literature." *College English*, 34.2, Marxist Interpretations of Mailer, Woolf, Wright and Others (November 1972). 178-79.
Trotsky, Leon. *Literature and Revolution*. Trans. Rose Strunsky. New York: Russell, 1957.
Vattimo, Gianni. *Hermeneutic Communism: From Heidegger to Marx*. New York: Columbia UP, 2011.
Žižek, Slavoj. *Living in the End Times*. New York: Verso, 2010.
—. *The Sublime Object of Ideology*. New York: Verso, 1989.

—. *Welcome to the Desert of the Real.* New York: Verso, 2002.

# 4

# Feminism

FOCUSES ON: the covert (unwritten) text in particular, as well as historical and biographical information, especially with regard to patriarchal influences.
BECAUSE: one of the goals of feminist critics is to reveal how patriarchal ideologies permeate and inform all aspects of society in hopes of attaining equality for all genders.
DEVELOPED IN: 1960s (as a cohesive school of literary criticism).
NOTABLE PRACTITIONERS:
  Simone de Beauvoir (1908-86)  Betty Friedan (1921-2006)
  Luce Irigaray (1930- )         Gloria Steinem (1934- )
  Kate Millet (1934- )           Hélène Cixous (1937- )
  Judy Brady (*née* Syphers) (1937- )  Germaine Greer (1939- )
  Elaine Showalter (1941- )      Julia Kristeva (1941- )
  Jo Freeman (1945- )            Camille Paglia (1947- )
  Christina Hoff Sommers (1950- )  bell hooks (1952- )
  Eve Ensler (1953- )            Judith Butler (1956- )
  Susan Faludi (1959- )          Naomi Wolf (1962- )
  Rebecca Walker (1969- )
IMPORTANT PREDECESSORS:
  Christine de Pizan (c. 1364- 1430)  Catharine Macaulay (1731-91)
  Abigail Adams (1744-1818)      Olympe de Gouges (1748-93)
  Mary Wollstonecraft (1759-97)  Matilda Joslyn Gage (1826-98)
  Virginia Woolf (1882-1941)
ADVANTAGES: offers important insight into the prevalence of patriarchal values in all aspects of social interaction, particularly with regard to works of literature.
DISADVANTAGES: like other approaches with a singular focus, the possibility exists for a feminist analysis to ignore other relevant facets of the text.

DEFINITION: the practice of interpreting a literary work through the lens of feminist theory with a conscious eye toward uncovering patriarchal ideologies within the text, often to raise awareness regarding the prevalence of these patriarchal values in an effort to effect change.

---

Feminist literary criticism is based upon the feminist movement, which advocates equal rights for women and men in all aspects of human life. As a unified school of literary critique, feminist criticism took hold in the 1960s. Feminism itself began centuries earlier, though it is difficult to pinpoint exactly when. Most scholars trace feminism's roots to the late eighteenth century. One could argue, though, that Mary Rowlandson's book, *A Narrative of the Captivity and Restoration of Mrs. Mary Rowlandson* (1682), laid the groundwork for the modern feminist movement over a century earlier. Some scholars suggest that feminism began with Christine de Pizan's writings of the early fifteenth century, particularly *Le Livre de la Cité des Dames* (1405; trans. *The Book of the City of Ladies*). We could even go back as far as the tenth century CE to see progressive feminist arguments within Sei Shōnagon's *The Pillow Book* (1002; trans. 1889).

No matter when we say feminism began, today we differentiate the progressing stages of the feminist movement in waves, beginning with the pioneering feminists of the late-eighteenth century. Most scholars recognize a transition into the first wave in the mid-nineteenth century, into the second wave in the mid-twentieth century and into the third wave in the early 1990s. As with literary periods and many of the theories that we discuss in this text, the delineations between the various waves are fluid, rather than rigid. What we have, instead, are common themes as well as works that stand out as significant representations of their respective time.

We should keep in mind, too, that the wave model is not perfect and it is not without debate; Shira Tarrant, for example, notes—rightly so—that our wave designations are aligned most specifically with the development of feminism in America, making these labels less relevant to feminism in other parts of the world. However, since the wave model is still the most common way of demarcating the progress of the feminist movement, a text such as this would best serve students by following this same formula, at least until a better system is introduced.

## Feminist Pioneers

The pioneering feminist movement was characterized by logical appeals arguing for equality in education and for basic human rights. One of the earliest feminist texts from this period was Catharine Macaulay's *Letters on Education* (1790). Macaulay's eight-volume *The History of England* (1763-1783) made her a renowned British historian. Though her reputation was later ruined with her marriage to a younger man, William Graham, she continued to write until her death in 1791. In *Letters on Education*, Macaulay argues that women are as intellectually capable as men and, moreover, if women were to receive the same education, their achievements would be equal to men's. While such a claim today would be indisputable, this wasn't the case in 1790. In the eighteenth century, it was commonly understood—by women as well as men—that women were weaker, more emotional, and less capable of rational thought than men. It was this prevailing belief that led to the institutional policies that subsequent feminists have been fighting against ever since.

## Revolution

The early stages of the feminist movement corresponded to the American and French revolutions in the late-eighteenth century. Abigail Adams worked behind the scenes in the 1770s and 1780s, writing numerous letters to her husband, John Adams, in support of property rights and education for women. While the Adamses kept the majority of their correspondence private, feminist thinkers became more conspicuous during the turmoil of the French Revolution. In France, there was a push by the French revolutionary leaders to establish an ideal society free of sovereign rule. As part of these efforts, contemporary thinkers were called upon to outline their plans for this new French state. An early result of these efforts was "*Déclaration des droits de l'homme et du citoyen*" (1789; trans. "Declaration of the Rights of Man and of the Citizen") composed by a committee of French thinkers including Jérôme Champion de Cicé and Charles Maurice de Talleyrand-Périgord. Their final draft was similar in many ways to the U.S. *Declaration of Independence* and included a seventeen-point plan designed to make all French men equal under the law:

> Article I: Men are born free and remain free and equal in rights. Social distinctions can be based only on public utility.
> [...]
> Article X: No one should be disturbed on account of his opinions, even religious, provided their manifestation does not upset the public order established by law.
> [...]
> Article XV: Society has the right to call for an account of his administration by every public agent.
> [...]

Article XVII: Property being a sacred and inviolable right, no one can be deprived of it, unless illegally established public necessity evidently demands it, under the condition of a just and prior indemnity.

The mention of women's rights in the document was conspicuously absent, and this fact was not lost on the early French feminist, Olympe de Gouges, responded with her "*Déclaration des droits de la femme et de la citoyenne*" (1791; trans. "Declaration of the Rights of Woman and the Female Citizen"). "Declaration of the Rights of Woman" followed the structure of "Declaration of the Rights of Man," including a seventeen-point plan of its own:

Article I: Woman is born free and lives equal to man in her rights. Social distinctions can be based only on the common utility.
[...]
Article X: No one is to be disquieted for his very basic opinions; woman has the right to mount the scaffold; she must equally have the right to mount the rostrum, provided that her demonstrations do not disturb the legally established public order.
[...]
Article XV: The collectivity of women, joined for tax purposes to the aggregate of men, has the right to demand an accounting of his administration from any public agent.
[...]
Article XVII: Property belongs to both sexes whether united or separate; for each it is an inviolable and sacred right no one can be deprived of it, since it is the true patrimony of nature, unless the legally determined public need obviously dictates it, and then only with a just and prior indemnity.

Though Gouges was a supporter of the revolution, her outspoken political activism led her to be declared an enemy of the state by the Jacobin party during the Reign of Terror and she was executed by guillotine in 1793.

Since France had been a powerful nation throughout the rule of Louis XVI, politicians and intellectuals throughout the western world paid close attention to the French Revolution. One of these intellectuals was the British writer, Mary Wollstonecraft. Wollstonecraft took issue with Talleyrand's presentation to the French National Assembly, "Report on Public Education" (1791). In the section of his report titled, "Education of Women," Talleyrand offers,

Article I. The girls will be able to be admitted to the primary Schools only until the age of eight years.
[...]
Article III. It will be provided, in every Department, to the means to form destined establishments to obtain to the girls that go out of the

primary Schools or first paternal education, the ease to learn from the suitable trades to their sex.
[...]
Article VIII. All the given instructions to the Students in the houses of public education, will stretch particularly to prepare the girls to the virtues of domestic life, and to the useful talents in the government of a family.

In other words, Talleyrand recommends that girls go to school only until they are eight years old (Article I), after which they should be given domestic training so that they will be better able to cook, clean and take care of their home and family (Article VIII), as all women are born to do (Article III).

Wollstonecraft had already gained some measure of respectability as a writer and a thinker by the time she published her response to Talleyrand, *A Vindication of the Rights of Woman* (1792). In this work, Wollstonecraft borrows from and expands upon Macaulay's earlier *Letters on Education* (a common and acceptable practice in the eighteenth century). Wollstonecraft frames her argument pragmatically, noting at one point that, if men want women to stay home and raise their young sons, wouldn't the women perform that job better if they were educated? As with the arguments of Macaulay and Olympe de Gouges, Wollstonecraft's assertions are irrefutable today. Still, it wasn't until the next century that young women were able to receive an education comparable to that of young men.

## The First Wave

As women began to gain more equality in education, the feminist movement shifted its focus to other areas of gender disparity. Like the feminist pioneers, women of the first wave utilized logic in their arguments. Where the pioneers argued for basic human rights like education, though, the women of the first wave argued for basic legal rights. The first wave feminist movement is marked by a call for equality in marriage, property rights and, what the first wave is perhaps best known for, equal voting rights. The push for the right to vote became more pronounced leading up to and after the 1870 ratification of the Fifteenth Amendment which granted all American men the right to vote.

Aside from noted suffragettes such as Susan B. Anthony and Elizabeth Cady Stanton, the first wave also gave us several renowned women writers. Whereas the literature of the pioneering feminists often mirrored the literature written by men, first wave writers progressively began to present issues from a feminine perspective. Writers like Matilda Joslyn Gage, Charlotte Perkins Gilman and Kate Chopin would have found a much less receptive audience a century earlier. Women's writing continued to progress in this vein with the first wave writers of the twentieth century, perhaps most famously with Virginia Woolf's *A Room of One's Own* (1929) and Simone de Beauvoir's *Le Deuxième Sexe* (1949; trans. 1953, *The Second Sex*; corrected ed., 2009).

*A Room of One's Own* is an extended essay based upon several lectures that Woolf delivered at Cambridge University. The premise of Woolf's essay is straightforward: all writers need a room of their own in which to contemplate and create their literary works. According to Woolf, men throughout history have had this quiet space, while women, in general, have not. It is because of this, rather than any perceived gender differences, that the literary geniuses throughout history have been predominately male. Men were given an education; women were not. Men had a place to write; women did not.

The most famous chapter in Woolf's text is the third, in which she expands upon this idea by envisioning a hypothetical sister for Shakespeare, named Judith. Judith is William's equal in all respects, except that she is female. Consequently, she doesn't receive the same education as young William and her parents actively—but gently—discourage her from pursuing her extraordinary gift for literary creation. It is more important, they continually insist, that she spend her time completing her daily chores, like mending the family's socks, rather than wasting her time reading or writing.

As a result, we never hear of Judith because Judith never has a chance to develop William's love of the theater or to even write one play. Examples of such wasted talent, Woolf concludes, surely exist throughout history because women, in their subordinate position, have never had the opportunities that men have had. Women have never had that room of their own.

## The Other Sex

Simone de Beauvoir expanded upon Woolf's argument in *The Second Sex*. While Beauvoir's book is similar in theme to *A Room of One's Own*, it is much more thorough than Woolf's essay and it is much more clinical in tone. In *The Second Sex*, we see a detailed history of sexual inequality throughout time and the consequences of the *Othering* of women. What this means is that, throughout history, men have been the primary or "normal" sex, making women, by extension, the *Other* sex, something other than normal. Seeing women as the outside Other led to the marginalization of women, relegating them to the periphery of society. And this marginalization contributed to the objectification of women which, in turn, led to the longstanding tradition of discrimination of women.

A longtime companion of Jean Paul Sartre, Beauvoir was a major figure in the existentialist movement of post-war France. This led to another significant assertion in her book: *l'existence précède l'essence* (existence precedes essence). Beauvoir shaped this common claim of existentialism into the idea that a female is not born a woman but, instead, "becomes one" through her exposure to society's socially-constructed gender-specific expectations. In other words, the things we think we "know" about gender differences are not always real, biological differences but, instead, ideas that we take to be real because society has told us, generation after generation, that these differences actually *are* real. From books, magazines, advertisements, etc., a young girl constantly encounters society's concept of what an ideal female is: girls are pretty, they play with dolls, they like the color pink, etc. It's not long before she unconsciously aspires toward that socially-constructed ideal. As the girl matures into adulthood, she is shaped by these societal expectations until she becomes the woman that society wants her to be. These expectations are so prevalent, in fact, that even the girl's parents unintentionally guide the girl to conform to them. Eventually, these preferred gender roles become obligatory. This process then continues in a self-perpetuating cycle: the girl becomes a mother who buys her daughter dolls to play with and pretty pink dresses to wear, while showing by example the expected role of an adult female by cooking, cleaning and shopping for her family.

Beauvoir's book was a significant text of the feminist movement and her ideas regarding marginalization and the social construction of gender roles continue to influence feminist thought even today.

## The Second Wave

Because of the distinct contrast between Beauvoir's book and anything that came before it, many scholars mark the publication of *The Second Sex* in 1949 as the beginning of feminism's second wave. Others see the second wave beginning a decade later, with another groundbreaking book, Betty Friedan's *The Feminine Mystique* (1963). Events that took place between the publication of these two books have also been noted, such as the report by President Kennedy's Commission on the Status of Women (1961) that identified discrimination against women in all aspects of American life. The introduction of the birth control pill in 1961 was also significant, as was Helen Gurley Brown's bestselling book, *Sex and the Single Girl* (1962).

Again, any number of arguments can be made regarding when one wave began and another ended. What can't be debated is the impact that Friedan, in particular, and also Gurley Brown had on the feminist movement and on women in general. Gurley Brown's book is in the genre of an advice book, similar to Wollstonecraft's *Thoughts on the Education of Daughters* (1787) from two centuries earlier. But where Wollstonecraft guides young women on things like "Moral Discipline," "Dress," "The Treatment of Servants," and "The Misfortune of Fluctuating Principles," Gurley Brown takes on subjects such as "How to be Sexy," "Money Money Money" and "The Affair: From the Beginning to the End."

Friedan's book is different. Her idea for *The Feminine Mystique* took shape after she surveyed her Smith College graduating class before her fifteen-year reunion. Friedan noticed that a substantial proportion of her classmates all suffered with the same problem, what Friedan termed "the problem that has no name." The women Friedan surveyed had all earned college degrees, and yet the vast majority of them felt a seething frustration at being relegated to the simple role of housewife and mother once they got married. In addition, most of these frustrated women also felt guilty for their frustration because they didn't realize other women felt the same way.

While Beauvoir's *The Second Sex* was directed more toward the academic community, Friedan's book was more accessible to a wider audience. As a result, *The Feminine Mystique* became a bestseller. It showed millions of women that their feelings weren't unique, which is why many consider it the spark that started the second wave of feminism. Still, many people—including many women—found the book objectionable. Though it may seem incomprehensible today, many women of the early sixties saw Friedan's book as threatening to the status quo that they were comfortable with. This tension between the struggle for change and the desire for stability continued throughout the second wave. Consequently, the second wave is commonly characterized as the most persistent and assertive period of the feminist movement.

Throughout history, significant societal change is often met with varying degrees of opposition, and the second wave brought about momentous changes not only in society, but more importantly, within the home. While women in the United States had been allowed to vote since 1920, the majority of American households still adhered to strict gender roles that most students would find difficult to comprehend today. This began to change in the sixties, but not without considerable resistance.

Conservatives referred to the movement as fascist or Stalinistic and used sobriquets such as "feminazi" to refer to feminist leaders. Some religious groups saw the second wave as contrary to the teachings of the Bible and the ideals of the Christian Church. When looked at in the context of its time and place in history, though, both the impassioned tone of feminism's second wave and its reactionary backlash are more easily understood as part of the process of change that repeats itself throughout history.

With this new look at gender roles in all aspects of society came a look, as well, at gender roles in literature. It is in the second wave, then, when we see feminism fully utilized as a serious and legitimate scholarly approach to literature. Theorists began looking closely at literature through a feminist lens. They studied, for example, the representation of female characters and how these characterizations perpetuate an inaccurate understanding of women.

Today, we have a vast assortment of entertainment options readily at hand—television, internet, computer games, etc. In past centuries, though, the dominant form of home entertainment was literature. And this entertainment medium was controlled almost entirely by men. In contrast to today, where we readily see women in a variety of roles (athlete, politician, soldier, astronaut, literary scholar, etc.), this wasn't the case just a century ago. There were writers who were women, of course, but the editors and the publishers—the people who decided what would be printed—were almost exclusively men.

Representations of women, then, even if they weren't written by men, were still "male-approved." What became clear to feminist scholars such as Woolf, Beauvoir and Elaine Showalter was that this system was not only defining and describing women, but shaping them as well.

To put it simply, if literature is our only source of entertainment, then literature will necessarily inform what we understand about the world. And when that literary industry is controlled by men, then everything that is produced by that industry is filtered through a male perspective, including the stories that are published and the characters within those stories. As a result, what readers—male and female—understand about women comes to them from these female literary characters who are generated from that male perspective. Before the twentieth century, in particular, this resulted in female characters who were weak, simpleminded, often impulsive and, ideally, obedient.

## Reading from a Feminist Perspective

As readers grew up to write their own stories (whether these new writers were men or women), their female characters were based upon these same simplistic stereotypes. Eventually, these stereotypes became accepted as "common knowledge" among women as well as men. A woman's understanding of who she was and how she should behave, then, was constructed by men's insufficient preconceptions of women. When women wrote their own stories, their female characters either followed these same conventions or their stories weren't published.

According to Showalter, this began to change around 1880. In *A Literature of Their Own* (1977), Showalter identifies three developmental phases in the evolution of women's literature: the Feminine, the

Feminist, and the Female. The Feminine phase, according to Showalter, dates from roughly 1840 to 1880 and is distinguished by women writers of the period disguising themselves as men, either on the page or, often, through masculine pseudonyms such as George Eliot (Mary Ann Evans) and Ellis, Acton, and Currer Bell (the Brontë Sisters). Showalter dates the next phase—Feminist phase—from 1880 to 1920 and characterizes it as a time when women were using "literature to dramatize the ordeals of wronged womanhood." She identifies Charlotte Perkins Gilman as a quintessential example of this period; Kate Chopin would be included here, as well. The third, and current, phase, according to Showalter, began in 1920, the year American women earned the right to vote. She sees the Female phase as neither imitative nor protest-driven but, instead, guided by a turn inward toward the experience of being a woman.

As part of this third, Female, phase, Showalter developed a new approach to feminist criticism that explores female writing from a female perspective. Showalter saw an inherent flaw in the traditional study of literature. As she notes in her essay, "Towards a Feminist Poetics" (1979):

> If we study stereotypes of women, the sexism of male critics, and the limited roles women play in literary history, we are not learning what women have felt and experienced, but only what men have thought women should be. [. . .] The critique also has a tendency to naturalize women's victimization by making it the inevitable and obsessive topic of discussion.

Showalter termed this new approach to feminist criticism, "Gynocritics," a word she adapted from the French *la gynocritique*.

Applying gynocritics to Kate Chopin's "The Story of an Hour," for example, the critic would look closely at how Louise's husband, Brently Mallard, is represented in the story. Is he a boorish, abusive lout, or is he a kind and caring husband who takes care of her? And yet, what does Louise realize about her marriage and herself after contemplating her husband's death? What does she eventually begin to whisper to herself? Why does she do this? Or, more specifically, why does Chopin have her character do this? And what is the diagnosis of the male doctor at the end of the story? Is it accurate? Again, why is this?

While Showalter was one of the first to employ a feminist approach to literature, she wasn't the only one. Not every feminist critic, though, followed Showalter's path. Other feminist critics, for example, were more interested in how women had been portrayed by past male authors. An early feminist text in this vein is Kate Millet's *Sexual Politics* (1970). In her book, Millet focuses specifically on the work of Jean Genet, D.H. Lawrence, Norman Mailer and Henry Miller and their representations of female characters. The goal of scholars like Millet was to uncover evidence of patriarchal ideals within literary texts to reveal the pervasiveness of these embedded gender norms throughout history. The word, patriarchy, refers to a society that is male-dominated in every way—politically, economically, socially and, especially, covertly through ideologies and societal beliefs, customs and mores. It's no secret that men have enjoyed economic and political control over women for millennia, but patriarchy infers an inconspicuous control that is even more pernicious because it becomes ingrained within the pattern of thought of every boy and girl and man and woman. To uncover evidence of a patriarchal mindset operating within a text, Millet and others engaged in close readings of traditionally canonical writings, paying particular attention to the covert text, often privileging it over the overt text, to reveal evidence of that patriarchal influence.

Working from this perspective, a feminist critic would quickly notice the relationship between Aylmer and his wife, Georgiana, in Hawthorne's "The Birthmark." While, in the beginning of the story, Georgiana sees her birthmark as "a charm," Aylmer sees it as a "defect." And it is his opinion that dominates. Instead of arguing with her husband or standing up for herself, Georgiana obediently submits to her husband's wishes to remove her "charm"—she, in fact, suggests it. She agrees to his experiment even though she had always seen the birthmark as an integral part of her identity and in spite of the fact that all of his past experiments were "mortifying failures." It's notable, too, that the text spends very little time explaining why Georgiana would subject herself to such danger; it is merely understood that she *will* relent because she is a good wife whose chief aim is to please her husband. If we were to reverse the roles of the characters, giving Aylmer the birthmark and making Georgiana the scientist, the patriarchal values operating within Hawthorne's text become more apparent. From a purely plot-based perspective, this version of the story wouldn't work because the reader would expect more debate from Aylmer about his birthmark (if he didn't ignore her suggestions altogether). Georgiana, as the scientist urging Aylmer to remove his birthmark, would be much less sympathetic than the character of Aylmer in Hawthorne's story. Feminist theorists would point to these and other examples as proof of unbalanced societal expectations between the genders.

As feminist criticism developed into an organized scholarly approach to literature, some theorists began to incorporate their interests and expertise from other areas into their feminist approaches. Annette Kolodny, for example, examines the role of social construction in shaping young women, particularly in her essay, "Dancing Through the Minefield." The poststructuralist theoretical feminists, as that cumbersome name implies, approached feminist criticism from a poststructuralist angle. More commonly known in the U.S. as the "French" feminists (which include Julia Kristeva, from Bulgaria, and Luce Irigaray, from Belgium, as well as the French theorist Hélène Cixous) these theorists found an inherent masculine bias within language. According to the French feminists, this bias resulted in the oppression of women through the repression of their natural feminine voice. Woolf spoke of this briefly in *A Room of One's Own*, identifying feminine versus masculine sentences, but Cixous' conclusions are more heavily influenced by Derrida's belief in the phallogocentric (or male-dominated) nature of written language.

In "The Laugh of the Medusa" (1976), Cixous used the term, *écriture féminine* (feminine writing) to describe how women can work to overcome this phallogocentric character of language. By engaging in *écriture féminine*, Cixous says, women can transcend the traditional male-created "rules" of writing and, instead, write from within, allowing the free-flowing, circular nature of their thoughts to come alive on the page.

A variety of approaches to feminist literary criticism developed during the second wave. While the various strands are diverse, it's important to note that they are all working toward common goals; some strands merely focus in other directions as they approach those goals.

However one views the second wave today, it is impossible to deny the progress made by the scholars, intellectuals, theorists and activists who equate themselves with the second wave. Most would argue that there is still progress to be made, but that doesn't discount the fact that the Western world is vastly different today than it was in 1950.

## The Third Wave

The third wave of feminism began in the early 1990s. Initially, it was often referred to as "post-feminism," but that name became problematic because it implied an end to feminism, rather than a continuation. Rebecca Walker popularized the term, "third wave," in her *Ms.* magazine article titled "Becoming the Third Wave" (1992). The term had already been in use before this, though, most notably in Naomi Wolf's *The Beauty Myth* (1991).

Compared to preceding waves, the third wave can seem to some as lacking a unified and significant goal. After all, the pioneering feminists fought for education and basic human rights, the feminists of the first wave earned basic legal rights and the right to vote, and the second wave feminists fought for equality in all aspects of human life. Measured against these standards, the third wave might appear to lack the same focus. What the third wave did do, though, was make feminism accessible to millions of women who felt underrepresented by the earlier feminist movements.

In the 1980s, there was a growing recognition among some women that the feminist movement spoke mostly to upper- and middle-class heterosexual white women. Theorists like Gloria Anzaldúa, Audre

Lorde, Cherrie Moraga and Barbara Smith, among others, noticed that the needs of poor women, non-heterosexual women and women of color were not being addressed by feminism's second wave.

The result of this was a third-wave body of theory that consciously works toward inclusiveness of all groups, regardless of race, class or gender identification. At the same time, third-wave feminism often reflects upon feminism itself—its successes as well as its shortcomings—in an effort to improve upon the mistakes of the past. The literary criticism of the third wave, then, is similar in approach to that of the second wave, but its focus encompasses a broader range of diverse women's issues including health, poverty, domestic violence and empowerment. Representations of women and self-image are brilliantly addressed in Naomi Wolf's *The Beauty Myth* and Eve Ensler's *The Good Body* (2004). Other third-wave feminists, including Susan Faludi and Christina Hoff Sommers, have studied feminism's effect on men, while others, like Barbara Ehrenreich, have looked more specifically at economic issues.

Still, feminist criticism of the third wave operates in much the same way as its predecessors. The third wave still uses a text to view women in a cultural context through their representation. And the third wave asks many of the same questions: What is femininity? What is masculinity? How much of what we "know" about gender is socially constructed? How are girls and women shaped by societal norms, mores and expectations? In what ways are women marginalized and objectified in literature? How do patriarchal values in society shape the representations of women in literature, and how do the representations of women in literature shape our understanding of women in society? What work by women authors belongs in the canon? And what part do literature, art and the media play in the stereotyping of gender roles?

## Implementation

Some theorists will argue that a traditional feminist critique should be political in tone, overtly promoting the stated goals of the feminist movement. While much of the analysis in the second wave used this approach, today a feminist analysis can take many forms. Some theorists use an approach similar to Showalter's gynocriticism, focusing on literature written by women. Other theorists favor an approach more along the style of Kate Millet's *Sexual Politics*, examining the portrayal of female characters in works written by men. Still others prefer to incorporate a psychoanalytic, Marxist, historical or linguistic slant to their analysis. Often, though, a feminist theorist today will not limit herself or himself to one particular style, preferring instead to remain open to whatever approach seems most applicable to the individual text.

A feminist analysis of a text follows, in many ways, the method used in a Marxist approach. Both begin with a close reading of the overt and the covert text, both often utilize historical and biographical research regarding the text, and both involve investigating the story for evidence of power structures at work within the text. The difference is in the nature of this power. While Marxism is interested in economic power and the subjugation of the economically disadvantaged, feminism is interested in power structures related to gender. In what ways, for example, does this text either perpetuate or undermine a patriarchal value system? Does a close reading of the covert text reveal the writer's bias regarding gender issues?

Most feminist readings will begin with other questions as well. For example, how are the female characters portrayed in the text? Do they play a primary or marginal role? Are they fully developed or one-dimensional? Are they strong or weak? Intelligent or simple-minded? Active or passive? Dominant or subservient? Along these same lines, how are the female characters viewed by other characters and by the narrator?

Feminist critics also examine how a text might reflect the gender attitudes of its time. In other words, how is the text a product of its history and, alternately, how might it have shaped history? What role, if any, does race play in the manifestation of these gender roles? How does the work fit into the scope of the literary canon? To put it simply, feminist theorists are interested in any issues related to gender issues.

In Chekhov's "Gooseberries," for example, women play only minor roles and they are treated dismissively by the narrator and the characters. Women in the story are reduced to objects, referred to not by name, but by their role. They function only to serve men and they are described only by their appearance. Nikolay's wife is "an elderly and ugly widow" and his cook is "a fat, barefooted woman" who "looked like a pig." Feminist critics would look first to see if the secondary male characters are handled in the same fashion and, if not, they would try to find the reasons for these characterizations.

Perhaps even more noteworthy from a feminist perspective is the treatment of Nikolay's wife. While Nikolay takes advantage of her so that he can acquire her wealth, Ivan, the narrator, makes little note of this startling fact. The wife, meanwhile, passively accepts this victimization. A feminist theorist might look to the story's historical milieu for answers. How were women treated in the Tsarist regime of 1898 Russia, when Chekhov published the story? A feminist taking a more psychoanalytic approach might wonder how Chekhov's life may have influenced the text, while a feminist reading with a Marxist slant might be more interested in the coronation of Nicholas II—and the subsequent Khodynka Tragedy—in 1896. A post-structuralist feminist would likely begin with the story's binary oppositions that are related to gender.

Comparing Chekhov's story to Chopin's "The Story of an Hour," we see a very different portrayal of the female characters. While, in "Gooseberries," the women are one-dimensional and marginalized, in Chopin's story, the protagonist is a fully-developed, thoughtful female character. Louise Mallard, while clearly constrained by her society's patriarchal influence, becomes awakened to her freedom from the subservient role placed upon her by society. The tragic ending, of course, comes when that freedom is suddenly taken from her.

In "The Yellow Wallpaper," Gilman's narrator is similarly inhibited by patriarchal attitudes. Her "rest cure" is prescribed by a male doctor and administered by her husband due to the prevailing attitude that women are weak and in need of care. In both Chopin's and Gilman's stories, a feminist critic might be particularly interested in the historical and biographical information surrounding those works. One might also notice that these two husbands are well-meaning, if naïve to their wives' innermost needs, reinforcing the argument that it is the patriarchy, rather than the individual husbands, that is responsible for the downfall of the stories' protagonists. In these two stories, then, we see the effects of patriarchal constraints on intelligent female characters.

Still, a feminist critic would point out, these women are less robust than their male counterparts. Louise Mallard, after all, has a weak heart and dies from the mere shock of seeing her husband. The confinement of Gilman's narrator results not in some form of mental clarity, but her descent into madness. A feminist theorist, then, might ask if these stories undermine the patriarchal value system or if they actually work to reinforce those beliefs responsible for the patriarchy.

Again, a feminist critique may take many forms. As with all critical approaches, it is up to the feminist thinker to determine what is most worthy of examination, remembering that any literary analysis is part of an ongoing conversation between like-minded scholars.

## Important Moments in Feminism

- 1002: Sei Shōnagon's *The Pillow Book*
- 1405: Christine de Pizan's *The Book of the City of Ladies*
- 1682: Mary Rowlandson's *A Narrative of the Captivity and Restoration of Mrs. Mary Rowlandson*
- 1789: French Revolution begins
- 1790: Catharine Macaulay's *Letters on Education*
- 1790: Nicolas de Condorcet's "For the Admission to the Rights of Citizenship For Women"
- 1790: Etta Palm d'Aelders' "Discourse on the Injustice of the Laws in Favor of Men, at the Expense of Women"

**1791:** Olympe de Gouges' "Declaration of the Rights of Woman and the Female Citizen"
**1792:** Mary Wollstonecraft's A Vindication of the Rights of Woman
**1848:** Elizabeth Cady Stanton drafts "The Declaration of Sentiments"
**1851:** Sojourner Truth's "Ain't I a woman?"
**1868:** first issue of *The Revolution*
**1879:** Matilda Joslyn Gage's "All The Rights I Want"
**1892:** Charlotte Perkins Gilman's "The Yellow Wallpaper"
**1893:** New Zealand grants women the right to vote
**1893:** Gage's *Woman, Church and State*
**1894:** Kate Chopin's "The Story of an Hour"
**1899:** Chopin's *The Awakening*
**1920:** Nineteenth Amendment of U.S. Constitution
**1929:** Virginia Woolf's *A Room of One's Own*
**1949:** Simone de Beauvoir's *The Second Sex*
**1960:** Sirimavo Bandaranaike becomes prime minister of Sri Lanka
**1961:** President Kennedy's Commission on the Status of Women
**1962:** Helen Gurley Brown's *Sex and the Single Girl*
**1963:** Betty Friedan's The Feminine Mystique
**1963:** the Equal Pay Act
**1966:** the National Organization for Women is founded
**1970:** Kate Millet's *Sexual Politics*
**1971:** first issue of *Ms.* magazine
**1972:** Title IX implemented as part of the Education Amendments of 1972
**1976:** Hélène Cixous' "The Laugh of the Medusa"
**1977:** Elaine Showalter's *A Literature of Their Own*
**1977:** Luce Irigaray's *This Sex Which Is Not One*
**1979:** Sandra Gilbert's and Susan Gubar's *The Madwoman in the Attic*
**1980:** Annette Kolodny's "Dancing Through the Minefield"
**1981:** Sandra Day O'Connor nominated to the U.S. Supreme Court
**1990:** Judith Bulter's *Gender Trouble*
**1991:** Susan Faludi's *Backlash*
**1991:** Naomi Wolf's *The Beauty Myth*
**1992:** Rebecca Walker's "Becoming the Third Wave"
**1996:** Eve Ensler's *The Vagina Monologues*
**2000:** Andrea Dworkin's *Scapegoat*
**2002:** Dworkin's *Heartbreak*
**2004:** Ensler's *The Good Body*
**2010:** Cordelia Fine's *Delusions of Gender*
**2011:** Peggy Orenstein's *Cinderella Ate My Daughter*

## Important Terms

gender
marginalization
the Other
phallocentrism

gynocriticism
objectification
patriarchy
social construction

## Study Questions

1. Both Charlotte Perkins Gilman's "The Yellow Wallpaper" and Kate Chopin's "The Story of an Hour" depict worlds governed by an unstated patriarchal mind-set wherein men seem, at least on the surface, to have greater powers of determination than women have (over self, social circumstances and the like). Pick a passage or a moment from each story and explain how the relationships between men and women are affected by this power.
2. The idea of the American Dream predates Franklin's *Autobiography* and, as such, began as a goal attainable primarily by white males only. Think about the American Dream from a feminist perspective as you consider the stories in the Appendices. What inferences can we make about each author's perception of the accessibility of the American Dream by reading their covert texts? Do they see the American Dream as obtainable? Or is it, to them, a fantasy still reserved exclusively for others?
3. From a story of your choice, pick the passages that you feel are best suited to a feminist reading. Take note of why you chose those passages, where each passage fits within the context of the entire narrative, and what the overall importance of the passage is in regards to feminism. What key words in the passage match up to key elements of feminism? Work with the text and feminist theory together. How can feminism help us better understand and appreciate the story you've chosen?
4. In Ambrose Bierce's "An Occurrence at Owl Creek Bridge," the narrator describes Peyton Farquhar's fateful meeting with a Federal scout:

> One evening while Farquhar and his wife were sitting on a rustic bench near the entrance to his grounds, a gray-clad soldier rode up to the gate and asked for a drink of water. Mrs. Farquhar was only too happy to serve him with her own white hands. While she was gone to fetch the water, her husband approached the dusty horseman and inquired eagerly for news from the front.

Reading this passage through the lens of feminism, list everything you can ascertain (about the characters, the narrator, the author) from reading this paragraph. What does this paragraph say about the

characters? About the author? What does it say about the meaning of Bierce's story as a whole? Point at least to one other passage in the text to support your claims.
5. From a feminist critical perspective, write a brief essay about a story of your choice that uncovers some truth about the story that isn't explicitly stated in the text. Examine all aspects of the story to find at least one significant truth that is implied but not actually written in the text. Perhaps you'd like to focus on the setting or the narrative situation. Maybe some truth about a character becomes more clear when looked at from a feminist perspective.

## Selected Bibliography

Angelou, Maya. *I Know Why the Caged Bird Sings*. New York: Ballantine, 2009.

Anzaldúa, Gloria, and Cherrie Moraga, Eds. *This Bridge Called My Back: Writings by Radical Women of Color*. Albany: Kitchen Table, 1984.

Baym, Nina. *Feminism and American Literary Theory: Essays*. Piscataway Township: Rutgers UP, 1992.

—. *Women's Fiction: A Guide to Novels by and about Women in America, 1820-70*. Urbana: Illinois UP, 1993.

Beauvoir, Simone de. *The Second Sex*. New York: Vintage, 2007.

Cixous, Hélène. "The Laugh of the Medusa." *Signs: Journal of Women in Culture and Society*, 1.4 (1976). 875-93.

Cixous, Hélène, and Catherine Clement. *The Newly Born Woman: Theory and History of Literature*. Minneapolis: Minnesota UP, 1986.

Ehrenreich, Barbara. *Nickel and Dimed: On (Not) Getting By in America*. New York: Metropolitan, 2001.

Eisenstein, Hester. *Contemporary Feminist Thought*. New York: Twayne, 1984.

Ensler, Eve. *The Good Body*. New York: Villard, 2004.

—. *The Vagina Monologues*. New York: Villard, 2007.

Faludi, Susan. *Backlash: The Undeclared War against American Women*. New York: Broadway, 2006.

—. *Stiffed: The Betrayal of the American Man*. New York: Harper, 2000.

Friedan, Betty. *The Feminine Mystique*. New York: Dell, 1984.

Freeman, Jo (Joreen). "The BITCH Manifesto." *Notes from the Second Year: Women's Liberation: Major Writings of the Radical Feminists*, Shulamith Firestone and Anne Koedt, eds. 1970.

Gage, Matilda Joslyn. "'All the Rights I Want.'" *The Essential Anthology of Literature by Women*. Ed. Shannon B. King. Tucson: Sabino Falls, 2012. 125-29.

—. "Is Woman Her Own?" *The Essential Anthology of Literature by Women.* Ed. Shannon B. King. Tucson: Sabino Falls, 2012. 123-24.

—. *Woman, Church and State.* Amherst, NY: Humanity, 2002.

Gilbert, Sandra M., and Susan Gubar. *The Madwoman in the Attic: The Woman Writer and the Nineteenth-Century Literary Imagination,* 2nd ed. New Haven: Yale UP, 2000.

—. *No Man's Land: The Place of the Woman Writer in the Twentieth Century.* New Haven: Yale UP, 1996.

Gouges, Olympe de. "Declaration of the Rights of Woman and the Female Citizen." Trans. Shannon B. King. *The Essential Anthology of Literature by Women.* Ed. Shannon B. King. Tucson: Sabino Falls, 2012. 28-30.

Greer, Germaine. *The Female Eunuch.* New York: Farrar, 2001.

—. *The Madwoman's Underclothes: Essays and Occasional Writings.* New York: Atlantic Monthly Press, 1994.

hooks, bell. *Ain't I a Woman: Black Women and Feminism.* Boston: South End, 1999.

Irigaray, Luce. *Speculum of the Other Woman.* Ithaca: Cornell UP, 1985.

—. *This Sex Which is Not One.* Ithaca: Cornell UP, 1985.

Jong, Erica. *Fear of Flying.* New York: New American, 2003.

Kolodny, Annette. "Dancing Through the Minefield: Some Observations on the Theory, Practice, and Politics of a Feminist Literary Criticism." *Critical Theory Since 1965.* Hazard Adams and Leroy Searle, Eds. Tallahassee: Florida State UP, 1986. 400-512.

Kristeva, Julia. *New Maladies of the Soul.* New York: Columbia UP, 1997.

—. *Desire in Language: A Semiotic Approach to Literature and Art.* New York: Columbia UP, 1980.

Macaulay, Catharine. *Letters on Education, with Observations on Religious and Metaphysical Subjects.* New York: Gale, 2002.

Millet, Kate. *Sexual Politics.* Champaign: Illinois UP, 2000.

Moi, Toril. *Sexual/Textual Politics: Feminist Literary Theory.* 2nd ed. New York: Routledge, 2002.

Paglia, Camille. *Sexual Personae: Art and Decadence from Nefertiti to Emily Dickinson.* New York: Vintage, 1991.

—. *Sex, Art, and American Culture: Essays.* New York: Vintage, 1992.

Pizan, Christine de. *Le Livre de la cité des dames.* Trans. Thérèse Moreau and Eric Hicks. Paris: Stock, 1975.

Rowlandson, Mary. *The Sovereignty and Goodness of God: Being a Narrative of the Captivity and Restoration of Mrs. Mary Rowlandson.* New York: Houghton Mifflin, 1930.

Showalter, Elaine. *A Literature of their Own: British Women Novelists from Brontë to Lessing.* Princeton: Princeton UP, 1998.

—. *Female Malady: Women, Madness and English Culture, 1830-1980.* New York: Virago, 1987.

—. *The New Feminist Criticism: Essays on Women, Literature, Theory.* Ed. Elaine Showalter. New York, Pantheon, 1985.
Smith, Barbara, Ed. *Home Girls: A Black Feminist Anthology.* Piscataway Township: Rutgers UP, 2000.
Steinem, Gloria. *Moving Beyond Words: Age, Rage, Sex, Power, Money, Muscles: Breaking the Boundaries of Gender.* New York: Touchstone, 1995.
—. *Outrageous Acts and Everyday Rebellions.* 2nd ed. New York: Holt, 1995.
Syphers, Judy. "Why I Want a Wife." *Ms.*, 1.1 (1972). 17.
Tan, Amy. *The Opposite of Fate: Memories of a Writing Life.* New York: Penguin, 2004.
Tarrant, Shira. *When Sex Became Gender.* New York: Routledge, 2006.
Tong, Rosemarie. *Feminist Thought: A More Comprehensive Introduction.* Boulder: Westview, 2008.
Walker, Rebecca. "Becoming the Third Wave." *Ms.* (January/February 1992). 39-41.
Weedon, Chris. *Feminist Practice and Poststructuralist Theory.* New York: Blackwell, 1996.
Wollstonecraft, Mary. *A Vindication of the Rights of Woman.* New York: Penguin, 1992.
Wolf, Naomi. *The Beauty Myth: How Images of Beauty Are Used Against Women.* New York: Harper, 2002.
Woolf, Virginia. *A Room of One's Own.* New York: Mariner, 1989.
—. *Selected Essays.* Oxford: Oxford UP, 2008.
Wurtzel, Elizabeth. *Bitch: In Praise of Difficult Women.* New York: Anchor, 1999.
—. *Prozac Nation: Young and Depressed in America: A Memoir.* New York: Riverhead, 1994.

# 5

# Structuralism

FOCUSES ON: the text and the components within, in relation to their place in a larger overarching system.
BECAUSE: structuralists are interested in how texts (or their parts) affect, are affected by, and conform to the rules of the systems of which they are part.
DEVELOPED IN: 1950s in Europe; 1960s in U.S.
NOTABLE PRACTITIONERS:
    Claude Levi-Strauss (1908-2009)    Roland Barthes (1915-1980)
    Roman Jakobson (1896-1982)    Northrop Frye (1912-1991)
    Mikhail Bakhtin (1895-1975)
IMPORTANT PREDECESSORS:
    Ferdinand de Saussure (1857-1913)
ADVANTAGES: provides a process to more fully understand all literary works, as well as the environment in which they are produced.
DISADVANTAGES: ignores the qualities of the individual literary text that make it unique.
DEFINITION: a critical approach to literature, based upon the linguistic theories of Ferdinand de Saussure, that focuses on how recurrent components relate and conform to larger literary, cultural or historical systems.

Relatively few literary scholars still utilize an exclusively linguistic-based structuralism to analyze a text. In fact, some textbook authors have begun eliminating altogether their chapters on structuralism. This is understandable. Besides the fact that few theorists still use traditional structuralism today, many of the core ideas that gave birth to structuralism have since been disproven. Still, it's important that we provide at least some brief background on structuralism simply because structuralism, in its brief heyday, transformed the study of literature and helped shape the way we look at texts today. We need to understand the basic principles of structuralism, then, as we move forward into other theories, particularly narratology—which is based on the structuralist model—and post-structuralism which, as the name implies, is best understood in relation to structuralist principles.

Structuralist literary theory owes its origins to Ferdinand de Saussure's *Course in General Linguistics* (1916; trans. 1959). The original text was actually an assemblage of five years' worth of lecture notes from Saussure's former students at the University of Geneva, compiled by Charles Bally and Albert Sechehaye after Saussure's death in 1913. While Saussure's book focuses on historical linguistics and semiotics, other scholars—particularly the French theorist Roland Barthes, the Russian theorist Roman Jakobson, and the French anthropologist Claude Lévi-Strauss—incorporated Saussure's ideas into their own work.

While many of his ideas have since been refuted by Chomsky and Holland, among others, Saussure's book was groundbreaking at the time and his work quite literally revolutionized linguistic study. *Course in General Linguistics* examines the fundamental elements of a language in order to identify a structural system under which that language operates. Historical linguists like Saussure work to understand a language by examining the fundamental parts that make up that language. When those fundamental parts are recognized, the goal—or, one of the goals—is to identify the underlying structure upon which that language operates.

## The Rules of Language

Saussure saw language as a system of individual components that conform to an established set of rules. That system, according to Saussure, must function as one and it must be able to accommodate new components, provided those new components conform to the same established rules. Think, for example, of English. Before we are even able to read, Saussure tells us, we have at least a limited sense of the structural rules of our language. A sentence must have, at least, a noun and a verb. Other parts of speech (adjectives, adverbs, direct objects, etc.) must be inserted in a certain order—following our understood structural rules—in order for the sentence to make sense. For example, we could say in English:

> Joe ate.
> Joe ate Cheetos.
> Joe ate Cheetos with Mary.
> Joe gracefully ate Cheetos with Mary.

Following our same structural rules, we could rearrange the words to say something like:

Mary ate Cheetos with Joe gracefully.

Or even:

Cheetos gracefully ate Joe with Mary.

We could even add new words to our language system:

Joe glomped Blobbledebob with Mary.

No matter how silly the sentence might be, as long as we follow our structural rules, we will still recognize it as a sentence in our language.
But we can't say:

Ate Joe.
Ate Cheetos Joe.
Gracefully ate Cheetos Joe Mary with.

We recognize immediately that these last examples don't follow our understood structural language rules. This is one of the reasons that foreign languages can be difficult to master for non-native speakers; not all languages follow the same structural rules as English. For example, in English, we might ask, "Do you speak English?" If we were to ask this in French, though, we might say, "*Parlez-vous anglais?*" which, when translated literally, would be closer to, "Do speak you English?" The structural rules governing French, in other words, are different from those we have in English.

## The Sign, the Signifier and the Signified

Saussure's study, of course, was much more advanced than these rudimentary examples might suggest. Saussure examined not just the overarching system of a language (what he called the *langue*), and the words and sentences spoken within the language (the *parole*), but he also identified the individual sounds, or phonemes, within different languages. To Saussure, individual words are what he calls "signs" and the sign is made up of the actual word itself (what he calls the "signifier") and our understanding of what that word describes (the "signified"). Theorists often represent it as a mathematical equation like this:

sign = (signifier) + (signified)

If we were to say, "Look at my hand," the word, "hand," in this sentence is the "sign," which consists of the four-letter word h-a-n-d (the "signifier") and it describes *the concept of* that thing on the end of our arm (the "signified"). (The structuralist term, "referent," is used to describe our actual hand.) If we were to look at the same word, but instead say, "Hand me a wrench," or, "I lost that hand of poker," the sign and signifier are the same, but the signified has changed. When we need assistance, we might say, "Give me a hand"; if someone were to applaud after hearing this, Saussure would say that our listener (deliberately or not) misunderstood the signified of the sign.

## The Nature of Words

It would be nearly impossible to condense all of Saussure's ideas into a few paragraphs, so, for the purpose of our needs here, we'll focus on those ideas that more directly relate to literary theory. Saussure argued that, for the most part, words are arbitrary. To put it another way, except for those words that sound like the things they describe (hum, buzz, ding, snap, crackle, pop, etc.) there is no reason that a word is developed to identify the thing it describes. (Saussure would say there is no inherent connection between the signifier and the signified.) There is no logical reason, for example, that the word, "hand," describes a hand. It could just as easily describe a table, or snow, or a cup of coffee.

Saussure also posited that the meaning of a word arises through its differential relationship with other words. We can only understand what a word means when we differentiate it from words that are similar to it—in meaning or sound. A floor is not a ceiling, it's not a wall, and it's not the ground. It's also not a door, a boor or a chore. A sculpture is not a painting, a photograph, or a collage. And it's not a sculptor, a culture or a vulture. We understand what a word *is*, according to Saussure, by knowing what it *isn't*. Structuralists saw that these differences often present themselves as binary oppositions (*up* is not *down*, *in* is not *out*, *hot* is not *cold*, etc.) which will become an important aspect of post-structuralist thought.

Most students find these ideas easy to grasp after some consideration. Students often have more trouble, though, with the structuralist belief that language not only describes our reality, but actually works to shape and create our reality. We see this articulated in the languages of the sciences. Animals are grouped according to certain characteristics. But the platypus is an example of an animal that doesn't fit neatly into any of our categories. In this case, language shaped our understanding of the animal world; our reality was that all animals belonged to one class or another, even though this wasn't the case. This is thoughtfully discussed in Umberto Eco's essay, "The Platypus" from his collection

*Kant and the Platypus* (1997; trans. 1999) In the same way, language shapes our understanding of the earth's composition (seven continents, five oceans, etc.) the solar *system* (stars, planets, moons, asteroids) and everything else.

In the language of political discourse, for example, politicians constantly use words to try to shape our reality. During a recent political campaign in the United States, opinion polls showed that most voters supported the Democrat's idea of "eliminating the Bush tax cuts for the wealthiest Americans" while many of these same voters adamantly opposed what the Republicans called "raising taxes on job creators"; both of these phrases, however, described the same thing. Similarly, political leaders find more support for a war action when it has a name like "Operation Iraqi Freedom," and that support is more likely to continue when the goal is to "spread democracy," and the consequences of war are described as "collateral damage," "friendly fire" and "enhanced coercive interrogation techniques."

## Barthes, Jakobson and Lévi-Strauss

All of this began to relate specifically to literary theory in the 1950s. Claude Lévi-Strauss had been studying myths among various indigenous cultures in remote parts of the world. Even though it would have been physically impossible (because of geography, etc.) for the divergent cultures to share their stories, Lévi-Strauss began to recognize a common pattern within the structures of these different cultures' myths. After a brief working relationship with Roman Jakobson (who had emigrated from Russia to Europe), Lévi-Strauss determined that the collection of myths he had been cataloguing followed the same structural patterns that Saussure had identified with language. Lévi-Strauss then concluded that these indigenous myths constituted their own kind of language and he incorporated Saussure's tools of linguistic study into his own study of myth.

Soon after this, Roland Barthes began using this same approach with literary texts. In contrast to Lévi-Strauss, Barthes' structuralist interests were more specifically focused on literature. In *S/Z* (1970), for example, Barthes recognizes five "codes" within a text: the hermeneutic code, the semic code, the symbolic code, the proairetic code and the cultural code. In his book, Barthes lists them "in order of their appearance, without trying to put them in any order of importance," but two codes that he spends a good deal of time on (and the two that are most relevant for our purposes) are the hermeneutic code and the proairetic code.

The hermeneutic code refers to an "enigma" which will be "distinguished, suggested, formulated, held in suspense, and finally disclosed."

In other words, the hermeneutic code creates suspense by providing a question that the reader wants answered. Murder mysteries often begin with just such a question: *Who killed the dead guy, and why?* Another story might incorporate the hermeneutic code with a scene that leaves the reader wondering *What's going on here?*

The proairetic code, on the other hand, describes all manner of actions "(*stroll, murder, rendezvous*)." The proairetic code creates suspense through action, whether those actions are "trivial, [. . .] melodramatic, [. . .] numerous or few." As an example, a story might say something like, *He just robbed (or punched, or insulted) that mean bad guy*, or, *She just hired a private investigator to spy on her husband. What's going to happen next?* If we read a good number of books (or watch a lot of movies), we will notice that most stories use either the hermeneutic or the proairetic code to create suspense. Creative writers, in particular, find it helpful to familiarize themselves with both.

In Poe's "The Cask of Amontillado," for example, we see the hermeneutic code at work in the story's opening: "The thousand injuries of Fortunato I had borne as best I could, but when he ventured upon insult, I vowed revenge." We are introduced immediately to the two main characters, but we are left to wonder about the exact nature of this "insult." And what will this "revenge" entail? (One could argue, though, that the question regarding the revenge could just as easily fit into the category of proairetic code.) In contrast, Ambrose Bierce begins his story, "An Occurrence at Owl Creek Bridge," utilizing primarily the proairetic code: "The man's hands were behind his back, the wrists bound with a cord. A rope closely encircled his neck." While we (briefly) wonder why Peyton Farquhar is about to be hanged (the hermeneutic code), and while the narrator hides from the reader the exact nature of Peyton Farquhar's escape, it is the proairetic code—action, after action, after action—that moves the story forward. As we read more and more stories (or watch more and more movies), we are better able to notice either the hermeneutic or proairetic code at work.

Structuralists also believe that, as with language, a similar system of components and rules applies to all types of human activity, whether that activity is cultural, social or literary. All human activity and behavior, in other words, could be studied as if it were a language, or a "text." As such, we are able to identify within each activity its system of signs and the rules that control it. We can then use Saussure's method to analyze that activity, whether the activity involves a literary text, a historical document, an indigenous culture, or anything. This allowed structuralists to view a literary text as not just a component of a larger system of its literary genre, but also as a component of its history and its culture. Chekhov's "Gooseberries," for example, could be viewed as a component of the genre system of short stories. It could also be seen as a part of the culture of late nineteenth-century Russia, it could be studied for the individual parts within the story itself, it could be compared to other stories within that story collection or it could be analyzed as part of Chekhov's entire body of work. In other words, a literary text could be studied in the context of any signifying system to which it belonged. This was a revolutionary idea when compared to the New Critics' belief that the text itself should be the only object of study for a proper literary analysis. Additionally, since structuralism provided nearly limitless avenues for analysis, structuralists concluded that there cannot be, as the New Critics argued, a single "correct" meaning to a text. Because of this, structuralism brought about a radical change in the theoretical study of literature.

Structuralist literary critics, then, might be interested in any aspect of a literary text with regard to how the text conforms to the rules of the theorist's chosen system. How do the parts of "The Cask of Amontillado," for example, or "The Yellow Wallpaper," fit into the larger genre (or *langue*) of the short story (or fiction in general)? How does Bierce's "An Occurrence at Owl Creek Bridge" function as part of the system of American Realism? How do the characters of Hawthorne's "The Birthmark" fit into the story itself? It is questions like these, regarding system components, that structuralists focus on. Narratologists look at system components as well, but where the components of structuralism can be part of any relevant system, narratologists are interested in those story components that are specifically related to the text and its narrative structure.

## NARRATOLOGY

**FOCUSES ON:** the narrative elements within the text, particularly with regard to how, when and where the story is told, and by whom.
**BECAUSE:** narratologists are interested in the individual parts that comprise a narrative, common to all narratives of the same type.
**DEVELOPED IN:** 1960s.
**NOTABLE PRACTITIONERS:**
    Dorrit Cohn (1924-2012)    Seymour Chatman (1928- )
    Gérard Genette (1930- )    Tzvetan Todorov (1939- )
    Gerald Prince (1942- )    Shlomith Rimmon-Kenan (1942- )
    Mieke Bal (1946- )    Jakob Lothe (1950- )
    James Phelan (1951- )
**IMPORTANT PREDECESSORS:**
    Aristotle (384 BCE-322 BCE)    Vladimir Propp (1895-1970)
    Roman Jakobson (1896-1982)
**ADVANTAGES:** Reveals the common structures within texts that most readers are unaware of.

**DISADVANTAGES:** Has its own unique vocabulary and ignores story specifics to focus on story structure.
**DEFINITION:** the theory of narrative, or the study of narrative structures.

---

Narratology is commonly considered a branch of structuralism, primarily because early narratologists used Saussure's methodology to analyze literature. Unlike traditional structuralists, though, narratologists limit their focus to components within a text and to how those components relate to similar components within other texts. Narratology studies the nature, form and function of narratives of all types; it looks at what all narratives have in common as well as what enables them to differ from each other.

One could easily argue that narratology began with Aristotle and his book, *Poetics*. In *Poetics*, Aristotle is looking at the individual parts of a story (in his case, in the form of a tragic play) to see where and how those parts fit together. (There is evidence to suggest that Aristotle also discussed comedy, possibly in a Part II to *Poetics*, but such a text no longer exists.) In the part of *Poetics* that still survives, Aristotle identifies six elements of a tragedy: plot, character, thought (what we now might call *theme*), diction (language), melody (music), and spectacle (which refers to things such as stage effects, costumes, acting, etc.).

To Aristotle, the play's plot is of primary importance; characters are secondary and should be created with the express goal of serving the plot (an opinion that is detestable to readers of "literary" fiction today). Aristotle also notes three key elements in a tragedy's plot: all tragic heroes must have some sort of tragic flaw (*hamartia*), the protagonist must at some point recognize the reality of his situation (*anagnorisis*), and the tragedy's protagonist should experience a reversal of fortune (*peripeteia*). When these elements work together effectively, the well-done tragedy will allow the audience to relate to the protagonist and then experience a release of emotions (a *catharsis*) by the time the play concludes.

While Aristotle's ideas on dramatic production have been refined over the last two thousand years, we still see his theories at work in nearly every movie and play produced today. He extolled the virtues of the three-act performance (the five-act play, described by Horace and presented by Shakespeare, is structured the same as the three-act play that Aristotle describes) and Aristotle gave us the outline for effective narrative that writers still use today.

## Vladimir Propp

The study of modern narratology, before it was called *narratology*, began with Vladimir Propp, a Russian Formalist. Propp published numerous essays throughout his career—many collected in *Theory and History of Folklore* (1984)—but he is best remembered for his pioneering book, *Morphology of the Folktale* (1928; trans. 1958). In *Morphology of the Folktale*, Propp uses a Formalist approach to analyze one hundred Russian fairy tales. Propp's book is the first comprehensive analysis of narrative structure in the modern era.

Upon dissecting the stories, Propp found that all the characters belonged in one of seven classification types: 1) the villain, 2) the dispatcher, 3) the magical helper, 4) the princess and/or her father, 5) the donor, 6) the hero, and 7) the false hero. In contrast to the conventional understanding of literary characters, Propp saw characters as mere pieces of a story that each serve some necessary purpose. The villain's "purpose," for example, is to oppose the hero, the dispatcher is a person or thing that sends the hero on his journey, and so on.

Propp also discovered that each story contained some combination of thirty-one different narrative actions (which he referred to as "functions"). None of the stories that Propp studied contained all thirty-one functions, but the functions all appeared in the same order that Propp identified (number IX, for example, when it appeared in a story, always came before number X, which always came before number XI, etc.). Propp determined that these functions are "basic components of the tale" that we need to extract from the story in order to see the story's structure. Propp identified the following narrative functions, always appearing in this order:

> I. One of the members of a family absents himself from home.
> II. An interdiction is addressed to the hero.
> III. The interdiction is violated.
> IV. The villain makes an attempt at reconnaissance.
> V. The villain receives information about his victim.
> VI. The villain attempts to deceive his victim in order to take possession of him or of his belongings.
> VII. The victim submits to deception and thereby unwittingly helps his enemy.
> VIII. The villain causes harm or injury to a member of a family.
> VIII a. One member of a family either lacks something or desires to have something.
> IX. Misfortune or lack is made known; the hero is approached with a request or command; he is allowed to go or he is dispatched.
> X. The seeker agrees to or decides upon counteraction.
> XI. The hero leaves home.
> XII. The hero is tested, interrogated, attacked, etc., which prepares the way for receiving either a magical agent or helper.
> XIII. The hero reacts to the actions of the future donor.
> XIV. The hero acquires the use of a magical agent.

XV. The hero is transferred, reaches, or is led to the whereabouts of an object of search.
XVI. The hero and the villain join in direct combat.
XVII. The hero is branded.
XVIII. The villain is defeated.
XIX. The initial misfortune or lack is liquidated.
XX. The hero returns.
XXI. The hero is pursued.
XXII. Rescued of the hero from pursuit.
XXIII. The hero, unrecognized, arrives home or in another country.
XXV. A difficult task is proposed to the hero.
XXVI. The task is resolved.
XXVII. The hero is recognized.
XXVIII. The false hero or villain is exposed.
XXIX. The hero is given a new appearance.
XXX. The villain is punished.
XXXI. The hero is married and ascends the throne.

Again, while none of Propp's stories included all thirty-one functions, these functions always occurred in this same order.

Propp summed up his findings with the following four observations:

1. Functions of characters serve as stable, constant elements in a tale, independent of how and by whom they are fulfilled.
2. The number of functions known to the fairy tale is limited.
3. The sequence of functions is always identical.
4. All fairy tales are of one type in regard to their structure.

This last point in particular was innovative in the study of literature. While theorists as far back as Aristotle had argued that a story *should* follow a certain structure, this was very different than Propp's assertion that stories already *did* conform to such a structure.

## Tzvetan Todorov

Tzvetan Todorov is credited with giving us the word, narratology, in his book, *Grammaire du Décaméron* (1969; *Grammar of the Decameron*). In it, Todorov analyzes Giovanni Boccaccio's *Decameron* through the lens of what we now refer to as structuralist narratology. Todorov's approach is decidedly structuralist in tone; in the same way that structural linguists worked with language, Todorov analyzed Boccaccio's stories, looking at them not in the traditional way theorists would analyze an individual story, but seeing them as different expressions of the possibilities within the structural framework of the language of the short story.

Todorov saw his book as an introduction into a new branch of science—*"la science du récit"* (the science of narrative). While Todorov's work is similar in many ways to the work Propp did four decades earlier, breaking stories down and looking at the structures within those stories, Todorov's ideas are much more advanced, particularly with his examination of plot. (Like Aristotle, Todorov emphasizes the importance of plot and sees it as key to an effective story.)

Propp's book wasn't translated into English until 1958, and it wasn't until the 1960s and 70s that narratology, as a field of study, began to gain momentum. This is when we had Todorov's *Grammaire du Décaméron* (1969) and Genette's *Narrative Discourse* (1972). Other books, such as Mieke Bal's *Narratology* (1985) and Gerald Prince's *A Dictionary of Narratology* (1987) were still several years away.

It might also help to keep in mind that many people study the structure of narrative without calling themselves narratologists (and perhaps without even realizing that what they're doing is akin to narratology). Robert McKee's book, *Story* (1999), is one example. While it is written primarily for movie screenwriters, a significant portion of the text focuses on the structure of narrative. Syd Field has written several screenwriting books in a similar vein as McKee. One could also include any of the scores of books available that focus on how to write fiction—if they have the word "plot" or "structure" in the title, more than likely they are discussing, in one form or another, many of the same issues that narratologists are discussing.

Narratology, of course, is a more in-depth study and it's more academic in tone, but it's doing, in essence, the same thing: studying the elements of a story that create suspense, excitement and intrigue—the elements of stories that make readers want to read stories and hear stories and watch stories on TV and in the movie theater.

## Modern Narratology

The majority of discussion regarding modern narratology begins with Gérard Genette; he is considered one of the original authorities on narratology. Genette's work is significant because it provides, as Jonathan Culler notes in Genette's forward, the first complete "systematic theory of narrative." In his book, *Narrative Discourse* (1972), Genette uses Proust's *A la recherché du temps perdu* (1913-1927; trans. 1922-1931, *Remembrance of Things Past*) to examine five different elements of a story: Order, Duration, Frequency, Mood and Voice. Related in the most simple terms, "Order" describes how the story is organized (chronologically or non-chronologically), "Duration" refers to how fast the story is narrated (are story events written in scene, or summarized, etc.?), "Frequency" describes how often story events are related or repeated,

"Mood" looks at the point of view from which the story is told, and "Voice" describes, specifically, who the narrator is.

One of the main difficulties for students first encountering narratology comes from narratology's new, complex vocabulary. This, for the most part, is unavoidable because narratologists identify the subtle differences between similar story elements. A first-person narrator, for example, could be telling his or her own story (a homodiegetic narrator with internal focalization, as in "The Cask of Amontillado" or "The Yellow Wallpaper"), or he could be telling the story of someone else (a homodiegetic narrator with external focalization, as in *The Great Gatsby* or *The Razor's Edge*. First-person narrators can be further distinguished in the stories by Poe and Gilman because the narrator of "The Yellow Wallpaper" has clearly undergone a significant change throughout the course of the story, while Poe's Montresor stays the same. These differentiations are developed even more when we consider when the narrator tells his or her story, how the narrator tells his story, and from where the narrator tells his story, etc. The vocabulary then, while difficult to navigate at first, actually simplifies things for narratologists.

Genette saw his book as merely the foundation for the study of narratology, expecting his work to be expanded and expounded upon. And it has been. Notable narratologists such as Mieke Bal, Shlomith Rimmon-Kenan, and Gerald Prince have all worked to refine and shape the study of narratology that we know today.

In simple terms, narratologists today are looking primarily at seven things: 1) Who is telling the story? 2) Who is he or she telling the story to? 3) Who is he telling the story about? 4) When is he telling the story (in relation to when it took place)? 5) From where is he telling the story (in relation to where it took place)? 6) What happens in the story? and 7) How is he telling the story (in what order is he telling the story? and at what speed is he telling different parts of the story?). We would be best served by looking at these questions more closely:

1) Who is telling the story?
    a) Is it a homodiegetic narrator (first-person), or a hetero-diegetic narrator (third-person)?
    b) Is it a monologic narrative with one unifying voice or consciousness? Or is it a dialogic/polyphonic (many-voiced) narrative (as in Faulkner's "A Rose for Emily")? (The monologic narrative is, by far, the most common.)

2) Who is he or she telling the story to?
    Who is the narratee (as opposed to the real reader and the implied reader)? (This isn't always explicitly clear.)

3) Who is he telling the story about?
    a) Who or what are the existents (actors or items of setting)?
    b) What is the focalization? It could be:
        i) a first-person narrator tells his own story (homodiegetic narrator with internal focalization),

ii) a first-person narrator tells a story he observed (a homodiegetic narrator with external focalization),
  iii) a third-person narrator who only describes characters' words and actions (heterodiegetic narrator with external focalization)
  iv) an omniscient narrator who has the authority to enter any character's mind and comment on any action (heterodiegetic narrator with zero focalization).
  v) a third-person limited narrator or free indirect discourse (heterodiegetic narrator with internal focalization).
4) When is he telling the story (in relation to when it took place)?
  a) What is the temporal distance? (how long before the story is narrated did the story events take place?) and
  b) What type of temporal narration is used? It could be:
    i) *Posterior narration*—a narration which follows the events being recounted; a subsequent narration. (What is commonly considered the traditional type of narration.)
    ii) *Anterior narration*—precedes in time the situations and events being narrated. Also called predictive narration. ("He will drive to the supermarket and buy some milk.")
    iii) *Intercalated narration*—a type of narration whereby a narrating instance is temporally situated between two moments of the action; characteristic of epistolary and diary narratives (also called an interpolated narrating).
    iv) *Simultaneous narration*—a narration in which the discourse takes place at the same time as the story events being related in the discourse.
5) From where is he telling the story (in relation to where it took place)?
  What is the physical (geographical) distance?
6) What happens in the story?
  What are the events (changes in state within the discourse—something a character does, or something that happens, like a snowstorm, tornado or traffic jam)?
7) How is he telling the story?
  a) What is the relationship between *story* (everything that happens in a fictional world) and *discourse* (how those story events are presented—the text, in other words)?
  b) In what order is he telling the story? Is it chronological or anachronous? Are there flashbacks? Flash forwards?
  c) At what speed is he telling different parts of the story? This refers to the five narrative tempos, which are (in descending order from infinity to zero) are: ellipsis, summary, scene, stretch and pause:
    i) Ellipsis—there is no discourse time; in other words, story events are skipped over in the discourse text. ("Three years later, he started working at the factory.")
    ii) summary—the written discourse time is shorter than the story time. ("He spent the next three years doing odd jobs until he got hired at the factory.")
    iii) scene—discourse time is equal to the story time (in other words, the narrator is describing events as if we were watching them unfold in real time—think of a scene in a movie).

iv) stretch—discourse time is greater than the story time it is recounting (several pages might describe a few brief seconds, as in "An Occurrence at Owl Creek Bridge").
v) pause—discourse time continues while there is no movement of story (this could be a description of a table, for example, or exposition, or a narrator's digression or commentary).

Again, narratologists are primarily interested in the structural components of a story rather than traditionally "analyzing" the story itself, but we can still utilize the tools of narratology to better conceptualize what is happening in a literary work as we look at it from any number of theoretical perspectives. The answers to these seven questions, then, can help us delve deeper into a literary text, regardless what critical approach we use.

## Implementation

While most narratologists focus their attention on the intricacies of narrative elements within a story (with essay titles like, "Intertextuality and the Collaborative Construction of Narrative" and "Munro's Handling of Description, Focalization, and Voice in 'Passion'"), understanding narratology can also help a reader grasp details within a story that he or she might otherwise overlook.

If we look carefully at the last paragraph in Poe's "The Cask of Amontillado," for example, we notice a temporal distance of roughly fifty years: "For the half of a century no mortal has disturbed them." If we combine this with the fact that much of the narration is rendered in scene, providing more specific detail than we could get with summary, then we begin to gain a richer understanding of the narrator. How has he remembered these events so vividly after fifty years, for example? Has he played them over and over in his mind all this time? And, if so, did he do this out of guilt, or pride?

From a narratological perspective, Bierce's "An Occurrence at Owl Creek Bridge" is notable for its vast difference between story time and discourse time. Story time, as noted, is the time it takes (within the world of the story) for the events of the story to take place. Discourse time, on the other hand, is the time it takes (outside the world of the story) for the narrator to describe those events. In "An Occurrence at Owl Creek Bridge," the story time after that last sentence of Part I—"The sergeant stepped aside"—is only a few seconds. The discourse time, though, covers the several minutes it takes us to read from that sentence to the last word of the story.

Note, too, the difference between the narrators in Bierce's story and King's "The Little Convent Girl." Both stories provide third-person narrators, but the information the narrators provide is very different. In

"An Occurrence at Owl Creek Bridge," we have access to Peyton Farquhar's thoughts, feelings and emotions. We see what he sees and feel what he feels. In "The Little Convent Girl," though, we have no such access to any of the characters. It is if we are sitting, unnoticed, on the boat watching the characters and eavesdropping on their conversation. Bierce's narrator (especially in Part I), also offers occasional opinions and thoughts that don't belong to any of the characters. King's narrator, again, relates only observable story events. Since there is nothing in the text to give us even the slightest hint about who King's narrator is, the narrator of "The Little Convent Girl" is a maximally covert (or third-person objective) narrator. That leaves it up to the reader to examine the covert (unwritten) text to infer for ourselves the reason for the girl's action in the end.

"The Yellow Wallpaper" and *Diary of a Madman* are similar in many ways. To begin, both stories employ intercalated narration. In other words, story events happen, then they are written about (just as in a posterior narration), then more story events happen, they are written about, and so on. Both of these narrators also incorporate, at times, simultaneous narration—story events in these moments are described as they happen. This brings us to the ending of, in particular, "The Yellow Wallpaper." What do you think happens—or is happening—at the end of the story? (Keep in mind that there is no right or wrong answer, as long as you're able to support your conclusion with evidence from the text.) If you want to argue that the narrator is deceased, for example, then you would want to explain how she is able to narrate the end of her own story.

Another similarity between "The Yellow Wallpaper" and *Diary of a Madman* is that both stories are told by unreliable narrators. Whenever we have a first-person narrator, we should always read that narration with a jaundiced eye, so to speak. We can imagine meeting a stranger at a train station, an airport, or at the end of a bar, etc. and that person tells us a story. At first, we are naturally inclined to believe what they tell us. But how do we know they are telling the truth? If our storyteller is someone like the narrator of "The Yellow Wallpaper," telling us about a woman who lives in her walls, we would hopefully suspect that such a narrator wouldn't necessarily be the best source for reliable information. It then becomes our job, as careful readers, to determine how much of her story we can believe.

In general, the further removed the narrator is from the characters, the more trustworthy that narrator becomes. On one end of the spectrum is the objective third-person narrator in King's "The Little Convent Girl." This narrator will, by nature, be the most reliable. After all, if the only information related by the narrator is facts, then there is no reason to distrust the narrator (though this assumption will be called into question when we get to the chapter on post-structuralism). On the other end of the spectrum, from a narratological perspective, is the least reliable narrator: a first-person narrator who tells his or her own story (like Poe's Montresor and Gilman's and Gogol's narrators in this text). It's not always clear when a first-person narrator is unreliable—and not all first-person narrators are unreliable—but one must keep in mind that the author made a conscious decision to employ a first-person narrator. The reader should, therefore, read such narratives carefully, looking for clues within the covert (unwritten) text that might explain why.

For example, when a narrator describes, like Gogol's Poprishchin, reading letters that two dogs have written to each other, we readers have to determine what is actually happening within the world of his story. What would we see, in other words, if we were a fly on the wall of Poprishchin's room? But what about a narrator like Poe's Montresor? Is he believable? He certainly isn't trustworthy, as Fortunato finds out by the end of the story, but can we, as readers, trust him to relate accurately his story's events? It might help, in this regard, to consider who we think Montresor is telling his story to. Who is the narratee, in other words? Since it isn't explicitly clear in the text, it is up to the reader to form his or her own opinion. Is it a priest—or a police officer—listening to a confession? Is it one of Montresor's grandchildren? Is it a random acquaintance on a carriage ride? Or perhaps it is Montresor's next victim. Literary criticism—from any theoretical perspective—can become a vibrant activity because questions such as these are not always possible to answer with certitude.

## Important Moments in Structuralism and Narratology

**1916:** Ferdinand de Saussure's *Course in General Linguistics*
**1925:** Victor Shklovsky's *Theory of Prose*
**1928:** Vladimir Propp's *Morphology of the Folktale*
**1958:** translation of Propp's *Morphology of the Folktale*
**1958:** Claude Lévi-Strauss' *Structural Anthropology*
**1959:** Saussure's *Course in General Linguistics* translated into English
**1964:** Lévi-Strauss' *The Raw and the Cooked*
**1966:** A.J. Greimas' *Structural Semantics*
**1969:** Tzvetan Todorov's *Grammar of the Decameron*
**1970:** *The Journal of Narrative Technique* founded
**1970:** Roland Barthes' *S/Z*
**1972:** Gérard Genette's *Narrative Discourse*
**1975:** Will Wright's *Sixguns and Society*
**1975:** Jonathan Culler's *Structuralist Poetics*
**1977:** Terrence Hawkes' *Structuralism and Semiotics*

1977: Julia Kristeva's *Desire in Language*
1978: Seymour Chatman's *Story and Discourse*
1978: Lévi-Strauss' *Myth and Meaning*
1982: Prince's *Narratology: The Form and Functioning of Narrative*
1983: Shlomith Rimmon-Kenan's *Narrative Fiction*
1983: Genette's *Narrative Discourse Revisited*
1984: Propp's *The Russian Folktale* published
1985: Society for the Study of Narrative Literature formed
1985: Mieke Bal's *Narratology*
1987: Gerald Prince's *A Dictionary of Narratology*
1996: Anna Wierzbicka's *Semantics: Primes and Universals*
1997: Umberto Eco's *Kant and the Platypus*
2000: Jakob Lothe's *Narrative in Fiction and Film*.

## Important Terms

To limit the confusion as much as possible in this introductory text, we'll try to avoid the narratological terms when a more conventional term already exists for, effectively, the same definition (for example, instead of using the term, "dramatized homodiegetic narrator with external focalization," we'll simply refer to it as a "first-person observer narrator"). For a complete list of narratological terms and their definitions, Gerald Prince's *A Dictionary of Narratology* is an excellent resource.

binary opposition
signifier
first-person observer narrator
third-person limited narrator
third-person omniscient narrator
monologic narrator
Narrative distance
  Physical distance
  Temporal distance
  Emotional distance
Plot
  Story
  Discourse
Narrative tempo
  Scene (mimesis)
  Exposition (diegesis)
  Summary
  Stretch
  Ellipsis

sign
signified
first-person participant narrator
third-person objective narrator
unreliable narrator
polyphonic narrator
Posterior narration
Anterior narration
Intercalated narration
Simultaneous narration

Story time
Discourse time

Flashback
Flash forward

## Study Questions

1. In Gilman's "The Yellow Wallpaper," we could find several binary oppositions related to gender, social class, weather, wisdom, confinement, respect, mental health and so on. If, as post-structuralists argue, there is a hierarchy inherent in every binary opposition, then where do you think Gilman places each of these binary elements on the hierarchical scale? What happens if we reverse these hierarchies? Do any of these binary oppositions contradict themselves or each other? What unique understanding can you derive from the story when considering it from a post-structuralist perspective, particularly in relation to the binary oppositions you identified? (As you formulate your response, you will likely find it helpful to first note all of the binary oppositions you can identify.)
2. As we noted, narratologists often approach a fictional text with several questions in mind, such as: Who is telling the story? Who is he or she telling the story to? Who is he telling the story about? When is he telling the story (in relation to when it took place)? From where is he telling the story (in relation to where it took place)? What happens in the story? and How is he telling the story (in what order is he telling the story? and at what speed is he telling different parts of the story?)?

    Once narratologists know the answers to these questions, they look again at the text in an attempt to determine why the author made his choices and what those choices can tell us, additionally, about the story. In "An Occurrence at Owl Creek Bridge," for example, why does Bierce choose a third-person limited narrator to tell his story? How would the story change if he had employed a third-person objective or third-person omniscient narrator? What effect would such a change have on other story elements (discourse time vs. story time, for example)?
3. Identify the type of narration (first-person participant, third-person omniscient, etc.) in each of the stories in this text. Then, with two of the stories, detail how they would be different if they employed each other's narrative type.
4. Which of these narrators would usually be the most reliable and which would be the least reliable, and why?: a) third-person objective, b) first-person participant, c) third-person limited.
5. From a narratological perspective, perform a close reading of Charlotte Perkins Gilman's "The Yellow Wallpaper."

    What does the story "tell" us, covertly, that we wouldn't have noticed without doing a narratological reading? How does narratology enhance our understanding of the text?

To answer this question, perhaps it would help to think about the following questions (find specific textual evidence to support each of your answers):

Why does Gilman choose a first-person narrator to tell her story? What can we glean from the story that the first-person narrator doesn't put on the page? How would the story change if she used the same narrator that Bierce uses? What if Gilman had used the same narrator that Chopin uses in "The Story of an Hour"? What if she'd used the narrator that is used in Sui Sin Far's "In the Land of the Free"?

6. Write a brief essay arguing either that Poprishchin is institutionalized throughout his narration or that he is only institutionalized sometime during his narration (if you choose the latter, you might be well-served by arguing for a specific date when he is institutionalized). Utilize the theoretical tools you have learned thus far and use textual evidence to support your claim.

You might find it helpful to examine the story's narrator and the narrative situation. What is implied but not actually written in the text? Maybe you'd like to focus on how the setting informs the story. For example, has the setting changed between the time of the story events recounted and the narrator's recounting of those events? Can we learn anything by considering the temporal distance between the narration and the story events the narrator describes?

## Selected Bibliography

Bal, Mieke. *Narratology: Introduction to the Theory of Narrative.* Toronto: Toronto UP, 2004.
Barthes, Roland. *Elements of Semiology.* New York: Hill and Wang, 1977.
—. *Empire of Signs.* New York: Hill and Wang, 1983.
—. *Mythologies.* New York: Hill and Wang, 1972.
—. *S/Z: An Essay.* New York: Hill and Wang, 1975.
—. *Selected Writings.* Waukegan, IL: Fontana, 1989.
—. *The Semiotic Challenge.* Berkeley: California UP, 1994.
Berlin, Brent, and Paul Kay. *Basic Color Terms: Their Universality and Evolution.* Palo Alto: CLSI, 1999.
Campbell, Joseph. *The Hero with a Thousand Faces.* Princeton: Princeton UP, 1972.
Campbell, Joseph, and Bill Moyers. *The Power of Myth.* New York: Anchor, 1991.
Chatman, Seymour. *Story and Discourse: Narrative Structure in Fiction and Film.* Ithaca: Cornell UP, 1980.
Chomsky, Noam. *Language and Mind.* New York: Columbia UP, 2006.

Culler, Jonathan. *Structuralist Poetics: Structuralism, Linguistics and the Study of Literature*. New York: Routledge, 2002.
Eco, Umberto. *Kant and the Platypus: Essays on Language and Cognition*. New York: Mariner, 2000.
Genette, Gérard. *Narrative Discourse: An Essay in Method*. Ithaca: Cornell UP, 1983.
—. *Narrative Discourse, Revisited*. Ithaca: Cornell UP, 1990.
Hawkes, Terrence. *Structuralism and Semiotics*. Berkeley: California UP, 1977.
Holland, Norman Norwood. *The Critical I*. New York: Columbia UP, 1994.
Innes, Robert E. ed. *Semiotics: An Introductory Anthology*. Bloomington: Indiana UP, 1985.
Kristeva, Julia. *Desire in Language: A Semiotic Approach to Literature and Art*. New York: Columbia UP, 1980.
Levi-Strauss, Claude. *Structural Anthropology*. New York: Basic, 1974.
—. *Myth and Meaning: Cracking the Code of Culture*. New York: Schocken, 1995.
—. *The Raw and the Cooked: Mythologiques, Volume 1*. Chicago: Chicago UP, 1983.
Lothe, Jakob. *Narrative in Fiction and Film*. Oxford: Oxford UP, 2003.
Messent, Peter. *New Readings of the American Novel: Narrative Theory and its Application*. Edinburgh: Edinburgh UP, 1998.
Pirsig, Robert M. *Lila: An Inquiry into Morals*. New York: Bantam, 1992.
Prince, Gerald. *A Dictionary of Narratology*. Lincoln: Nebraska UP, 1987.
—. *Narratology: The Form and Functioning of Narrative*. New York: Mouton de Gruyter, 1982.
Propp, Vladimir. *The Morphology of the Folktale*. Austin: Texas UP, 1990.
—. *Theory and History of Folklore*. Minneapolis: Minnesota UP, 1997.
Rimmon-Kenan, Shlomith. *Narrative Fiction*. London: Routledge, 1983.
Saussure, Ferdinand de. *Course in General Linguistics*. New York: Columbia UP, 2011.
Scholes, Robert. *Structuralism in Literature: An Introduction*. New Haven: Yale UP, 1974.
Shklovsky, Victor. *Theory of Prose*. Normal, IL: Dalkey, 1991.
Todorov, Tzvetan. *Genres in Discourse*. Cambridge: Cambridge UP, 1990.
—. *Grammaire du Décaméron*. The Hague: Mouton, 1969.
—. *Introduction to Poetics*. Minneapolis: Minnesota UP, 1981.
—. *The Fantastic: A Structural Approach to a Literary Genre*. Ithaca: Cornell UP, 1975.

Wierzbicka, Anna. *Semantics: Primes and Universals*. Oxford: Oxford UP, 1996.
Wright, Will. *Sixguns and Society: A Structural Study of the Western*. Berkeley: California UP, 1997.

# 6

# Post-Structuralism

**FOCUSES ON:** only the text.
**BECAUSE:** by focusing on only the text, we open up the text to reveal its innumerable interpretations.
**DEVELOPED IN:** 1960s.
**NOTABLE PRACTITIONERS:**
    Roland Barthes (1915-1980)    Jacques Derrida (1930-2004)
    Michel Foucault (1926-84)
**IMPORTANT PREDECESSORS:**
    Claude Levi-Strauss (1908-2009)    Roland Barthes (1915-1980)
**ADVANTAGES:** provides readers with the tools to formulate their own unique interpretation of a text.
**DISADVANTAGES:** while the concepts of post-structuralism are not overly complicated, the terminology in many of the primary texts can be challenging for students.
**DEFINITION:** a method of literary analysis, derived from structuralism, which argues that our understanding of all forms of reality is unstable and constantly changing.

---

Of all the literary theories in this text, post-structuralism is one of the more difficult to explain in simple and precise terms. It comes after structuralism, of course—we see its emergence in the late sixties with the work of Jacques Derrida and Roland Barthes—and, in some ways, it is a continuation of structuralist ideas. In many other ways, though, post-structuralism is a critique of and reaction to structuralism.

As we remember, structuralism saw itself as a logical and scientific approach to knowledge through an analysis of the underlying structures upon which that knowledge is based. We understand what a love story is, for example, because it follows the same structural pattern that is common to all love stories. We know what a protagonist is because he or she functions as all protagonists do. Structuralists saw these underlying structures as inherent to a thing. Whether that thing is a story, a language, or a body of knowledge, structuralists saw the structure as a constant foundational element upon which that thing is based.

Post-structuralists believed that our understanding of these underlying structures is flawed. They argued that structures aren't intrinsic to a thing but, instead, perceived by and created by human beings and, therefore, subject to human biases and misinterpretations. In other words, the structures that we think we see in all love stories are not necessarily there, but only perceived by our fallible human minds. Furthermore, according to post-structuralists, people from different cultures and from different times might identify different structures at work in the same story. This same idea applies to all structures, whether those structures are in stories, languages or anything.

Critiques of structuralism began in Europe in the early 1960s. One example is Umberto Eco's *Opera aperta* (1962; trans. 1989, *The Open Work*). Most scholars in the United States, though, mark the beginning of post-structuralism with a 1966 symposium at Johns Hopkins University. The symposium's title was, "The Languages of Criticism and the Sciences of Man: The Structural Controversy." It was here that Jacques Derrida first delivered his pioneering lecture, "Structure, Sign and Play in the Discourse of the Human Sciences." In 1966, structuralism was still a recent development in U.S. academia (Saussure's *Course in General Linguistics*, after all, hadn't been translated into English until 1959). The Johns Hopkins conference was conceived as an introduction of structuralism to the United States. Derrida's lecture, though, revealed flaws in the structuralist model and anticipated a future after structuralism.

One thing that Derrida (and, later, Roland Barthes) found problematic about structuralist literary criticism was that, when a structuralist reads a story, he or she is always looking at it from a structuralist perspective. He reads a story, in other words, then decides what it means, and *then* he looks for the structures that shaped the text. Following such an approach, according to Derrida, will lead the reader to ignore (consciously or unconsciously) any parts of the story that don't contribute to that pattern.

For example, a Marxist who studies a literary work might unconsciously notice meaning that is related to class conflict between the rich and the poor; a Freudian might overlook Marxist ideas in the same text and notice what the text implicitly says about an author's childhood. A structuralist looking for patterns, according to Derrida, will approach a text in the same way, recognizing structural patterns at the expense of other aspects of the text, or even seeing structures that aren't necessarily there.

Post-structuralists saw another flaw with structuralism that was more fundamental. Structuralists look for patterns (or structures) within texts. Logically, though, for a structure to exist at all, it would have to be in existence before the text is created. After all, a text—or anything—can't conform to a structure if the structure isn't there first (just like a homebuilder can't tile the bathroom or carpet the living room before he builds the floors and walls). Structuralism, then, relies on the implication that a text is based upon an underlying structure that existed before the text—any text—is created. This idea, though, contradicts the structuralists' own belief that language precedes thought, making the core idea of structuralism a logical impossibility. If (as the structuralists say) we are unable to conceive of something like a structure before we have the language to describe it (and thus make it real), then how can language be based upon a structure, when the structure, by its very nature, would have to exist before language in order for language to conform to it? In other words, how could language have always conformed to a structure when language first had to create the structure that it conforms to?

Since structuralists saw structures at work throughout the human and natural world, this question applied to all aspects of human understanding. Post-structuralism, then, as a philosophical study, critiques the structuralist understanding of the origin of knowledge (where does knowledge come from and how do we know what we know?). Post-structuralists found that a model of knowledge based upon structures (structuralism) and a model of knowledge based upon experience (phenomenology) were both inadequate. This resulted in the recognition that knowledge is much more ambiguous than we had always believed.

But post-structuralism didn't reject all of the ideas of structuralism. One primary area of commonality regarded the importance of language. Both structuralism and post-structuralism saw language as essential to reality. Language controls our knowledge, according to the structuralists and post-structuralists, because we can only think of things we have the words to describe (which leads to the idea that nothing can exist without language).

The two approaches differ, though, in their understanding of the nature of language. Structuralists see language, for all intents and purposes, as relatively unchanging. Meanings of words might change over time and in different contexts, but what a word means today is usually what a word will mean tomorrow and beyond. Post-structuralists, on the other hand, saw language as constantly in flux—changing not just from year to year or day to day, but from moment to moment, place to place and person to person. This is an important distinction. If language is constantly changing, then our reality is constantly changing.

What this means for literary theorists is that we have innumerable interpretations of every text. Not only that, but post-structuralists argue that one thing—one word, one phrase, etc.—can mean one thing to one reader and something completely different to another reader. It could even mean two (or more) different things to the same reader or one thing to a reader one day and something else to that same reader another day. A common way to prove this is to provide a seemingly simple sentence for interpretation, such as:

> The teacher thinks this chapter is difficult.

While it may seem like a straightforward statement, post-structuralists would argue that there are a number of equally valid meanings to this one sentence. If we emphasize the word *teacher*, for example, as in, "The *teacher* thinks this chapter is difficult," this could suggest that, while the *teacher* thinks it's difficult, somebody else—or everybody else—disagrees. Putting emphasis on the word, *thinks*, could imply that that the teacher is only guessing and he doesn't know for sure (possibly because he hasn't gauged anybody's reaction to the chapter, or maybe he hasn't even read it himself). Emphasizing the word, *this*, might mean that, even though this particular chapter is difficult, none of the other chapters are. Emphasizing the word *chapter* may imply that, while the chapter is difficult, the topic it discusses is actually quite easy. And what do we mean by difficult? Difficult to read? Difficult to comprehend? Or difficult like a sleep-deprived toddler coming down from a sugar high? Add to that the fact that we don't know who the teacher is, what chapter he's talking about (or even what book it's in), and we end up with a variety of possible meanings for this one sentence.

We could do this same thing with every sentence we encounter (*we* could do it, but you can't; we *could* do it, but why would we want to? etc.). And if we can arrive at this many equally valid interpretations of one sentence, imagine how many interpretations are possible in a short story or a novel that contains hundreds of sentences. When we add to this the structuralist idea that each word in a language is arbitrary, which makes (according to the post-structuralists) all of a language arbitrary, then we are left with the conclusion that there can never be one absolute meaning to anything.

Along these same lines, meaning will also be affected by the difference between the world at the time the text was written and the world at the time the text was read. (There will always be a difference between the two, even if it's infinitesimal—reality will always have changed at least slightly between the time of the writing and the time of the reading.) Post-structuralists would argue, then, that it isn't possible for all readers to agree on a single definitive interpretation of a text that is unquestionably superior to all other interpretations. Even if we have a good interpretation today, tomorrow we might have a better one.

For post-structuralists, a text can only "exist" as it is read. In contrast to the New Critics who saw in each text only one "correct" meaning (no matter when it was written or when it's read), post-structuralists believe that the text's meaning depends upon a variety of factors. The most important of these are 1) who reads it (what is this one reader's reality, compared to another reader's?) and 2) when and where they read it (what is the reality of the world at the time of one reading, compared to the reality at the time of another reading?). Consequently, any interpretation arrived at through a careful reading of a text would have to be considered as valid as any other interpretation.

As one might imagine, such a realization brought about a significant shift in the theoretical study of literature. What we were left with, then, was an approach to literature that was based upon uncertainty.

## The Death of the Author

While some might see a text's undecidability as problematic, Roland Barthes saw it as liberating. In "The Death of the Author" (1968), Barthes argues for a literary approach that embraces, rather than rejects, this post-structuralist understanding of reality.

In his essay, Barthes criticizes the reader's tendency to consider aspects of the author's identity—the author's political views, historical context, religion, ethnicity, psychology, or other biographical or personal attributes—to understand the author's work. For Barthes, this is a flawed and lazy way of reading. When using this author-centric method of analysis, the author's life becomes the definitive "explanation" of the work. Barthes says, "To give a text an Author [and assign a single, corresponding interpretation to it] is to impose a limit on that text." According to Barthes, readers must separate a literary work from its creator in order to liberate the text from interpretive tyranny, for each piece of writing contains multiple layers and meanings.

Aside from this, Barthes notes, there is an elemental problem with an author-centric approach: it's impossible to know what the author truly intended. Even if the author writes an essay called "This is What this Story is About," that doesn't mean that the essay is accurate. The author might be dishonest (for any number of reasons). It's also possible that the author doesn't understand his own motivations (a brief glimpse of reality TV can illustrate the human mind's capacity for self-delusion and denial). We can make assumptions about the writer's unconscious (as in psychoanalysis) or estimate the impact of the writer's economic class (Marxism), but we can never determine, with certainty, how anything regarding the author might have shaped the text.

"The Death of the Author" suggests that the essential meaning of a work depends upon the impressions of the reader, not the "passions" or "tastes" of the writer. Barthes believes that "a text's unity lies not in its origins," or its creator, "but in its destination," the audience. He suggests that we should think of the author as simply a "scriptor," rather than an author (author/authority). The scriptor exists to produce but not to explain the work and "is born simultaneously with the text, is in no way equipped with a being preceding or exceeding the writing, [and] is not the subject with the book as predicate." In other words, we should think of a writer as someone who merely writes down the text as it is dictated to him from some other source. This will allow us to see the text as it is, rather than as a product of the author's internal or external motivations.

Barthes argues that every literary work is "eternally written here and now," each time it is read, because meaning lies in "language itself" and in its impressions on the reader. When we see the author as an uninvolved scriptor, we don't read a text looking for its "single 'theological' meaning (the 'message' of the Author-God)." Instead, we realize that writing is comprised of "a multi-dimensional space," that cannot be "deciphered," but only "disentangled." And when we refuse to "assign a 'secret,' ultimate meaning" to a text, it liberates that text ("an activity that is truly revolutionary since to refuse meaning is, in the end, to refuse God and his hypostases—reason, science, law").

The death of the author, then, signals the rebirth of the reader, an idea we'll see expanded upon with reader-response criticism, a theoretical school that develops shortly after post-structuralism.

## Michel Foucault

Michel Foucault approached post-structuralism more from a philosophical, rather than literary, perspective. Foucault was a leading French historian, philosopher and social theorist. His ideas influenced the shape of French thought in a variety of fields, including literary theory, from the sixties until well after his death in 1984.

According to Foucault, all that we know is controlled in every way by our language, our communication and our ideology. Like many post-structuralists, he believed that our very perception of reality is guided by language—the idea that we can't perceive something unless we have the words to describe it. Language also controls us, the argument goes, by the way it works on its most basic level. For example, if language operates under a system of binary oppositions as the structuralists suggest—hot is not cold; up is not down; on is not off—then, Foucault says, we will become conditioned to understand the world according to this same formula: you are either rich or poor; you are either liberal or conservative; you are either nice or mean, etc. What we think of as reality, then, is actually a "reality" that is filtered through our language.

Foucault goes on to suggest that our "reality" is also filtered through our culture and our cultural codes (our social mores and our societal sense of right and wrong). This means that people are created by their culture and their language. People exist only as parts of their society; they get their meaning, reality and self-image only through the various social groups they belong to (their group of coworkers; their softball or bowling team; or, if he or she is a "loner," he understands what a "loner" is from what he sees on TV or reads in books and magazines). In other words, it is our language, communication and beliefs that create our sense of self; without these, we have no sense of self.

Foucault also tells us that we have multiple belief systems that continually appear and disappear. These belief systems make up our temporary reality. For example, several centuries ago, part of our "reality" involved the sun, stars and planets all revolving around the earth; our "reality" now is very different and, several centuries in the future, that part of our "reality" might be different again. Foucault believed that there was no logical reason for these changing belief systems; he believed that they simply changed by random chance. He saw the same randomness in the progression of history and of evolution. While we normally see history as an inevitable chain of events leading us to where we are now, Foucault argued that this view of history is flawed. We see history this way, Foucault believed, because our human minds are conditioned (by language) to ascribe structure, meaning and significance to these random events. To Foucault, all the events of history and all the developments of evolution have merely been the result of chance, and nothing more.

Foucault's philosophical conclusions, then, were of significant influence to the post-structuralist theme of uncertainty.

## Deconstruction

Any thorough conversation about post-structuralism will eventually lead to the topic of deconstruction (it's not uncommon, in fact, to hear the two terms used interchangeably). Deconstruction is a term coined by Jacques Derrida in his book, *De la grammatologie* (1967: trans. 1976, *Of Grammatology*). While Derrida has been accused of engaging in "terrorism of obscurantism" (Michel Foucault) and employing "pretentious rhetoric" (Noam Chomsky) to hide his "low level of philosophical argumentation" (John Searle), no one can deny that he has had a profound effect on literary theory as we know it. It may be true that Derrida has found resistance to his ideas on the nature of knowledge, but nearly all literary scholars today utilize at least some aspects of deconstruction in their approaches to texts.

There is a progression of thought within Derrida's body of work that no summary could adequately encapsulate. The reader who is interested in further explanation, then, should make liberal use of the suggested readings at the end of this chapter. We should note here, though, a couple of common misconceptions regarding Derrida and deconstruction. The first involves a well-known quote from Derrida's book, *Of Grammatology*: "*il n'y a pas de hors-texte*," which is usually translated as, "there is nothing outside the text." This is often misconstrued to suggest that Derrida believes language is so important that everything else is inconsequential. What Derrida is actually saying here, however, is that *everything is text*. Our reality and everything that we think we know—about ourselves, about our natural and created world—is actually a reality that is filtered through language. The consequence of this statement, of course, is that, if we need to rethink our approach to language—how it works, how we know what we know, etc.—then we need to rethink our understanding of *everything*.

Another popular misunderstanding has to do with what, exactly, deconstruction is. While deconstruction is often considered a literary theory, Derrida didn't see it that way. For him, deconstruction was a reading strategy—a new way to approach a text—and, as such, it could be utilized in conjunction with any literary theory. It would be inaccurate to call deconstruction a literary theory then, at least from Derrida's point of view.

Still, it is not an easy task to define what deconstruction is. Even Derrida had trouble in this regard, offering a number of different definitions over the years. In the essay, "Et cetera" (2000), from later in Derrida's career, he offers this in lieu of a definition:

> Each time that I say "deconstruction and X" (regardless of the concept or the theme), this is the prelude to a very singular division that turns this X into, or rather makes appear in this X, an impossibility that becomes its proper and sole possibility, with the result that between the X as possible and the "same" X as impossible, there is nothing but a relation of homonymy, a relation for which we have to provide an account [. . . any definition] can be possible only as impossible, as the impossible, that is, unconditionally.

Here Derrida is saying, in his uniquely verbose way, that he can't define deconstruction because it's impossible to accurately define anything.

Two years later, when asked again for a definition of deconstruction, he tells us,

> I want to underline rather than efface our surrounding technical conditions, and not feign a "naturality" which doesn't exist [. . .] because one of the gestures of deconstruction is to not naturalize what isn't natural—to not assume that what is conditioned by history, institutions, or society is natural.

In other words, Derrida suggests that one of the goals of deconstruction is to recognize that much of what we accept as "fact" is actually based upon constructed beliefs that may or may not be true. One example of this would be western society's view of women. As recently as the last century, it was common "knowledge" that women were weaker than men, more emotional than men, and less capable of rational thought than men. (The belief in these "facts" led to an institutionalized discrimination of women that wouldn't be tolerated today: women couldn't vote, own property, receive a top-quality education, and so on.) The women's movements of the twentieth century helped Western society realize that many of the differences between men and women weren't actual biological differences but were, instead, socially constructed beliefs that were passed down from generation to generation. These beliefs were then reinforced and made real by societal customs and mores. Consequently, many of the "facts" that everyone in the nineteenth century "knew" about women turned out to be inaccurate.

Derrida would argue that, if we looked closely at everything we "know" today, we would find that many, if not all, of our current "facts" are constructed in the same way. In this sense, then, deconstruction is a way to read a text without assuming that any previously-held notions about the text are correct, accurate or "natural." In its simplest terms, deconstruction does just what the word implies: it takes a story apart to examine how its constituent pieces work together to create meaning. The goal of deconstruction—if you could say that deconstruction has a goal—is to dig deeply inside a text to reveal the instability inherent within that text. To do this, we begin by examining the most fundamental aspects of our language.

Part of this examination involves meticulous attention to the text's binary oppositions. Structuralism taught us, among other things, about words' relationships to one another. We know what *hot* is because it's not *cold*; we know what *day* is because it's not *night*, etc. More than that, though, is the understanding that each half of these pairs exists because of the other. If everything in our world were the same temperature, there would be neither hot nor cold; we would have no concept of a thing such as temperature because the temperature would always be constant. If we somehow were to live our whole lives floating unencumbered in space, we would have no concept of up or down or day or night. We need *day* for *night* to exist and we can't have *up* if we don't have a *down*.

Levi-Strauss recognized in these binaries a hierarchical order—one is always considered preferable to the other—rich is better than poor; fast is better than slow; strong is better than weak. Derrida found these hierarchies problematic. One binary that was particularly troubling for him was the relationship between speech and writing. Throughout the history of Western civilization, Derrida notes, there has existed a hidden bias for speech over writing. As evidence of this, post-structuralists often point to John 1:1 of the Christian Bible: "In the beginning was the Word, and the Word was with God, and the Word was God." We also see philosophers from as far back as Plato expressing a similar preference for speech. In other words, according to Derrida, Western scholarship throughout history has privileged speech over text, making it the center of the structure we call language.

Inherent in this binary of speech / writing, according to Derrida, is another binary: presence / absence (here / there). Presence is characteristic of speech while absence is characteristic of writing. (After all, in order for our speech communication to be heard, we must be present with our audience; likewise, the thinking goes, there is no need to write to someone when they are within speaking distance.) Derrida saw this binary of presence / absence as the reason behind the preference for speech over text and he called this approach to language logocentrism. (To illustrate the dominant male position in Western language, Derrida coined another term: phallogocentrism—or phallocentrism.)

But Derrida didn't see speech as better than text (he didn't want to privilege text over speech, either; he saw them both as equally fundamental to language). To convey this, he gave us his term, *différance*. *Différance* provided a way for Derrida to discuss, and then erase, this hidden bias for voice over text. In spoken French, the words, *différence* and *différance* sound nearly identical (identical enough that you would need to hear the words in context to tell them apart) but, when written, we can tell the two apart immediately—there's the letter *a* where we usually see an *e*. What Derrida wanted to show with *différance* is that writing is just as valid a form of language as speech. While any number of homonyms could be used to prove this point (in French, there are *vers*, *verre*, and *vert*, and in English we have there, their and they're, etc.), Derrida chose *différance* to suggest not only difference, but deferral. Derrida wants to remind us that when we grasp and understand meaning, this does not happen simultaneously (as the structuralist model claims). If we understand words in relation to their difference with one another as the structuralist and post-structuralist models both suggest, then meaning comes to us as a progression of thought; we think of a word (and its signifier), and then we think of another word, and another signifier, on and on until we have an endless chain of signification. And this happens countless times every day, with every person who uses language.

As a result, meaning is constantly changing and language is constantly in a state of flux. According to Derrida, this makes it impossible to have a definitive interpretation of any text—and, if everything *is* text, this means we can't truly know anything.

## Deconstructing the Center

Derrida further recognized that all areas of Western thought—art, science, philosophy, etc.—have relied upon their own underlying guiding principle. Derrida called these principles "centers." (Using the language of structuralism, he also refers to the center as a "transcendental signified.") The purpose of this center, according to Derrida, is to balance and organize the structure while limiting the activity (what Derrida calls "play") within the structure. In philosophy, this organizing center is often called Truth; in monotheistic religions, this center is the creator-God. In literature, the center is the story's primary conflict. Throughout the history of Western thought, these underlying centers were understood to be fundamental elements of their respective structures.

According to Derrida, this center, as conceived, exists both inside and outside of the structure. In "Structure, Sign and Play in the Discourse of the Human Sciences," Derrida notes:

> it has always been thought that the center, which is by definition unique, constituted that very thing within a structure which governs the structure, while escaping structurality. This is why classical thought concerning structure could say that the center is, paradoxically, *within* the structure and *outside* it. The center is at the center of the totality, and yet, since the center does not belong to the totality (is not part of the totality), the totality *has its center elsewhere*. The center is not the center.

In the Judeo-Christian tradition, for example, God creates the heavens and earth while existing outside of it. The author of a story, who is outside of the text, creates the central conflict upon which the story is designed. Derrida recognizes this as a problem. How can a center be a fundamental constituent of a structure—meaning that it was inside the structure from the beginning—yet have its origins outside that same structure? Derrida concludes, then, that the center is not a naturally-occurring component of a structure, but rather a human construct designed to impose order upon an unstructured system. It is this train of thought that leads to Derrida's process "decentering" a text.

Decentering is a method of examining a text without regard for any perceived intentions of the text. Or, as Derrida says in *Writing and Différance*, it is "the stated abandonment of all reference to a center, to a subject, to a privileged reference [or] to an origin." If we think of children's stories, for example, they usually conclude with some sort of "happy" ending—Hansel and Gretel return home; the little engine makes it over the mountain; green eggs and ham are delicious. "Cinderella," "Snow White" and "Beauty and the Beast" all end with a prince and princess living happily ever after. When we examine a story like "Cinderella" with this "happy" ending in mind, we can see how the symbolism, the stylistic choices and the events in the story all lead to this happy ending: the stepmother and stepsisters were mean, the fairy godmother appears, the prince finds the glass slipper, etc.

Derrida argues that, when we go back and analyze the Cinderella story, we only imagine that these story elements lead to the ending because we've already decided that the ending is a happy one. This is what he means by the story's center: the story revolves around the binary opposition of the beginning and the end (unfulfilled young woman in the beginning / happy princess in the end). Derrida wants us to consider how our understanding of the story would change if the marriage between the prince and princess was not a good thing. What if, for example, the prince and princess spent their married lives happily torturing and sadistically abusing their subjects? Their happy conclusion would result in a sad outcome for everyone else. (In this simple example, of course, the process sounds depressing, but Derrida wants us to apply these steps to all stories, thereby considering a positive ending for those stories that finish sadly.) Keep in mind, too, that Derrida isn't suggesting that every happy story from our childhood is actually a tragedy in disguise; his intention is merely to open us up to the vast interpretative potential within a text. When we accept all the possibilities as equally plausible, we have successfully decentered the text and we are now able to evaluate the story, unhindered by preconceptions.

## Implementation

In its most simple terms, deconstructing a text is a three-step process:
1) identify the binary oppositions and determine their hierarchal positions,
2) temporarily invert those hierarchies and analyze the story from that perspective
3) analyze the story again, accepting all hierarchal arrangements as equally plausible.

To begin step one, we want to first identify the binary related to the story's center. Most stories, remember, revolve around the problem in the beginning and the resolution of that problem in the end. The majority of love stories, for example, are resolved by a romantic pairing of some sort, so a common central binary in a love story would be "single / paired" (or words to that effect). An escape story, as the term suggests, will be resolved with an escape, making that binary "imprisoned / free." The center of Hawthorne's "The Birthmark" balances the binary of "life / death."

Once we have identified the center, the focus then becomes other binaries within the text. Obviously, if we argue that every word in our language has a corresponding opposite, it wouldn't be feasible to identify every binary opposition in a story. A practical deconstructive reading, then, will focus on a few of the most relevant binaries (different theorists, though, will have different views on what is most relevant, and it is this diversity of opinion which makes each deconstructive reading unique). Binaries a reader might find relevant in Hawthorne's story are "perfection / imperfection," "nature / technology," "dominance / subservience," "beauty / ugliness," and so on. We can also incorporate deconstruction with another critical approach—like feminism, Marxism or psychoanalysis—and seek out binaries applicable to that theory.

In the second step, we temporarily invert the hierarchies of the binary oppositions that we found in step one, beginning with the story's center. What this means is, we now imagine that our love story suggests that it's better to be single than to be in a relationship and our escape story implies that it's better to be imprisoned than to be free. When we do this, we might see that, well, it sure seems a lot easier to be single; you certainly wouldn't have to deal with the heart-wrenching drama that inevitably arises at the end of the second act. When we invert the hierarchies in the escape story, we should more easily recognize the benefits of the regimented prison lifestyle and the unique bonds that are formed among the inmates. A story like *The Great Gatsby*, for example, could be read as the story of a healthy marriage that was almost ruined by an unwelcome interloper. Hawthorne's "The Birthmark" might become a happy story of science's triumph over nature. The goal of deconstruction's second step is to see other interpretations that are possible within a text.

The third step of a deconstructive reading is to read the text again, this time acknowledging that all the hierarchal arrangements from steps one and two are equally valid. This allows for, as Derrida calls it, "free play" within the structure of the story. This free play permits us to merge any combination of the hierarchies we found in step one with any grouping of the hierarchies we got from step two, resulting in a seemingly limitless number of possible interpretations. Deconstruction, then, wants us to ask, *How does the meaning of the text change if good isn't better than evil and love isn't better than hate?*

It is in this third step that we also ask questions such as: What "facts" in a text are actually facts? What is in the text (the overt content) and what is excluded (the covert text)? What is marginalized in the text? Where and how does the text contradict itself? Does anything in the covert text contradict the overt text? How does the story's title contribute to—or obscure—meaning? Answers to these questions can help us uncover even more insights into the text. It is then up to us, as we deconstruct a text, to sort through and scrutinize our findings so that we may form our own unique conclusions.

Deconstruction gives us a regimented process whereby we can see the wide array of ways we can read and understand a story. We might come to the conclusion, for example, that Hawthorne's Georgiana is suicidal. Maybe Poe's Montresor is a hero instead of a villain. Gilman's narrator could be completely sane, and her diary could be a fictionalized part of an intricate plot to murder her husband. As long as we use accurate textual evidence to back up our claims, a post-structuralist would argue that our analysis is just as valid as anyone else's.

## Important Moments in Post-Structuralism

**1916:** Ferdinand de Saussure's *Course in General Linguistics*
**1958:** Claude Lévi-Strauss' *Structural Anthropology*
**1962:** Umberto Eco's *Opera aperta* (*The Open Work*)
**1966:** Jacques Derrida's lecture "Structure, Sign and Play in the Discourse of Human Sciences"
**1967:** Barthes' *Elements of Semiology*
**1967:** Derrida's *Of Grammatology*
**1967:** Derrida's *Speech and Phenomena*
**1967:** Derrida's *Writing and Difference*
**1968:** Roland Barthes' "The Death of the Author"
**1968:** Eco's *La struttura assente* (*The Absent Structure*)
**1969:** Michel Foucault's *The Archaeology of Knowledge*
**1972:** Derrida's *Positions*
**1973:** Barthes' *The Pleasure of the Text*
**1975:** Foucault's *Discipline and Punish*
**1980:** Foucault becomes visiting professor at UC-Berkeley
**1981:** Foucault lectures at UCLA
**1982:** Foucault teaches at the University of Vermont
**1991:** Derrida's *Acts of Literature*

## Important Terms

| | |
|---|---|
| binary opposition | center |
| decenter | deconstruction |
| *différance* | logocentrism |
| phallocentrism | play |
| transcendental signified | |

## Study Questions

1. In Gilman's "The Yellow Wallpaper," we could find several binary oppositions related to gender, social class, weather, wisdom, con-

finement, respect, mental health and so on. If, as post-structuralists argue, there is a hierarchy inherent in every binary opposition, then where do you think Gilman places each of these binary elements on the hierarchical scale? What happens if we reverse these hierarchies? Do any of these binary oppositions contradict themselves or each other? What unique understanding can you derive from the story when considering it from a post-structuralist perspective, particularly in relation to the binary oppositions you identified? (As you formulate your response, you will likely find it helpful to first note all of the binary oppositions you can identify.)

2. Consider either Chekhov's "Gooseberries" or Gogol's "Diary of a Madman" through the critical lenses of both post-structuralism and one other theory of your choice. How would these two readings compare? What can you gain from a post-structuralist reading that you can't get from the other reading, and vice-versa? Base your analysis on at least two specific scenes from the story as you develop your argument.

3. Poe's narrator in "The Cask of Amontillado" relates at one point:

> "Come," I said, with decision. "We will go back; your health is precious. You are rich, respected, admired, beloved; you are happy as once I was. You are a man to be missed. For me it is no matter. We will go back; you will be ill and I cannot be responsible. Besides, there is Luchesi—"
> 
> "Enough," he said; "the cough is a mere nothing; it will not kill me. I shall not die of a cough."

What is the significance of this passage to the overall story? How would a post-structuralist reading contribute to your understanding of this excerpt in relation to the story as a whole? What other theoretical approach would you utilize to reinforce your interpretation of this passage?

4. Using the tools you learned in this chapter, deconstruct a common object or text that you see in your everyday life. It could be a television show, movie or advertisement that you see frequently, it could be a sign or a symbol that you often encounter, or it could even be a behavior or pattern of behavior that you witness regularly.

5. Write a brief essay about Sui Sin Far's "In the Land of the Free" that uncovers some truth about the story that isn't explicitly stated in the text. As we deconstruct the text, what can the story tell us that we might not have seen otherwise? What have you discovered from your deconstructive reading that can give the reader a better appreciation for the piece?

You might begin by examining the story's narrator and the narrative situation. What is implied but not actually written in the text? Or perhaps you'd like to discuss who the narrator is telling the story to and where that narratee is at the time of narration. Maybe you'd like to focus on how the setting informs the story. For example, has the setting changed between the time of the story events recounted and the narrator's recounting of those events? Can we learn anything by considering the temporal distance between the narration and the story events the narrator describes?

## Selected Bibliography

Atkins, G. Douglas. *Reading Deconstruction: Deconstructive Reading*. Lexington: Kentucky UP, 1985.
Bakhtin, Mikhail. *The Dialogic Imagination: Four Essays*. Austin: Texas UP, 1982.
—. *Problems of Dostoevsky's Poetics*. Minneapolis: Minnesota UP, 1984.
—. *Toward a Philosophy of the Act*. Austin: Texas UP, 1993.
Barthes, Roland. *Camera Lucida*. New York: Hill and Wang, 2010.
—. *Critical Essays*. Evanston: Northwestern UP, 1972.
—. *Elements of Semiology*. New York: Hill and Wang, 1977.
—. *Image-Music-Text*. New York: Hill and Wang, 1978.
—. *The Pleasure of the Text*. New York: Hill and Wang, 1975.
—. *Roland Barthes by Roland Barthes*. New York: Hill and Wang, 2010.
—. *S/Z: An Essay*. New York: Hill and Wang, 1975.
Bloom, Harold, Paul de Man, Jacques Derrida, Geoffrey Hartman and J. Hillis Miller, eds. *Deconstruction and Criticism*. New York: Continuum, 2004.
Caputo, John D. *Deconstruction in a Nutshell: A Conversation with Jacques Derrida*. New York: Fordham UP, 1996.
Culler, Jonathan. *On Deconstruction: Theory and Criticism After Structuralism*. Ithaca: Cornell UP, 2008.
Derrida, Jacques. *Acts of Literature*. London: Routledge, 1991.
—. *Dissemination*. Chicago: Chicago UP, 1983.
—. *Of Grammatology*. Baltimore: Johns Hopkins UP, 1998.
—. *The Post Card: From Socrates to Freud and Beyond*. Chicago: Chicago UP, 1987.
—. *Speech and Phenomena: And Other Essays on Husserl's Theory of Signs*. Evanston: Northwestern UP, 1973.
—. "Structure, Sign, and Play in the Discourse of the Human Sciences." *The Structuralist Controversy: The Languages of Criticism and the Sciences of Man*. Ed. Richard Macksey and Eugenio Donato. Baltimore: Johns Hopkins UP, 2007. 247-65.
—. *Writing and Difference*. Chicago: Chicago UP, 1980.
Eco, Umberto. *The Open Work*. Cambridge: Harvard UP, 1989.
Foucault, Michel. *The Archaeology of Knowledge*. New York: Routledge, 2002.

Frye, Northrup. *Anatomy of Criticism*. Toronto: Toronto UP, 2007.
Holland, Norman Norwood. *The Critical I*. New York: Columbia UP, 1994.
—. Dynamics of Literary Response. New York: Norton, 1975.
Miller, J. Hillis. *Fiction and Repetition: Seven English Novels*. Cambridge: Harvard UP, 1985.
Morson, Gary Saul. *Mikhail Bakhtin: Creation of a Prosaics*. Palo Alto: Stanford UP, 1990.
Norris, Christopher. *Deconstruction and the Interests of Theory*. Leicester: Leicester UP, 1992.
—. *Deconstruction: Theory and Practice*. London: Methuen, 1984 .
Taylor, Mark C., ed. *Deconstruction in Context: Literature and Philosophy*. Chicago: Chicago UP, 1986.

# 7

# Postmodernism

**FOCUSES ON:** any element of the text or the reading or writing experience, most often in literary works from the postmodern period or works that contain narrative strategies commonly associated with the postmodern period.
**BECAUSE:** postmodern theory encompasses a wide range of fields, so a postmodern theorist might find any aspect of a text worthwhile for study.
**DEVELOPED IN:** 1960s.
**NOTABLE PRACTITIONERS:**
    Jean-François Lyotard (1924-98)    Gilles Deleuze (1925-95)
    Ihab Hassan (1925- )    Michel Foucault (1926-84)
    Jean Baudrillard (1929-2007)    Jürgen Habermas (1929- )
    Felix Guattari (1930-92)    John Barth (1930- )
    Umberto Eco (1932- )    Fredric Jameson (1934- )
    Charles Jencks (1939- )    Slavoj Žižek (1949- )
    Brian McHale (1952- )
**IMPORTANT PREDECESSORS:**
    Friedrich Nietzsche (1844-1900)    Ludwig Wittgenstein (1889-1951)
    Martin Heidegger (1889-1976)    Georges Bataille (1897-1962)
    Roland Barthes (1915-1980)    Jacques Derrida (1930-2004)
    Richard Rorty (1931-2007)
**ADVANTAGES:** offers a thought-provoking view of literature and everything in the world around us.
**DISADVANTAGES:** the concepts of postmodernism can be confusing for anyone unfamiliar with the numerous subjects that shaped postmodernist thought, particularly philosophy and the nature of scientific inquiry in the nineteenth and twentieth centuries.
**DEFINITION:** (see below).

People often equate postmodernism with post-structuralism. Some scholars even regard them as synonymous. It's easy to see why. Many postmodern theorists, after all, incorporate the post-structuralist concepts of Derrida and Foucault into their own studies. But postmodernism and post-structuralism have different focuses. While post-structuralist studies are limited, for the most part, to literature, postmodernism spans a variety of areas including art, architecture, fashion, literature, music, philosophy, religion, and even sports studies.

Others consider post-structuralism to be a branch of the larger field of postmodernism. But post-structuralism came first. According to Charles Jencks, the first known use of the term, "post-modern," was by John Watkins Chapman, a painter, in the 1870s. Chapman's idea of "post-modern," though, was very different than the postmodernism that we know today. As Jencks notes, postmodernism in its current context didn't arrive in the literary world until Ihab Hassan's *The Dismemberment of Orpheus* (1971), five years after Derrida's groundbreaking lecture at Johns Hopkins. Consequently, most scholars today regard postmodernism and post-structuralism as distinct, but closely related, bodies of thought.

## The Postmodern Period

As far as we know, no one has yet developed a thorough definition of postmodernism that all scholars can agree upon. In one connotation, postmodernism simply refers to a literary and artistic period. In this sense, postmodernism isn't complicated. It follows modernism, naturalism, realism, etc. It is exemplified in the conceptual art, digital art and performance art of the 1960s, 70s and 80s. We recognize it in the architecture of Frank Gehry and Philip Johnson, and in the literature of Kathy Acker, Donald Barthelme and Thomas Pynchon, among others.

But even this simple understanding of postmodernism is a source of disagreement. Not everyone agrees which works of art, literature, etc. fall into the modern period and which are postmodern. Samuel Beckett's *Waiting for Godot* (1952; trans. 1954), as one example, is considered postmodern by some scholars and modern by others. There is also no consensus regarding when the postmodern period began. Some say it started with the onset of World War II. Others believe it began at the end of the war. Still others place it in the 1950s or 1960s. Charles Jencks is more specific. He dates the beginning of postmodernism at 3:32 p.m. on July 15, 1972. This is when the first stage of demolition was completed at the Pruitt-Igoe housing project in St. Louis. To Jencks, the Pruitt-Igoe was a quintessential example of modernist architecture and its failure (only two decades after its construction) represented the failure of modernism. Thus, for Jencks, the postmodern period began. Many significant texts that we now identify as postmodern, though, were published before the destruction of the Pruitt-Igoe. These include Pynchon's *The Crying of Lot 49* (1966), Barthelme's *Snow White* (1967) and Barth's *Lost in the Funhouse* (1968), as well as numerous aleatory ("shuffle") texts such as Marc Saporta's *Composition No. 1* (1962; trans. 1963) and Julio Cortázar's *Hopscotch* (1963; trans. 1966).

Scholars, then, find it difficult to pinpoint when the postmodern period began and when (or if) it ended. Most agree that it spanned the 1970s and 80s and that it reached its peak during that time. Still, the parameters of the postmodern period remain undetermined.

## Defining Postmodernism

Postmodernism also refers to a body of theoretical work that developed during the postmodern period. This is the postmodernism that scholars struggle to define. Some say it's impossible. Others try. Gary Aylesworth describes postmodernism as:

> a set of critical, strategic and rhetorical practices employing concepts such as difference, repetition, the trace, the simulacrum, and hyperreality to destabilize other concepts such as presence, identity, historical progress, epistemic certainty, and the univocity of meaning.

Charles Jencks calls it "a wide cultural movement (since the 1960s) which has its *soi-disant* variants in every field (including science and dance)." Terry Eagleton is perhaps more clear. He defines postmodernism as a method of thought that is

> suspicious of classical notions of truth, reason, identity, and objectivity, of the idea of universal progress or emancipation, of single frameworks, grand narratives or ultimate grounds of explanation.

Fredric Jameson, Brian McHale, Slavoj Žižek and many others have all offered their own definitions of postmodernism. Probably the most commonly accepted definition, though, comes from Jean-François Lyotard. In *The Postmodern Condition* (1979; trans. 1984), Lyotard says, "Simplifying to the extreme, I define postmodern as incredulity toward metanarratives." To understand his definition, of course, we need to know how Lyotard differentiates between narratives and metanarratives.

## Metanarratives

A narrative is a depiction of events. It could be anything from a novel to a news story or an anecdote we tell our friends. Lyotard is most interested in two types of narratives. One type portrays significant events in the history of human progress. The other describes important moments in the development of human knowledge.

A narrative of human progress could be an account of early man's first use of a tool. It could also depict the development of agriculture, the invention of the automobile, or the mission to the moon by Apollo 11. Narratives that chart human knowledge include the development of Copernicus' model of the universe, Darwin's theory of evolution and Einstein's theory of relativity.

A metanarrative, on the other hand, is an implicit grand narrative that combines smaller narratives into one large story. These smaller narratives work together to suggest that they are part of an interconnected chain of events that progresses from the beginning, through the present, to a seemingly inevitable future. The metanarrative of human progress, for example, might begin with early humans living in caves. It would include narratives describing the use of fire, the invention of the wheel, and the development of more advanced tools. Later, it would show how we moved into cities, invented machines, created computers, and how, one day, we'll live in a peaceful utopia with flying cars and intergalactic cruise ships. The metanarrative of human knowledge has a comparable structure: complete ignorance, followed by the origin of various myths, Newton's laws, the big bang theory, etc., until we reach a future moment when we know the absolute Truth of the universe.

There are numerous metanarratives about nearly every subject. The Marxist metanarrative, for example, charts the history of economic systems that will one day lead to the end of capitalism and the rise of an economy based upon shared wealth. Religions have their own metanarratives. So do countries and social movements. Even big businesses have metanarratives:

> Mr. Smith started with a dream and a vision. With hard work and determination, he turned XYZ Corporation into a Fortune 500 company. In five years, XYZ Corp. will be the largest manufacturer of widgets in the world.

Nearly every culture, group or entity has a metanarrative that follows a similar pattern.

## The Incredulity toward Metanarratives

According to Lyotard, though, these metanarratives aren't real. They merely seem real because they consist of events that produce a narrative pattern and ignore or exclude anything that doesn't conform to that pattern. This creates the illusion that these isolated and random historical moments are part of a progressive chain of events that leads to a logical conclusion. But, postmodernists argue, we could use real historical narratives to generate almost any metanarrative we choose. We could take reports of alien cow abductions, animal-rights protests, and diseases like E. coli and mad cow disease, for example, and arrange them into a metanarrative that suggests cows will one day rule the world.

Not only that, but once these individual narratives are arranged into a grand metanarrative, the narratives within the metanarrative become legitimized. By simply being a part of the metanarrative, in other words, even a questionable "historical fact" will seem more credible. If we were to argue that E. coli is an experimental disease developed by cows in their quest to wipe out humanity, we would sound idiotic. But, when this E. coli narrative is just one link in our metanarrative that predicts a cow revolution, this ridiculous "fact" could seem plausible.

While this is an outlandish example, it illustrates how postmodernists view all metanarratives. After all, metanarratives are constructed of historical events. And, postmodernists point out, our knowledge of historical events is limited to second-hand narrative accounts that we either hear or read. This makes all historical facts as dubious as our silly "fact" about E. coli. When the parts that make up the grand metanarrative are unreliable, then the metanarrative becomes untrustworthy as well.

This becomes problematic when we consider the pervasive nature of metanarratives. Metanarratives tell us who we are, where we come from and where we're going. They dictate our definitions of truth and justice. They establish guidelines for acceptable behavior and they regulate cultural production. They determine what knowledge is legitimate and how it is evaluated. They influence what pursuits are worthwhile and what choices are admirable. In other words, metanarratives shape the way we live, what we know and even how we think. For Lyotard, this cultural imperialism is inherent in metanarratives.

Even worse, according to Lyotard, is that metanarratives are shaped and circulated by those in positions of power. Ancient Egypt provides one example. Their historical metanarrative charted the bloodline of the gods to the pharaohs. This, in turn, allowed the pharaohs to wield power and to amass wealth while maintaining their rule for thousands of years. But one needn't be descended from gods in order to perpetuate a favorable metanarrative. Anyone who is an authority figure in a group, a community or a culture has the power to advance his or her own metanarrative.

This includes, of course, politicians. Whenever a politician speaks passionately about the values upon which his or her country was founded, that politician is advancing a metanarrative. Early postmodernists witnessed this with the rise of Nazi Germany before World War II. Using selected moments from Germany's past, the Nazis produced a metanarrative that envisioned a future ruled by "pure" Germans. They then convinced their citizenry that the path to that future included World War II and the Holocaust. Lyotard would argue that it was the successful propagation of the Nazi metanarrative that facilitated these atrocities.

Postmodernists, then, found all metanarratives to be untrustworthy. When postmodernists rejected metanarratives, they rejected the prevalent modernist beliefs that accompanied them. They refused to believe, in other words, that human "progress" is leading us toward a utopian future or that scientific discoveries are bringing us closer to an absolute Truth. This reaction expressed itself not only in literature, but also in art, architecture, philosophy, history and the sciences.

## The Rise of *le petit récit*

As postmodernists turned away from grand metanarratives, according to Lyotard, they turned toward numerous *"petits récits"* or little narratives. These are the stories of individuals within a society. When the control of knowledge shifted to the masses, it changed the way we see the world. Information was no longer passed down from authorities who defined reality for the rest of us. And, more importantly, knowledge could no longer be used by those in power to suppress the populace.

Postmodernism's preference for little narratives brought increased acceptance to nontraditional forms of understanding. The views of those outside the establishment began to gain notice and consideration. Today, we might refer to this as the crowdsourcing of knowledge. It affected not just literature, but all aspects of Western life. The contemporary New Age movement, the renewed interest in homeopathic medicine, the advances in the personal computer and the noticeable changes in art, music and architectural design all resulted from postmodernism's shift in the way knowledge was disseminated .

There is a clear difference between modernist thought and the little narratives of postmodernism. For a lighthearted example of this, we could compare the modernist documentary, *Reefer Madness* (1936), to a film from the postmodern period, *Nice Dreams* (1981). While these two works discuss the same subject, it's clear from watching *Reefer Madness* that the information it provides is misleading, at best. This highlights another outcome of the adoption of little narratives: increased skepticism toward established "experts." There was a growing sense during the postmodern period that those in power were either ill-informed, incompetent or blatantly dishonest. The Vietnam War left many to question the government's motives, its competence, and its integrity, leading to a decade of anti-war protests in the U.S. In France, frustration with the government of Charles de Gaulle led to nationwide strikes by students and workers. These protests in May, 1968 nearly crippled the country.

For Lyotard, the rejection of metanarratives brought about the significant changes that we now associate with postmodernism. We see it in the renunciation of narrative conventions in literature, stylistic conventions in art, and the conventions of design in architecture.

## Deleuze and Guattari

Scholars today credit two French thinkers, Gilles Deleuze and Félix Guattari, with shaping much of the early postmodern thought. Deleuze, a philosopher, and Guattari, a psychologist, collaborated on a number of works. The most significant of these, *Capitalism and Schizophrenia*, consists of two volumes, *Anti-Oedipus* (1972; trans. 1977) and *A Thousand Plateaus* (1980; trans. 1987). These two books influenced theoretical discourse throughout the postmodern period.

One of the main concerns in *Anti-Oedipus* is to understand how we develop a desire for our own oppression. As Deleuze and Guattari put it,

> the fundamental problem of political philosophy is still precisely the one that Spinoza saw so clearly, and that Wilhelm Reich rediscovered: "Why do men fight for their servitude as stubbornly as though it were their salvation?" How can people possibly reach the point of shouting: "More taxes! Less bread!"? As Reich remarks, the astonishing thing is not that some people steal or that others occasionally go out on strike, but rather that all those who are starving do not steal as a regular practice, and all those who are exploited are not continually out on strike: after centuries of exploitation, why do people still tolerate being humiliated and enslaved, to such a point, indeed, that they *actually want* humiliation and slavery not only for others but for themselves?

Like Reich, Deleuze and Guattari argue that people are not innocently misled into becoming subservient to a fascist regime. Indeed, "at a certain point, under a certain set of conditions," we want to be controlled. It is precisely this "perversion of the desires of the masses" that Deleuze and Guattari address in *Anti-Oedipus*.

To answer this fundamental question, Deleuze and Guattari provide a reframing of both psychoanalysis and Marxism on a mechanistic model. They reimagine both desire and the object of that desire as machines that work together to produce reality. Their argument, in essence, is that a capitalist society works in conjunction with the Oedipal complex to make us willing servants to an oppressive regime. This begins with the nuclear family.

According to Deleuze and Guattari, the nuclear family programs us as children to love and desire oppression. The stern discipline we receive from our parents—in which we are inhibited from fulfilling many of our desires—conditions us to equate oppression with love. As we grow into adulthood, we come to want and love the repressive discipline of a fascist regime (whether that fascism is the government of Hitler, a modern democracy in which the majority of wealth belongs to one percent of the population, or a love bond in which one person controls the other). To enable us to recognize this pattern, Deleuze and Guattari outline a process of schizoanalysis wherein the analyst works like a "mechanic" to diagnose and reconfigure—or "deterritorialize"—our desiring-machines.

In *A Thousand Plateaus*, the second volume of *Capitalism and Schizophrenia*, Deleuze and Guattari propose a new "image of thought" modeled on the rhizome. The modernist model, they note, was based upon the tree—the "tree of knowledge." The tree model suggests binary thought that emanates from a defined center (the tree's trunk). For Deleuze and Guattari, the rhizome more accurately characterizes how thought actually works.

In the plant world, a rhizome is an underground stem that grows horizontally and produces shoots and roots at random intervals. Ginger is a rhizome. So are bamboo, Bermuda grass and couch grass. Deleuze and Guattari expand their definition to include not only bulbs and tubers, but also rats, influenza, and the relationship between a wasp and an orchid. Nearly anything that moves horizontally, in other words, and creates modifications at random intervals, is rhizomatic.

Deleuze and Guattari provide the characteristics of a rhizome:

1 and 2. Principles of connection and heterogeneity.
3. Principle of multiplicity.
4. Principle of asignifying rupture.
5 and 6. Principle of cartography and decalcomania.

In an effort to clarify their points, they offer a summary of these characteristics:

> unlike trees or their roots, the rhizome connects any point to any other point, and its traits are not necessarily linked to traits of the same nature [. . .]. It has neither beginning nor end, but always a middle (*milieu*) from which it grows and which it overspills. [. . .] Unlike the tree, the rhizome is not the object of reproduction [. . .]. The rhizome operates by variation, expansion, conquest, capture, offshoots.

For Deleuze and Guattari, this is an apt description for the way we think.

In other words, thought is naturally decentered, fragmentary, prone to lead in random directions, and not always coded in language. This is contrary to the structuralist model that sees thought move in a linear fashion from one language sign to the next. As Deleuze and Guattari show, though, our way of thinking is more complex than that. Thoughts often "sprout" from any number of places, rather than develop in an orderly fashion from a cohesive center. And, when we think, we incorporate a "multiplicity of codes." We utilize not just language, but also music, images, etc. (Which explains Deleuze and Guattari's rhizomatic analogy of the wasp and orchid—two diverse species working together: the wasp randomly pollinates orchids the way a picture or song randomly influences our thoughts.) Thus, the rhizome, in all its forms, provides a better representation of thought than the structuralist—modernist—"tree."

Furthermore, when we reevaluate thought, we also need to reevaluate the products of thought, particularly historical accounts. As Deleuze and Guattari note, "History is always written from the sedentary point of view and in the name of a unitary State apparatus." In other words, recorded history emanates from a center, in this case the State. The actual lived history, by contrast, follows the pattern of the rhizome, with countless real living people involved. No single historical account, then, can accurately or adequately portray real historical events as they were lived. We see again, then, the skepticism identified by Lyotard.

Deleuze and Guattari changed the way we think about human behavior and the way we think about thought itself. Because of this, they are still regarded as quintessential postmodern theorists.

## Postmodern Hyperreality

Jean Baudrillard sees the transition from modernism to postmodernism in a slightly different way than many of his contemporaries. For Baudrillard, modernism was characterized by its capitalist modes of production. This changed in the postmodern period. Postmodern society is shaped by consumption rather than production. And this consumption is based on a foundation of simulated reality.

Baudrillard argues that, in the postmodern period, we moved into a state of hyperreality. He believes that we have come to accept simulations of reality in place of real objects, real events, etc. For us, Baudrillard says, these simulations have become more real than the actual real things they simulate. This happens in four stages:

1. the reflection of a basic reality (the representation of reality is an accurate depiction of the reality it represents).
2. masks and perverts basic reality (the representation is clearly a distortion of reality).
3. masks the absence of a basic reality (the representation leads you to believe it depicts reality, but that reality never existed in the first place).

4. bears no relation to any reality whatever: it is its own pure simulacrum (the representation makes no effort to depict reality).

A common clarification of Baudrillard's stages includes a television newscast in the first stage, a reality show in the second stage, a television comedy in the third, and an animated show in the fourth stage. If we imagine a trip to the grocery store, genetically-modified blueberries would be a first-stage simulation of organic blueberries. Blueberry Pop Tarts and blueberry pie filling represent the second stage. Blueberry-flavored Craisins ("dried cranberries infused with blueberry juice") are the third stage, and Boo Berry cereal is the fourth stage.

Baudrillard refers to the representations in these third and fourth stages as simulacra. A simulacrum (singular) is a representation that corresponds to no underlying reality. Television comedies and animated shows are simulacra, then, as are blueberry-flavored Craisins, Boo Berry cereal, and countless other items at the grocery store, the shopping mall, and nearly everywhere we look.

In other words, according to Baudrillard, we are surrounded by false representations of reality. These simulacra are so pervasive, in fact, that we don't even notice them. Still, they shape all aspects of our lives, including the way we act and what we think. In *Simulacra and Simulation* (1981; trans. 1994), Baudrillard discusses Jorge Luis Borges' flash fiction piece, "On Rigor in Science." Borges' story describes cartographers who drew a map of an empire "whose size was that of the Empire, and which coincided point for point with it." Eventually, the map is discarded, but its tattered ruins continue to be "inhabited by Animals and Beggars." For Baudrillard, in today's world, we live upon the map while the real world "slowly rot[s] across the extent of the map."

Baudrillard believes that the postmodern period is marked by a prevalence of these simulacra. We are living, in other words, on Borges' map while the "desert of the real" crumbles to pieces from neglect. Hyperreality in the form of supermodels, professional sports, and amusement parks have replaced our authentic lives. In a frequently quoted passage, Baudrillard says,

> Disneyland is presented as imaginary in order to make us believe that the rest is real, when in fact all of Los Angeles and the America surrounding it are no longer real, but of the order of the hyperreal and of simulation. It is no longer a question of a false representation of reality (ideology), but of concealing the fact that the real is no longer real, and thus of saving the reality principle.

For Baudrillard, the real world in the postmodern age is a dreary wasteland that we avoid by living in a hyperreal world, surrounded everywhere by simulated reality.

## Fredric Jameson

Fredric Jameson views postmodernism from a Marxist perspective. Widely regarded as America's preeminent Marxist theorist, Jameson is also a leading authority on postmodernism. For Jameson, postmodernism "expresses the inner truth" of late capitalism.

Also referred to as consumer, multinational and postindustrial capitalism, late capitalism emerged after World War II. It is a multinational business model that includes international banking and stock exchanges, computer automation, the worldwide outsourcing of labor, and global gentrification. According to Jameson, late capitalism brought with it fleeting tastes in fashion and style, pervasive media and advertising, commodity fetishism, new models of consumption ("'culture' has become a product in its own right"), and a host of other issues that made extensive change inevitable.

Throughout much of the postmodern period, scholars and theorists disagreed about what, exactly, postmodernism was. Was it an extension of modernism? Was it an ideology? A style? A passing fad? To Jameson, postmodernism is a literary period that is clearly distinguishable from modernism. Jameson believes that the cultural products of postmodernism—art, film, literature, music and architecture—are "specific reactions against the established forms of high modernism." From this perspective, Jameson notes, we could place the demarcation between modernism and postmodernism at the point when modernist texts—once considered scandalous—were accepted by academia and added to the canon.

One characteristic of postmodernism, according to Jameson, is that it erodes the boundaries between "high culture and so-called mass or popular culture." This is a significant departure from modernism where scholars made a clear distinction between the work of Herman Melville, for instance, and a Superman comic book. Jameson believes that postmodernism also altered the nature of theoretical discourse. Whereas literary and art theory were once unconnected to social theory, philosophy, history, etc., this changed with the postmodern period. These separate studies combined into one theoretical study that postmodernists refer to simply as "theory."

In several essays and in books such as *Postmodernism, or, The Cultural Logic of Late Capitalism* (1991), Jameson outlines other key features of postmodernism that differentiate it from modernism. These include pastiche, depthlessness, the "waning of affect," a crisis in historicity, and the expanding role of new technologies. In Jameson's view, the move from parody (the imitative mocking of another's style) to pastiche (a neutral imitation) was caused by what he calls the "death of the subject." He is referring to the distinct styles of modernist writers like D.H. Lawrence, Faulkner, and others, whose writing is easy to identify.

For Jameson, such individuality is lacking from postmodern works. Since parody mocks a contemporary writer's unique style, parody is lost in a postmodern period where "stylistic innovation is no longer possible." Thus, the parody of the modern period has been replaced by the pastiche we find in works like Andy Warhol's iconic *Campbell's Soup Cans* (1962).

Literary and artistic works from the postmodern period, according to Jameson, are also marked by their depthlessness. Jameson describes depthlessness as the loss of a deeper context behind a work of art. He illustrates this by comparing Vincent Van Gogh's modernist painting, *A Pair of Boots* (1887) to Andy Warhol's postmodern *Diamond Dust Shoes* (1980). For Jameson, Van Gogh's painting suggests a profound story behind the scene: a "world of agricultural misery, of stark rural poverty, and the whole rudimentary human world of backbreaking peasant toil, a world reduced to its most brutal and menaced, primitive and marginalized state." Warhol's *Diamond Dust Shoes*, by comparison, doesn't operate on this level. There is nothing within the image to connect Warhol's shoes to the "larger lived context of the dance hall or the ball, the world of jetset fashion or glamour magazines." Without this deeper context, Jameson argues, Warhol's painting is simply "a random collection of dead objects hanging together on the canvas like so many turnips."

The lack of depth in postmodernism leads to another postmodern trait: the "waning of affect." To Jameson, postmodern works don't stir us the way that modern works do. Van Gogh's *A Pair of Boots* shows us the misery of poverty. Picasso's *Guernica* makes us feel the horror, pain and senselessness of war. Without a deeper context, postmodern works have lost the ability to affect us in this way.

Not only did postmodernism usher in a waning of affect, it also brought us a waning sense of history. Jameson believes that our society has gradually lost its "capacity to retain its own past." We now live in "a perpetual present," in a state of constant change, feeling no need to preserve the traditions of past generations. While Jameson sees a number of reasons for this, he argues that advanced media technologies have played a significant role. The developments of cable television, satellite communication and portable video cameras have turned the media into an omnipresent and inescapable fact of our existence. Jameson suggests that the news media's very function is to transform recent events "as rapidly as possible into the past." The media works, then, "to serve as the very agents and mechanisms for our historical amnesia."

Jameson acknowledges that we could find numerous works from the modern period that include the postmodern features he identifies—pastiche, depthlessness, etc. What distinguishes their use as postmodern devices is the way they are positioned within the postmodern period. In the modern period, these traits played only minor or secondary roles. In the postmodern period, by contrast, they become the dominant characteristics. As Jameson notes, "we have something new when they become the central features of cultural production."

## Modernism vs. Postmodernism

Some scholars find it useful to understand postmodernism by differentiating it from modernism. Those who prefer this method most often refer to Ihab Hassan's influential work, *The Dismemberment of Orpheus: Toward a Postmodern Literature* (1971). In his book, Hassan provides a table of the differences he identifies between modern and postmodern literature:

| Modernism | Postmodernism |
|---|---|
| Romanticism / Symbolism → | Pataphysics / Dadaism |
| Form (conjunctive, closed) → | Antiform (disjunctive, open) |
| Purpose → | Play |
| Design → | Chance |
| Hierarchy → | Anarchy |
| Mastery / Logos → | Exhaustion / Silence |
| Art Object / Finished Work → | Process / Performance / Happening |
| Distance → | Participation |
| Creation / Totalization → | Decreation / Deconstruction |
| Synthesis → | Antithesis |
| Presence → | Absence |
| Centering → | Dispersal |
| Genre / Boundary → | Text / Intertext |
| Semantics → | Rhetoric |
| Paradigm → | Syntagm |
| Hypotaxis → | Parataxis |
| Metaphor → | Metonymy |
| Selection → | Combination |
| Root / Depth → | Rhizome / Surface |
| Interpretation / Reading → | Against Interpretation / Misreading |
| Signified → | Signifier |
| *Lisible* (Readerly) → | *Scriptable* (Writerly) |
| Narrative / *Grande Histoire* → | Anti-narrative / *Petit Histoire* |
| Master Code → | Idiolect |
| Symptom → | Desire |
| Type → | Mutant |
| Genital / Phallic → | Polymorphous / Androgynous |
| Paranoia → | Schizophrenia |
| Origin / Cause → | Difference-Difference / Trace |

God the Father→ | The Holy Ghost
Metaphysics→ | Irony
Determinacy→ | Indeterminacy
Transcendence→ | Immanence

Hassan makes it clear that these differences are not stable. They are likely to change as the postmodern period progresses. As he notes, the differences will continue to "shift, defer, even collapse." Still, he argues that the "rubrics in the right column point to the postmodern tendency, the tendency of indetermanence," thus bringing us closer to an "historical and theoretical definition."

## Implementation

Most postmodern literary criticism focuses on literary works of the postmodern period or on earlier works that utilize postmodern literary strategies. Consequently, postmodern readings of books like Laurence Sterne's *Tristram Shandy* (1767) are nearly as common as postmodern readings of texts from the late twentieth century.

Some of the more common postmodern strategies are:

> depthlessness: superficiality in art and literature. It is characterized in works that neither demand nor invite covert readings or deep interpretations. Fredric Jameson suggests that Andy Warhol's *Diamond Dust Shoes* illustrates depthlessness, in contrast to Vincent Van Gogh's *A Pair of Boots*.
> elliptical narration: a nonlinear narrative that progresses in a more circular fashion rather than in the conventional sense. A notable example is Samuel Beckett's *Waiting for Godot*.
> erasure: when something in a narrative is presented—to get the reader emotionally or intellectually invested—and then taken away, as in: Postmodernism provides an ~~insane~~ ~~confusing~~ interesting way to look at things.
> fragmentation: as the term implies, it is the breaking up into parts of either story elements or the postmodern "self." Aleatory literature (also known as shuffle literature) could be described this way.
> interruption of narration: the narration of the story is interrupted, usually by the implied author or the narrator. For example, Part One of Donald Barthelme's *Snow White* ends with a list of fifteen questions, including:
>> 1. Do you like the story so far? Yes ( ) No ( )
>> 9. Has the work, for you, a metaphysical dimension? Yes ( ) No ( )
>> 14. Do you stand up when you read? ( ) Lie down? ( ) Sit? ( )
>
> metafiction: fiction that overtly reminds the reader that he or she is reading a fictional story. There are numerous examples, but one most students might be familiar with is William Goldman's *The Princess Bride*.

the mixing of genres: the inclusion of poetry, nonfiction or drama—or drawings, photographs or even a music CD—in a novel, for example.
non-narrative techniques: this includes things like song lyrics, lists, etc. as part of the exposition. In Nabokov's *Lolita*, the narrator lists all of Lolita's classmates from a class roster.
pastiche: imitation of a previous work or author without the satiric mocking that is inherent in parody.

Beginning with strategies such as these, a postmodern critique can lead in any number of directions. It could argue that Miguel de Cervantes' use of metafiction in *Don Quixote* (1605-1615) was the inspiration for *Lost in the Funhouse* (1968) by John Barth, or that Laurence Sterne's *Tristram Shandy* (1759-1767) should be considered a work of postmodern fiction for its non-linear narration and its liberal use of pastiche.

One could also examine how a postmodern text reflects its historical, political, or socioeconomic context, or how it shaped the world of art, music or fashion. In other words, as is the case with many of our critical approaches, a postmodern critique can be as unique as the scholar undertaking it.

## Important Moments in Postmodernism

1953: Ludwig Wittgenstein's *Philosophical Investigations*
1953: premiere of Samuel Beckett's *Waiting for Godot*
1959: Alain Robbe-Grillet's *Jealousy*
1963: Kurt Vonnegut's *Cat's Cradle*
1962: Marc Saporta's *Composition No. 1*
1962: Umberto Eco's *Opera aperta*
1963: Julio Cortázar's *Rayuela* (trans. 1966, *Hopscotch*)
1966: Thomas Pynchon's *The Crying of Lot 49*
1967: Donald Barthelme's *Snow White*
1968: Vonnegut's *Welcome to the Monkey House*
1968: student and worker strikes in France
1968: John Barth's *Lost in the Funhouse*
1969: Vonnegut's *Slaughterhouse Five*
1971: Ihab Hassan's *The Dismemberment of Orpheus*
1972: demolition of Pruitt-Igoe housing development
1972: first issue of the postmodern literary journal *boundary 2*
1972: Deleuze's and Guattari's *L'Anti-Œdipe* (*Anti-Oedipus*)
1973: Pynchon's *Gravity's Rainbow*
1977: Charles Jencks' *The Language of Postmodern Architecture*
1979: Jean-François Lyotard's *The Postmodern Condition*
1980: Deleuze's and Guattari's *Mille plateau* (*A Thousand Plateaus*)
1981: Jean Baudrillard's *Simulacra and Simulation*
1983: Fredric Jameson's "Postmodernism and Consumer Society"

**1984:** Jameson's essay, "Postmodernism, or, The Cultural Logic of Late Capitalism"
**1986:** Baudrillard's *America*
**1988:** Milorad Pavić's *Landscape Painted with Tea*
**1991:** Jameson's *Postmodernism* expanded and published as a book
**1993:** Frederick Barthelme's *The Brothers*
**1996:** David Foster Wallace's *Infinite Jest*
**2002:** Baudrillard's *The Spirit of Terrorism*

## Important Terms

commodity fetishism
desiring-machine
hyperreality
metafiction
pastiche
simulacrum
waning of affect

depthlessness
deterritorialization
late capitalism
metanarrative
rhizome
simulation

## Study Questions

1. Using real historical narratives, construct a preposterous metanarrative that concludes in some unforeseeable future. Make it as outlandish as possible, ending with the most ridiculous implications that you can think of for the metanarrative's future conclusion.
   or:
   Using, again, real historical events, as well as events from your own life, construct a metanarrative of your life that suggests a future in which you are a notable figure in some capacity other than your current field of study.
2. Identify two texts of your choice—one from the modern period and one from the postmodern period—that utilize some of the same postmodern strategies outlined in this chapter. Discuss how the two texts differ in their use of the same strategies. How are they the same?
3. In one hour of a normal day—or on your next shopping excursion—identify as many simulacra as you can find. Choose between two and five of these and discuss how they separate you from what Baudrillard calls the "desert of the real."
4. From your own experience, identify and discuss at least five examples where you believe that Deleuze and Guattari's concept of the rhizome accurately (or inaccurately) illustrates the process of human thought.
5: In a short essay of five hundred to six hundred words, answer the following question: Where would you place the demarcation be-

tween the modern and postmodern literary periods? Use specific texts and historical information to justify your answer.

6: In *Postmodernism*, Fredric Jameson discusses how late capitalism shaped the creative work of the postmodern period. In a short essay (five hundred to six hundred words), describe how you think late capitalism has influenced the art, music and literature of the twenty-first century.

## Selected Bibliography

Baudrillard, Jean. *America*. Trans. Chris Turner. New York: Verso, 2010.
—. *The Gulf War Did Not Take Place*. Bloomington: Indiana UP, 1995.
—. *Simulacra and Simulation*. Trans. Sheila Faria Glaser. Ann Arbor: Michigan UP, 1995.
—. *The Spirit of Terrorism*. Trans. Chris Turner. New York: Verso, 2002.
Cortázar, Julio. *Hopscotch*. Trans. Gregory Rabassa. New York: Pantheon, 1987.
Crimp, Douglas. *On the Museum's Ruins*. Boston: MIT, 1995.
Crowther, Paul. *Defining Art, Creating the Canon: Artistic Value in an Era of Doubt*. Oxford: Oxford UP, 2012.
—. *Meanings of Abstract Art: Between Nature and Theory*. New York: Routledge, 2012.
—. *The Phenomenology of Modern Art: Exploding Deleuze, Illuminating Style*. New York: Continuum, 2012.
Deleuze, Gilles, and Felix Guattari. *A Thousand Plateaus: Capitalism and Schizophrenia*. Trans. Brian Massumi. Minneapolis: Minnesota UP, 1987.
—. *Anti-Oedipus: Capitalism and Schizophrenia*. Trans. Robert Hurley. New York: Penguin, 2009.
Eagleton, Terry. *The Illusions of Postmodernism*. New York: Blackwell, 1996.
Eco, Umberto. *Faith in Fakes: Travels in Hyperreality*. Chennai: Minerva, 1995.
—. *Foucault's Pendulum*. Trans. William Weaver. New York: Mariner, 2007.
—. *The Open Work*. Trans. Anna Cancogni, Cambridge: Harvard UP, 1989.
Federman, Raymond. *Critifiction: Postmodern Essays*. Albany: SUNY, 1993.
Foucault, Michel. *The Archaeology of Knowledge*. Trans. A M. Sheridan Smith. New York: Routledge, 2002.

—. *Death and the Labyrinth: The World of Raymond Roussel*. Trans. Charles Ruas. Berkeley: California UP, 1987.
Gass, William H. *Fiction and the Figures of Life*. Boston: Goodine, 1989.
Gellner, Ernest. *Postmodernism, Reason and Religion*. New York: Routledge, 1992.
Habermas, Jürgen. *Moral Consciousness and Communicative Action*. Trans. Christian Lenhardt and Shierry Weber Nicholsen. Boston: MIT, 2001.
—. *The Theory of Communicative Action: Lifeworld and System: A Critique of Functionalist Reason*. Trans. Thomas McCarthy. Boston: Beacon, 1985.
Hassan, Ihab. *The Dismemberment of Orpheus: Toward a Postmodern Literature*. Madison: Wisconsin UP, 1982.
—. *The Postmodern Turn: Essays in Postmodern Theory and Culture*. Columbus: Ohio State UP, 1987.
—. *Paracriticisms: Seven Speculations of the Times*. Urbana: Illinois UP, 1985.
Huyssen, Andreas. *After The Great Divide: Modernism, Mass Culture, Postmodernism*. Bloomington: Indiana UP, 1987.
—. *Twilight Memories: Marking Time in a Culture of Amnesia*. New York: Routledge, 1994.
—. *Modernity and the Text*. New York: Columbia UP, 1989.
Jameson, Fredric. *The Cultural Turn: Selected Writings on the Postmodern, 1983-1998*. New York: Verso, 2009.
—. *Postmodernism, or, the Cultural Logic of Late Capitalism*. New York: Verso, 1990.
Jencks, Charles. *The Language of Post-modern Architecture*. New York: Rizzoli, 1977.
—. *Post-Modernism*. New York: Rizzoli, 1988.
Johnson, B.S. *The Unfortunates*. New York: New Directions, 2009.
Laclau, Ernesto. *On Populist Reason*. New York: Verso, 2007.
Lyotard, Jean-François. *The Postmodern Condition: A Report on Knowledge*. Trans. Brian Massumi. Minneapolis: Minnesota UP, 1984.
McHale, Brian. *Postmodernist Fiction*. New York: Routledge, 1987.
—. *Constructing Postmodernism*. New York: Routledge, 1993.
Norris, Christopher. *Uncritical Theory: Postmodernism, Intellectuals and the Gulf War*.
Pavić, Milorad. *Landscape Painted with Tea*. New York: Vintage, 1991.
Robbe-Grillet, Alain. *Jealousy*. Trans. Richard Howard. London: Alma, 2012.
Rorty, Richard. *Consequences of Pragmatism: Essays 1972-1980*. Minneapolis: Minnesota UP, 1982.
—. *Philosophy and the Mirror of Nature*. Princeton: Princeton UP, 2012.

Saporta, Marc. *Composition No. 1: a Novel.* Trans. Richard Howard. New York: Simon and Schuster, 1963.
Vattimo, Gianni. *The End of Modernity: Nihilism and Hermeneutics in Postmodern Culture.* Baltimore: Johns Hopkins UP, 1991.
—. *Dialogue with Nietzsche.* New York: Columbia UP, 2008.
—. *A Farewell to Truth.* New York: Columbia UP, 2011.
Žižek, Slavoj. *The Sublime Object of Ideology.* London: Verso, 1989.

# 8

# Reader-Response Criticism

**FOCUSES ON:** the reader's interpretation of and reaction to the text.
**BECAUSE:** reader-response critics believe we cannot fully understand a literary work without considering the reader's interaction with the text.
**DEVELOPED IN:** 1960s.
**NOTABLE PRACTITIONERS:**
- Hans-Robert Jauss (1921-97)
- Wolfgang Iser (1926-2007)
- David Bleich (1936- )
- Stanley Fish (1938- )
- Robert Crosman (1940- )
- Peter J. Rabinowitz (1944- )
- James Phelan (1951- )
- Lisa Zunshine (1968- )
- Michael Riffaterre (1924-2006)
- Norman Holland (1927- )
- Judith Fetterley (1938- )
- Susan Rubin Suleiman (1939- )
- Gerald Prince (1942- )
- Steven J. Mailloux (1950- )
- Richard Gerrig (1959- )

**IMPORTANT PREDECESSORS:**
- I. A. Richards (1893-1979)
- Georges Poulet (1902–1991)
- Louise Rosenblatt (1904-2005)
- Walker Gibson (1919-2009)
- C. S. Lewis (1898-1963)
- Hans-Georg Gadamer (1900-2002)
- Roland Barthes (1915-80)
- Wayne C. Booth (1921-2005)

**ADVANTAGES:** clarifies the importance of the reader in formulating a thorough analysis of a literary work.
**DISADVANTAGES:** some scholars argue that reader-response criticism overlooks socioeconomic and gender issues; others feel that the focus on the reader comes at the expense of attention to the text.
**DEFINITION:** various methods of literary analysis that consider the reader's understanding of the text to be a necessary component of interpretation.

Reader-response criticism arose as theorists began to question what role, if any, the reader plays in the meaning of a text. The idea of considering the reader—and how a literary work affects the reader—goes back at least as far as ancient Greece. Plato famously saw poetry as inferior to philosophy because of poetry's dangerous ability to incite our basest emotions. The reader's role in generating meaning, though, didn't gain widespread attention until the 1960s.

In the English-speaking world, new criticism dominated literary theory for the first half of the twentieth century. This method involved an unwavering focus on only the text itself, based on the new critical belief that a literary text was an objective work of art with only one true meaning. Reader-response theorists questioned this method. How is it, they wondered, that different readers—even educated readers with the same training—can arrive at vastly divergent interpretations of the same text? And how can we decide which interpretation is "correct"? Reader-response theorists believe that a literary work is shaped by the reader's experience. Not only can readers impart meaning onto a text, they believe, but it's inevitable that they will. Reader-response criticism, then, argues that we cannot fully understand a literary work until we understand how the reader interprets it.

The new critics disagreed. Because reader-response criticism moved the focus away from the text and toward the reader, new critics worried that it would plunge literary criticism toward anarchy. That hasn't happened. Reader-response criticism has, however, changed the shape of all future methods of literary criticism by forcing us to reevaluate our methods of analysis.

## Why Worry about the Reader?

For those students unfamiliar with reader-response criticism, the idea of a reader imparting meaning onto a written text might sound ridiculous. The text is already there, after all; the reader can't simply go in and change the words. But each literary text is created to be read by real readers, and each of those readers approaches the text from his or her own unique perspective. It would be impossible for all of those perspectives to be identical.

We could imagine, for example, hearing the following on our car's radio:

> The storm is coming.

If this is all we hear before the signal is replaced by static, it's up to us to determine what it means. If we are driving toward ominous clouds, we would understand the sentence to be a warning about severe weather. If we follow politics, we might recognize a reference to an upcoming election season. For sports fans, it could mean that the Seattle Storm basketball team will be in town for a game. We could also hear it as part of an advertisement, a commentary, or even a euphemism. The meaning of this sentence, in other words, depends upon who we are, where we are, and the circumstances in which we hear it.

This applies to literature as well. What a literary work means for one reader can be quite different from what it means for another. Reader-response theorists argue that we need to account for these differences when we analyze any literary work.

Obviously, this presents a problem. With countless potential readers, how could we possibly interpret literature with the reader in mind? Reader-response criticism understands this, and provides guidelines for such interpretation. Reader-response theorists disagree, though, on what those guidelines are.

## Before Reader-Response

While Stanley Fish is commonly considered our first reader-response theorist, earlier scholars guided literary analysis toward a reader-centered approach. Walker Gibson's conception of the mock reader in 1950 blurred the boundaries between the reader, the writer and the text. Wayne C. Booth raised awareness about the role of the reader in *The Rhetoric of Fiction* (1961). In his book, Booth distinguishes between the implied author and the unreliable narrator. He also outlines the techniques that writers use to coerce readers to become invested in a story.

Many scholars, though, feel that I.A. Richards sowed the seeds of reader-response criticism decades earlier. While Richards was teaching at Cambridge, he provided his students with thirteen poems to analyze. Some of the poems were poorly-written pieces by students and others were written by renowned poets. Richards presented the poems to his students without letting them know who the authors were.

Richards found that his students' interpretations differed significantly. He published these findings as part of his book *Practical Criticism* (1929). While this exercise was part of Richards' work as a new critic, he nevertheless illustrated the divergent preconceptions that readers bring to literary texts. In Richards' essay, "The Interaction of Words" (1942), he stakes out a position more closely aligned with a reader-centered approach. He argues, in effect, that poetry takes shape within the reader's mind. This view contradicted the new critical belief in the objective and autonomous text.

In retrospect, we can also see Louise Rosenblatt's *Literature as Exploration* (1938) as another move toward reader-response criticism. Rosenblatt conceived a model of reading that involves a transaction between the reader and the text. Because of each reader's unique collection of knowledge and life experiences, each reader will respond differently to any written work. Even the same reader, reading a text a second time, will have a different reading experience because that reader will have changed at least a little. These ideas would later become characteristic of reader-response criticism. Still, in *Literature as Exploration*, Rosenblatt doesn't yet abandon the new critical view of the literary text as autonomous and objective. Because of this, most scholars hesitate to refer to her book as true reader-response criticism.

However we position Richards and Rosenblatt, we do credit them with one important milestone in the advent of reader-response criticism. Their work inspired, at least in part, the new critics W. K. Wimsatt and Monroe Beardsley to compose their essay, "The Affective Fallacy" (1949). It was this essay, more than any other, that reader-response theorists would directly challenge.

## Stanley Fish v. the Affective Fallacy

Many students recognize Wimsatt and Beardsley for their essay, "The Intentional Fallacy" (1946), but "The Affective Fallacy" is more relevant to reader-response theorists. As prototypical new critics, Wimsatt and Beardsley saw literature as objective and autonomous. For them, a literary work has only one meaning and this meaning exists within the text itself. The author's intention is not relevant to meaning (as they discuss in "The Intentional Fallacy"). The reader's reaction is also irrelevant (their argument in "The Affective Fallacy"). To Wimsatt and Beardsley, nothing matters but the text. For them, the affective fallacy is the "confusion between the poem and its *results*." Such confusion, they believe, "ends in impressionism and relativism."

This "impressionism and relativism" worried new critics the most. New criticism began as an organized system of analyzing literature. It was an attempt to apply the strategies of scientific inquiry to literary study. Before new criticism, literary analysis consisted of an assortment of various approaches with no definitive goal in mind. For literary analysis to maintain its recently acquired status as a serious academic study, new critics felt that it was necessary to remain faithful to new criticism's roots. Wimsatt and Beardsley wrote "The Affective Fallacy" to preserve the integrity of literary analysis. To Wimsatt and Beardsley, a reader-centered approach was not only foolish, but it undermined the scholarly efforts of past and present new critics.

Stanley Fish disagreed. Fish was an outspoken opponent of new criticism and one of the earliest advocates of a reader-centered approach. This is why most scholars see him as the originator of reader-response criticism. Contrary to the new critics, Fish argued that we can't fully understand a work of literature without understanding its effect on the reader. It is the reader, after all, who encounters the text and for whom the text is written.

Fish first makes the case for a reader-centered approach in his book, *Surprised by Sin: The Reader in* Paradise Lost (1967). To Fish, readers *experience* a text rather than passively receive it. Fish undertakes a meticulous reading of Milton's text, guiding us step-by-step through his progression of thought to prove his conclusions. As he points out in the case of Milton's work, the reader is steered toward one emotional response, then another, and often again toward a third or fourth, all within the same passage. The experience of reading these passages, Fish says, is analogous to typing the wrong letter on a typewriter:

> Even as the finger presses the wrong key, something in the mind flashes a warning signal [. . .] and one simultaneously participates in and analyzes a failure in co-ordination.

The reader, in other words, becomes an active agent in the meaning of Milton's text. Not only that, but *Paradise Lost* seems designed to produce a reading experience that parallels the text's content. If that is the case, Fish argues, then how can we possibly ignore the effect the text has upon the reader?

## The Source of Meaning

Still, at this point in his career, Fish sees the text as the source of the reader's emotional responses. The design of the text, in other words, guides the reader's reaction. This is reflected in his famous dictum that reader-response criticism changes the emphasis from what literature *means* to what literature *does*.

Fish modifies this aspect of his approach in *Is There a Text in this Class?* (1980). In this later book, he argues that these responses aren't inherent in the text, but, instead, are derived from within the reader. In a famous example, he discusses a list of theorists' names he wrote on the chalkboard for his class on linguistics and literary criticism. The students in this class, of course, recognized the words for what they were written to be—a reading list for the upcoming assignment:

> Jacobs—Rosenbaum
> Levin
> Thorne
> Hayes
> Ohman (?)

The next class Fish taught in the same room, however, was a group of students studying religious poetry from seventeenth-century England.

Fish told this second group of students that the list was a religious poem. These students then intently understood it as such. They offered a number of interpretive possibilities: the poem is a hieroglyph, shaped either like a cross or an altar; Jacobs suggests Jacob's ladder, Rosenbaum is read as "an obvious reference to the Virgin Mary"; Thorne refers to Christ's crown of thorns, etc.

Fish concludes from this exercise that it is solely from the reader, not the text, that meaning is generated. As he sees it, excellent reading doesn't involve finding what is in the text, but creating what we can prove is in the text. When we interpret a literary work, we construct it, rather than decode it. While Fish's experimental methods will come to be questioned by later reader-response theorists, his argument nevertheless solidified the interest in reader-response analysis.

## Interpretive Communities

Though Fish sees meaning as generated from the reader, he recognizes that outside influences shape the reader's interpretation. He found it notable that all of his linguistics students recognized the writing on the board as a reading assignment while his poetry students recognized it as a poem. To explain this, Fish developed the concept of interpretive communities.

An interpretive community is a loosely formed group that shares similar strategies for interpreting texts. These texts can be literary or non-literary, and individuals are members of several overlapping interpretive communities at once. An interpretive community could be comprised of one's family, classmates, friends, coworkers, or even those with whom he or she shares a similar hobby. In today's world, this could also include internet groups interested in various games, movies, music, etc.

It is from these interpretive communities that we receive our cues on how to read and understand the world. A literature student with a passion for NASCAR racing and gourmet cooking will be a member of interpretive communities devoted to those interests. And that student will likely interpret a poem differently than an engineering student whose hobbies include quantum physics and internet cat memes. As Fish shows, even students at the same university, majoring in the same subject, can belong to opposing interpretive communities and therefore understand a text quite differently.

To demonstrate the power of interpretive communities, Fish provides an example of a college student raising his hand during a lecture. Someone from another culture, who had never been in a classroom, would be unfamiliar with the meaning of this gesture. It is only through our interpretive communities that we understand that this student is asking to speak, as opposed to simply waving hello, requesting to use the restroom (as might be the case in an elementary school), or any number of other possibilities. We know what it means to raise our hand in a college classroom only because we've gained this knowledge through our interpretive communities.

To Fish, the influence of interpretive communities should ease any fears about a reader-centered approach leading to interpretive anarchy. After all, even though readers create the meanings within texts, Fish says, the meanings they make have been shaped by "culturally derived interpretive categories" (their interpretive communities). A textual interpretation can never be unique or idiosyncratic, according to Fish, because it will always be derived from an "institutional structure of which the 'see-er' was an extending agent." Readers may create the meaning, in other words, but the meaning they create is a product of their interpretive communities (which are shaped by various societal codes, beliefs and patterns of behavior).

## The Reception Aesthetics of the Constance School

While Fish was refining his reader-response theory in the U.S., scholars in Germany were developing their own reader-centered approach. Professors at the University of Konstanz (Constance), most notably Wolfgang Iser and Hans Robert Jauss, made up what would come to be known as the Constance School. Drawing on the work of German philosophers—particularly Kant, Husserl, Heidegger and Gadamer—the Constance School studied how readers and texts interact. Since their focus was on how a text is received, they referred to their work as *rezeptionsästhetik*, or reception aesthetics.

Iser's primary interest is the way in which individual readers actively construct meaning as they read. For Iser, a literary work has two poles: the artistic and the aesthetic. The artistic pole refers to the author's text and the aesthetic pole is "the realization accomplished by the reader." By reading, the reader makes it possible for the text to realize its full existence. Iser accepts that it is the author who writes the story and populates it with his or her own words and ideas. But, he reminds us, when that story is read, "the reader becomes the subject who does the thinking." As such, a text will be interpreted in different ways by different readers—just as a Mozart concerto will sound much different if it's performed by the London Philharmonic Orchestra as opposed to Justin Bieber.

Iser believes that these differences come about as readers fill in the "gaps" in texts. By "gaps," Iser is referring to those actions or descriptions of characters and settings that are not included in the written text. No literary work, after all, can describe everything that happens and everything that exists in the world of the story. It is up to the reader, then, to fill in the blanks with his or her own mental images. A character described as a sultry brunette, for example, might conjure up an image of Jessica Alba for one reader and Beyoncé Knowles—or Taylor Lautner—for another. Such gaps aren't limited to physical descriptions, however; they occur throughout the progression of a story's plot as well.

In "The Cask of Amontillado," we are not only left to imagine the appearance of the characters, the nature of Fortunato's insult and to whom Montresor is speaking, but also when this insult took place, how often Montresor and Fortunato have met since then, and what, if any, words were exchanged during these meetings. And that is just in the first two paragraphs. In good literature, according to Iser, countless gaps are necessary to allow the reader to participate actively—via his or her imagination—in the fulfillment of the story. The reader will only become involved in a text—and therefore fulfill the text's intentions—when his or her imagination is activated. And the reader's imagination is only activated as he or she fills the gaps within the text.

## Filling the Gaps

A number of factors determine how a reader will fill these gaps. Obviously, all readers have different life experiences and different stores of knowledge, so divergent readings are inevitable in this sense. But these readings remain confined "within the limits of the written text." Iser argues that we get cues on how to read a story (and thus on how to fill the gaps) from the story itself. Conventions of storytelling, literary devices and genre conventions all work to create a framework within which we perform (often unconsciously) our role as active readers. We expect, for example, that the description of a silent moonlit night, when written in a love story, will precede some significant development in a loving relationship. The same description in a horror story, however, would suggest that something bad is about to happen. In this example, our understanding of genre conventions, in conjunction with the text, produces a response in us as we read. Our reading experience is similarly active when we encounter literary devices such as symbolism, allusion or parallelism.

Good writers, according to Iser, utilize our knowledge of these literary conventions to keep us actively involved in the reading process. They use our knowledge of literary conventions against us, so to speak, by continuously leading us to expect one thing before giving us something else. Most of us are familiar with moments in books or movies when something unexpected happens. Iser believes these moments are explained by the writer's manipulation of our knowledge of literary conventions. The skilled author knows what we expect to see, makes us think it is about to happen, and then surprises us by giving us something different. Good writing involves the constant negotiation between the evocation of expectations and the surprise when those expectations go unfulfilled. This results in defamiliarization (in the same sense that it was described by the Russian formalists), and this defamiliarization, to Iser, is what creates good literature.

For Iser, again, these moments originate in the text rather than in the reader. This contrasts with the view of other reader-response theorists (such as Fish in his later work) who believe that the reader is solely responsible for generating meaning. For this reason, Iser's approach was more palatable for the new critics and therefore more widely accepted by the academic community.

## Reception and History

Whereas Iser was interested in the individual reader's reception of a text, his colleague of the Constance School, Hans Robert Jauss, applied reception theory to literary history. Rather than focusing on the individual reader, Jauss wanted to know how groups of readers responded to literary works in different places and at different moments throughout history.

Jauss was a proponent of historical approaches to literature, but he felt all previous methods were incomplete. The problem he saw was that literary historians tended to arrange literary works "according to the chronology of great authors" or according to a perceived "tendency [or] genre." Such an approach, according to Jauss, fails to recognize history as it was actually lived because it overlooks the role of the reader in shaping literary history.

For Jauss, literature does not progress through time as a broken chain of significant moments that we can chart by connecting the dots. Instead, literature evolves on a continuum, led forward by works that, when first read, exceed the boundaries of what is considered acceptable—either in form or in content—and alter the expectations of readers. As the expectations of readers change, authors then produce works that accommodate those changes. An essential component in this process is, obviously, the reader (often reacting as a group, similarly to Fish's interpretive community). Because of this, Jauss felt that literary analysis is neither complete nor accurate unless it considers the role of the audience.

## The Horizon of Expectations

Jauss developed a revised approach to literary history that incorporated the reader's reception of a text. Central to Jauss' approach were his concepts of a "horizon of expectations" and aesthetic distance. A horizon of expectations, simply put, is what a reader expects to happen in a story. This includes everything regarding setting, characters' actions, character development, and the progression of plot. A horizon of expectations is based upon the reader's understanding of genre and literary conventions, and it is shaped by all the elements of the reader's world—education, social conditions, societal norms, etc.—that are unique to that reader in his or her particular time and place in history. Aesthetic distance measures the difference between the horizon of expectations (what the reader expects to read) and what actually happens in the story.

Based upon these ideas, Jauss formulated seven theses as the basis for his approach:

1) literature is, and has always been, shaped by its reception.
2) it is possible for us to ascertain, objectively, what readers' expectations are.
3) by examining a literary work's horizon of expectations, we can determine its historical influence and aesthetic quality.
4) we can reconstruct the horizon of expectations that existed during a work's creation to see how the work could have been received by its original readers.
5) reception aesthetics can help us discover a literary work's historical position and significance.
6) following the model of structural linguistics, we can understand the reception of a literary work at just one point in history (synchronically) as well as throughout history (diachronically).
7) we need to recognize that literary history is independent from, but intertwined with, general history.

Jauss uses the example of Flaubert's *Madame Bovary* (1856). Today, of course, we see the story as quite tame by our standards. The book's original audience, though, was so shocked by the content that Flaubert stood trial in 1857 for "offending public morals." However, the French readers' horizon of expectations soon shifted, reducing the aesthetic distance of *Madame Bovary* and making texts with similar content acceptable. As proof of this, Jauss points to the novel, *Fanny* (1858), by Ernest Feydeau. Feydeau's novel contained much of the same subject matter as *Madame Bovary*, yet the same French audience that rejected Flaubert's story turned Feydeau's novel into a bestseller.

Flaubert's work also altered the audience's horizon of expectations with regard to literary conventions. Readers originally felt Flaubert's narrative technique was too unconventional (the aesthetic distance between the text's style and the readers' horizon of expectations was too great). But as writers began to incorporate aspects of Flaubert's narration into their own work, readers finally came to accept, then expect, Flaubert's style of prose. This, in turn, eventually led to dissatisfaction with Feydeau's hackneyed writing and its "flowery style." As a result, Feydeau's work ultimately faded into obscurity while *Madame Bovary* endured as a classic work of French prose. This chain of events, according to Jauss, was precipitated by the reception of the audience.

American cinema provides a more distilled illustration of this same concept. Acceptable (and credible) action-movie antagonists were once clichéd stereotypes of Native Americans. As the worldviews of moviegoers changed, so did their horizons of expectations. Film studios then emulated these changes (with the guidance of test screenings and focus groups). Consequently, movie villains have since included Russian spies, robots, religious extremists, etc., that coincide with the audience's currently predominant worldview.

As the worldviews of audience members change, the audience's tastes will also change (or, evolve to "sanction a new canon of expectations") and readers will gradually turn away from once-popular styles, modes of characterization and content. This, in turn, will prompt writers to adapt their work to accommodate the audience's changing tastes. According to Jauss' model, literature progresses through history in a perpetual cycle, kept in motion by the constant interaction between texts and the audience's reaction to those texts.

## Reading Psychologically

Some reader-response theorists prefer a more specific focus on the psychology of the individual reader. Because they are interested in the reader's unique subjective interaction with the text, they are often grouped together as subjectivists. We see this method exemplified in the work of Norman Holland and David Bleich.

Most scholars see the origins of this subjectivist branch of reader-response in the work of Louise Rosenblatt. Rosenblatt's *Literature as Exploration* (1938) notably discussed the uniqueness of each reading of a text—even subsequent readings conducted by the same reader. With the predominance of new criticism during this time, however, Rosenblatt's book garnered little attention when it was first published. It would be another thirty years before theorists revisited the psychological approach to reader-response criticism.

Contrary to the hope of some students, the subjectivist strand of reader-response is not a freewheeling, anything goes approach. It does not, in other words, give students *carte blanche* to merely describe their feelings about a story and call that a subjective reader-response analysis. Subjective analyses are based on thorough and thoughtful research. While subjectivists do utilize individual responses in their work, they most often use these in conjunction with several such responses and other research as part of a larger project.

Norman Holland, for example, sets out to combine psychological analysis with the close reading strategies developed by new critics. He wants to know how "we meet ourselves in the books we read." Holland's work is based on the belief that it isn't the story that provides a unified structure for the reader to uncover (a story, after all, is nothing more than various blotches of ink on a page) it is the reader who imposes his or her own unity onto a text. He sees two reasons for this. First, we humans seem inherently wired to seek out and find unity in all things. We also have an innate need to find a center around which this unity revolves. In a story, this center might be structural (a pattern of plot), symbolic (a unifying symbol), thematic (a central theme), etc.

In *5 Readers Reading* (1975), Holland studies the psychological responses of five students as they interact with texts. He analyzes the students' individually as they each discuss the same story, Faulkner's "A Rose for Emily." (In an appendix, he also provides these readers' responses to Fitzgerald's "Winter Dreams" and Hemingway's "The Battler.") What Holland found is that four principles guide the way "readers read to fit their personalities." These principles are:

1) Style Seeks Itself
2) Defenses Must Be Matched
3) Fantasy Projects Fantasies
4) Character Transforms Characteristically

For Holland, his research proved that we can't make assumptions about how an audience might respond to a text until we study how individual readers respond to that same text. From this, he concludes that we need to study the individual reader's response before we can truly understand a literary work.

David Bleich takes a slightly different approach than Holland. In the 1970s, Bleich and Holland engaged in a number of (sometimes contentious) written debates regarding the direction of subjective criticism. Bleich places even more emphasis than Holland on the importance of the reader in textual interpretation. While Holland feels that the reader's response is necessary for us to understand a text, he nevertheless sees the text as the starting point from which this response arises.

Bleich's model, on the other hand (first outlined in his book, *Readings and Feelings* (1975) and modified in *Subjective Criticism* (1978), begins not with the text, but with the reader's personal feelings. It isn't until after we study the individual reader's feelings that we move toward the reader's "feelings about literature" and then on to the topics of literary importance and the communal nature of interpretation.

For Bleich, this communal interpretation is key. He believes that our individual responses shape—and are shaped by—our social interactions, specifically in the classroom. As we share our responses with others, we edit our own interpretations, adding to and subtracting from (or "negotiating") them. Through this negotiation, we eventually arrive at a socially acceptable, "validated" analysis. Observers of the process, according to Bleich, will begin to recognize patterns in readers' perception and thus understand how these patterns are relevant to reading.

## Authorial Reading

One complaint against reader-response criticism—voiced by Terry Eagleton and Mary Louise Pratt, among others—is that it ignores the important social and political aspects of texts. We see these concerns addressed in the work of Peter J. Rabinowitz. As Rabinowitz notes, other reader-response methods focus on the reader either during the reading process or after the reading is complete. Rabinowitz feels this approach is incomplete. He believes that readers' textual interpretations are shaped by the cultural beliefs and societal values that influence them before they even encounter the text. As such, it's important to Rabinowitz that we also consider the reader before he or she reads.

As part of this process, Rabinowitz differentiates between three different types of reading audience: the actual audience (the "flesh-and-blood people who read the book"), the narrative audience (those who accept the narrative situation presented in the story), and the authorial audience (the readers that the writer imagines will read the story).

While other theorists have accounted for the actual audience (using terms like real reader, historical reader, etc.), Rabinowitz's narrative audience and authorial audience are slightly unique. The narrative audience consists of those readers who are able and willing to suspend their disbelief when reading a story. This includes those of us (most of us) who can accept the fictional existence of a fairy godmother in *Cinderella*—to use Rabinowitz's example—while understanding that fairy godmothers don't exist in real life.

The authorial audience, by contrast, is purely hypothetical. It is made up of those imagined readers that the author believes he or she is writing for. Since nobody can know who will make up the actual audience, the author has to base his or her authorial choices on assumptions of who these readers might be. These assumptions guide writers of children's books, for example, to design content that is very different from what we'd find in romance novels, detective stories or literary fiction.

Rabinowitz argues that we should read each story as if we are members of the story's authorial audience. He calls this authorial reading. Authorial reading allows us to understand the author's intention in all aspects of a story's composition (this is the same authorial intention that the new critics, Wimsatt and Beardsley, argue against in their essay, "The Intentional Fallacy").

Rabinowitz advocates authorial reading for a number of reasons. First, since most of us already speculate on the author's intention as we read—whether we realize it or not—it's important to have a strategy to do so. Authorial reading also helps us see an author's culture and his or her opinions about that culture. More important, perhaps, is that authorial reading gives us a foundation upon which to build interpretations from other theoretical perspectives. In this sense, authorial reading can help us, for example, identify bourgeois or misogynistic texts and differentiate them from satiric works.

Authorial reading can be difficult, however. It requires us to reconstruct the social or historical milieu of an author and to determine which hypothetical readers the author is writing for. Sometimes a text will suggest who its authorial audience is (through its content and language, etc.), but often we must determine the authorial audience with "an intuitive mix of experience and faith, knowledge and hunch—plus a certain amount of luck" (an educated guess, in other words). It's theoretically possible, of course, for a reader to find an authorial audience that is identical to him- or herself, but this is rare. More often, even with recent texts, the authorial audience will have social or political beliefs that differ from our own. We might also encounter an authorial audience with beliefs that are not shared with anybody in any of our interpretive communities (Rabinowitz uses the example of an authorial audience from Ancient Greece, where the belief in their pantheon of gods is not shared by anyone today).

Rabinowitz identifies four types of rules that govern the way we undertake an authorial reading: rules of notice, rules of signification, rules of configuration, and rules of coherence. Rules of notice are guidelines to suggest what aspects of a text we should pay particular attention to (beginnings, endings and titles are always important, for example). The rules of signification help us determine the importance of the textual aspects that we identified through the rules of notice (if a story's title is "The Yellow Wallpaper," we know the wallpaper will be significant). Rules of configuration help us recognize the expectations we have about texts, based upon our knowledge of literary devices and story elements among various genres (we expect the good guy to catch the bad guy in a detective story). Rules of coherence push for a textual interpretation that uncovers the text's best version possible (though not everybody will agree on the same "best" version).

While authorial reading provides a number of advantages in its own right, Rabinowitz also sees it as the means to a more significant goal: interpreting the misreadings of literary texts. Rabinowitz defines a misreading as an interpretation "in which the reader *aims* at joining the authorial audience, but fails." This can happen in several ways—an incorrect reading of symbols, a misapplication of genre rules, etc.—but Rabinowitz is most interested in how misreadings can inform our understanding of a culture. The misreadings of a text provide clues we can use to uncover the cultural values and dominant ideologies within a society. If we were to find, for example, that Kate Chopin's authorial audience read "The Story of an Hour" as a happy story of triumph for Brently Mallard over the ungrateful Louise, that could suggest a patriarchal ideology that borders on misogyny.

Rabinowitz sees a culture's values and ideologies as important because they shape the reader's worldview, which in turn shapes the reader's interpretation of texts. By retracing the reader's steps, so to speak, we can reconstruct that reader's political, cultural and socioeconomic climate to develop a clear picture of the reader's—and the author's—world. For Rabinowitz, then, the reader provides a path through which we can illuminate the values and socioeconomic conditions surrounding a text and its interpretation.

## Implementation

There are a variety of reader-response approaches, but not all of them are practical for student applications. The subjective methods suggested by Holland and Bleich, for example, both require an impartial observer to record and analyze the psychological responses of several other readers of the text. Fish's approach looks at readers' interactions with their interpretive communities and the way these interactions determine meaning. This is best done objectively, studying the interactions of others rather than analyzing ourselves.

While those methods might not work for most students, there are other options available. The approach the student chooses depends primarily upon one's personal preference. Students interested in literary history might prefer Jauss' method. This would help us see how Poe's "The Cask of Amontillado" fits within—or shaped—the continuum of literary history. Iser's method of reception aesthetics would allow us to analyze Poe's use of literary conventions and textual gaps that give his audience a worthwhile active reading experience. Here, for example, we would look at the ways in which Poe continuously subverts our expectations—most conspicuously in his neglect to name the insult that sets in motion the story's gruesome chain of events.

If we were to apply Rabinowitz's process to Poe's story, for example, our first step would be to position ourselves as part of Poe's authorial audience. In other words, we want to imagine that we are one of the readers Poe specifically targeted as he wrote his story. The difficulty here is that we must not only imagine that we are a reader in 1846, but we must also determine which specific 1846 audience Poe thought he was writing for. What social class did his intended audience consist of?

Were they laborers? Scholars? Readers of popular fiction? What level of education did they have? What did their typical days consist of?

We would note that the U.S. was a much different country during this time. America was made up of only twenty-eight states. California, Nevada, Utah and Arizona—and parts of Colorado, New Mexico and Wyoming—still belonged to Mexico. The American Civil War was fifteen years away. It would be nearly seventy years before women were able to vote. Nobody had electricity, indoor plumbing was a luxury, and it was common for children younger than ten to work in factories and coal mines. A popular form of entertainment consisted of reading poetry in front of the fireplace. Contemporary writers included Hawthorne, Longfellow and Tennyson. Imagining what it was like during this time can be a good first step toward envisioning Poe's intended audience.

Sometimes a text will suggest who its authorial audience is. At the very least, we can narrow the possibilities with a few preliminary observations. We can tell almost immediately, for example, that Poe didn't write his story for children. While the discussion of revenge wouldn't rule out all young readers, the vocabulary and writing style would. We also know from the subject matter that this isn't a story for readers who prefer popular love stories, and the short story form tells us, quite simply, that it wasn't written for those who read only novels. We can gain other insights in the same way. To identify a more specific audience, though, requires us to do some research.

We know that Poe was an established writer and literary critic by 1846; his 1845 poem, "The Raven," was an instant popular success. In imagining Poe's intended audience, we would also consider that Poe had a number of literary rivalries with other authors. These often took place in print. One writer in particular, Thomas Dunn English, was engaged in an ongoing written (and, on at least one occasion, physical) confrontation with Poe in the 1840s. A few months before Poe wrote "The Cask of Amontillado," English published his novel, *1844, or, The Power of the S.F.* In the book, Poe is caricatured as a lying misogynistic alcoholic. Many scholars see "The Cask of Amontillado" as a response to English's novel. If we read Poe's story in this way, we could conclude that its authorial audience consists of members of the literary establishment who would recognize any veiled references to English.

The choice we make with regard to the authorial audience will affect how we approach the text. If we establish that Poe's intended audience is the literary establishment, then we would naturally examine the text for characterizations of—and parallels to—Thomas Dunn English. On the other hand, if we see the authorial audience as simply readers of popular fiction, we would instead focus on plot elements and literary devices that the story utilizes to appeal to that audience.

Once we've positioned ourselves as part of Poe's authorial audience, we can turn our attention to Rabinowitz's four rules of authorial reading.

Rules of notice guide us to take note of certain aspects of the story. Some of these textual elements will be noteworthy regardless of the piece we are analyzing (Rabinowitz suggests, for example, that we always pay attention to beginnings, endings and titles, as well as conspicuous literary devices and conventions). In Poe's story, we would also look for any suggestions of Thomas Dunn English within the story (provided we see the literati as Poe's authorial audience). We might then determine that Fortunato is Poe's fictional depiction of English. Seeing the text in this way could give deeper meaning to such things as the characterization of Fortunato as an incompetent wine snob (Fortunato says, after all, that Luchresi "'cannot distinguish Sherry from Amontillado,'" not realizing that Amontillado is a type of Sherry). It might also lead us to reconsider to whom it is that Montresor addresses his tale.

Rabinowitz's rules of signification direct us to determine the significance of those textual aspects that we have taken note of. Here, we would study the irony that Poe sprinkles throughout his story and the symbolism of such things as Montresor's coat of arms. Through the rules of configuration, we can recognize the literary devices and plot elements that we have learned to expect from short stories in general and Poe's stories in particular. Rules of coherence suggest that we should always work toward uncovering the best possible interpretation that the story has to offer.

As Rabinowitz notes, the rules he identifies don't provide a prescriptive method of reading that we follow one after another. Rather, he suggests that we take in the text as a whole, applying each rule where appropriate. Any parallels we find between Fortunato and Thomas Dunn English, for example, would fit into all four categories. We would consider them with the rules of notice because parallels are literary conventions that we should always take note of. We would include them in the rules of signification because any parallel to English, in our reading, will be significant to our understanding of the text. Rules of configuration also apply because parallels involve the structural pattern of the text. And, in the case of "The Cask of Amontillado," parallels to English fall under the category of rules of coherence because, in our authorial reading, an adequate analysis of the story would have to include any references to Poe's rival.

Finally, we can study the scholarship and criticism that has accompanied Poe's story. The way people read (or misread) a text can show us the values and beliefs that were dominant in that reader's culture. In the late twentieth century, for example, scholars began to conclude that the "insult" Montresor references was homoerotic in nature (a failed love affair, perhaps, or a rape, etc.). Whether we see such interpretations as accurate analyses or misreadings, they nevertheless demonstrate a change in cultural attitudes and beliefs since 1846, when such interpretations weren't considered. Any reading, in other words, can reveal clues about the critic's culture; as we compare these readings through history (a method suggested by Hans Robert Jauss) we can see the changes that take place in a culture through time.

A reader-centered analysis, then, can take many forms, depending upon the method we use and the decisions we make while employing that method.

## Important Moments in Reader-Response Criticism

**1929:** I.A. Richard's *Practical Criticism*
**1938:** Louise Rosenblatt's *Literature as Exploration*
**1960:** Hans-Georg Gadamer's *Truth and Method*
**1961:** Wayne C. Booth's *The Rhetoric of Fiction*
**1967:** Stanley Fish's *Surprised by Sin*
**1968:** Norman Holland's *The Dynamics of Literary Response*
**1969:** Hans Robert Jauss's "Literary History as a Challenge to Literary Theory"
**1971:** Umberto Eco's *The Role of the Reader*
**1970:** Wolfgang Iser's lecture "The Affective Structure of the Text"
**1972:** Iser's *The Implied Reader*
**1972:** Fish's *Self-Consuming Artifacts*
**1973:** Gerald Prince's "Introduction to the Study of the Narratee"
**1975:** Holland's *5 Readers Reading*
**1975:** David Bleich's *Readings and Feelings*
**1976:** Iser's *The Act of Reading: A Theory of Aesthetic Response*
**1976:** Fish's "Interpreting the Variorum"
**1977:** Hans Robert Jauss' *Aesthetic Experience and Literary Hermeneutics*
**1978:** Hans Robert Jauss' *Toward an Aesthetic of Reception*
**1978:** Rosenblatt's *The Reader, The Text, The Poem*
**1980:** Fish's *Is There a Text in This Class?*
**1980:** Jane Tompkins' *Reader-Response Criticism*
**1984:** Robert C. Holub's *Reception Theory*
**1985:** Jane Tompkins' *Sensational Designs*
**1987:** Peter Rabinowitz's *Before Reading*
**1989:** Jauss' *Question and Answer: Forms of Dialogic Understanding*
**1989:** James Phelan's *Reading People, Reading Plots*
**1992:** Holland's *The Critical I*
**2006:** Bleich's "The Materiality of Reading"

## Important Terms

actual audience                aesthetic distance
authorial audience             authorial reading

gaps
ideal reader
implied reader
narratee
postulated reader

horizon of expectations
implied author
interpretive community
narrative audience
real reader

## Study Questions

1. Identify at least three different interpretive communities that you belong to. Then, outline the differences each of those communities would have in the interpretation of your favorite short story.
2. Find five "gaps" that you must fill—and how you fill them—in your reading of the story of your choice. Then, discuss with your friends or classmates how they fill those same gaps.
3. Who is the authorial audience of "The Story of an Hour"? Describe at least three important characteristics of this audience. What can you gain from an authorial reading that you couldn't gain from a different type of analysis?
4. Describe how your interpretation of a text has been "negotiated" in a classroom or a social setting as described by Bleich.
5. In "The Story of an Hour," while Louise is alone in her room, she says to herself, "Free! Body and soul free!" In a brief essay (five hundred to eight hundred words), describe the differences and similarities you find in this line when reading it from the method outlined by Iser, the method outlined by Jauss and the method outlined by Rabinowitz.

## Selected Bibliography

Bleich, David. *Readings and Feelings: An Introduction to Subjective Criticism*. Urbana: NCTE, 1975.
—. *Subjective Criticism*. Baltimore: Johns Hopkins UP, 1978.
Booth, Wayne C. *The Rhetoric of Fiction*. Chicago: Chicago UP, 1983.
Eco, Umberto. *The Role of the Reader: Explorations in the Semiotics of Texts*. Bloomington: Indiana UP, 1979.
Fish, Stanley. *Is There a Text in this Class? The Authority of Interpretive Communities*. Cambridge: Harvard UP, 1982.
—. *Self-Consuming Artifacts: The Experience of Seventeenth-Century Literature*. Pittsburg: Duquesne UP, 1998.
—. *Surprised by Sin: The Reader in* Paradise Lost. Berkeley: California UP, 1972.
Freund, Elizabeth. *The Return of the Reader: Reader-Response Criticism*. New York: Routledge, 2002.

Holland, Norman Norwood. *5 Readers Reading*. New Haven: Yale UP, 1975.
—. *The Critical I*. New York: Columbia UP, 1994.
—. *The Dynamics of Literary Response*. New York: Columbia UP, 1989.
Holub, Robert C. *Reception Theory*. New York: Routledge, 2002.
Iser, Wolfgang. *The Act of Reading: A Theory of Aesthetic Response*. Baltimore: Johns Hopkins UP, 1980.
—. *The Implied Reader: Patterns of Communication in Prose Fiction from Bunyan to Beckett*. Baltimore: Johns Hopkins UP, 1978.
—. *The Range of Interpretation*. New York: Columbia UP, 2001.
Jauss, Hans-Robert. *Aesthetic Experience and Literary Hermeneutics*. Minneapolis: Minnesota UP, 1982.
—. *Toward an Aesthetic of Reception*. Minneapolis: Minnesota UP, 1982.
Mailloux, Steven. *Interpretive Conventions: The Reader in the Study of American Fiction*. Ithaca: Cornell UP, 1984.
Ong, Walter. *Orality and Literacy*. New York: Routledge, 2002.
Phelan, James. *Reading People, Reading Plots: Character, Progression, and the Interpretation of Narrative*. Chicago: Chicago UP, 1989.
Poulet, Georges. "Phenomenology of Reading." *New Literary History* 1.1 (October 1969). 53-68.
Rabinowitz, Peter. *Before Reading: Narrative Conventions and the Politics of Interpretation*. Ithaca: Cornell UP, 1987.
Rosenblatt, Louise. *Literature as Exploration*. New York: MLA, 1995.
—. *The Reader, The Text, The Poem: The Transactional Theory of the Literary Work*. Carbondale: Southern Illinois UP, 1994.
Tompkins, Jane P. *Reader-Response Criticism: From Formalism to Post-Structuralism*. Baltimore: Johns Hopkins UP, 1980.
—. *Sensational Designs: Cultural Work of American Fiction, 1790-1860*. Oxford: Oxford UP, 1985.

# 9

# New Historicism

**FOCUSES ON:** the overt and covert text, as well as biographical information and all manner of historical documents from the same period.
**BECAUSE:** new historicists aim to understand and explain the reciprocal relationship between literature and history.
**DEVELOPED IN:** 1980s.
**NOTABLE PRACTITIONERS:**
    Jerome McGann (1937- )    Stephen Greenblatt (1943- )
    Catherine Gallagher (1945- )    Louis A. Montrose (1946- )
    John Guillory (1952- )
**IMPORTANT PREDECESSORS:**
    Raymond Williams (1921-88)    Michel de Certeau (1925-86)
    Michel Foucault (1926-84)    Clifford Geertz (1926-2006)
    Hayden White (1928- )    Pierre Bourdieu (1930-2002)
**ADVANTAGES:** when done properly, it can reveal fascinating historical information regarding the text, author or world in which the text was written.
**DISADVANTAGES:** to do it properly requires a significant commitment to historical research; also, a new historicist reading tends to ignore the unique literary aspects of the text.
**DEFINITION:** a method of literary analysis that elucidates a text's complex relationship with the time and place in which it was written.

---

As the name suggests, new historicism was a new way to analyze literature from a historical point of view. Part of this involves a sort of anthropological study of a culture from a literary perspective, leading some new historicists to prefer calling it "cultural poetics" instead of "new historicism."

The term, new historicism, probably comes from Michael McCanles in an essay he wrote in 1980. Most scholars, though, credit Stephen Greenblatt with shaping new historicism into the literary theory that we know today. As new historicism was developing, Greenblatt was a professor at UC Berkeley, commonly considered the place where new historicism originated. It was in Berkeley, in 1983, where Greenblatt and his colleagues founded the literary journal, *Representations*, still the foremost journal of new historicist thought. While the focus of early new historicists was the literature of the early modern, or Renaissance, period, new historicism soon expanded into other literary interests. Indeed, the techniques of new historicism can be applied to any literary period.

Before new historicism, most theorists still practiced new criticism or had recently converted to post-structuralism. New historicists found both of these approaches inadequate. (The New Critics, remember, viewed a text as autonomous in order to uncover its one true meaning; post-structuralists, likewise, focused primarily on the text, but they did so to find the text's many possible meanings.) New historicists felt that literary analysis was incomplete unless it took into account an author's cultural environment. This belief coincided with a changing climate throughout academia. The years after the Vietnam War saw rapid transformations in the United States and the world. In the face of an increasingly global economy and a computerized world, there developed a growing sense that any liberal arts education needed a cultural studies component that included women and people of color. New historicism, as Greenblatt points out, reflected this "recent inclusion of groups that in many colleges and universities had hitherto been marginalized, half-hidden, or even entirely excluded from the professional study of literature."

By the mid-eighties, new historicism had become one of the most popular approaches to literary analysis. This was due in part to the success of Greenblatt's work and partly to the accessibility of new historicist ideas. In contrast to post-structuralism, for example, the fundamental concepts of new historicism were relatively easy to grasp. As such, it offered an inclusive approach that both students and professors could embrace.

While new historicism became immensely popular in a relatively short time, it was not without its detractors. Much of the criticism came from scholars still aligned with new criticism. Many new critics still viewed the approaches of feminism, Marxism, post-structuralism and psychoanalysis as specialized studies that were unworthy of serious consideration. New historicism's prevalence, though, made it impossible to ignore. The new critics saw new historicism as a serious threat to what they considered true literary scholarship. Since the new critics believed that all attention should be focused on the text itself, they felt that any research of a text's history was not only a waste of time, but that it also diverted attention away from their own method of literary analysis. As such, new critics attacked new historicism as "a lunge toward barbarism" perpetrated by "ethnic minorities and leftist faculty" bent on sending the country toward "cultural suicide." What these critics failed to appreciate, though, was that new historicism not only satisfied the need for a more inclusive study of literature but also elucidated literature more thoroughly than any autonomous approach ever could.

## New Historicism: Defined?

New historicists generally oppose defining new historicism, believing that doing so would limit the possible directions that a new historicist reading can take. Fortunately for us, they are more willing to outline its methods. Many of the early new historicists began their careers as new critics, so new historicists often utilize the close reading strategies of new criticism. The difference is that new historicists apply these strategies to texts of all types, whereas the new critics focused only on literary texts. Catherine Gallagher describe it as a parallel analysis of "literary and nonliterary texts as constituents of historical discourses" with no preconceptions regarding which influenced the other.

Harold Veeser, as well, has identified five key assumptions that underlie nearly all new historicist analyses:

1. every expressive act is embedded in a network of material practices;
2. every act of unmasking, critique, and opposition uses the tools it condemns and risks falling prey to the practice it exposes;
3. literary and non-literary "texts" circulate inseparably;
4. no discourse, imaginative or archival, gives access to unchanging truths nor expresses inalterable human nature;
5. a critical method and a language adequate to describe culture under capitalism participate in the economy they describe.

According to Veeser, new historicists analyze an act or an event to reveal and understand the numerous forces at work within a society. In so doing, they are better able to determine how these factors shaped the work they are studying which, in turn, reveals new information about the society. In other words, Veeser tells us, new historicism provides "a new awareness of how history and culture define each other." This is important, new historicists argue, because no literary analysis can be accurate unless we understand the literary work in relation to its historical and cultural environment.

## Old vs. New Historicism

Scholars have approached literature from a historical perspective for hundreds of years—most notably, perhaps, with regard to the work of

Shakespeare. The previous historical approaches, however, differed from new historicism in their understanding of literature's relationship to history. In the introduction to his book, *The Power of Forms in the English Renaissance* (1982), Stephen Greenblatt delineates the differences between new historicism the earlier literary historicism.

While Greenblatt's introduction is brief, it nevertheless outlines the fundamental beliefs that would go on to guide new historicist thought. In short, these beliefs are:

1) literature not only *reflects* history, but it shapes and influences history as well.
2) a theorist's interpretation of literature—historical or otherwise—is unavoidably influenced by the theorist's own biases, experiences, preconceptions and historical milieu.
3) furthermore, what we think of as historical "facts" would be better understood as interpretations of historical events that are colored by the historian's own biases, experiences, etc.

To prove these points, Greenblatt explicates an example of the "old historicism": a 1939 lecture by John Dover Wilson. Wilson was the leading Shakespearean scholar of his day and his work represented the authoritative voice of the previous historical approach. In his lecture, "The Political Background of Shakespeare's *Richard II* and *Henry IV*," Wilson argues that "*Richard II* is not at all subversive but rather a hymn to Tudor order." Greenblatt disagrees. He notes that, in the months preceding the Essex uprising in 1601, Shakespeare's *Richard II* had been transformed into a sort of call to arms for the supporters of Robert Devereux, the Second Earl of Essex, in his attempt to overthrow the Queen. While the play itself was written with no seditious intentions, it had been appropriated by—and performed many times for—the supporters of Devereux in order to incite rebellion.

Queen Elizabeth and Robert Devereux both understood the power that literature has to affect history. (When discussing the Essex uprising—and Devereux's resultant beheading—Elizabeth famously said, "I am Richard II, know ye not that?") Indeed, we see numerous examples today of history being shaped by literature—whether in the form of inspiring troubled individuals to commit acts of violence or encouraging fans of a popular author to dress as their favorite character for the latest book or movie release. The earlier historical approaches overlooked this aspect of literature.

In the same essay, Greenblatt also points out that Wilson had a vested interest in viewing the play as though it strongly opposed rebellion. Greenblatt says,

> We might [. . .] look closely at the relation between Dover Wilson's reading of *Richard II*—a reading that discovers Shakespeare's fears of

chaos and his consequent support of legitimate if weak authority over the claims of a ruthless usurper—and the eerie occasion of his lecture.

Greenblatt suggests that Wilson equates the actions of Shakespeare's Bolingbroke with those of Hitler in 1939; consequently, Wilson's understanding of Bolingbroke—either consciously or unconsciously—is colored by this comparison.

Furthermore, according to Greenblatt, our record of history itself is tinged with the same type of bias that Wilson displays. Greenblatt uses the term, "historian's interpretation," to describe what we commonly think of as historical "fact." While this is often more subtle than Wilson's reading of *Richard II*, it is nevertheless an unavoidable consequence of any human documentation. New historicism, then, followed the recognition that our understanding of history and literature—and their relationship to each other—had been flawed.

## Foucault and Power

One influence for this revised understanding of history was the French philosopher, Michel Foucault. From the 1970s until his death in 1984, Foucault frequently lectured at UC Berkeley. It is no coincidence that new historicism was developing at Berkeley during this time.

Foucault studied under Louis Althusser at the top university in Paris. Althusser's Marxist leanings shaped Foucault's early studies. Foucault later disavowed Marxism as impractical, but we still see traces of Althusser's Marxist influence in Foucault's thought.

Much of Foucault's work—especially his later work—focuses on power. Foucault's concept of power is different from our conventional understanding of the term. It is more pervasive than the power attained through force. And it is more insidious than the economically derived power perceived by Marxism. At its most basic, Foucault's power is the relationship between individuals, entities or institutions in which one is able to influence another. What makes Foucault's power different is the way in which it manifests itself. For Foucault, power is more than repressive strength. It is more than the ability of person or an institution to control us physically. Power, as Foucault sees it, operates in nearly all social interactions.

Power is expressed through State directives (laws, speed limits, etc.). It controls localized communication (a sales transaction at the grocery store, a conversation with the automobile mechanic). It even controls us through inanimate constructions (pathways to guide where we walk, benches and alcoves that determine where we sit and relax). Power can also take the form of disciplinary control. It trains us in school to behave "properly," to follow directions, and to speak only after given permission.

Power can also take a more subtle form. This type of power involves the spread of knowledge. "Knowledge," in this sense, is any belief that is commonly accepted by a society. It doesn't have to be factually accurate. We once "knew," for example, that the earth was flat and that it was orbited by the sun. According to Foucault, an institution like a school not only conditions acceptable behavior, but also teaches us how to think, what to think, and what type of thinking is valid. In other words, the school—in this example—controls what we know and how we think. The teacher gives us his or her version of facts and tells us which of those "facts" are worth knowing. We experience a similar circulation of knowledge, in varying degrees, in every one of our social interactions. It happens at school, at work, and even in lighthearted conversations with our friends.

## Foucault and Discourse

Knowledge is distributed through discourse, which in turn reinforces power. Discourse is the means of communicating a social group's ideology; it encompasses not only the group's unique vocabulary and modes of expression, but also its worldview and patterns of behavior. In short, a discourse is a social group's language of beliefs and ideas. In today's politics, for example, the discourse of conservatives is different from the discourse of liberals, which is also different from the discourse of libertarians. While these three political groups are living at the same period of time in the same part of the world, with access to the same information, they nevertheless all have a different understanding of the world, a different set of values and at least a slightly different vocabulary. The same is true for the various social groups we belong to. The discourse of our immediate family is different from the discourse of our circle of college friends, just as the discourse of our book club is different from the discourse of our church group, athletic team or secret society.

In other words, innumerable discourses exist simultaneously. This is not only true of today's world, but it has been true of every period of time in recorded history. What Foucault pointed out—which caught the attention of the new historicists—was that historical events were most often recorded from the perspective of only one of the multiple discourses that existed in a given time. And that discourse was often the one sanctioned by the State. Thus, the American Revolution is understood in the U.S. as a battle for freedom while, in Britain, it could be depicted as something entirely different. Furthermore, not only were historical events, as they happened, recorded from the perspective of a single discourse, the future historian—years or centuries later—will describe those same events from the biased perspective of his or her own discourse (as Greenblatt notes with regard to John Dover Wilson's reading of Shakespeare's *Richard II*). The implication here, of course, is that what we have always thought of as historical fact is actually just one interpretation of history that has been filtered through the discourses of both the historian (which itself has been shaped by a variety of discourses) and the person who originally documented the event.

New historicists, then, analyze any historical document with the understanding that it presents only one (very limited) view of the time in which it was created.

## Clifford Geertz: Culture as Text

The corpus of new historicist thought has been inspired by an eclectic mix of scholars from a variety of fields. Besides Foucault, these include the historian Hayden White, the Marxist theorist Raymond Wilson, and sociologists Pierre Bourdieu and Michel de Certeau. For new historicists, the work of Clifford Geertz is particularly significant. According to Greenblatt, Geertz developed the methods of analysis and explication that would become hallmarks of new historicism.

Geertz was a cultural anthropologist who specialized in ethnic cultures. His work was innovative in many respects, beginning with his research process. Geertz immersed himself in the societies he studied. He participated in their rituals and daily activities while recording his observations. As he analyzed these cultures, Geertz employed an approach similar to what one might use on a literary text. In a practical application of Derrida's post-structuralist proposition that everything is text, Geertz "read" a culture the same way one would read a work of literature.

Greenblatt saw that reading a culture as a text led to a variety of possibilities for the historical study of literature. For one, ignored or forgotten texts could now be analyzed with the same seriousness as texts that were considered classics. These rediscovered texts can give us a more complete understanding of our canonical works. They help us recognize themes common to all literature of a period and they provide evidence of their influence upon our literary classics. For the new historicist, reading a culture as a text also involves researching all manner of material produced during a particular period. Aside from literary texts, this includes news articles, advertisements, political tracts, court records, etc. Or, as Gallagher and Greenblatt put it, new historicists study the

> rabble of half-crazed religious visionaries, semiliterate political agitators, coarse-faced peasants in hobnailed boots, dandies whose writings had been discarded as ephemera, imperial bureaucrats, freed slaves, women novelists dismissed as impudent scribblers, learned women excluded

from easy access to the materials of scholarship, scandalmongers, provincial politicians, charlatans, and forgotten academics.

New historicists hope to develop a more complete understanding of an author's physical and cultural environment. Following Geertz's example, the practice of studying numerous texts of all types became de rigueur for any new historicist.

## Geertz's Thick Description

Geertz's work also provided the framework through which new historicists could clarify their conclusions. Geertz illustrates his academic essays with "thick description," a term he borrows from the philosopher Gilbert Ryle. A thick description is similar in style to a detailed depiction in a literary work. As opposed to a thin description, which is a mere recounting of an action or an event, a thick description puts that event in context—why it is happening, what its intended consequences and actual consequences are, and how it might impact the larger social group. Ryle famously highlights the need for thick description when discussing a hypothetical person's blink of an eye: is it an involuntary twitch? a flirtatious or a conspiratorial wink? a parody of someone else's wink (and if so, is that parody friendly or malicious), etc. Thick description helps us understand the meaning and context of these and other gestures, which helps us more fully understand a culture. Following the lead of Geertz and Ryle, new historicists employ thick description to recreate a more accurate representation of the world in which a literary work was created.

As we "read" these gestures, however, we encounter an issue common to all readings of texts; namely, no two theorists will read a text in the same way. Much like Foucault, Geertz understood that each reading of a text (or a culture as a text) represents little more than the subjective interpretation of one person and, at best, explains only one aspect of that culture. As such, no single reading of a culture can be complete; each reading comes from the unique position of the theorist doing the reading. It is necessary for us, then, to construct our understanding of a culture from an amalgamation of several different readings. New historicists adopted this approach in their historical analysis of literature, which further underscores their need to examine numerous texts of all types.

## Implementation

New historicism wants us to form as complete a picture as possible of the world that an author inhabited. Doing so will allow us to understand the author's literary work in the context of its time. While this involves reading the literary work alongside contemporaneous texts (in the post-structuralist sense that everything is text), it's up to the individual theorist to decide how to go about that. One scholar might read a story and then seek out and study texts from the time that the story was written. Another scholar might be interested in a specific period—the early Victorian period, for example, or Russia's Golden Age—and would therefore begin by studying that period. More often, though, analysis of the literary work coincides with the study of parallel texts; as we get deeper into our research of the parallel texts, we realize that further analysis of the literary work is needed, and vice versa. However one undertakes the process, the steps of a new historicist analysis remain the same: a close reading of the literary work, a thorough study of any texts that coincide with that work, and an explication of what we uncovered.

If we were to perform a new historicist analysis on Chekhov's "Gooseberries," for example, we could begin by seeking out any Russian texts from around 1898, when the story was published. This includes newspaper and magazine articles, advertisements, political pamphlets, and personal journals, as well as Chekhov's own writings (his published works as well as diaries, letters or even notes or lists he may have scribbled). While we could examine anything from before or throughout Chekhov's life, the scope of our study would be determined by our thesis. If we were to argue, for example, that Chekhov's body of work, including "Gooseberries," was an inevitable product of Russia's Tsarist system of government, then our research might expand to everything produced in Russia from the eighteenth century to 1917, when the reign of Nicholas II ended. If we want to identify Chekhov's influences, our research might cover a similar span of time. The student writing a new historicist analysis of "Gooseberries," though, would probably want to limit his or her study to the years more immediately surrounding the story's publication.

The lines of inquiry that new historicists pursue are as diverse as the theorists themselves. Our studies could reveal, for example, that Chekhov modeled all of his characters after people in his life. Or we could discover that the story's setting describes a place with personal significance to Chekhov—in which case we might find further meaning in the characters' interaction with their setting and with each other. Perhaps something in the story suggests that "Gooseberries" was inspired by the 1896 Khodynka Tragedy that followed the coronation of Nicholas II. It could be, too, that we find something unique about the framed narrative that Chekhov uses in the story, or perhaps he employs a method of characterization that would come to be utilized by all successive Russian writers.

Using new historicism, we could also focus on Chekhov himself. Our study of secondary texts might uncover something interesting about Chekhov's life that other scholars had overlooked. Maybe diary entries or private letters will reveal that the circumstances of Chekhov's childhood or his adult life were different than we thought. A new historicist reading done in this fashion can uncover all manner of information which can then inform our understanding of the author's literary work. A new historicist reading, in other words, can approach its subject from numerous angles, based upon the theorist's interests.

Some prefer to use a new historicist approach in conjunction with another theoretical perspective such as Marxism, feminism, psychoanalysis, etc. A scholar applying new historicism with a Marxist focus would study the socioeconomic circumstances surrounding the publication of Chekhov's story. This includes the financial status of Chekhov and his family as well as the conditions in Russia during this time. Nineteenth-century Russia was stable in the sense that the Romanov family had ruled for centuries; however, the country underwent significant change throughout Chekhov's lifetime. Chekhov grew up under the reformist reign of Tsar Alexander II. In 1881, though, when Chekhov was twenty-one, Alexander III came to power and reversed many of the social improvements instituted by his predecessor. Though Russia's serfs remained free, there was still a significant discrepancy between the poorest and the wealthiest of the country's citizens. Bankruptcy, in fact, had forced Chekhov to finish his schooling alone in Taganrog while his father moved the rest of the family to Moscow to avoid debtor's prison. A new historicist reading from a Marxist perspective would look deeper into topics such as these.

Applying a feminist slant to a new historicist reading of the story would shift our attention to Chekhov's portrayal of women. As with all new historicist readings, we wouldn't examine just the story in question; we'd also consider his other works. In this case, we would want to know if the women in "Gooseberries" are characteristic of female characters in Chekhov's other stories. How many of Chekhov's women are static characters differentiated solely by their appearance? How many are treated dismissively? How often are they relegated to minor roles? Do they have occupations other than as cooks, maids or housewives? From our study of other Russian texts from this period, we would then determine how Chekhov's depiction of women compares to the common attitude toward women in Chekhov's world.

Juxtaposing new historicism with feminism could also lead us to Chekhov's relationships with women. Taking this approach, we might identify a moment in Chekhov's body of work when his portrayals of women changed from fully developed dynamic characters to the flat, static women we see in "Gooseberries." If that is the case, we could comb through Chekhov's letters and journals for evidence of a significant event such as a personal misfortune, perhaps, or a failed love affair. Alternatively, we might discover evidence that Chekhov was a forward thinking champion of women's rights, which might suggest that any negative depictions of women should be read as satire. What we want to do with any new historicist reading is uncover some new information about the author, his text or his world which will give us a fuller understanding of his work. New historicism provides us with countless avenues through which we can do that.

Once we have completed our research and formulated our thesis, we are ready to explicate our findings in a critical essay. Following the lead of Greenblatt, many early new historical analyses began with an anecdote infused with thick description. Often, it was an anecdote that seemed to bear little relevance to the issue at hand. Originally, this served two purposes: first, it helped the reader form a more complete understanding of the environment in which an author existed and, second, it illustrated the pervasiveness of the power that Foucault identified. While Greenblatt was masterful at employing the anecdote, this wasn't the case with all new historicists. Consequently, the anecdote became an object of derision for those opposed to new historicism and it became less common in new historicist analyses. Today, new historicist analyses are similar in form to those using other theoretical perspectives.

One primary difference, though, between a new historicist essay and that of another approach—aside from the content—is the new historicist's willingness to communicate his or her biases and preconceptions. Since new historicists understand recorded history as interpretations of historical events that are shaped by the various discourses described by Foucault, they recognize the need to clarify their own position. While such clarification is a necessary component of any true new historicist analysis, it is often simply a matter of the theorist acknowledging his or her research interests, identifying the motivations behind the project and outlining how it began. Once that is accomplished, the new historicist is free to follow whatever course he or she prefers.

## Important Moments in New Historicism

**1966:** Michel Foucault's *The Order of Things: An Archaeology of the Human Sciences*
**1969:** Michel Foucault's *Archaeology of Knowledge*
**1971:** Michel Foucault's "The Discourse on Language"
**1980:** Stephen Greenblatt's *Renaissance Self-Fashioning: From More to Shakespeare*
**1981:** Jonathan Goldberg's *Endlesse Worke: Spenser and the Structures of Discourse*
**1982:** Greenblatt's *The Power of Forms in the English Renaissance*

**1983:** first issue of the journal *Representations*
**1983:** Jerome J. McGann's *A Critique of Modern Textual Criticism*
**1983:** Jonathan Goldberg's *James I and the Politics of Literature: Shakespeare, Donne, and Their Contemporaries*
**1985:** Catherine Gallagher's *The Industrial Reformation of English Fiction: Social Discourse and Narrative from 1832-1867*
**1985:** Jerome J. McGann's *The Beauty of Inflections: Literary Investigations in Historical Method and Theory*
**1986:** Jonathan Goldberg's *Voice Terminal Echo: Postmodernism and English Renaissance Texts*
**1989:** Harold Aram Veeser's *The New Historicism*
**1991:** Jerome J. McGann's *The Textual Condition*
**1992:** Jonathan Goldberg's *Sodometries: Renaissance Texts, Modern Sexualities*
**1994:** Catherine Gallagher's *Nobody's Story: The Vanishing Acts of Women Writers in the Marketplace, 1670-1920*
**1996:** Louis Montrose's *The Purpose of Playing: Shakespeare and the Cultural Politics of the Elizabethan Theater*
**2001:** Stephen Greenblatt's and Catherine Gallagher's *Practicing New Historicism*
**2005:** Greenblatt's *Will in the World: How Shakespeare Became Shakespeare*
**2006:** Louis Montrose's *The Subject of Elizabeth: Authority, Gender, and Representation*

## Important Terms

| | |
|---|---|
| anecdote | context |
| discourse | power |
| text | thick description |

## Study Questions

1. Analyze a story of your choice from the perspective of new historicism and one other theoretical approach of your choice. How do the two readings compare? Which theory do you think provides the most rewarding analysis, and why? Use specific examples from the story as you develop your response.
2. In "The Story of an Hour," the narrator says,

> She knew that she would weep again when she saw the kind, tender hands folded in death; the face that had never looked save with love upon her, fixed and gray and dead. But she saw beyond that bitter moment

a long procession of years to come that would belong to her absolutely. And she opened and spread her arms out to them in welcome.

How does this passage affect the meaning of the story, and how does the context of the writer's milieu affect the meaning of this passage? Use textual and critical evidence to make your argument.
3. Compare the depiction of women in Hawthorne's "The Birthmark" and Sui Sin Far's "In the Land of the Free." To what degree are any differences the result of the time and place in which each story was written? What differences can we attribute to the gender of the authors? What else can you identify that would explain any disparity in characterization?
4. After reading either "An Occurrence at Owl Creek Bridge" or "The Yellow Wallpaper," perform some preliminary research on the story and the author to determine in which direction you would take a new historicist analysis of the piece. Would you focus primarily on the author? On his or her cultural environment? On the effect the story had on its readership and the world? Or would you pursue another avenue of interest? Explain the reasons for your decision.
5. Using a story of your choice, write a brief essay (four hundred to six hundred words) that examines some truth about the piece that you could only uncover through a new historicist reading. Perhaps you'd like to discuss the author, the setting or the narrative situation. Maybe you'd rather incorporate a feminist, Marxist or psychoanalytic perspective into your analysis. Or maybe you'd like to study the author's influences and develop an argument based upon your findings. Whatever your topic, your conclusion should be something that could not be gleaned from the story alone.

## Selected Bibliography

Bourdieu, Pierre. *The Field of Cultural Production*. New York: Columbia UP, 1993.
—. *Outline of a Theory of Practice*. Cambridge: Cambridge UP, 1977.
—. *Homo Academicus*. Palo Alto: Stanford UP, 1990.
—. *Language and Symbolic Power*. Cambridge: Harvard UP, 1999.
Dollimore, Jonathan. *Radical Tragedy: Religion, Ideology and Power in the Drama of Shakespeare and His Contemporaries*. Durham: Duke UP, 2003.
Foucault, Michel. *Archaeology of Knowledge and The Discourse on Language*. New York: Vintage, 1982.
—. *The Order of Things: An Archaeology of the Human Sciences*. New York: Vintage, 1984.
Gallagher, Catherine, and Stephen Greenblatt. *Practicing New Historicism*. Chicago: Chicago UP, 2000.

—. "Marxism and The New Historicism." *The New Historicism*. Ed. H. Aram Veeser. London: Routledge, 1989. 37-48.
Geertz, Clifford. *The Interpretation of Cultures*. New York: Basic, 1977.
—. *Local Knowledge: Further Essays In Interpretive Anthropology*. New York: Basic, 1985.
Goldberg, Jonathan. *Voice Terminal Echo: Postmodernism and English Renaissance Texts*. London: Methuen, 1986.
Greenblatt, Stephen. "Towards a Poetics of Culture." *The New Historicism*. H. Aram Veeser, ed. London: Routledge, 1989. 1-14.
—. *Hamlet in Purgatory*. Princeton: Princeton UP, 2002.
—. *Learning to Curse: Essays in Early Modern Culture*. New York: Routledge, 2007.
—. *The Power of Forms in the English Renaissance*. Ed. Stephen Greenblatt. Norman: Pilgrim, 1982.
—. *Renaissance Self-Fashioning: From More to Shakespeare*. Chicago: Chicago UP, 2005.
—. *Will in the World: How Shakespeare Became Shakespeare*. New York: Norton, 2004.
Hamilton, Paul. *Historicism: The New Critical Idiom*. New York: Routledge, 2003.
Holderness, Graham. *The Shakespeare Myth*. Manchester: Manchester UP, 1988.
Levinson, Marjorie, ed. *Rethinking Historicism*. New York: Blackwell, 1989.
McGann, Jerome. *The Beauty of Inflections: Literary Investigations in Historical Method and Theory*. Oxford: Oxford UP, 1988.
—. *A Critique of Modern Textual Criticism*. Charlottesville: Virginia UP, 1992.
—. *Historical Studies and Literary Criticism*. Madison: Wisconsin UP, 1986.
—. *Social Values and Poetic Acts: The Historical Judgment of Literary Works*. Cambridge: Harvard UP, 1988.
—. *The Textual Condition*. Princeton: Princeton UP, 1991.
Montrose, Louis A. "Professing the Renaissance: The Poetics and Politics of Culture." *The New Historicism*. Ed. H. Aram Veeser. London: Routledge, 1989. 15-36.
—. *The Purpose of Playing: Shakespeare and the Cultural Politics of the Elizabethan Theater*. Chicago: Chicago UP, 1996.
Morris, Wesley. *Toward a New Historicism*. Princeton: Princeton UP, 1972.
Veeser, Harold Aram, ed. *The New Historicism*. London: Routledge, 1989.
White, Hayden. *Metahistory: The Historical Imagination in Nineteenth-Century Europe*. Baltimore: Johns Hopkins UP, 1975.

Wicke, Jennifer A. *Advertising Fictions: Literature, Advertisement, and Social Reading*. New York: Columbia UP, 1988.

Wilson, Richard, and Richard Dutton, eds. *The New Historicism Reader*. London: Routledge, 1994.

# 10

# Postcolonialism

FOCUSES ON: the covert and the overt text, particularly with regard to themes of power in all its forms (intellectual, political, artistic, etc.) relating to citizens of present and former colonized and colonizing nations.

BECAUSE: postcolonial scholars study the numerous consequences of colonization that had been overlooked for centuries.

DEVELOPED IN: 1950s (as anti-colonialism; the term "postcolonialism" wasn't common until the 1980s).

NOTABLE PRACTITIONERS:

Kwame Nkrumah (1909-72)
Albert Memmi (1920- )
Frantz Fanon (1925-61)
Chinua Achebe (1930-2013)
Ngũgĩ wa Thiong'o (1938- )
Gareth Griffiths (1943- )
Bill Ashcroft (1946- )
Dipesh Chakrabarty (1948- )
Declan Kiberd (1951- )

Aimé Césaire (1913-2008)
Ousmane Sembène (1923-2007)
Anibal Quijano (1928- )
Edward W. Said (1935-2003)
Gayatri Chakravorty Spivak (1942- )
Helen Tiffin (1945- )
Walter Mignolo (1947- )
Homi K. Bhabha (1949- )
Elleke Boehmer (1961- )

IMPORTANT PREDECESSORS:

Antonio Gramsci (1891-1937)   Michel Foucault (1926-84)

ADVANTAGES: provides a view of a text that is different from the traditional Western perspective and illustrates how those affected by colonialism might interpret a particular literary work.

DISADVANTAGES: as postcolonial theorists tend to prioritize literature's social value, the unique literary and artistic aspects of a text can be overlooked.

DEFINITION: a method of critical analysis that focuses on the lingering economic, political and psychological issues that result from and continue after the end of a society's colonization.

Postcolonialism encompasses a variety of fields that examine the wide-ranging human consequences of the colonization of a culture or society. These consequences begin when an area is first colonized and continue long after the colonized group has attained independence.

Colonization has been a reality of civilizations throughout recorded history. The ancient Egyptians colonized southern Canaan as early as the third millennium BCE. The ancient Phoenicians, Greeks and Romans—as well as the Aztecs and Incas in Central and South America—all colonized other areas. Postcolonial theorists, though, focus on the European colonialism that began in the fifteenth century CE and spread throughout the globe. It is the remnants of these colonial expansions, they argue, that shape our world even today.

Other approaches to literature fail to account for the numerous effects of colonization. Postcolonial theorists tell us, though, that ignoring these issues often results in the marginalization of colonized and formerly colonized groups. This, in turn, leads to the perpetuation of stereotypes and patterns of prejudicial behavior. The first goal of postcolonialism, then, is to help us understand literary works from the perspective of those affected by colonialism. As postcolonialism evolves, scholars continue to discover new consequences of colonialism that affect us all.

## The Beginnings of Postcolonialism

One could argue that postcolonialism has its roots in 1890 with George Washington Williams' open letter to King Leopold of Belgium. Formally titled "An Open Letter to His Serene Majesty Léopold II, King of the Belgians and Sovereign of the Independent State of Congo," the letter exposes the atrocities committed against the Congolese people by Leopold's gendarmerie. The Congo Free State was a Belgian colony established by Leopold in order to extract ivory and rubber for his personal profit. In the process, Leopold's men enslaved everyone in the region, maintaining control by murdering millions of the area's inhabitants.

Leopold's exploitation of the Congolese peoples inspired various writers, thinkers and social reformers to compose diverse works revealing the inherent horror of colonial rule. The most recognizable of these was Joseph Conrad's *Heart of Darkness* (1899). Despite its unfortunate shortcomings (later identified by Chinua Achebe), the book nevertheless exposed Leopold's crimes to the reading public. A year later, The Reverend William Henry Sheppard, who had personally confirmed the reports of George Washington Williams, published a report in *The New York Times*. That same year, the British journalist Edmund D. Morel began writing weekly magazine articles denouncing Leopold's crimes.

The investigation of the Congo by the British diplomat Roger Casement led to the detailed Casement Report (1904). Mark Twain offered a sardonic exposition on the exploitation of the Congolese in *King Leopold's Soliloquy* (1905) and Vladimir Lenin's *Imperialism, the Highest Stage of Capitalism* (1917) argues that the horrors of colonialism are the inevitable result of capitalism.

Still, most scholars trace the beginnings of postcolonialism to the loosely defined field of anti-colonialism of the 1950s. During this time, a number of fictional and nonfictional works addressed colonialist issues. Aimé Césaire's *Discours sur le colonialisme* (1950; trans. 1972, "Discourse on Colonialism") advocates a policy of decolonization. He refutes the common Western perception that equates colonization with civilization. Césaire argues that a "civilization" that engages in colonization cannot be a moral or a healthy civilization.

Frantz Fanon's *Peau noire, masques blancs* (1952; trans. 1967, *Black Skin, White Masks*) is a scholarly examination of the psychological effects—dependence, hopelessness, self-contempt, etc.—that colonial racism has on people of color. As such, it became an influential text for both African American studies and postcolonialism. In 1959, Fanon published *L'An V de la Révolution Algérienne* (trans. 1965, *Studies in a Dying Colonialism*), a collection of essays focused on the colonial revolution in Algeria. Fanon's most recognized work, *Les Damnés de la Terre* (1961; trans. 1963, *The Wretched of the Earth*), argues that colonialism is enabled by both racial and social class prejudices. As such, he believes that colonial rule will only end through violent means, similar in many ways to the socioeconomic revolution described by Marx.

Albert Memmi's *Portrait du colonisé, précédé par Portrait du colonisateur* (1957; trans. 1965, *The Colonizer and the Colonized*) provides vivid portrayals of both colonists and their colonial subjects. His thorough descriptions were accurate enough that colonized peoples throughout the world recognized themselves in Memmi's depictions. Through his analysis, Memmi shows that these two opposed groups are interconnected in ways that previous thinkers had failed to recognize. Memmi finally concludes that the colonial system is inherently unsustainable. This led imperialists to see the book as a provocative call to arms. Many feared it would further inspire revolutionaries in the ongoing Algerian War of Independence.

Chinua Achebe's *Things Fall Apart* (1958) presents a fictionalized account of colonization from the perspective of the colonized. The book depicts the changes that take place in a fictional Nigerian village after the arrival of Christian missionaries and British colonists. Originally written in English, Achebe's acclaimed novel was one of the first texts to expose issues of colonialism to the English-speaking world.

These texts had various degrees of impact on the social and political aspects of decolonization movements throughout the world. At the time of their publication, however, they didn't significantly change the direction of literary criticism. Now, though, scholars recognize them as the earliest works of postcolonial thought.

## Voices from the Heart of Darkness

As anti-colonialism gave way to the more palatable sounding "colonialist discourse" in the sixties and seventies, the academic community gradually began to pay more attention to postcolonial issues. This was due to a number of factors. For one, new historicism's popularity and the resurgence of Marxism paved the way for any literary approach that analyzed the interrelationship between literature and culture. The increased globalization of the world, too, facilitated Western awareness of the issues facing those living in non-Western societies. It also helped that the publication of works addressing colonial issues continued throughout the sixties and seventies. Notable among these was Jean Rhys' *Wide Sargasso Sea* (1966) which, by giving voice to the "madwoman in the attic" from Charlotte Brontë's *Jane Eyre* (1847), led readers to rethink the portrayal of non-Western characters in other classic literary works. Still, most academics weren't prepared for Chinua Achebe's second Chancellor's Lecture at the University of Massachusetts in 1975.

Achebe's lecture was titled "An Image of Africa: Racism in Conrad's *Heart of Darkness*." In it, he suggests that *Heart of Darkness* (1899) is an "offensive and totally deplorable" book and that Conrad himself "was a bloody racist." Achebe offers a number of examples to make his point, beginning with the contrast between the novel's depiction of its African and its European characters. He also notes the narrator's use of language that had since been considered offensive.

To Achebe, Conrad presents Africa as an untamed hell on earth and his African characters as primitive, mysterious savages. He believes the book provides an "image of Africa as 'the other world,' the antithesis of Europe and therefore of civilization, a place where man's vaunted intelligence and refinement are finally mocked by triumphant bestiality." According to Achebe, Conrad paints his African characters as inferior to the civilized, cultured European ideal. This is important because, for many readers, the characterizations in *Heart of Darkness* are as close as they'll ever get to an actual person from Africa. Their indelible understanding of African people, then, would be shaped by Conrad's descriptions. By dehumanizing the people of Africa, Achebe argues, Conrad fosters among his Western readers a belief that Africans are somehow less human than the civilized and educated people of Europe. This belief, in turn, will inevitably lead to prejudiced behavior toward colonized peoples.

His larger argument, though, is that Western society has long overlooked the racism inherent in Conrad's novel, and similar works, because "white racism against Africa is such a normal way of thinking that its manifestations go completely undetected." While many scholars found Achebe's argument enlightening, a number of traditionalist academics reacted defensively. At the time, *Heart of Darkness* was a favored assigned text for many college professors. To them, Achebe was not only suggesting, in effect, that fans of Conrad's novel were racists, but that the way they had been reading literature was intrinsically flawed. After all, though Achebe focuses on Conrad's book in particular, the implication is that all literature in the Western canon should be examined in a similar fashion.

Part of the disagreement stemmed from the traditionalists' view (passed down from formalist approaches) that literature should be judged for its artistic merit alone, apart from any historical, political or social context. These traditionalists felt that it would be better to address Achebe's concerns in fields like sociology, philosophy or political science—anything but literature. Postcolonial theorists, though, argue that it's important to discuss such issues whenever we encounter them, regardless of the field of study. These opposing views led some to criticize what they felt was Achebe's misreading of Conrad's text. Others took umbrage at Achebe's tone (at one point, he calls attention to the racist beliefs of the noted European humanitarian, Albert Schweitzer, who unfortunately remarked, "The African is indeed my brother but my junior brother"). For the next several years, scholars vigorously debated various aspects of Achebe's lecture.

Whether one agreed or disagreed with Achebe, no one could deny that his ideas sparked discussion on the merits of colonialist discourse. However, it wasn't enough to convince many professors to adopt a colonialist approach to their study of literature. It would be a few more years before that happened.

## Edward Said and Orientalism

Most scholars identify Edward Said's third book, *Orientalism* (1978), as the text that inaugurated our modern study of postcolonialism. By the time the book was published, Said was already a prominent literary theorist. He was considered an authority on both Joseph Conrad (*Joseph Conrad and the Fiction of Autobiography*, 1966) and literary criticism (*Beginnings: Intention and Method*, 1975). In *Orientalism*, Said analyzes how the Western perception of the East and the Middle East manifests itself through our beliefs, our politics and our culture. As a Palestinian-born Christian who was educated at Princeton and Harvard, Said's distinct background provided a unique perspective on the subject.

*Orientalism* was published as rising tensions in the Arab-Israeli conflict focused renewed attention on the Middle East. This made the book a critical and commercial success. It also expanded Said's influence to other areas including history, anthropology, politics and the Middle East. Unfortunately, it also brought him virulent criticism. He received repeated death threats and his university office was burned. Because he offered an analysis of the Middle East that contrasted the one offered by Western media and politicians, his detractors argued that he supported terrorism, despite his moderate views. In spite of this, Said is credited with spurring the reevaluation of Western perceptions of the non-Western world.

Said offers two related definitions for Orientalism. In the first, he defines it as the academic study of Eastern and Middle Eastern cultures by those from the West. ("The Orient" was once a common term used to describe the vast area between eastern Asia and northern Africa.) According to Said, this study began with Napoleon's 1798 invasion of Egypt. Besides his vast military force, Napoleon brought with him 150 scientists, historians and engineers to catalog any information they could uncover regarding Egypt and its people. Thus began a trend among other European imperialists. The ultimate goal was to learn as much as possible about a country in order to defeat and control its people more efficiently.

Said also describes Orientalism as the consistent Western perception of these non-Western cultures. This perception is propagated through the media, literature, art, popular culture, political discourse, etc., and it draws a clear binary distinction between the Western world and the vastly different Eastern *Other*. Said contends that what we know about "the Orient" has been passed down from Western scholars whose understanding of the region was limited. More often than not, this understanding was also shaped by some combination of political, racial and religious bias. The problem with this (aside from lumping billions of diverse peoples into one common stereotype) is that everything we are told about the area and its people is wrong. We have been taught nothing but a recycled body of misinformation that bears little resemblance to reality. In other words, the "Orient" that we know is merely a product of the Western imagination. As such, according to Said, our perception of this area says more about ourselves than it does about the actual East and Middle East.

Said offers numerous examples of the anti-Islamic bias that permeates news reports, popular entertainment and even academic work from supposed experts. While bias in political rhetoric is expected; the same bias in academic scholarship is more pernicious, Said claims, because it is presented as factual knowledge. Thus, Said deconstructs the publications of past and present "Orientalist" scholars. Most notable among these is Said's scathing analysis of Bernard Lewis, who was then considered one of the world's foremost scholars on the Middle East. What Said finds is a troubling pattern of prejudiced representations wherein the Arab people are depicted as uncivilized, illogical, weak (yet also threatening) and inherently prone to terrorism.

Such misrepresentations are problematic, Said argues, because they perpetuate a belief in Western and European superiority in all aspects of human life. This, in turn, fosters the type of mindset that led to Western imperialism—the need for an enlightened, reasonable, and strong guiding hand to set boundaries and provide stability. Said maintains that this attitude guides our politics and foreign policy even today. To him, it's clear that the United States, for the most part, sees the Arab and Muslim people "as either oil suppliers or potential terrorists." This is because our scholars and news reporters depict them as "crude, essentialized caricatures of the Islamic world presented in such a way as to make that world vulnerable to military aggression."

Said would continue this argument throughout his career, most specifically in his next two books, *The Question of Palestine* (1979) and *Covering Islam* (1981). *The Question of Palestine* examines all aspects of the conflict in the Middle East from a Palestinian perspective. *Covering Islam*, on the other hand, focuses on the Western perception of Islam and how the West uses that perception. Said begins with Foucault's belief that knowledge is disseminated through discourse. The media outlets that control our discourse, therefore, provide us with their manufactured image of the Islamic world. When that image of Islam is used as a rhetorical device (as it often is; Said gives the example of a U.S. television commercial) the image is then proliferated and reinforced.

Said's later book, *Culture and Imperialism* (1993), is often considered his finest work of literary criticism. In it, he uses a postcolonial approach to discuss art's interrelationship with imperialism. The book draws on numerous examples of classic nineteenth- and twentieth-century European literature—Jane Austen, Joseph Conrad, Charles Dickens, etc.—as well as Verdi's opera, *Aida*, to reveal how art both reflects and reinforces (or criticizes) imperialist ideologies. Because of its thoroughness and breadth, *Culture and Imperialism* became a model for future postcolonial analyses of literature.

It would be difficult to overstate Said's influence on postcolonial studies. His body of work guided postcolonial theorists to reexamine not only the Western perceptions of the Middle East, but the Western perceptions of the entire non-Western world.

## The Silent Subaltern

As Bill Ashcroft, Gareth Griffiths and Helen Tiffin suggest, colonized people can never speak freely. Any literature written during a period of colonization was produced "on government paper with government ink and press," making it clear that it had "the aid and support of the superintendent." Because of this, colonial subjects were effectively silenced. Gayatri Chakravorty Spivak argues that similar circumstances apply even after a country's colonization has ended.

Spivak describes herself as a Marxist, a feminist and a deconstructionist. Still, she is most often associated with postcolonialism, considered one of the foremost postcolonial scholars in the world. Born in Kolkata, India, in 1942, Spivak had firsthand knowledge of India during and after the end of British colonial rule. She attended graduate school at Cornell in the U.S. and soon gained recognition in the academic community for her translation of Jacques Derrida's *De la grammatologie* (1967; trans. 1976, *Of Grammatology*). A decade later, she achieved worldwide acclaim with her theoretical essay, "Can the Subaltern Speak?" (1985).

In "Can the Subaltern Speak?" (first conceived in a 1983 lecture), Spivak discusses Michel Foucault's concept of power with regard to the subaltern. ("Subaltern" was used by Antonio Gramsci to describe the disenfranchised proletariat; Spivak's subaltern are the forgotten masses of the colonized lower class who have "limited or no access to cultural imperialism"). Disagreeing with a published conversation between Foucault and Gilles Deleuze, Spivak makes the case that the subaltern have no voice.

In short, the needs, beliefs and ideas of the subaltern are ignored because the subaltern have no power to speak. Sympathetic Westerners can't speak for the subaltern, either. Despite their good intentions, Westerners still perceive the world through the lens of imperialism and therefore can never truly understand the subaltern perspective. As proof of this, Spivak points to the British ban on *sati*. *Sati* was a traditional Indian funeral practice wherein a widow would immolate herself on her deceased husband's funeral pyre. It was banned by the British in the nineteenth century. As Spivak notes, outlawing *sati* may have saved many women's lives, but it also took from Indian widows the ability to act as they chose, rendering them powerless and silent.

Spivak further asserts that Western intellectuals are unwittingly complicit in the continued oppression of the subaltern. She argues, in effect, that even intellectual efforts to support the subaltern have the unintended consequence of classifying all subaltern peoples as one homogeneous group (a process she calls essentializing). When we essentialize these infinitely diverse individuals as one group (a group that seems to need our support and whose situation warrants our concern), it perpetuates the stereotype of all subaltern peoples as weak, ineffectual and unable to speak for themselves.

To complicate matters, this essentialism will happen even if the subaltern try to speak for themselves. Since the powerless subaltern can only be heard if they speak with a collective voice, it is impossible for them to be heard without becoming essentialized as a result. There is little hope for the subaltern, then, except for what Spivak calls "strategic essentialism," purposely essentializing one's own group when it would be politically advantageous to do so. This is a process she recommends for limited use by subaltern women, who are doubly oppressed as subaltern and as women.

## Homi K. Bhabha and Hybridity

The work of Homi K. Bhabha continues in the vein of Said and Spivak. Bhabha was born in Mumbai, India, and, like Spivak, received his early education there. He earned graduate degrees at Oxford University and taught at several prestigious universities before accepting a professorship at Harvard in 2001. Bhabha explicates his theoretical approach in numerous academic essays. That approach is shaped by a variety of influences. Aside from his postcolonial predecessors, his work also incorporates the ideas of Lacan, Marx, Bakhtin, Foucault and, in particular, Derrida.

While Bhabha is a devotee of Derrida, he opposes most binary oppositions that suggest absolute perspectives. He finds theoretical absolutes to be inadequate in real-world practice. For example, in theory, we can easily identify a binary opposition between oppressor and oppressed. In practice, however—with actual people (oppressor and oppressed)—the distinction isn't so clear. Thus, instead of "Orient and Occident," "oppressor and oppressed, centre and periphery, negative image and positive image," Bhabha sees an almost infinite array of possibilities between binary poles.

For Bhabha, these "in-between" spaces are important. They give us a place between where we can identify ourselves and understand our place in society. Part of this identification involves Bhabha's concept of hybridity. Hybridity is the blend of contradictory consciences existing within a person simultaneously. Bhabha sees this exemplified in both the colonizer and the colonized. Once a person is subject to colonial rule, he or she will unavoidably develop within himself aspects of the colonizer's identity. These aspects could include anything: styles of dress, standards of acceptable behavior, language, etc. (For Bhabha, unlike Spivak, the subaltern *can* speak, but they often do so by mimicking or parodying their oppressors.) On one hand, then, the colonized subject feels compelled to resist his imperialist oppressor while, on the other hand, he becomes more like the colonizer he opposes. The colonized will eventually become a hybrid form of who he was, combined with who his oppressor is. Once this happens, he has lost his original identity, never to regain it.

In time, the colonized will lose aspects of his pure culture (such as the *sati* practice discussed by Spivak). He will no longer be a member of his original culture and, because of his inferior status as a colonial subject, he can never be a member of the imperialist culture either. He exists in a state of "unhomeliness" between two opposing—and inaccessible—cultures. Bhabha calls this area the "Third Space of enunciation." Here, the colonized subject is left alone to determine his own unique identity.

Ironically, the colonizing imperialist experiences a similar transformation. He will take on identity traits of the colonized—habits of language, patterns of thought, etc.—(though, in his case, he often does so in an effort to rule more effectively). Still, the result is the same: a hybrid identity accompanied by a loss of culture. When both the colonized and the colonizer lose their original or "pure" culture, the hybridization of cultures becomes inevitable. The result of this is that binaries of cultural separation—Orient and Occident, Us and Them—eventually become irrelevant. As Bhabha puts it, when we explore the hybridity of ourselves and our culture, we can "elude the politics of polarity and emerge as the others of our selves." Hybridization will one day render the colonizer indistinguishable from his colonized subject.

According to Bhabha's model, then, colonization, by its very nature, is unsustainable; the colonizer cannot rule unless he has an inferior, different Other to rule over.

## The Postcolonial West

While we normally associate colonialism with the area Said describes as "The Orient," we shouldn't forget that European colonialism stretched into the Western world as well. British colonization of Ireland, for example, formally began after the conclusion of the Nine Years War (1594-1603) and continued for centuries. This led to unrest between the two countries that persisted well into the second half of the twentieth century. Postcolonial Irish theorists like Declan Kiberd argue that, while the Irish were predominantly white Christians like their English colonizers, they nevertheless suffered oppression similar to other colonial subjects.

Kiberd provides a thorough look at Ireland and Irish literature through the lens of postcolonialism in his substantial book, *Inventing Ireland* (1995). Kiberd argues that Ireland was "invented" by not only the Irish and the nostalgic Irish diaspora, but also by the colonizing English. England, according to Kiberd, used Ireland as "a foil to set off English virtues, as a laboratory in which to conduct experiments, and as a fantasy-land in which to meet fairies and monsters." Kiberd's masterful postcolonial analysis of Irish literary classics begins from this premise.

Of course, European colonialism reached across the Atlantic as well. At one time, the entire Western Hemisphere was under the control of various European governments. While North America is commonly considered outside the purview of postcolonialism, this isn't the case with Latin America. (Decolonization efforts in the U.S., for example, weren't undertaken by the indigenous population, but by descendents of the colonizing Europeans; many of the issues that would be studied by a U.S. postcolonialism are addressed in the field of Native American Studies.) While there are fields of study throughout Central and South America that resemble Native American Studies in the U.S., they are more regional in nature and not generally recognized outside of their immediate areas.

## Decoloniality

Anibal Quijano and Walter Mignolo have produced significant work on the effects of colonialism in Latin America. They often refer to their own work—especially their later work—as decolonial aesthetics, or decoloniality, rather than postcolonialism. They differentiate between the two because, in their view, decoloniality moves beyond the purely theoretical scope of postcolonialism to engage in concrete social reform. These efforts include actively supporting the rights of indigenous peoples throughout Central and South America. Still, postcolonial theorists worldwide have embraced their work and incorporated it into the body of postcolonial thought.

Quijano, a sociologist from Peru, illustrates the effects of colonialism from a sociological perspective with his concept of the "coloniality of power." Coloniality of power describes the structures of social hierarchy that result from colonialism and continue long after colonization has officially ended. Indigenous peoples across the globe most commonly determined social hierarchy according to gender—with males often considered dominant. Colonialism changed that. With colonialism, phenotypic (or physical) differences such as skin color became the primary determinant of social dominance. As Quijano notes, "race and racial identity were established as instruments of basic social classification." Colonialism also brought about hierarchical divisions along economic lines—based upon the Eurocentric capitalist model. Thus, the social order in a colonized area began with the European colonizer at the top. Below this were those who looked or acted most like—or were most helpful to—the imperialists. At the bottom were the indigenous peoples who looked and acted least like—and had no interest in acquiescing to—their European colonizers.

Even after the period of colonization ended, according to Quijano, these same hierarchal structures continued. Indeed, this hierarchical dynamic facilitated the abuse of the indigenous Putumayo people of Peru by the Peruvian Amazon Company. The Peruvian Amazon Company enslaved and tortured the Putumayo to extract rubber from Peru's rainforest. Roger Casement, author of the Casement Report detailing the cruelty in the Congo Free State, found that the abuse of the Putumayo was as bad as that suffered by the Congolese. While the Peruvian Amazon Company had a British board of directors, it was presided over by Julio César Arana, a Peruvian industrialist who would later become a successful politician. According to Quijano, such an outcome is the inevitable consequence of colonialism.

Walter Mignolo, from Argentina, incorporates Quijano's coloniality of power in his own decolonial and postcolonial studies. In contrast to Quijano, Mignolo's approach is decidedly literary. This is due to his background in literary theory and semiotics. Mignolo's approach begins by looking at colonialism from a historical perspective. He sees the roots of colonialism in the European Renaissance that began in the fourteenth century. Advancements in art, science and the humanities fostered a belief in the superiority of all aspects of European life. This hubris led to a sense of entitlement with regard to the "undeveloped" and "uncivilized" areas of the world. In addition, the papal bull *Dum Diversas* (1452), issued by Pope Nicholas V, gave Portugal the divine authority to invade western Africa and to enslave all "[Muslims], pagans and any other unbelievers."

Colonialism soon became a competition between European powers to control the largest possible share of the globe and reshape it in their own image. Ignored in all of this, of course, were the subjugated masses under colonial control. Before colonialism, each of these areas had their own systems of government, economics and education, as well as their own religions, languages and worldviews. European colonists replaced these various indigenous systems and beliefs with their own modern European versions, which they believed were better. Eventually, Eurocentrism became dominant throughout the world.

As Mignolo reminds us, nearly every aspect of our lives today is based upon a Eurocentric model. This includes our literary theory (even postcolonialism). Mignolo believes that we need a new paradigm for reading literature—and understanding the world—that isn't derived from Eurocentrism. Decolonialists want us to recognize and accept non-Eurocentric methods of discourse. In other words, they believe we need to decolonize our knowledge as well as our lands and our resources. Only then will we truly be able to understand literature from a postcolonial perspective.

## Implementation

Probably the most widely recognized postcolonial analysis of a literary work is Chinua Achebe's reading of *Heart of Darkness* by Joseph Conrad. In it, Achebe highlights aspects of Conrad's text that readers had long overlooked or ignored, namely its offhand depictions of the African characters as uncivilized, savage and subhuman. When we undertake a postcolonial analysis, we examine the overt and covert text for evidence of prejudicial attitudes toward colonized peoples. With a story like Rudyard Kipling's "Lispeth," for example, we could begin by examining Kipling's depictions of his characters.

One approach would be to undertake this step systematically, underlining every instance of characterization in the text. Early in the story, the descriptions seem innocuous. The protagonist, an indigenous "Hill girl" from India, is described as "lovely," with a "Greek face" and "pale, ivory" skin and, "for her race, extremely tall." Later, the narrator makes reference to her "uncivilized Eastern instincts," noting that she is "a savage by birth." The Chaplain's wife refers to her repeatedly as a "heathen" and an "infidel." By the end of the story, Lispeth has become a "bleared, winkled creature, so like a wisp of charred rag."

Defenders of Kipling would acknowledge these racist undertones in the story. But they would point out that it is the white English characters—the Chaplain's wife and the traveling Englishman—who the narrator presents as deceitful, hypocritical, insensitive, petty and superficial. They would argue, then, that Kipling's story demonstrates a favorable attitude toward India's colonized subjects.

The postcolonial response to such an argument would be that, while the Englishman and the Chaplain's wife are presented unfavorably, they are nevertheless presented as civilized, intelligent and educated. A postcolonial reading would also note that Lispeth's innocence further underscores her lack of development as a human being. After all, the superficiality that the Chaplain's wife exhibits is a decidedly human behavior. The innocence of Lispeth isn't characteristic of a sophisticated woman, but of an untrained animal that is incapable of such machinations.

Throughout the story, in fact, Lispeth is presented as subhuman. Kipling repeatedly differentiates her from the average English woman. Lispeth is strong enough to carry a grown man for miles; she doesn't "walk in the manner of English ladies"; she acts on impulse and instinct, rather than logic and reason; she has no concept of impropriety, seeing no need to hide her feelings; and she has no chance to marry an Englishman because the English are "of superior clay."

Kipling's narrator implies, too, that Lispeth's beauty comes from her English and Christian upbringing. Early in the story, the narrator tells us, "Whether Christianity improved Lispeth, or whether the gods of her own people would have done as much for her under any circumstances, I do not know; but she grew very lovely." This question is answered before the story ends: "She [Lispeth] took to her own unclean people savagely [. . .] in a little time, she married a wood-cutter who beat her, after the manner of paharis, and her beauty faded soon."

It is not just Lispeth, though, but all "Hill people" that Kipling depicts as lesser forms of human. For the narrator, a beautiful young woman from Lispeth's locale "is worth traveling fifty miles over bad ground to look upon." The implication, of course, is that most young women from this area are unattractive. Kipling's Hill people are "unclean," "infamously dirty," and jealous of Lispeth because she had "become a memsahib and washed herself daily."

The casual manner with which the narrator presents such depictions repeatedly throughout the story suggests that the author shares these views. Reading "Lispeth" from a postcolonial perspective would almost certainly lead us to conclude that Kipling harbors an obvious disdain for the indigenous peoples of India. A postcolonial reading, then, not only illustrates how the victims of colonization understand literature and the world, but how others view these colonized subjects.

## Important Moments in Postcolonialism

- **1890:** George Washington Williams' open letter to Leopold II of Belgium
- **1905:** Mark Twain's "King Leopold's Soliloquy"
- **1917:** Vladimir Lenin's *Imperialism, the Highest Stage of Capitalism*
- **1950:** Aimé Césaire's "Discourses on Colonialism"
- **1952:** Frantz Fanon's *Black Skin, White Masks*
- **1957:** Albert Memmi's *The Colonizer and the Colonized*
- **1958:** Chinua Achebe's *Things Fall Apart*
- **1961:** Fanon's *The Wretched of the Earth*
- **1966:** Jean Rhys' *Wide Sargasso Sea*
- **1975:** Chinua Achebe's lecture "An Image of Africa: Racism in Conrad's *Heart of Darkness*"
- **1977:** Syed Hussein Alatas' *The Myth of the Lazy Native*
- **1978:** Edward Said's *Orientalism*
- **1983:** Ashis Nandy's *The Intimate Enemy*
- **1985:** Gayatri Chakravorty Spivak's "Can the Subaltern Speak?"
- **1986:** Ngũgĩ wa Thion'o's *Decolonising the Mind*
- **1988:** David Cairns' and Shaun Richards' *Writing Ireland*
- **1989:** Homi K. Bhabha's "The Commitment to Theory"
- **1992:** Walter Mignolo's "The Darker Side of the Renaissance"
- **1993:** Said's *Culture and Imperialism*
- **1994:** Bhabha's *The Location of Culture*
- **1995:** Declan Kiberd's *Inventing Ireland*
- **1999:** Mignolo's *Local Histories/Global Designs*
- **2000:** Anibal Quijano's "Coloniality of Power"
- **2011:** Mignolo's *The Darker Side of Western Modernity*

## Important Terms

colonialism
decolonization
essentialism
imperialism
marginalization
Othering
power
unhomeliness

coloniality of power
double consciousness
hybridity
in-betweenness
neocolonialism
postcolonialism
subaltern

## Study Questions

1. A postcolonial reading will be most fruitful on those texts that are set in, or include characters from, colonized or formerly colonized areas. Identify five stories that you think would provide a productive postcolonial reading. Discuss why you chose each of these texts.
2. Perform a postcolonial analysis on one of the texts you selected in the previous question.
3. Edward Said has two primary definitions for Orientalism. In one, Orientalism is the Western perception of non-Western cultures, disseminated through Western art, media, popular culture, etc. Find five examples of literature, movies or works of art that perpetuate a simplified understanding of a non-Western culture. What stereotypes do these works generate? Do you think the stereotypes are accurate? Why or why not?
4. When a student leaves home to attend college, he or she experiences some of the same effects described by Homi Bhabha's hybridity. What are these similarities? What are the differences? Describe how the life of a new college student can help us better understand, in these terms, the experience of someone subjected to colonial rule.
5. In "Lispeth," after Lispeth placed the injured Englishman on the sofa, she told the Chaplain's wife, "This is my husband. I found him on the Bagi Road. He has hurt himself. We will nurse him, and when he is well, your husband shall marry him to me." In a brief essay (five hundred to eight hundred words), explain (from a postcolonial perspective) why the Chaplain's wife "shrieked with horror" in response.

## Selected Bibliography

Achebe, Chinua. *Hopes and Impediments: Selected Essays*. New York: Anchor, 1990.
—. *Things Fall Apart*. New York: Anchor, 1994.

Alatas, Syed Hussein. *The Myth of the Lazy Native: A Study of the Image of the Malays, Filipinos and Javanese from the 16th to the 20th Century and Its Function in the Ideology of Colonial Capitalism.* New York: Routledge, 2010.
Anderson, Benedict. *Imagined Communities: Reflections on the Origin and Spread of Nationalism.* London: Verso, 2006.
Ankerl, Guy. *Coexisting Contemporary Civilizations: Arabo-Muslim, Bharati, Chinese and Western.* Geneva: INU Press.
Ashcroft, Bill, Gareth Griffiths and Helen Tiffin. *Key Concepts in Post-Colonial Studies.* New York: Routledge, 1998.
—. *The Empire Writes Back: Theory and Practice in Post-Colonial Literature.* New York: Routledge, 2000.
Ashcroft, Bill, Gareth Griffiths and Helen Tiffin, eds. *The Post-Colonial Studies Reader.* London: Routledge, 1995.
Amin, Samir. *L'eurocentrisme: Critique d'une idéologie.* Paris: Anthropos, 1988.
Balagangadhara, S. N., *"The Heathen in his Blindness...": Asia, the West, and the Dynamic of Religion.* Boston: Brill, 1994.
Bhabha, Homi K. *The Location of Culture.* New York: Routledge, 2004.
—. *Nation and Narration.* New York: Routledge, 1990.
Cairns, David, and Shaun Richards. *Writing Ireland: Colonialism, Nationalism, and Culture.* New York: Macmillan, 1988.
Césaire, Aimé. *Discourse on Colonialism.* New York: Monthly Review, 2001.
Chambers, Iain, and Lidia Curti, eds. *The Post-Colonial Question: Common Skies, Divided Horizons.* New York: Routledge, 1996.
Chatterjee, Partha. *The Nation and its Fragments: Colonial and Postcolonial Histories.* Princeton: Princeton UP, 1993.
Dabashi, Hamid. *Iran: A People Interrupted.* New York: The New Press, 2008.
Dean, Bartholomew Crispin, and Jerome Meyer Levi, eds. *At the Risk of Being Heard: Indigenous Rights, Identity, and Postcolonial States.* Ann Arbor: Michigan UP, 2003.
Fanon, Frantz. *Black Skin, White Masks.* New York: Grove, 2008.
—. *The Wretched of the Earth.* New York: Grove, 2005.
Foucault, Michel. *Language, Counter-Memory, Practice: Selected Essays and Interviews.* Ithaca: Cornell UP, 1980.
Gandhi, Leela. *Postcolonial Theory: A Critical Introduction.* New York: Columbia UP: 1998.
Guevara, Ernesto. *Colonialism is Doomed.* Havana: Cuban Ministry of External Relations, 1965.
Hashmi, Alamgir. *The Commonwealth, Comparative Literature and the World: Two Lectures.* Islamabad: Gulmohar, 1988.
Hountondji, Paulin J. *African Philosophy: Myth & Reality.* Bloomington: Indiana UP, 1986.

Janmohamed, Abdul R. *Manichean Aesthetics: The Politics of Literature in Colonial Africa*. Amherst: Massachusetts UP, 1983.
Kiberd, Declan. *Inventing Ireland*. Cambridge: Harvard UP, 1997.
Lenin, Vladimir Ilyich. *Imperialism, the Highest Stage of Capitalism*. Eastford, CT: Martino, 2011.
Mannoni, Octave. *Prospero and Caliban: The Psychology of Colonization*. Ann Arbor: Michigan UP, 1991.
Mbembe, Achille. *On the Postcolony*. Berkeley: California UP, 2001.
Memmi, Albert. *The Colonizer and the Colonized*. Boston: Beacon, 1991.
Mignolo, Walter D. *The Darker Side of the Renaissance: Literacy, Territoriality, & Colonization*. Ann Arbor: Michigan UP, 2003.
—. *The Darker Side of Western Modernity: Global Futures, Decolonial Options*. Durham: Duke UP, 2011.
—. *The Idea of Latin America*. New York: Wiley, 1991.
—. *Local Histories/Global Designs: Coloniality, Subaltern Knowledges, and Border Thinking*. Princeton: Princeton UP, 2012.
Mignolo, Walter D., and Árturo Escobar, eds. *Globalization and the Decolonial Option*. New York: Routledge, 2009.
Mudimbe, V.Y. *The Invention of Africa: Gnosis, Philosophy, and the Order of Knowledge*. Bloomington: Indiana UP, 1988.
Nandy, Ashis. *The Intimate Enemy: Loss and Recovery of Self Under Colonialism*. Oxford: Oxford UP, 2010.
—. *Regimes of Narcissism, Regimes of Despair*. Oxford: Oxford UP, 2013.
—. *Traditions, Tyranny, and Utopias: Essays in the Politics of Awareness*. Oxford: Oxford UP, 1993.
Quijano, Anibal. "*Colonialidad del Poder, Cultura y Conocimiento en América Latina.*" *Disposito* 24.51 (1999). 137-48.
—. "Coloniality of Power, Eurocentrism, and Latin America." Trans. Michael Ennis. *Nepantla: Views from South* 1.3 (2000). 533-80.
—. *Modernidad, identidad y utopia en America Latina*. Quito, Ecuador: El Conejo, 1990.
—. *Nationalism and Capitalism in Peru: A Study in Neo-Imperialism*. Trans. Helen R. Lane. New York: Monthly Review Press, 1972.
Retamar, Roberto Fernández. *Caliban and Other Essays*. Minneapolis: Minnesota UP, 1989.
Said, Edward Wadie. *Beginnings: Intention and Method*. New York: Columbia UP, 1985.
—. *Covering Islam: How the Media and the Experts Determine How We See the Rest of the World*. New York: Vintage, 1997.
—. *Culture and Imperialism*. New York: Vintage, 1994.
—. "Nationalism, Colonialism, and Literature: Yeats and Decolonization." Dublin: Field Day, 1988.
—. *Orientalism*. New York: Vintage, 1979.
—. *The Question of Palestine*. New York: Vintage, 1992.

—. *The World, the Text, and the Critic.* Cambridge: Harvard UP, 1983.
Singh, Amritjit, and Peter Schmidt, eds. *Postcolonial Theory and the United States: Race, Ethnicity, and Literature.* Oxford: Mississippi UP, 2000.
Spivak, Gayatri Chakravorty. *A Critique of Postcolonial Reason: Toward a History of the Vanishing Present.* Cambridge: Harvard UP, 1999.
—. "Can the Subaltern Speak? Speculations on Widow-Sacrifice." *Wedge* 7/8 (Winter/Spring 1985). 120-30.
—. *The Postcolonial Critic: Interviews, Strategies, Dialogues.* New York: Routledge, 1990.
—. *Selected Subaltern Studies.* Oxford: Oxford UP, 1988.
Thion'o, Ngũgĩ wa. *Decolonising the Mind: The Politics of Language in African Literature.* Melton, Suffolk, UK: James Currey, 2011.
—. *In the Name of the Mother: Reflections on Writers and Empire.* Melton, Suffolk, UK: James Currey, 2013.

# 11

# Ethnic Studies

Ethnic literary criticism is a branch of the interdisciplinary field of Ethnic Studies and it includes African American, Asian American, Latina/o, and Native American criticism. America has a long history of outstanding literature produced by writers of non-European descent. Many of those works, however, were initially ignored or considered unworthy of academic consideration. On those rare occasions when a work by a non-white author was taken seriously, it was analyzed from the traditional Eurocentric perspective. As a result, even those works that did receive scholarly attention were often misunderstood and unappreciated because they didn't conform to traditional expectations of "quality" literature.

This began to change in the 1960s. In the wake of the Civil Rights Movement and the growing American counterculture, people started to note that Americans of European heritage were disproportionately represented in all fields of academic study. In history, science, art and literature, the contributions of people of color were either treated dismissively or overlooked entirely. Dissatisfaction with education's Eurocentric myopia gained wide attention with the East L.A. Blowouts in March, 1968. Over fifteen thousand students from predominantly Latina/o high schools in Los Angeles participated in mass walkouts to protest the Anglocentric focus of the Los Angeles school system.

In the fall of the same year, college students organized a similar strike at San Francisco State College (now San Francisco State University). This strike was organized by the Black Students Union and the Third World Liberation Front, a coalition of ethnic student groups that included the Asian American Political Alliance, the Latin American Students Organization, the Native American Students Union, the Philippine-American Collegiate Endeavor, and *El Renacimiento* (the Renaissance, an Hispanic student organization). It would become the longest student strike in U.S. history. The striking students presented the administrators with a list of fifteen demands that included the reinstatement of George Murray, a suspended English instructor; the development of an ethnic studies department; the implementation of an enrollment policy that admitted more ethnic students; and the hiring of a more ethnically diverse faculty.

In the midst of the SFSC strike, the TWLF branch at Cal-Berkeley began its own strike on January 22, 1969. The demands of the Berkeley protesters were similar to those at SFSC. On March 7, 1969, administrators at Cal-Berkeley officially established its Department of Ethnic Studies, the first of its kind in the country. The SFSC strike ended on March 21, and ushered in SFSC's College of Ethnic Studies. Gradually, other colleges followed suit. Within ten years, ethnic studies courses were offered at over four hundred colleges across the country.

The aim of ethnic studies programs is to increase our understanding of racialized groups in today's world. This includes recognizing the past contributions and struggles of people of color as well as appreciating our modern world from a non-Eurocentric perspective. Consequently, such departments include a variety of fields such as history, political science, media, gender, art and literature. Out of this arose a more structured body of ethnic literary criticism.

As ethnic groups in America face many of the same issues as the subaltern of postcolonial areas, America's ethnic criticisms share many similarities and concepts not only with each other, but also with postcolonial theory. Still, each have grown out of their own individual traditions with unique beliefs and diverse expectations and challenges. Ethnic literary criticism seeks to develop a process wherein literature is analyzed and understood from these unique perspectives. As is the case with many other approaches to literature, there has been some debate about the best way to accomplish that.

## AFRICAN AMERICAN CRITICISM

**FOCUSES ON:** the covert and the overt text, as well as historical and biographical information, as it relates to works by or about African Americans.

**BECAUSE:** African American criticism is interested in the depictions of African Americans and how those depictions speak to, shape and reflect the African American experience.

**DEVELOPED IN:** 1960s.

**NOTABLE PRACTITIONERS:**
Sterling Allen Brown (1901-89)
Toni Morrison (1931- )
Amiri Baraka (1934- )
Maya Angelou (1928-2014 )
Michael Cooke (1934-90)
Wole Soyinka (1934- )

Sonia Sanchez (1934- )          Maulana Karenga (1941- )
Wilson J. Moses (1942- )        Houston A. Baker, Jr. (1943- )
Barbara Christian (1943- )      Werner Sollors (1943- )
Alice Walker (1944- )           Barbara Smith (1946- )
Hazel V. Carby (1948- )         Henry Louis Gates, Jr. (1950- )
Robert B. Stepto (1950- )       Dexter Fisher
Deborah E. McDowell (1951- )    bell hooks (1952- )
Rita Dove (1952- )              Cornel West (1953- )
Anthony Appiah (1954- )         Chinua Achebe (1930-2013)

**IMPORTANT PREDECESSORS:**
Jupiter Hammon (1711-1806)      Ignatius Sancho (1729-1780)
Olaudah Equiano (1745-97)       Phillis Wheatley (1753-84)
Harriet Ann Jacobs (1813-97)    William Wells Brown (1814-84)
Frederick Douglass (1818-95)    Alexander Crummell (1819-98)
Harriet E. Wilson (1825-1900)   George Washington Williams (1849-91)
Booker T. Washington (1856-1915) W.E.B. Du Bois (1868-1963)
Carter G. Woodson (1875-1950)   Alain LeRoy Locke (1885-1954)
Zora Neale Hurston (1891-1960)  Jean Toomer (1894-1967)
Langston Hughes (1902-67)       Richard Wright (1908-1960)
Ralph Ellison (1914-94)         James Baldwin (1924-87)
Frantz Fanon (1925-61)          Lorraine Hansberry (1930-65)

**ADVANTAGES:** allows literature by or about African Americans to be analyzed on its own terms, rather than through the traditional Eurocentric perspective.

**DISADVANTAGES:** as Henry Louis Gates, Jr. notes, any theoretical approach that focuses on race or ethnicity has the potential to essentialize that group and thus perpetuate a belief in genetic racial or ethnic differences.

**DEFINITION:** a method of literary analysis that examines works written by or about African Americans, analyzing the depictions of African Americans and the effects of those depictions on the African American community.

---

Of all the ethnic approaches to literature, African American criticism is the most recognizable. This is due in part to the long, vibrant history of African American literature that dates back to America's colonial period.

In 1760, Jupiter Hammon became the first African American to be published in the U.S. with his poem, "An Evening Thought: Salvation by Christ with Penitential Cries." Phillis Wheatley's *Poems on Various Subjects, Religious and Moral* (1773) was the first full book to be published by an African American. African American publications increased in the nineteenth century with writers such as Frederick

Douglass, William Wells Brown, Harriet Wilson, Harriet Jacobs and George Washington Williams.

The twentieth century saw publications from African American writers increase exponentially during the Harlem Renaissance of the 1920s and 1930s and again during the civil rights era of the 1940s and 1950s. Works by African American writers gradually gained notice from the literary establishment (though these works were still being analyzed from a Eurocentric perspective). Gwendolyn Brooks was the first African American to win the Pulitzer Prize with her poetry collection, *Annie Allen* (1949). Ralph Ellison won the National Book Award for his novel, *Invisible Man* (1952). By 1969, when the first school of ethnic studies had been established at San Francisco State College, the body of African American literature had been established.

## W.E.B. Du Bois

African American literary criticism has a long history as well. While such work didn't coalesce into a structured body of criticism until the 1960s, discussions concerning the direction of African American literature had been ongoing for several decades. A notable contributor in this regard was W.E.B. Du Bois. Du Bois was one of the preeminent African American thinkers of the early twentieth century. The first African American to earn a Ph.D. from Harvard, Du Bois would go on to help found the NAACP as well as the Niagara Movement, a group that worked for equal rights for African Americans.

Du Bois is perhaps best known today for his collection of essays, *The Souls of Black Folk* (1903). The book examines African American life at the turn of the century from a historical and a sociological perspective. Du Bois saw a classical education as the best avenue toward equality with white people. As such, he offers a pointed critique of Booker T. Washington and the "Atlanta Compromise," which he saw as Washington's conciliatory approach toward racial injustice. While *The Souls of Black Folk* doesn't address literature and literary criticism directly, it does discuss the issues that African American writers would face throughout the twentieth century. This includes Du Bois' concept of the African American's double consciousness.

Similar to Homi Bhabha's later concept of hybridity, Du Bois' double consciousness describes how African Americans navigate through white America behind a veil that hides their true selves. As a result, African Americans unavoidably develop a double consciousness—one that allows them to survive in a white world and another that more closely resembles their true selves. Du Bois describes it as a "second-sight in this American world,—a world which yields him no true self-consciousness, but only lets him see himself through the revelation of the other world." It gives all African Americans the peculiar feeling of always "measuring one's soul by the tape of a world that looks on in amused contempt and pity." Du Bois concludes that "To be a poor man is hard, but to be a poor race in a land of dollars is the very bottom of hardships."

## The Role of African American Literature

Du Bois moved closer to literary criticism with an article in the *Los Angeles Times*, "A Negro Art Renaissance" (1925). In it, he predicted a burgeoning output of African American literature. His prediction was accurate. The Harlem Renaissance of the 1920s and 1930s produced a prolific body of work that shaped art, literature and music throughout the twentieth century.

In 1926, the official journal of the NAACP, *The Crisis*, published a seven-volume symposium entitled *The Negro in Art: How Shall He Be Portrayed?* Perhaps the best remembered of these symposium pieces is Du Bois' essay, "Criteria of Negro Art." In it, he outlines his suggestions for African American art and literature. Most notable among these is Du Bois' belief that African American art and literature should present African Americans in the best possible light. Doing so, he felt, would make the transition toward equality more palatable for white Americans. Once white America is able to accept the idea of equality, Du Bois believed, then it would be much easier to move in that direction.

Not everyone agreed. Richard Wright, for example, felt that literature should accurately depict the reality of the African American experience. Only by truthfully portraying all aspects of African American life—even its darkest aspects—could one fulfill the artistic endeavor of literature. Similar debates continued throughout the Harlem Renaissance and well into the 1960s.

## The Stages of African American Literature

One benefit of establishing ethnic studies programs in colleges across the country is that it affords professors the opportunity to engage in ethnic studies research that they wouldn't otherwise have the time or inclination to engage in. The result was a greater body of work related to ethnic studies that began to appear in the 1970s and 1980s. One such project was Michael G. Cooke's *Afro-American Literature in the Twentieth Century* (1984). Cooke analyzes the development of twentieth century African American literature from a historical perspective.

Cooke identifies four stages of African American literature in the twentieth century. The "self-veiling" stage, borrowing Du Bois' metaphor, is characterized by literature that is written to be indistinguishable from the work of white authors. According to Cooke, writers like James Weldon Johnson, Charles Chesnutt and Nella Larsen wrote with the understanding that their work had to imitate the white authors of the time in order to be published.

In Cooke's second stage, "solitude," writers like Zora Neale Hurston, Richard Wright and Ralph Ellison worried less about hiding behind a figurative veil and focused on their own self-realization. For many, this happens in a way similar to the discovery made by Ellison's invisible man by the end of his narration, or Hurston's Janie, who first realizes she is black as she examines a photograph of her class.

In contrast to the "self-veiling" stage, the literature of the "kinship" stage is characterized by language, dialect and literary devices that are unique to African American literature. Cooke sees this differentiation as a means to identify oneself in an effort to connect with a community of likeminded people. For Cooke, this is exemplified in the poetry of Michael Harper and the essays of Eldridge Cleaver.

Cooke's final stage, "intimacy," is marked by the freedom to write in whatever way best suits the writer's needs. No longer must an African American author writer as if he or she were white ("self-veiling"), or as a means to clearly represent the African American community. In the "intimacy" stage, the author can utilize any literary models that suit his or her purposes, regardless of any unspoken racial implications. Cooke sees this stage clearly represented in the work of Robert Hayden and Alice Walker.

For Cooke, the significance of these literary stages lies in the fact that each progressing stage reflects the state of affairs of the African American population. The "self-veiling" stage took place while African Americans lived, as Du Bois noted, behind a veil that hid their double consciousness. The literary stage of "solitude" coincided with the African American search for identity, just as the "kinship" stage developed during the organizational movements of the Civil Rights era and the stage of "intimacy" paralleled the empowerment of a new generation born after the end of government-sanctioned segregation. Cooke sees African American literature, in other words, as intertwined with the African American experience.

## Signifyin(g)

Students who are new to ethnic criticism might wonder why we should want to read from a particular ethnic perspective. How is such a reading different from the way we normally read? Henry Louis Gates, Jr. provides an answer to such questions in his pioneering study, *The Signifying Monkey* (1988).

Gates takes the title of his book from a popular character of African American folk tales. The signifying monkey is a trickster character drawn from Esu-Elegbara, a deity in the Yoruba religion of Africa. In most of his stories, the signifying monkey creates some type of discord between a lion and an elephant through duplicitous conversations with each of them. It is these duplicitous dialogues that form the basis of Gates' concept of signifyin(g). Drawing on his studies of both structuralism and post-structuralism, Gates sees signifyin(g) as language in which "the sign itself appears to be doubled [but] only the signifier has been doubled and (re)doubled, a signifier in this instance that is silent, [...] a 'sound-image' *sans* the sound."

In its simplest terms, signifyin(g) is the art of saying one thing while meaning another. A familiar example would be when someone insults another person while pretending to compliment that person to a third party (who recognizes the insult). As Gates notes, signifyin(g) was common among African American slaves. While they needed to maintain an outward appearance of obedience, they could still communicate their true feelings through signifyin(g) linguistic practices.

In literature, of course, signifyin(g) can take on more complex forms. By the twentieth century, signifyin(g) had developed into a common trope in African American literature. Gates provides numerous examples where it manifests itself "as explicit theme, as implicit rhetorical strategy, and as a principle of literary history." Ralph Ellison, for example, in his novel, *Invisible Man*, signifies on Richard Wright's novel *Native Son*. As Gates notes, Ellison disagreed with Wright about the best way to convey, in literature, the African American experience. Wright employed the pessimistic realism of the naturalism movement while Ellison preferred the literary devices of the modern period. According to Gates, Ellison subtly expresses this disagreement in his novel with his title (*son* vs. *man*), his characterization, and his plot development. Then, a generation later, Ishmael Reed "successfully critiques both realism and modernism" by signifyin(g) on both Wright and Ellison, as well as Zora Neale Hurston, James Baldwin and others. African American writers have repeated this pattern throughout the twentieth century.

Gates argues that this tradition of signifyin(g) is an important element of African American literature and it needs to be recognized and understood in order to fully appreciate works by African American writers. A traditional Eurocentric reading will overlook such nuance and betray a "tone deafness to the black cultural voice." When we apply a more sophisticated reading to African American literature, based on an African American perspective, we realize that many of these overlooked works are worthy of inclusion in the Western canon.

## Reconsidering the Canon

For Gates, inclusion in the *Western* canon is essential. Because of the uniqueness of African American literature, some scholars argued for a separatist Afrocentric education to counterbalance education's longstanding Eurocentric bias. As part of these efforts, a push was made to develop a literary canon consisting solely of writers of African descent. Some proponents of Afrocentricity further argued that these literary works should be taught by African and African American professors. One goal of Afrocentricity was to empower Africans and the African diaspora with the self-awareness to recognize that racial differences are not biologically determined but, instead, have been socially constructed through centuries of Eurocentric dominance of thought.

Molefi Asante defines Afrocentricity as "a mode of thought and action in which the centrality of African interests, values, and perspectives predominate. [. . .] it is the placing of African people in the center of any analysis of African phenomena." According to Wilson J. Moses, Afrocentricity emanated from the work of Melville J. Herskovits in the 1930s. Herskovits was an anthropologist who gained distinction as one of the first white scholars to study Africa and the African diaspora from a non-Eurocentric perspective. He also established America's first African Studies program at Northwestern University in 1948. Afrocentricity gained wider notice in the 1980s, due in large part to the work of Molefi Asante. Asante's *Afrocentricity* (1980) and *The Afrocentric Idea* (1987) helped elucidate Afrocentricity for those unfamiliar with its ideas. In short, Afrocentric studies seek to end the marginalization and misrepresentation of African peoples and their descendents. It does this by presenting the culture and history of Africa and the African diaspora from an Afrocentric perspective.

While it's easy to see the merit in Afrocentricity's goals, Gates suggests that such efforts are ultimately counterproductive. Gates believes that scholarly interest and expertise shouldn't be determined by one's race. For him, Afrocentricity's insistence that only black scholars should teach African and African American literature is "as ridiculous as if someone said I couldn't appreciate Shakespeare because I'm not Anglo-Saxon." Such restrictions not only exclude many potential scholars and researchers, but they also limit the reach of the literary works that Afrocentric theorists champion.

A more pervasive problem, perhaps, is that Afrocentric studies inevitably draw a demarcation between the Eurocentric white male and the essentialized Other. Just as Gayatri Spivak notes with regard to the subaltern of postcolonial areas, even the most well-intentioned efforts to unite a group based on race or ethnicity can essentialize that group. Essentialism, in turn, paves the way for the continuation of unfavorable racial comparisons in the form of racist attitudes and beliefs.

But Afrocentricity isn't the only approach that can lead to essentialism. Indeed, essentialism can become a very real consequence of any ethnic study. As Gates notes, when we try to use "*race* as a term for an essence, as did the Negritude movement, for example [. . .], we yield too much, such as the basis of a shared humanity." For Gates, the best approach is to use Derrida's concept of speaking "'the other's language without renouncing our own.'" In other words, we should use "the most sophisticated critical theories and methods generated by the Western tradition to reappropriate and to define our own 'colonial' discourses."

Many scholars today find it important to balance the need for African American studies with the understanding that such work can lead to essentialism. For Gates, the answer is to broaden our criteria for inclusion in a Western canon that becomes more accessible for writers of non-European descent. This allows us to read these works on their own terms, acknowledging their difference while recognizing their equal worth.

## Contemporary African American Criticism

While Gates' work is perhaps the most recognized among contemporary African American literary theorists, several other scholars continue to make significant contributions in the field as well. Barbara Christian, Deborah E. McDowell and Mary Helen Washington approach African American criticism from a feminist perspective. Each highlights in her own way the unique challenges African American women face, including the problems associated with being doubly marginalized as African Americans and as women.

Houston A. Baker, Jr. examines African American literary works in their historical context and traces the aesthetic development of African American literature through history. In the 1980s, he engaged Gates in an ongoing dialogue regarding the best direction of African American literary criticism. Baker argued for a more Marxist approach. He felt that a text's social and historical context were necessary considerations in any critique of African American literature. Gates preferred a more traditional approach that kept the majority of focus on the text. Literary scholars in all fields followed their discussion. As the debate continued into the next decade, both Baker and Gates gradually moved closer to each other's position.

Other African American theorists focus on the representation of African Americans in the works of white authors, in much the same way that Chinua Achebe approached Conrad's *Heart of Darkness*. A notable work in this vein is Toni Morrison's *Playing in the Dark: Whiteness and the Literary Imagination* (1992). Morrison argues that the mere presence of African Americans in the U.S. has distinctively shaped

America's literary canon. As she puts it, the "championed characteristics" of American literature ("individualism, masculinity, social engagement versus historical isolation," etc.) developed in response to "a dark, abiding, signing Africanist presence." She illustrates this in her explication of works by Poe, Twain, Cather, Hemingway and others. Through her analysis, she shows that the American literary canon should logically include works by African Americans.

Today, scholars can focus their criticism in any direction they wish. Because of this, African American criticism has grown into a wide-ranging field, analyzing innumerable aspects of literature by or about African Americans.

## Important Moments in African American Criticism

- **1760:** Jupiter Hammon's "An Evening Thought: Salvation by Christ with Penitential Cries"
- **1773:** Phillis Wheatley's *Poems on Various Subjects, Religious and Moral*
- **1782:** Ignatius Sancho's *The Letters of the Late Ignatius Sancho, an African*
- **1789:** Olaudah Equiano's *The Interesting Narrative of the Life of Olaudah Equiano*
- **1845:** Frederick Douglass' *Narrative of the Life of Frederick Douglass*
- **1858:** William Wells Brown's *The Escape; or, A Leap for Freedom*
- **1859:** Harriet Wilson's *Our Nig*
- **1861:** Harriet Jacobs' *Incidents in the Life of a Slave Girl*
- **1883:** George W. Williams' *The History of the Negro Race in America from 1619–1880*
- **1901:** Booker T. Washington's *Up from Slavery*
- **1903:** W.E.B. DuBois' *The Souls of Black Folk*
- **1910:** *The Crisis*, magazine of the NAACP, founded
- **1921:** Langston Hughes' "The Negro Speaks of Rivers"
- **1923:** Jean Toomer's *Cane*
- **1925:** Alain LeRoy Locke's anthology *New Negro*
- **1937:** Hurston's *Their Eyes Were Watching God*
- **1940:** Richard Wright's *Native Son*
- **1948:** The Program of African Studies founded at Northwestern University
- **1952:** Ralph Ellison's *Invisible Man*
- **1965:** The Black Arts Movement begins
- **1968:** Third World Liberation Front goes on strike at San Francisco State College
- **1969:** Third World Liberation Front strikes at UC Berkeley
- **1969:** UC Berkeley establishes an Ethnic Studies Department

**1969:** SFSC establishes School of Ethnic Studies
**1972:** The National Association for Ethnic Studies is founded
**1973:** The Society for the Study of the Multi-Ethnic Literature of the United States (MELUS) is founded
**1974:** first issue of *MELUS* literary journal
**1979:** Dexter Fisher and Robert B. Septo's *Afro-American Literature: The Reconstruction of Instruction*
**1980:** Houston A. Baker, Jr. publishes *The Journey Back*
**1982:** Henry Louis Gates, Jr. republishes Harriet Wilson's 1859 book, *Our Nig*
**1983:** Chinua Achebe's "An Image of Africa"
**1984:** Baker's *Blues, Ideology, and Afro-American Literature*
**1984:** Michael G. Cooke's *Afro-American Literature in the Twentieth Century*
**1987:** Gates' *Figures in Black*
**1987:** Gates' *The Signifying Monkey*
**1988:** Barbara Christian's "The Race for Theory"
**1992:** Toni Morrison's *Playing in the Dark*

## ASIAN AMERICAN CRITICISM

**FOCUSES ON:** the covert and the overt text, as well as historical information, in works by or about Asian Americans.
**BECAUSE:** Asian American criticism wants to understand, analyze and explain the Asian American experience on its own terms.
**DEVELOPED IN:** 1960s.
**NOTABLE PRACTITIONERS:**

Lawson Fusao Inada (1938- )
Frank Chin (1940- )
Jeffery Paul Chan (1942- )
David Hsin-fu Wand
Shawn Wong (1949- )
King-Kok Cheung (1955- )
Lisa See (1955- )
Rey Chow (1957- )
Lois-Ann Yamanaka (1961- )
Rachel C. Lee (1965- )
Jhumpa Lahiri (1967- )
David Leiwei Li

Maxine Hong Kingston (1940- )
Bharati Mukherjee (1940- )
Shirley Geok-lin Lim (1944- )
Sau-ling Cynthia Wong (1946- )
Amy Tan (1952- )
Gish Jen (1955- )
David Henry Hwang (1957- )
Elaine Kim (1957- )
Susan Koshy
Chang-rae Lee (1965- )
Han Ong (1968- )
lê thi diem thúy (1972- )

**IMPORTANT PREDECESSORS:**

Sui Sin Far (1865-1914)
Bhagat Singh Thind (1892-1967)
Bienvenido Santos (1911-96)

Yone Noguchi (1875-1947)
Toshio Mori (1910-1980)
Carlos Bulosan (1913-56)

Louis Hing Chu (1915-70)   Hisaye Yamamoto (1921-2011)
John Okada (1923-1971)    Yuji Ichioka (1936-2002)
**ADVANTAGES:** moving away from the traditional Eurocentric perspective helps us recognize the many permutations of anti-Asian bias and prejudice that operate throughout our society.
**DISADVANTAGES:** as with all ethnic approaches, Asian American criticism can essentialize the entire diverse Asian American community and reinforce misguided stereotypes and prejudices.
**DEFINITION:** a method of literary analysis that examines, from an Asian American perspective, literary works written by or about Asian Americans.

---

Because of the similarities in their approaches to texts, Asian American criticism, Latina/o criticism, and Native American criticism are often lumped together with African American criticism as one body of theoretical study. The problem with such an approach, of course, is that it ignores the unique histories from which each of these diverse fields developed. Even the singular category of Asian American criticism can be problematic. It encompasses writers and thinkers from over twenty different countries, thus failing to recognize the diversity of these different cultures—and the vast differences among people within each of these ethnic groups.

The historian Yuji Ichioka is credited with coining the term "Asian American" in the 1960s. While this classification essentializes whole groups of diverse peoples, most see it as a positive development, similar to Gayatri Spivak's strategic essentialism. By joining together, the disparate groups of Asian Americans have much more influence to affect change politically, socially and economically. As the past experiences of Asian American peoples have proven, positive change is nearly impossible without such influence.

Peoples of Asian descent have a long history in the United States that predates America's independence from England. Evidence suggests that sailors from China and the Philippines resided on our continent's west coast by at least the sixteenth century and historical records list one "East Indian" as a citizen of Jamestown, Virginia, in 1635. By the late eighteenth century, Filipino sailors had formed a small settlement in Louisiana and, by 1860, Chinese immigrants alone accounted for nearly ten percent of California's population. Asian Americans have fought for the U.S. in every major military conflict since 1812. Up to ninety percent of the workers who built the transcontinental railroad were of Asian descent and it was Asian immigrants who modernized California's agriculture industry in the nineteenth century. Still, Americans of Asian descent have been viewed as "outsiders" and "perpetual foreigners" throughout America's history, making Asian Americans the targets of discrimination even today.

## "Give me your tired, your poor, your European"

By most accounts, resentment toward Asian immigrants—particularly Chinese immigrants—began during California's Gold Rush. Before this, Chinese immigrants were viewed favorably as ideal workers and model citizens. After gold was discovered in 1848, however, railroads and coal mining companies were eager to expand. To keep their labor costs low, they recruited thousands of Chinese laborers to work in California.

The influx of new arrivals brought increased competition for gold and for jobs. Many of the newly-arrived white settlers blamed Chinese workers for the lack of opportunities. Violence against Chinese people soon followed. Chinese miners were regularly robbed, beaten and murdered. An 1856 editorial in the Shasta County *Republican* noted that "Hundreds of Chinamen have been slaughtered in cold blood" between 1851 and 1856. The Chinese massacre of 1871 in Los Angeles and the San Francisco Riot of 1877 left over twenty Chinese immigrants tortured and murdered and hundreds of Chinese homes and businesses burned. Rather than prosecute most of these crimes, the California government passed discriminatory laws designed to discourage further Asian immigration.

Such discrimination wasn't limited to California, however. Oregon's new state constitution (1859) prohibited land ownership by any "Chinaman." The vitriolic anti-Asian speeches of labor agitator Denis Kearney attracted huge audiences even on the East Coast. American residents of Asian descent were ruled ineligible for U.S. citizenship in 1878. The federal government's Chinese Exclusion Act of 1882 outlawed the immigration of Chinese laborers. Three years later, an angry mob of white men and women in Wyoming attacked Chinese miners in what came to be known as the Rock Springs Massacre. At least twenty-eight Chinese workers were murdered and the Chinatown area of Rock Springs was destroyed. Sixteen white rioters were initially arrested, but neither local, state, nor federal prosecutors ever charged anyone with a crime. Similar attacks soon followed throughout the West and in the Deep South.

Individual and institutionalized racism against people of Asian origin continued through the next century. The Geary Act (1892) extended the Chinese Exclusion Act and required all Chinese residents of the U.S. to carry an identification card. Those who didn't were either deported or imprisoned. The Immigration Act of 1924 effectively outlawed the immigration of any person of Asian descent, regardless of their home country. By 1925, fourteen states had alien land laws that prohibited Asian residents from owning land. Anti-Asian bias became so pervasive that it often went unnoticed by even the most progressive thinkers.

## Yellow Peril

After the Rock Springs Massacre, large-scale violence against people of Asian descent became less common. Still, discrimination was prevalent. Much of this prejudice arose from fear. Labor leaders who resented Asian workers began to scare Americans to oppose Asian immigration. Almost every day, European Americans were warned about the horrifying consequences of continued Asian immigration. This "yellow peril" would take American jobs, defile American women and destroy the American way of life. Even worse, Americans were told, Christianity would be replaced by some strange form of Asian paganism. As a result, all good Christian Americans would be condemned to eternal damnation.

Throughout the first half of the twentieth century, some variation of this fear was expressed regularly in literature, the media and popular culture. The vast newspaper network of William Randolph Hearst used regular anti-Asian editorials and frightening cartoons to make "yellow peril" familiar to every American household. Fiction writers depicted doomsday scenarios precipitated by Asian villains in countless short stories and novels. This trope began with M.P. Shiel's *The Yellow Danger* (1898), and included works such as Émile Driant's *L'Invasion Jaune* (1905; trans. *The Yellow Invasion*), G. G. Rupert's *The Yellow Peril* (1911), Philip Francis Nowlan's *Armageddon 2419 A.D.* (1928) and Robert A. Heinlein's *Sixth Column* (1941). Nearly every American who could read was exposed to some version of this fearmongering. This fear grew in World War II. In 1942, President Roosevelt signed Executive Order 9066, authorizing the forced removal of over 120,000 Japanese Americans to internment camps for the duration of the war.

While state-sponsored discrimination against Asian peoples ostensibly ended with the Immigration and Nationality Act of 1965, Asian Americans continued to experience racism on every level. The murder of Vincent Chin in 1982 is just one example. Chin, a Chinese American, was beaten to death by two Detroit autoworkers who were angry about the success of Japanese automobile manufacturers. Even though two off-duty police officers witnessed the attack, Chin's murderers were not sentenced to any jail time. For the Asian American community, little seemed to change in the hundred years since the Rock Springs Massacre.

## Yellowface

America's attitude toward Asian Americans has probably been best exemplified by Hollywood. The movie industry's tacit endorsement of prejudice, bigotry and discrimination directed at Asian groups reflected the sentiment of most Americans. Not only have Asian Americans been significantly underrepresented in Hollywood productions but, in works that have had Asian characters, those representations were almost always simplistic and demeaning racist caricatures laden with negative stereotypes. Even worse, perhaps, is that many of these Asian characters were portrayed by white actors wearing "yellowface"—makeup and prosthetics to make them look Asian.

It would be difficult to identify Hollywood's most shameful representation of an Asian character simply because there are so many to choose from: Luise Rainer's O-Lan in *The Good Earth* (1937), Mickey Rooney's I.Y. Yunioshi in *Breakfast at Tiffany's* (1961), David Carradine's Kwai Chang Caine in *Kung Fu* (1972-75), Gedde Watanabe's Long Duk Dong in *Sixteen Candles* (1984), Rob Schneider's Asian minister in *I Now Pronounce You Chuck & Larry* (2005), Christopher Walken's Feng in *Balls of Fire* (2007), Emma Stone's Allison Ng in *Aloha* (2015), etc. Most incomprehensible, though, is that these distasteful practices continue in the twenty-first century. Even though blackface has been considered unacceptable since the 1960s, Hollywood still—unapologetically—employs yellowface today.

## The Problem with the "Model Minority"

It's not only negative caricatures that are problematic, however. "Positive" stereotypes can be troublesome as well. In his *New York Times* magazine essay, "Success Story: Japanese American Style" (1966), sociologist William Petersen used the term "model minority" to describe Japanese Americans. Though subsequent researchers have questioned Petersen's findings, the label stuck. Even today, Asian Americans are held up as the "model minority" in American society: disciplined, hardworking, intelligent and successful.

But there are a number of problems with such a stereotype, even when it seems complimentary. Aside from being accompanied by unrealistic expectations, the model minority label reduces all Asian Americans to one-dimensional versions of real people. This further perpetuates the belief that all Asian Americans are identical and, as Gordon H. Chang notes, clearly differentiated from white Americans and other minority groups. Others argue that, since the model minority label is supposedly positive, racist behavior is often overlooked when directed at Asian Americans. This becomes particularly disconcerting when we consider the history of Asian immigrants in America.

Asian American literary theory, then, examines simplistic and inaccurate representations of Asian and Asian American characters, whether those depictions are positive or negative.

## Frank Chin and Authenticity

The author and literary scholar Frank Chin has been one of the most outspoken critics of inauthentic portrayals of Asian American characters. Chin first gained recognition in the 1970s as a pioneering Asian American playwright. His play, *Chickencoop Chinaman* (1972), was the first major New York play produced by a writer of Asian descent. A year later, he founded the Asian American Theater Company in San Francisco. He then wrote and produced *The Year of the Dragon* (1974), published several works of fiction, and served as coeditor of two major anthologies of Asian American literature: *Aiiieeeee!* (1974) and *The Big Aiiieeeee!* (1991).

Chin sees inauthentic representations of Asian Americans common in all types of literary works, even those written by Asian Americans. In the introduction to *Aiiieeeee!*, Chin and his coeditors claim that

> Every Chinese American book ever published in the United States of America by a major publisher has been [. . .] the [product] of white racist imagination, not fact, not Chinese culture, and not Chinese or Chinese American literature.

Chin takes particular issue with well-known works by David Henry Hwang, Maxine Hong Kingston and Amy Tan. Chin argues that these writers anglicize well-known Chinese folk tales in their published works to satisfy a white audience. To do so, they must "fake all of Asian American history" to maintain their stories' continuity. According to Chin, this leads to continued misinformation regarding Chinese history and Asian Americans in general.

This misinformation includes the idea that the first Asian immigrants had no intention of remaining in the U.S.; that Asian cultures are unacceptably misogynistic; and that Asian cultures oppose individualism, civil disobedience and core American values. When mistaken beliefs such as these circulate, it reinforces the idea of the Asian American as the perpetual foreigner. Consequently, Asian Americans continue to be viewed as outsiders, making them easier targets for racism and discrimination.

It's important, then, for white America to better understand and accept Asian Americans as they truly are. For Chin, a necessary step in this process is to accurately portray Asian Americans in literature and in film.

## Important Moments in Asian American Criticism

1820: Chinese merchants and sailors begin immigrating to U.S.
1865: Central Pacific Railroad begins recruiting Chinese workers for transcontinental railroad
1868: Fourteenth Amendment gives citizenship to babies born in U.S.
1882: Chinese Exclusion Act signed
1886: Rock Springs massacre in Wyoming
1899: Sui Sin Far's "A Chinese Ishmael"
1902: Yone Noguchi's *The American Diary of a Japanese Girl*
1903: Korean Friendship Association founded by Dosan Ahn Chang Ho
1909: Sui Sin Far's "Leaves from the Mental Portfolio of an Eurasian"
1912: Sui Sin Far's *Mrs. Spring Fragrance*
1924: Johnson-Reed Act (Immigration Act) ratified
1930: Watsonville Riots in California
1942: Executive Order 9066 forces Japanese Americans into internment camps
1946: Carlos Bulosan's *America is in the Heart*
1957: John Okada's *No-No Boy*
1961: Louis Hing Chu's *Eat a Bowl of Tea*
1968: Immigration and Nationality Act of 1965 enacted
1968: Third World Liberation Front goes on strike at San Francisco State College
1969: Third World Liberation Front strikes at UC Berkeley
1969: UC Berkeley establishes an Ethnic Studies Department
1969: SFSC establishes School of Ethnic Studies
1971: *Amerasia Journal* founded
1971: Bharati Mukherjee's *The Tiger's Daughter*
1972: The National Association for Ethnic Studies is founded
1973: The Society for the Study of the Multi-Ethnic Literature of the United States (MELUS) is founded
1974: first issue of *MELUS* literary journal
1974: David Hsin-fu Wand's anthology *Asian American Heritage*
1974: Jeffery Paul Chan et al. publish *Aiiieeeee!*
1975: Maxine Hong Kingston's *The Woman Warrior*
1978: Edward Said's *Orientalism*
1980: Kingston's *China Men*
1982: Elaine Kim's *Asian American Literature*
1982: Theresa Hak Kyung Cha's *Dictee*
1988: David Henry Hwang's *M. Butterfly*
1989: Amy Tan's *The Joy Luck Club*
1990: Jessica Hagedorn's *Dogeaters*

1991: Sucheng Chan's *Asian Americans*
1991: Rey Chow's *Woman and Chinese Modernity*
1991: David O'Brien's and Stephen Fugita's *The Japanese American Experience*
1993: King-Kok Cheung's *Articulate Silences*
1993: Chow's *Writing Diaspora*
1993: Sau-ling Cynthia Wong's *Reading Asian American Literature*
1995: students at Northwestern University go on hunger strike to establish Asian American Studies program
1997: David Leiwei Li's "Race, Gender, Class and Asian American Literary Theory"
1998: *Journal of Asian American Studies* founded
1998: David Leiwei Li's *Imagining the Nation*
1998: Chow's *Ethics after Idealism*
1999: Rachel C. Lee's *The Americas of Asian American Literature*
1999: Robert G. Lee's *Orientals*
2005: Susan Koshy's *Sexual Naturalization*
2006: Chow's *The Age of the World Target*
2008: Koshy's and S. Radhakrishnan's *Transnational South Asians*

## LATINA/O CRITICISM

**FOCUSES ON:** the covert and the overt text, as well as historical and biographical information, as it relates to works by or about Latina/os.
**BECAUSE:** Latina/o criticism examines how Latina/os are portrayed in literature and analyzes how those portrayals reflect and shape America's understanding of the Latina/o community.
**DEVELOPED IN:** 1960s.
**NOTABLE PRACTITIONERS:**
   Octavio Paz (1914-98)            Gloria E. Anzaldúa (1942-2004)
   Juan Bruce-Novoa (1944-2010)     Luz Maria Umpierre (1947- )
   Gustavo Pérez Firmat (1949- )    Juan Flores
   Ramón Saldívar (1949- )          Frances Aparicio (1955- )
   José David Saldívar              Suzanne Oboler
   Ilan Stavans (1961- )            Arlene Dávila
**IMPORTANT PREDECESSORS:**
   George I. Sánchez (1906–1972)    Américo Paredes (1915-99)
   César Chávez (1927-93)           Oscar Zeta Acosta (1935-74)
**ADVANTAGES:** allows us to understand literature from a Latina/o perspective, rather than through the traditional Eurocentric lens.

DISADVANTAGES: as is the case with other ethnic approaches, Latina/o criticism could potentially essentialize the Latina/o community and thus seem to sanction stereotyping and prejudice.

DEFINITION: a method of literary analysis that examines literary works from a Latina/o perspective.

---

Latina/o criticism developed in response to the discrimination and prejudice that the Latina/o community has faced for much of America's history. In the early years of the United States, the American Southwest was a territory of Spain, and then Mexico, before it came under U.S. control in the mid-nineteenth century. During this time, citizens of Mexican and Spanish origin far outnumbered Anglo settlers. As a result, the first Latina/o residents of the U.S. enjoyed some measure of political influence and social prestige.

As the U.S. spread west—particularly after the discovery of gold in California—Latina/o residents soon found themselves in the minority. It wasn't long before state legislators sympathetic to Latina/o issues were replaced by politicians with an Anglocentric agenda. These new lawmakers passed several discriminatory laws that favored Anglo settlers and marginalized everybody else. Latina/os were victimized at all levels of society by the Anglo majority. By 1860, most Latina/o farmers had lost their land and Latina/o miners had been forced out of their mining claims. Latina/o families who had recently owned or managed expansive ranches now struggled to survive in menial jobs that Anglo settlers refused to do.

This continued throughout the nineteenth century. Latina/os became subject to increasingly discriminatory laws that left them disenfranchised and socially and economically disadvantaged. They were often segregated from Anglo populations, unable to attend the same schools or churches and prohibited from using the same restrooms or living in the same neighborhoods. Latina/o laborers faced harsh conditions while working for lower and lower wages. Latina/os suspected of crimes were frequently lynched by Anglo mobs. Police and government officials ignored—and often perpetrated—all manner of crimes against members of the Latina/o community.

## Organizing the Latina/o Community

In the early twentieth century, Latina/os began to organize. In 1903, Mexican and Japanese farm workers joined together to form the Japanese-Mexican Labor Association. One of the JMLA's first orders of business was the Oxnard Strike of 1903, a strike of Southern California's sugar beet laborers. While the strike succeeded in earning the workers higher wages, it did little to lessen the discrimination against the Latina/o community. Segregation continued. Lynchings were still common. Throughout the first half of the twentieth century, the U.S. federal government either overlooked or facilitated the oppression of the Latina/o community. The government-sanctioned "Mexican Repatriation" of the 1930s forced up to two million Latina/os—over half of whom were American citizens—to leave their homes in the U.S. and "relocate" to Mexico. "Operation Wetback" of the 1950s had similar results. The Zoot Suit Riots of 1943 and the Felix Longoria affair after World War II served as further reminders that many Americans still held a contemptuous view of Latina/os.

Throughout this period, the Latina/o community persevered in its quest for equality. In 1911, *El Primer Congreso Mexicanista* (the First Mexican Congress) was held in Laredo, Texas. The goal was to combat the civil and social abuses faced by Latina/os. As part of this endeavor, the group formed *La Gran Liga Mexicanista de Beneficencia y Protección* (the Great Mexican League for Benefit and Protection). Similar groups took shape as Latina/os realized they needed to organize in order to survive. Of these, *El Congreso del Pueblo de Habla Española* (the Congress of Spanish-Speaking Peoples) (1938) is significant because it was the first nationwide effort to consolidate Latina/os of various ethnic origins.

Many of these early groups were social service organizations that provided food, clothing and health care to struggling Latina/o families. Other groups formed to educate Latina/os about their rights and obligations as American citizens. These efforts led to early childhood education for Latina/o children and to a number of significant court cases. The judgments handed down in *Mendez v. Westminster* (1946) and *Delgado v. Bastrop ISD* (1948) helped end the segregation of Latina/o public school students; *Hernandez v. Texas* (1954) determined that Latina/o citizens are due equal protection under the 14th Amendment.

Most organizations, though, focused on workers. By the 1930s, the vast majority of farm laborers in the Southwest were Latina/o men, women and children who worked in hazardous conditions for less than nine cents per hour (about $1.50 today). In California alone, over forty farm labor unions were active between 1928 and 1940. When bargaining efforts with owners failed, the organized workers were able to go on strike to persuade employers to provide higher wages and better working conditions. According to Devra Weber, "Between April and December 1933, thirty-seven strikes, involving 50,000 workers, erupted in California's agricultural fields." Most of these strikes met with violent resistance from the Anglo farm owners. Some strikes failed; others succeeded. Still, oppressive conditions for farm laborers have persisted, bringing about new labor organizations and more strikes that have continued into the twenty-first century.

## Latina/o Students Strike

It was in this spirit of organization that the East L.A. Blowouts began. In the mid-sixties, prejudice against Latina/o high school students in Los Angeles was common and obvious. Students weren't allowed to speak Spanish in school. Teachers and guidance counselors steered Latina/o students—even straight-A students—away from college and toward menial low-wage vocational careers. The schools that served Latina/o students were overcrowded and in disrepair. Many didn't have indoor lunchrooms and all had insufficient libraries. The schools' curricula and textbooks ignored Latina/o issues and the Latina/o contributions to American history. As a result, over half of L.A.'s Latina/o high school students dropped out before graduating. Those who did graduate averaged an eighth-grade reading level.

By 1968, Latina/o high school students in Los Angeles organized to protest this institutionalized discrimination. The students' strike began on March 1. Eventually, over fifteen thousand students—from Belmont, Garfield, Jefferson, Lincoln, Roosevelt, Venice, Wilson, and several other area high schools—joined in. Police in riot gear tried to disperse many of these peaceful demonstrations by beating and arresting students or by forcibly escorting them inside to their principals' offices. The list of grievances that the students presented to the board of education included thirty-nine proposed changes to academics, administration, facilities and the rights of students. When the strike ended, the board of education agreed with almost all of the requests. They also determined, though, that a lack of funding made many of those modifications impossible.

Within a year, college students would go on strike at San Francisco State College and UC-Berkeley, bringing about the country's first department of ethnic studies and the first college of ethnic studies. It was from these beginnings that ethnic studies and Latina/o criticism began.

## Contemporary Latina/o Criticism

Latina/o criticism explores a wide range of interests. This is due, at least in part, to the diversity of Latina/o peoples. Most scholars recognize "Latina/o" to describe anyone with origins from Cuba, Mexico, Puerto Rico, Spain, or Central or South America, regardless of race. This includes over twenty different countries, each with unique people, cultures and social conditions. The issues faced by a native of Cuba, for example, might be very different from those faced by a native of Mexico, Costa Rica or Ecuador. As one might imagine, then, Latina/o criticism could focus in a number of unique directions.

Much of the Latina/o theoretical work of the 1970s and eighties incorporates the work of Derrida and Foucault in a post-structuralist reading of texts. We also see Foucault applied in service to an historical approach to Latina/o criticism. Some Latina/o theoretical work studies the representations of Latina/os in literature and how culture shapes—and is shaped by—those representations. Some examines the effects of exile on Latina/os and their literature. There is also a significant body of Latina/o theory devoted to the unique social issues faced by various Latina/o communities. Still other Latina/o criticism analyzes literature from a postcolonial perspective.

More recently, we see Latina/o theory framed by the growing popularity in the U.S. of anti-immigration efforts and English-only movements. California's Proposition 187 (1994) was designed to deny immigrants the right to get health care, public education, and any other social services. In Arizona's "Chandler Roundup" (1997), police arrested any Latina/o person—legal U.S. citizen or not—who wasn't carrying identification. In 2005, the U.S. House of Representatives passes HR 4437, which authorized, among other things, the construction of a wall between the U.S. and Mexico. Arizona's SB 1070 (2010) required police to check the identification of any Latina/o citizen throughout the state. The same year, Arizona also passed HB 2281, which outlawed ethnic studies programs in public schools. In 2011, Alabama passed HR 56, a law similar to Arizona's SB 1070.

Latina/o theory that focuses on such legislation examines both the causes and the effects of these efforts on literature and analyzes how literary works either reflect or respond to these efforts.

## Important Moments in Latina/o Criticism

1911: *El Primer Congreso Mexicanista* in Laredo, Texas
1929: the League of United Latin American Citizens (LULAC) founded
1929: the U.S. begins its program of "Mexican Repatriation"
1938: *El Congreso del Pueblo de Habla Española* in Los Angeles
1940: George I. Sánchez's *Forgotten People*
1943: Zoot Suit Riots
1946: *Mendez v. Westminster*
1948: American G.I. Forum founded
1949: Felix Longoria Affair
1950: Octavio Paz's *El Laberinto de la Soledad* (*The Labyrinth of Solitude*)
1954: "Operation Wetback" implemented by the U.S. INS
1954: *Hernandez v. Texas*
1962: National Farm Workers Association founded by César Chávez and Dolores Huerta
1967: *El Grito* founded by Octavio Romano and Nick Vaca

1968: East L.A. Blowouts
1968: Third World Liberation Front goes on strike at San Francisco State College
1969: Third World Liberation Front strikes at UC Berkeley
1969: UC Berkeley establishes an Ethnic Studies Department
1969: SFSC establishes School of Ethnic Studies
1969: El Plan de Santa Bárbara adopted at UC Santa Barbara
1972: The National Association for Ethnic Studies is founded
1973: The Society for the Study of the Multi-Ethnic Literature of the United States (MELUS) is founded
1974: first issue of *MELUS* literary journal
1986: Werner Sollors' *Beyond Ethnicity*
1987: Gloria E. Anzaldúa's *Borderlands/La Frontera*
1990: Ramón Saldivar's *Chicano Narrative*
1991: José David Saldívar's *The Dialectics of Our America*
1991: Héctor Calderón's and José David Saldívar's *Criticism in the Borderlands*
1993: José Rabasa's *Inventing America*
1993: UCLA student hunger strike in support of Chicana/o Studies
1994: Gustavo Pérez Firmat's *Life on the Hyphen*
1994: passage of Proposition 187 in California
1994: Helena Maria Viramontes' *Under the Feet of Jesus*
1995: Ilan Stavans's *The Hispanic Condition*
1995: Suzanne Oboler's *Ethnic Labels, Latino Lives*
1997: "Chandler Roundup" in Chandler, Arizona
1999: Román De la Campa's *Latin Americanism*
2005: Walter D. Mignolo's *The Idea of Latin America*
2005: H.R. 4437 passes U.S. House of Representatives
2006: Elizabeth Jacobs' *Mexican American Literature*
2008: Werner Sollors' *Ethnic Modernism*
2010: Arizona passes SB 1070
2010: Arizona passes HB 2281
2011: Alabama passes HB 56
2013: Raúl Coronado's *A World Not to Come*

# NATIVE AMERICAN CRITICISM

**FOCUSES ON:** the covert and the overt text, as well as historical information, in works by or about Native Americans.

**BECAUSE:** Native American criticism studies the portrayals of Native Americans in order to root out inaccuracies and to reexamine the canon with Native American literature in mind.

**DEVELOPED IN:** 1960s.

**NOTABLE PRACTITIONERS:**
Elizabeth Cook-Lynn (1930- )
Jack D. Forbes (1934-2011)
Simon J. Ortiz (1941- )
William Least Heat Moon (1939- )
Raymond J. DeMallie (1946- )
Alfred Young Man (1948- )
Craig S. Womack
Charlene Teters (1952- )
Luana Ross
Greg Sarris (1959- )
Taiaiake Alfred (1964- )
Sherman Alexie (1966- )
Vine Deloria, Jr. (1933-2005)
Gerald Vizenor (1934- )
Paula Gunn Allen (1939-2008)
Arnold Krupat (1941- )
Ward Churchill (1947- )
Trudie Lamb-Richmond
Jace Weaver
Devon A. Mihesuah (1957- )
Allison Hedge Coke (1958- )
Robert Warrior
James Thomas Stevens (1966- )
Daniel Heath Justice

**IMPORTANT PREDECESSORS:**
Samson Occom (1723-92)
William Apess (1798–1839)
John Rollin Ridge (1827-67)
Charles Eastman (1858-1939)
Zitkala-Ša (1876–1938)
Black Hawk (1767-1838)
George Copway (1818-69)
Sarah Winnemucca (1844-91)
S. Alice Callahan (1864-94)
John J. Neihardt (1881-1973)

**ADVANTAGES:** provides a better understanding of and appreciation for Native Americans and their contributions to our body of literature and to society as a whole.

**DISADVANTAGES:** Native American criticism has the potential to essentialize and negatively stereotype the numerous diverse indigenous communities of North America.

**DEFINITION:** a method of literary analysis that examines works written by or about Native Americans in an effort to understand and explain the experience and worldview of Native American peoples.

---

Native American criticism is unique from other ethnic approaches because the experience of Native Americans has been different than that of other ethnicities in America. The countless atrocities committed against Native Americans have been well documented. The barbarous enslavement of indigenous peoples by Spanish colonists was first chronicled by Bartolomé de las Casas in *Brevísima relación de la destrucción de las Indias* (1542; 1583, trans. *A Brief Account of the Devastation of the Indies*). While las Casas' report was the first of its kind, it wouldn't be the last.

In the next centuries, Native Americans faced repeated attempts at genocidal extermination. During the Siege of Fort Pitt (1763), British General Jeffrey Amherst and Colonel Henry Bouquet conspired to kill the Delaware and Shawnee tribes by providing them with smallpox-infected blankets. Colonial and state governments across the expanding nation offered sizeable rewards for the scalps of indigenous men, women and children. Custer's infamous Last Stand began as an attempt to murder every Native person his cavalry could find—a goal that was realized at the Wounded Knee Massacre fourteen years later. Pierre Wibaux, a cattle baron in Montana, tried to wipe out the Sioux Nation by slaughtering every buffalo in the Northern Great Plains.

Other efforts at solving "the Indian problem" appeared more diplomatic but still resulted in appalling consequences. Andrew Jackson's Indian Removal Act (1830) led to thousands of deaths on the Trail of Tears. "Indian schools" set up by the corrupt Bureau of Indian Affairs focused on eliminating Native Americans through a process of assimilation and acculturation. Native children were taken to boarding schools hundreds of miles from their homes and forced to forget their families' cultures, traditions and languages. The establishment of the reservation system came with promises that the government would provide food, security and basic human necessities. These promises were not kept.

Today, on many reservations, over ninety percent of residents live in poverty, unemployment rates remain above eighty percent, and the rates of many deadly diseases are over five times the national average. Disregard for Native cultures continues in the form of government oppression, educational neglect and the exploitation of tribal lands and resources.

## The Origins of Native American Criticism

Most early research of America's indigenous cultures was conducted to help conquer Native American peoples and control their lands. By the early twentieth century, such research became unnecessary; the "Indian Wars" had concluded and most Native Americans had been relocated to small reservations. Consequently, the study of Native Americans shifted from a military endeavor to an academic pursuit.

Until the mid-twentieth century, the majority of scholars interested in Native American studies were anthropologists like Franz Boas and Claude Lévi-Strauss. Very few literary scholars showed any interest in Native American literature during this time. Consequently, if Native American literature was studied at all, it was most often studied from an anthropological perspective. And this study was usually limited to the transcription of Native American oral narratives.

According to Robert M. Nelson, later scholars such as Karl Kroeber and Dell Hymes began to read these transcriptions as works of literature. These efforts brought literary credibility to Native American oral traditions. From here, the academic study of Native American literature was born.

## Native American Literary Traditions

Today, according to the U.S. government, there are fewer than six hundred Native American tribes in the United States. Before first contact with Europeans, there were over one thousand. We will never know the exact number because countless indigenous nations were likely lost to European diseases before colonists first witnessed their presence.

What we do know is that each of these populations had their own unique language. Many of these languages had deeply intricate grammatical structures that rivaled ancient Latin in complexity. There were also numerous—perhaps numbering in the hundreds—indigenous sign language systems that allowed for intertribal communication. However, few indigenous populations throughout the Americas utilized a structured system of written communication. Because of this, the bulk of Native Americans' literary history consists of oral narratives passed down for centuries.

The most common types of oral narratives categorized by scholars are folktales, legends, memorates and myths. Folktales are fictional stories, often for children, which provide some moral or a lesson to live by. Legends involve specific places, and usually include humans or supernatural beings associated with that place, such as stories explaining the formation of Devil's Tower in Wyoming. Memorates are first-hand narratives of supernatural encounters. Myths describe the creation of the world or significant events during the world's earliest years. Each indigenous population in North America had its own unique oral tradition, making Native American storytelling both vibrant and diverse.

There is also a long history of Native Americans writing in English. The earliest of these were autobiographical texts written by Native Americans who had since converted to Christianity. Samson Occom's autobiographical account of his conversion, "A Short Narrative of My Life" (1768), was the first work written by a Native American to be published in English. William Apess and George Copway continued this trend in the next century. But the nineteenth century also saw Native Americans writing in opposition to the Eurocentric development of indigenous lands. The first work in this vein was *Life of Ma-ka-tai-me-she-kia-kiak* (1833) by the Sauk warrior Black Hawk.

By the middle of the nineteenth century, Native Americans were publishing fiction, nonfiction and poetry. In the early twentieth century, several Native Americans were producing notable work. Alexander Posey's satirical Fus Fixico letters (1902-08) ridiculed the U.S. government's appropriation of Native lands. Zitkala-Ša was an essayist and political activist. Christal Quintasket and John Milton Oskison both wrote a number of fictional works. Charles Eastman was a writer, a social activist and a physician. John Joseph Matthews' nonfiction account of Osage life, *Wah'kon-tah* (1929) became a bestseller. Still, most in the academic community continued to ignore literature by Native American writers.

## The Native American Literary Renaissance

The years between World War II and 1968 were relatively quite ones for Native American authors. Aside from work by writers like D'Arcy McNickle and John Joseph Matthews, Native American literature during this time gained little notice. The publication of N. Scott Momaday's *House Made of Dawn* (1968), though, sparked a renewed interest in Native American literature. Some scholars, such as Kenneth Lincoln, mark this as the beginning of the Native American Renaissance.

Other works by Native American authors were soon to follow. Duane Niatum, James Welch, Leslie Marmon Silko, and Gerald Vizenor are all identified by Lincoln as writers in the first wave of the Native American Renaissance. In the second wave, Lincoln includes Joy Harjo, Barney Bush, Simon J. Ortiz, Louise Erdrich, Paula Gunn Allen, and nila northSun. According to Suzanne Lundquist, the Native American Renaissance is characterized by the recovery of Native American customs, the reexamination of Native American texts, and the resurgence of traditional Native American forms of storytelling. Lincoln believes that this Renaissance was aided by the fact that, for the first time in America's history, a full generation of Native Americans had, in the preceding decades, completed an English-only education. This education included literature courses, fueling an interest in writing for those who were so inclined.

Before long, literary journals and anthologies were published that focused exclusively on Native American writers. The Native American Renaissance then led to a reevaluation of literary theory and the literary canon, with the Native American perspective in mind.

## Contemporary Native American Theory

Like other ethnic approaches, one aim of Native American literary criticism is to reevaluate the literary canon. For Eurocentric literary scholars, the canon is as an unchangeable collection of texts that are indisputably worthy of scholarly attention. Native American theorists, though, believe that the canon should remain in a constant state of flux, always under construction.

Part of this reevaluation includes the incorporation of Native American literature. As scholars such as Arnold Krupat point out, the U.S. has been indelibly shaped by its indigenous cultures. Any discussion of American literature, then, would be incomplete if it ignored the contribution of Native American authors or overlooked the fundamental role of Native American modes of storytelling. For Native American theorists, it would be impossible to fully understand American literature without first recognizing how Native peoples have shaped America.

While Native American theory shares with other ethnic approaches the goal of canon revision, it is also unique. As Elvira Pulitano notes, today's Native American criticism is different because it, ideally, integrates Native American oral traditions and it examines literature through a Native American worldview. According to Penelope Myrtle Kelsey, early versions of Native American theory approached literature from the typical Eurocentric theoretical perspective. But there were several problems with this. For one, the Eurocentric template fails to account for the diversity of Native American peoples. It also fails to address issues of culture and sovereignty. Most importantly, perhaps—at least with regard to literary analysis—is that it fails to recognize Native American literary devices, and fails to grasp the intricacies of Native American thought and the subtleties of Native American humor and innuendo. In other words, when Native American criticism follows the Eurocentric model, a thorough and accurate reading becomes impossible.

This is one reason why Elizabeth Cook-Lynn has been an outspoken advocate for autonomous Native Studies departments in colleges throughout the U.S. Only then, according to Cook-Lynn, will we have a body of Native American criticism that has been untainted by Eurocentric modes of thought. In essays like "Who Stole Native American Studies?" (1997) and "How Scholarship Defames the Native Voice . . . and Why" (2000), Cook-Lynn argues that Native American theory has been guided by political and financial concerns rather than by authentic scholarly interest. In her view, Native American criticism is more comparable to postcolonialism than to other ethnic approaches. After all, she reminds us, Native Americans have suffered the same consequences of European colonialism as other colonized peoples. Even today, Native Americans deal with discrimination, poverty, unemployment, inadequate health care, corrupt reservation governments and the continued exploitation of their lands and resources.

In *New Indians, Old Wars* (2007), Cook-Lynn argues that Native American theorists have been distracted from these important issues, focusing instead on matters of secondary importance. As a result, U.S. history continues to emphasize only those Native Americans who were complicit in the colonization of America and the genocide of its indigenous populations. As Cook-Lynn sees it,

> the need to challenge the literary or historical academy is not felt by native writers, scholars, and historians because the inevitable (and magical?) yet oppressive structures and imaginations of dependence still beckon us.

In too many cases, major American Indian fictionists submit to the old fictions, still writing the same story taught by oppressors, stories of intermarriage and concubinage blurring racial and political distinctions to create a population ripe for colonial rule.

Cook-Lynn has little hope that any of this will change until native American scholars can work independently, free from the Eurocentric constraints of the history, anthropology and English departments that now control them.

## Important Moments in Native American Criticism

1768: Samson Occom's *A Short Narrative of My Life*
1828: first printing of *Cherokee Phoenix*
1829: William Apess' *A Son of the Forest*
1830: Indian Removal Act signed by Andrew Jackson
1833: Black Hawk's *Life of Ma-ka-tai-me-she-kia-kiak*
1854: John Rollin Ridge's *The Life and Adventures of Joaquín Murieta*
1883: Sarah Winnemucca's *Life Among the Paiutes*
1891: S. Alice Callahan's *Wynema*
1899: Simon Pokagon's *Ogimawkwe Mitigwaki*
1947: George Copway's *The Life, History, and Travels of Kah-Ge-Ga-Gah-Bowh*
1901: Zitkala-Ša's *Old Indian Legends*
1902: Charles Eastman's *Memories of an Indian Boyhood*
1911: Eastman's *The Soul of the Indian*
1921: Zitkala-Ša's *American Indian Stories*
1924: Zitkala-Ša's "Oklahoma's Poor Rich Indians"
1929: John Joseph Matthews' *Wah'kon-tah*
1930: Frank Bird Linderman's *Plenty-Coups: Chief of the Crows*
1932: John G. Neihardt's *Black Elk Speaks*
1968: Third World Liberation Front goes on strike at San Francisco State College
1968: N. Scott Momaday's *House Made of Dawn*
1968: American Indian Movement (AIM) founded
1969: Third World Liberation Front strikes at UC Berkeley
1969: UC Berkeley establishes an Ethnic Studies Department
1969: SFSC establishes School of Ethnic Studies
1969: UCLA founds its American Indian Studies Center
1969: Vine Deloria's *Custer Died for Your Sins: An Indian Manifesto*
1969: Momaday's *House Made of Dawn* awarded Pulitzer Prize
1970: first Convocation of American Indian Scholars held at Princeton
1970: AIM's Thanksgiving-day seizure of the *Mayflower II*

**1972:** The National Association for Ethnic Studies is founded
**1973:** Wounded Knee incident
**1973:** The Society for the Study of the Multi-Ethnic Literature of the United States (MELUS) is founded
**1974:** first issue of *MELUS* literary journal
**1974:** *American Indian Quarterly* literary journal established
**1974:** Vine Deloria's *The Indian Affair*
**1977:** Leslie Marmon Silko's *Ceremony*
**1978:** Robert F. Berkhofer's *The White Man's Indian*
**1980:** founding of the scholarly journal *SAIL (Studies in American Indian Literature)*
**1980:** Gretchen M. Bataille's and Charles L. P. Silet's *The Pretend Indians*
**1981:** Leslie Marmon Silko's *Storyteller*
**1982:** William Least Heat Moon's *Blue Highways*
**1984:** Louise Erdrich's *Love Medicine*
**1984:** Ward Churchill's and Elisabeth Lloyd's *Culture versus Economism*
**1985:** *Wičazo Ša Review* founded
**1989:** *Journal of Indigenous Studies* established
**1990:** Mary Crow Dog's *Lakota Woman*
**1992:** Arnold Krupat's *Ethnocriticism*
**1993:** Churchill's *Struggle for the Land*
**1993:** Robert M. Nelson's *Place and Vision*
**1994:** Gerald Vizenor's *Manifest Manners*
**1994:** Robert Allen Warrior's *Tribal Secrets*
**1995:** Russell Means' *Where White Men Fear to Tread*
**1995:** Deloria's *Red Earth, White Lies*
**1995:** Sherman Alexie's *Reservation Blues*
**1997:** Jace Weaver's *That the People Might Live*
**1997:** Leslie Marmon Silko's *Yellow Woman*
**1997:** Churchill's *A Little Matter of Genocide*
**1998:** Vizenor's *Fugitive Poses*
**1999:** Craig S. Womack's *Red on Red*
**2003:** MariJo Moore's *Genocide of the Mind*
**2003:** Elvira Pulitano's *Toward a Native American Critical Theory*
**2004:** Churchill's *Kill the Indian, Save the Man*
**2005:** *AlterNative* academic journal founded
**2005:** Robert Allen Warrior's *The People and the Word*
**2008:** Craig S. Womack, Daniel Heath Justice and Christopher B. Teuton publish *Reasoning Together*
**2008:** Penelope Myrtle Kelsey's *Tribal Theory in Native American Literature*
**2009:** Womack's *Art as Performance, Story as Criticism*
**2010:** Weaver's *Notes from a Miner's Canary*

2011: Elizabeth Cook-Lynn's *A Separate Country*

## Implementation

Considering the various branches of ethnic studies, a theoretical analysis with an ethnic focus can lead in any number of directions. Besides the four most commonly identified categories of ethnic criticism—African American, Asian American, Latina/o, and Native American criticisms—there are numerous emphases within each of these branches. All ethnic critiques, however, share a common interest in the representations of characters from a particular ethnic group. Because of this, ethnic critiques are usually limited to literary works by or about members of one or another of these groups. The best ethnic readings also share another similarity: they are undertaken by scholars with a thorough understanding of the racialized group they are studying. Whether that understanding comes from experience or research, it provides the theorist with the foundation upon which to build his or her analysis.

For Henry Louis Gates, Jr., his deep knowledge of African American literary traditions helps him to identify and explain the use of signifyin(g) in African American discourse. He then offers signifyin(g) as one example to support his argument for expansion of the canon. Frank Chin's familiarity with Chinese society allows him to recognize inaccurate portrayals of Chinese history and folklore. Chin knows, for example, that the story of Fa Mulan is as common to Chinese children as any fairy tale is to an American child of European descent. He uses this knowledge to critique the anglicized versions of Chinese folk tales in works by Amy Tan, Maxine Hong Kingston and David Henry Hwang. Elizabeth Cook-Lynn's understanding of America's indigenous cultures reinforces all of her scholarly work. This gives her credibility when she criticizes Native American authors who, in her view, overlook the continued oppression of Native Americans.

But ethnic readings aren't limited to texts written by authors of a particular racialized group. Ethnic analyses can also delve into works by white writers. Critiques in this vein are often similar to Chinua Achebe's analysis of Joseph Conrad's *Heart of Darkness*. As such, they involve a close reading of the covert text to uncover the author's hidden biases with regard to race and ethnicity. Most scholars see Toni Morrison's theoretical work as a notable representation of this type of analysis. In assorted essays and in books such as *Playing in the Dark* (1992), Morrison highlights the dehumanization of African Americans in Hemingway, the othering of African Americans in Poe, the use of African Americans as literary devices in Cather and Twain, and the role of blackness in Melville.

Still other ethnic readings seek to understand a literary work within its historical, cultural or economic context. Readings such as these might incorporate new historicism or Marxism. An ethnic critique could also examine a text from the perspective of feminism, psychoanalysis, post-structuralism or reader-response theory. There are few limits, in other words, on the shape an ethnic analysis can take.

## Important Terms

Africanism
allotment
Chinese Exclusion Act
double consciousness
Indian Removal Act
model minority
signifyin(g)
yellowface

Afrocentricity
assimilation
Dawes Act
essentialism
indigenousness
perpetual foreigner
yellow peril

## Study Questions

1. Identify and explain three or more examples of signifyin(g) that you have encountered recently. How do your examples compare to those identified by Gates?
2. Toni Morrison argues that all American literature has been indelibly shaped by the same African American presence that shaped the United States. Similarly, there are Asian American, Latina/o, and Native American scholars who recognize the influence of their own respective cultures. Identify at least three stories that illustrate what these scholars mean. In what way or ways do these texts exemplify the influence of one or another ethnic group?
3. From an ethnic theoretical perspective, analyze the character of Aminadab in Nathaniel Hawthorne's "The Birthmark." Who is this character? What role does he play? What significance does he serve to the story? Provide specific examples from the text in your response.
4. Consider Sui Sin Far's "In the Land of the Free" through the lenses of ethnic criticism and one other theoretical perspective. How would these two readings compare? What can you gain from an ethnic reading that you couldn't gain from a different type of analysis, and vice-versa? How might these two perspectives complement each other? Use specific examples from the story as you develop your position.
5. From the perspective of ethnic criticism, write a brief essay on the story of your choice in which you determine the author's hidden bi-

ases with regard to race and ethnicity. What do the characters say about these issues? How do the characters interact with each other? Which characters are the most and the least developed? How are racialized characters described in the story? Are they dynamic or static characters? What roles do they play?

## Selected Bibliography

Achebe, Chinua. *Hopes and Impediments: Selected Essays.* New York: Anchor, 1990.
Angelou, Maya. *I Know Why the Caged Bird Sings.* New York: Ballantine, 2009.
Appiah, Kwame Anthony. *Cosmopolitanism: Ethics in a World of Strangers.* New York: Norton, 2007.
—. *The Ethics of Identity.* Princeton: Princeton UP, 2007.
—. *The Honor Code: How Moral Revolutions Happen.* New York: Norton, 2011.
Asante, Molefi Kete. *Afrocentricity: The theory of Social Change.* Chicago: African American Images, 2003.
—. *The Afrocentric Idea.* Philadelphia: Temple UP, 1998.
Baker, Jr., Houston A. *Black Studies, Rap, and the Academy.* Chicago: Chicago UP, 1995.
—. *Blues, Ideology, and Afro-American Literature.* Chicago: Chicago UP, 1987.
—. *I Don't Hate the South: Reflections on Faulkner, Family, and the South.* New York: Oxford UP, 2007.
—. *The Journey Back.* Chicago: Chicago UP, 1984.
Carby, Hazel V. *Reconstructing Womanhood: The Emergence of the Afro-American Woman Novelist.* New York: Oxford UP, 1989.
—. *Race Men.* Cambridge: Harvard UP, 2000.
Chow, Rey. "The Interruption of Referentiality: Poststructuralism and the Conundrum of Critical Multiculturalism." *The South Atlantic Quarterly*, 101.1 (Winter 2002). 171-86.
Christian, Barbara. *Black Feminist Criticism: Perspectives on Black Women Writers.* Westport: Praeger, 1980.
—. *New Black Feminist Criticism, 1985-2000.* Ed. Gloria Bowles, M. Giulia Fabi and Arlene Keizer. Urbana–Champaign: Illinois UP, 2007.
Cooke, Michael G. *Afro-American Literature in the Twentieth Century.* New Haven: Yale UP, 1986.
Du Bois, W.E.B. *Black Reconstruction in America: 1860-1880.* Piscataway: Transaction, 2013.
—. *The Philadelphia Negro: A Social Study.* Philadelphia: Pennsylvania UP, 1995.

—. *The Souls of Black Folk*. Oakland: Eucalyptus, 2013.
Fanon, Frantz. *Black Skin, White Masks*. New York: Grove, 2008.
—. *The Wretched of the Earth*. New York: Grove, 2005.
Fisher, Dexter, and Robert B. Septo, eds. *Afro-American Literature: The Reconstruction of Instruction*. New York: MLA, 1990.
Gates Jr., Henry Louis. *Figures in Black: Words, Signs, and the "Racial" Self*. New York: Oxford UP, 1989.
—. *Loose Canons: Notes on the Culture Wars*. New York: Oxford UP. 1992
—. *The Signifying Monkey: A Theory of African-American Literary Criticism*. Oxford: Oxford UP, 1989.
—. *Tradition and the Black Atlantic: Critical Theory in the African Diaspora*. New York: Basic, 2010.
—. *The Trials of Phillis Wheatley: America's First Black Poet and Her Encounters with the Founding Fathers*. New York: Basic, 2010.
Gates Jr., Henry Louis, and Cornel West. *The African American Century: How Black Americans Have Shaped Our Country*. New York: Free Press. 2000.
hooks, bell. *Ain't I a Woman?: Black Women and Feminism*. Brooklyn: South End, 1999.
—. *Feminist Theory: From Margin to Center*. Brooklyn: South End, 2000.
—. "Postmodern Blackness." *Postmodern Culture* 1.1 (September 1990).
—. *We Real Cool: Black Men and Masculinity*. New York: Routledge, 2003.
McDowell, Deborah E. *"The Changing Same": Black Women's Literature, Criticism, and Theory*. Bloomington: Indiana UP, 1995.
—. *Leaving Pipe Shop*. New York: Norton, 1998.
Morrison, Toni. "Introduction." *The Adventures of Huckleberry Finn*. Ed. Shelley Fisher Fishkin. New York: Oxford UP, 1996. xxxii-xli.
—. *Playing in the Dark: Whiteness and the Literary Imagination*. New York: Vintage, 2007.
Walker, Alice. *In Search of Our Mothers' Gardens: Womanist Prose*. New York: Mariner, 2003.
West, Cornel. *Keeping Faith: Philosophy and Race in America*. New York: Routledge, 2008.
—. *Race Matters*. New York: Vintage, 1994.

---

Adachi, Jeff, dir. *The Slanted Screen*. CAAM, 2007.
Bonacich, Edna, and Lucie Cheng. *Labor Immigration under Capitalism: Asian Workers in the United States Before World War II*. Berkeley: California UP, 1984.
Bulosan, Carlos. *America is in the Heart*. Seattle: Washington UP, 1973.
Cha, Theresa Hak Kyung. *Dictee*. Berkeley: California UP, 2009.

Chan, Jeffery P. et al., eds. *Aiiieeeee!: An Anthology of Asian American Writers*. New York: Plume, 1997.
—. *The Big Aiiieeeee!: An Anthology of Chinese American and Japanese American Literature*. New York: Plume, 1991.
Chan, Sucheng. *Asian Americans: An Interpretive History*. Boston: Twayne, 1991.
—. *Income and Status Differences Between White and Minority Americans*. Lewiston, PA: Edwin Mellen, 1990.
Cheung, King-Kok. *Articulate Silences*. Ithaca: Cornell UP, 1993.
—. Ed. *Words Matter: Conversations with Asian American Writers*. Honolulu: Hawaii UP, 2000.
Chin, Frank. *Born in the USA: A Story of Japanese America, 1889-1947*. Lanham, MD: Rowman & Littlefield, 2002.
—. *Bulletproof Buddhists and Other Essays*. Honolulu: Hawaii UP, 1998.
—. *The Chickencoop Chinaman/The Year of the Dragon: Two Plays*. Seattle: Washington UP, 1981.
—. *The Chinaman Pacific & Frisco R.R. Co*. Minneapolis: Coffee House, 1988.
—. *Donald Duk*. Minneapolis: Coffee House, 1991.
—. *Gunga Din Highway*. Minneapolis: Coffee House, 1995.
Chow, Rey. *The Age of the World Target: Self-Referentiality in War, Theory, and Comparative Work*. Durham: Duke UP, 2006.
—. *Ethics after Idealism: Theory-Culture-Ethnicity-Reading*. Bloomington: Indiana UP, 1998.
—. *Woman and Chinese Modernity: The Politics of Reading between West and East*. Minneapolis: Minnesota UP, 1991.
—. *Writing Diaspora: Tactics of Intervention in Contemporary Cultural Studies*. Bloomington: Indiana UP, 1993.
Chu, Louis. *Eat a Bowl of Tea*. New York: Lyle Stuart, 2002.
Daniels, Roger. *The Politics of Prejudice: The Anti-Japanese Movement in California and the Struggle for Japanese Exclusion*. Berkeley: California UP, 1962.
Hagedorn, Jessica. *Dogeaters*. New York: TCG, 2002.
Hakuta, Kenji. *Mirror of Language: The Debate on Bilingualism*. New York: Basic, 1986.
Hwang, David Henry. *M. Butterfly*. New York: DPS, 1998.
Kim, Elaine. *Asian American Literature: An Introduction to the Writings and Their Social Context*. Philadelphia: Temple UP, 1984.
Kingston, Maxine Hong. *China Men*. New York: Vintage, 2011.
—. *The Woman Warrior: Memoirs of a Girlhood Among Ghosts*. New York: Vintage, 1989.
Kitano, Harry, and Roger Daniels. *Asian Americans: Emerging Minorities*. New York: Prentice, 1988.
Koshy, Susan. *Sexual Naturalization: Asian Americans and Miscegenation*. Palo Alto: Stanford UP, 2005.

Koshy, Susan, and S. Radhakrishnan. *Transnational South Asians: The Making of a Neo-Diaspora*. Oxford: Oxford UP, 2008.
Lee, Rachel C. *The Americas of Asian American Literature: Gendered Fictions of Nation and Transnation*. Princeton: Princeton UP, 1999.
Lee, Robert G. *Orientals: Asian Americans in Popular Culture*. Philadelphia: Temple UP, 1999.
Li, David Leiwei. *Imagining the Nation: Asian American Literature and Cultural Consent*. Palo Alto: Stanford UP, 2000.
—. "On Ascriptive and Acquisitional Americanness: The Accidental Asian and the Illogic of Assimilation." *Contemporary Literature* 45.1 (Spring 2004). 106-34.
—. "Race, Gender, Class and Asian American Literary Theory." *Race, Gender & Class* 4.3 (1997). 40-53.
Ng, Fae Myenne. *Bone*. New York: Hyperion, 2008.
O'Brien, David, and Stephen Fugita. *The Japanese American Experience*. Bloomington: Indiana UP, 1991.
Omi, Michael, and Howard Winant. *Racial Formation in the United States: From the 1960s to the 1980s*, New York: Routledge, 1986.
Okada, John. *No-No Boy*, Seattle: Washington UP, 1980.
Okihiro, Gary et al., eds. *Reflections on Shattered Windows: Promises and Prospects for Asian American Studies*. Pullman: Washington State UP, 1988.
Said, Edward. *Orientalism*. New York: Vintage, 1979.
Sandmeyer, Elmer C. *The Anti-Chinese Movement in California*. Champaign: Illinois UP, 1991.
Srikanth, Rajini. *The World Next Door: South Asian American Literature and the Idea of America*. Philadelphia: Temple UP, 2004.
Sui Sin Far. *Mrs. Spring Fragrance*. Champaign: Illinois UP, 1995.
Takaki, Ronald. *Pau Hana: Plantation Life and Labor in Hawaii, 1835-1920*, Honolulu: Hawaii UP, 1987.
—. *Iron Cages: Race and Culture in 19th Century America*. Oxford: Oxford UP, 1990.
Tsai, Shih-shan. *The Chinese Experience in America*. Bloomington: Indiana UP, 1986.
Wand, David Hsin-fu, ed. *Asian American Heritage: An Anthology of Prose and Poetry*. New York: Pocket Books, 1974.
Wong, Sau-ling Cynthia. *Reading Asian American Literature: From Necessity to Extravagance*. Princeton: Princeton UP, 1993.

---

Alvarez Borland, Isabel. *Cuban-American Literature of Exile: From Person to Persona*. Charlottesville: Virginia UP, 1998.
Anzaldúa, Gloria E. *Borderlands/La Frontera: The New Mestiza*. San Francisco: Aunt Lute, 2012.

—. ed. *Making Face, Making Soul/Haciendo Caras: Creative and Critical Perspectives by Feminists of Color.* San Francisco: Aunt Lute, 1990.
Aparicio, Frances, ed. *Latino Voices.* Brookfield: Millbrook, 1994.
—. *Listening to Salsa: Gender, Latin Popular Music, and Puerto Rican Cultures.* Middletown, Wesleyan UP, 1998.
Avelar, Idelber. *The Untimely Present: Postdictatorial Latin American Fiction and the Task of Mourning.* Durham: Duke UP, 1999.
Brogan, Kathleen. *Cultural Haunting: Ghosts and Ethnicity in Recent American Literature.* Charlottesville: Virginia UP, 1998.
Calderón, Héctor, and José David Saldívar, eds. *Criticism in the Borderlands: Studies in Chicano Literature, Culture, and Ideology.* Durham: Duke UP, 1991.
Christian, Karen. *Show & Tell: Identity as Performance in U.S. Latina/o Fiction.* Albuquerque: New Mexico UP, 1997.
Coronado, Raúl. *A World Not to Come: A History of Latino Writing and Print Culture.* Cambridge: Harvard UP, 2013.
Dávila, Arlene. *Culture Works: Space, Value and Mobility Across the Neoliberal Americas.* New York: New York UP, 2012
—. *Latino Spin: Public Image and the Whitewashing of Race.* New York: New York UP, 2008
—. *Latinos Inc.: Marketing and the Making of a People.* Berkeley: California UP, 2001.
Davis, Mike. *Magical Urbanism: Latinos Reinvent the U.S. Big City.* New York: Verso, 2001.
De la Campa, Román. *Cuba on My Mind: Journeys to a Severed Nation.* New York: Verso, 2002.
—. *Latin Americanism.* Minneapolis: Minnesota UP, 1999.
Flores, Juan. *The Diaspora Strikes Back: Caribeño Tales of Learning and Turning.* New York: Routledge, 2007.
—. *From Bomba to Hip-Hop: Puerto Rican Culture and Latino Identity.* New York: Columbia UP, 2000.
Flores, William V., and Rina Benmayor, eds. *Latino Cultural Citizenship: Claiming Identity, Space and Rights.* Boston: Beacon, 1997.
Fox, Geoffrey. *Hispanic Nation: Culture, Politics, and the Constructing of Identity.* Tucson: Arizona UP, 1997.
Gugelberger, Georg M., ed. *The Real Thing: Testimonial Discourse and Latin America.* Durham: Duke UP, 1996.
Jacobs, Elizabeth. *Mexican American Literature: The Politics of Identity.* New York: Routledge, 2009.
Laó-Montes, Augustín, and Arlene Dávila. *Mambo Montage: The Latinization of New York.* New York: Columbia UP, 2001.
Limón, José. *Dancing with the Devil: Society and Cultural Poetics in Mexican-American South Texas.* Madison: Wisconsin UP, 1994.
—. *Mexican Ballads, Chicano Poems: History and Influence in Mexican-American Social Poetry.* Berkeley: California UP, 1992.

Mignolo, Walter D. *The Darker Side of Western Modernity: Global Futures, Decolonial Options.* Durham: Duke UP, 2011.
—. *The Idea of Latin America.* New York: Wiley, 2005.
—. *Local Histories/Global Designs: Coloniality, Subaltern Knowledges, and Border Thinking.* Princeton: Princeton UP, 2012.
Moraga, Cherrie, and Gloria E. Anzaldúa, eds. *This Bridge Called My Back: Writings by Radical Women of Color.* New York: Kitchen Table/Women of Color Press, 1984.
Novas, Himilce. *Everything You Need to Know About Latino History.* New York: Plume, 1994.
Oboler, Suzanne. *Ethnic Labels, Latino Lives: Identity and the Politics of (Re)Presentation in the United States.* Minneapolis: Minnesota UP, 1995.
O'Gorman, Edmundo. *The Invention of America: An Inquiry into the Historical Nature of the New World and the Meaning of Its History.* Bloomington: Greenwood, 1961.
Omi, Michael, and Howard Winant. *Racial Formation in the United States: From the 1960s to the 1980s.* New York: Routledge, 1986.
Padilla, Félix M. *Latino Ethnic Consciousness: The Case of Mexican Americans and Puerto Ricans in Chicago.* Notre Dame: Notre Dame UP, 1985.
Paz, Octavio. *The Labyrinth of Solitude and other Writings.* New York: Grove, 1994.
—. *Children of the Mire: Modern Poetry from Romanticism to the Avant-Garde.* Trans. Rachel Phillips. Cambridge: Harvard UP, 1974.
Pérez Firmat, Gustavo. *Do the Americas Have a Common Literature?* Durham: Duke UP, 1990.
—. *Idle Fictions: The Hispanic Vanguard Novel, 1926–1934.* Durham: Duke UP, 1993.
—. *Literature and Liminality: Festive Readings in the Hispanic Tradition.* Durham: Duke UP, 1985.
—. *Life on the Hyphen: The Cuban-American Way.* Austin: Texas UP, 2012.
Quijano, Aníbal. *Modernidad, identidad y utopia en America Latina.* Quito, Ecuador: *Editorial el Conejo,* 1990.
Rabasa, José. *Inventing America: Spanish Historiography and the Formation of Eurocentrism.* Norman: Oklahoma UP, 1994.
Richard, Nelly. *The Insubordination of Signs: Political Change, Cultural Transformation, and Poetics of the Crisis.* Trans. Alice A. Nelson and Silvia R. Tandeciarz, Durham: Duke UP, 2004.
Saldívar, José David. *Border Matters: Remapping American Cultural Studies.* Berkeley: California UP, 1997.
—. *The Dialectics of Our America: Genealogy, Cultural Critique, and Literary History.* Durham: Duke UP, 1991.

Saldivar, Ramón. *Chicano Narrative: The Dialectics of Difference*. Madison: Wisconsin UP, 1990.
—. *The Borderlands of Culture: Américo Paredes and the Transnational Imaginary*. Durham: Duke UP, 2006.
Sánchez, George I. *Forgotten People: A Study of New Mexicans*. Albuquerque: New Mexico UP, 1940.
Sandoval, Anna Marie. *Toward a Latina Feminism of the Americas: Repression and Resistance in Chicana and Mexicana Literature*. Austin: Texas UP, 2009.
Sollors, Werner. *Beyond Ethnicity: Consent and Descent in American Culture*. New York: Oxford UP, 1986.
—. *Ethnic Modernism*. Cambridge: Harvard UP, 2008.
—. ed. *The Invention of Ethnicity*. New York: Oxford UP, 1991.
Stavans, Ilan. *The Hispanic Condition: Reflections of Culture and Identity in America*. New York: Harper, 2001.
—. *Spanglish: The Making of a New American Language*. New York: Harper, 2004.
Ugarte, Michael. *Shifting Ground: Spanish Civil War Exile Literature*. Durham: Duke UP, 1989.
Weber, Devra. *Dark Sweat, White Gold: California Farm Workers, Cotton, and the New Deal*. Berkeley: California UP, 1996.

---

Apess, William. *A Son of the Forest: The Experience of William Apes, a Native of the Forest, Comprising a Notice of the Pequod Tribe of Indians*. New York: Apes, 1829.
Berkhofer, Robert F. *The White Man's Indian: Images of the American Indian from Columbus to the Present*. New York: Vintage, 1979.
Black Hawk. *Life of Ma-ka-tai-me-she-kia-kiak or Black Hawk: Embracing the Tradition of His Nation; Indian Wars in which He has been Engaged; Cause of Joining the British in their Late War with America, and its History; Description of the Rock River Village; Manners and Customs; Encroachments by the Whites, Contrary to Treaty; Removal from his Village in 1831: with an Account of the Cause and General History of the Late War; his Surrender and Confinement at Jefferson Barracks and Travels Throughout the United States*. Trans. Antoine Leclair. Cincinnati: Patterson, 1833.
Callahan, S. Alice. *Wynema: A Child of the Forest*. Lincoln: Nebraska UP, 1997.
de las Casas, Bartolomé. *A Short Account of the Destruction of the Indies*. New York: Penguin, 1992.
Cook-Lynn, Elizabeth. *A Separate Country: Postcoloniality and American Indian Nations*. Lubbock: Texas Tech UP, 2012.

—. *Anti-Indianism in Modern America: A Voice from Tatekeya's Earth.* Urbana–Champaign: Illinois UP, 2007.
—. *New Indians, Old Wars.* Urbana–Champaign: Illinois UP, 2007.
—. *Why I Can't Read Wallace Stegner and Other Essays: A Tribal Voice.* Madison: Wisconsin UP, 1996.
Cook-Lynn, Elizabeth, and Mario Gonzalez. *The Politics of Hallowed Ground: Wounded Knee and the Struggle for Indian Sovereignty.* Urbana–Champaign: Illinois UP, 1998.
Copway, George. *Indian Life and Indian History, by an Indian Author.* Boston: Albert Colby, 1858.
—. *The Life, History, and Travels of Kah-Ge-Ga-Gah-Bowh (George Copway): A Young Indian Chief of the Ojebwa Nation, a Convert to the Christian Faith, and a Missionary to His People for Twelve Years; With a Sketch of The Present State of the Ojebwa Nation, in Regard to Christianity and Their Future Prospects. Also an Appeal; With All The Names of the Chiefs Now Living, Who Have Been Christianized, and the Missionaries Now Laboring among Them.* Albany: Weed and Parsons, 1847.
—. *Life, Letters and Speeches.* Lincoln: Nebraska UP, 2006.
Deloria Jr., Vine. *American Indian Policy in the Twentieth Century.* Norman: Oklahoma UP, 1992.
—. *Custer Died for Your Sins: An Indian Manifesto.* Norman: Oklahoma UP, 1988.
—. *God Is Red: A Native View of Religion.* Golden, CO: Fulcrum, 2003.
—. *Red Earth, White Lies: Native Americans and the Myth of Scientific Fact.* Golden, CO: Fulcrum, 1997.
Deloria Jr., Vine, and Sandra L. Cadwalader, eds. *The Aggressions of Civilization: Federal Indian Policy Since the 1880s.* Philadelphia: Temple UP, 1984.
Deloria Jr., Vine, and Clifford M. Lytle. *The Nations Within: The Past and Future of American Indian Sovereignty.* Austin: Texas UP, 1998.
Dennis, Helen May. *Native American Literature: Towards a Spatialized Reading.* New York: Routledge, 2006.
Dewing, Rolland. *Wounded Knee II.* Chadron, NE: Great Plains Network, 1995.
Drinnon, Richard. *Facing West: The Metaphysics of Indian-Hating and Empire-Building.* Norman: Oklahoma UP, 1997.
Eastman, Charles A. *Indian Boyhood.* New York: Dover, 1971.
—. *The Soul of the Indian: An Interpretation.* Lincoln, NE: Bison, 1980.
Harjo, Joy, and Gloria Bird, eds. *Reinventing the Enemy's Language: Contemporary Native Women's Writings of North America.* New York: Norton, 1998.
Hopkins, Sarah Winnemucca. *Life Among the Paiutes: Their Wrongs and Claims.* Whitefish, MT: Kessinger, 2010.

Justice, Daniel Heath. *Our Fire Survives the Storm: A Cherokee Literary History*. Minneapolis: Minnesota UP, 2006.
Kelsey, Penelope Myrtle. *Tribal Theory in Native American Literature: Dakota and Haudenosaunee Writing and Indigenous Worldviews*. Lincoln: Nebraska UP, 2010.
Kroeber, Karl. *Artistry in Native American Myths*. Lincoln: Nebraska UP, 1998.
—, ed. *Native American Storytelling: A Reader of Myths and Legends*. New York: Wiley, 1991.
—, ed. *Traditional Literatures of the American Indian: Texts and Interpretations*. Lincoln: Nebraska UP, 1981.
Krupat, Arnold. *Ethnocriticism: Ethnography, History, Literature*. Berkeley: California UP, 1992.
—. *The Voice in the Margin: Native American Literature and the Canon*. Berkeley: California UP, 1989.
Krupat, Arnold, ed. *New Voices in Native American Literary Criticism*. Washington: Smithsonian, 1993.
Lévi-Strauss, Claude. *The Story of Lynx*. Trans. Catherine Tihanyi. Chicago: Chicago UP, 1996.
Lincoln, Kenneth. *Native American Renaissance*. Berkeley: California UP, 1985.
Linderman, Frank B. *Plenty-Coups: Chief of the Crows*. Lincoln, NE: Bison, 2002.
—. *Pretty-shield: Medicine Woman of the Crows*. Lincoln, NE: Bison, 2003.
Lundquist, Suzanne Evertsen. *Native American Literatures: An Introduction*. New York: Consortium, 2004.
Maddox, Lucy. *Removals: Nineteenth-Century American Literature and the Politics of Indian Affairs*. New York: Oxford UP, 1991.
Matthews, John Joseph. *Sundown*. Norman: Oklahoma UP, 1988.
—. *Twenty Thousand Mornings: An Autobiography*. Norman: Oklahoma UP, 2012.
—. *Wah'kon-tah: The Osage and The White Man's Road*. Norman: Oklahoma UP, 1981.
Momaday, N. Scott. *House Made of Dawn*. New York: Harper, 2010.
Moore, MariJo, ed. *Genocide of the Mind: New Native American Writing*. New York: Nation, 2003.
Neihardt, John G. *Black Elk Speaks: Being the Life Story of a Holy Man of the Oglala Sioux*. Lincoln: Nebraska UP, 1988.
—. *When the Tree Flowered: The Story of Eagle Voice, a Sioux Indian*. Lincoln: Nebraska UP, 1991.
Nelson, Robert M. *Leslie Marmon Silko's Ceremony: The Recovery of Tradition*. New York: Peter Lang, 2008.
—. *Place and Vision: The Function of Landscape in Native American Fiction*. New York: Peter Lang, 1993.

Pokagon, Simon. *Ogimawkwe Mitigwaki (Queen of the Woods)*. East Lansing: Michigan State UP, 2011.
Pulitano, Elvira. *Toward a Native American Critical Theory*. Lincoln: Nebraska UP, 2003.
Ridge, John Rollin. *The Life and Adventures of Joaquín Murieta, the Celebrated California Bandit*. Norman: Oklahoma UP, 1977.
Silko, Leslie Marmon. *Ceremony*. New York: Penguin, 1986.
—. *Yellow Woman and a Beauty of the Spirit: Essays on Native American Life Today*. New York: Simon and Schuster, 1997.
Swann, Brian, ed. *On the Translation of Native American Literatures*. Washington: Smithsonian, 1992.
Treuer, David. *Native American Fiction: A User's Manual*. Minneapolis: Minnesota UP, 2006.
Vizenor, Gerald. *Fugitive Poses: Native American Indian Scenes of Absence and Presence*. Lincoln: Nebraska UP, 2000.
—. *Manifest Manners: Narratives on Postindian Survivance*. Lincoln: Nebraska UP, 1999.
Warrior, Robert Allen. *The People and the Word: Reading Native Nonfiction*. Minneapolis: Minnesota UP, 2005.
—. *Tribal Secrets: Recovering American Indian Intellectual Traditions*. Minneapolis: Minnesota UP, 1994.
Weaver, Jace. *Notes from a Miner's Canary: Essays on the State of Native America*. Albuquerque: New Mexico UP, 2010.
—. *That the People Might Live: Native American Literatures and Native American Community*. New York: Oxford UP, 1997.
Weaver, Jace, Craig S. Womack and Robert Warrior. *American Indian Literary Nationalism*. Albuquerque: New Mexico UP, 2006.
Womack, Craig S. *Art as Performance, Story as Criticism: Reflections on Native Literary Aesthetics*. Norman: Oklahoma UP, 2009.
—. *Red on Red: Native American Literary Separatism*. Minneapolis: Minnesota UP, 1999.
Wong, Hertha Dawn. *Sending My Heart Back Across the Years: Tradition and Innovation in Native American Autobiography*. New York: Oxford UP, 1992.
Zitkala-Ša. *American Indian Stories, Legends, and Other Writings*. New York: Penguin, 2003.
—. *Dreams and Thunder: Stories, Poems, and The Sun Dance Opera*. Lincoln, NE: Bison, 2005.
—. *Old Indian Legends*. London: Forgotten, 2008.

# 12

# Queer Theory

FOCUSES ON: the overt and the covert text, specifically with regard to issues of sexual orientation.
BECAUSE: queer theorists are interested in the way gender identity and sexual orientation are presented and discussed in literature; they see the study of literary texts as one avenue through which to end the marginalization of and discrimination against persons of all sexual orientations.
DEVELOPED IN: 1980s
NOTABLE PRACTITIONERS:
    Michel Foucault (1926-84)
    Monique Wittig (1935-2003)
    Teresa de Lauretis (1938- )
    Marilyn Frye (1941- )
    Paula Bennett (1945- )
    Guy Hocquenghem (1946-88)
    Karla Jay (1947- )
    David Halperin (1952- )
    Lauren Berlant (1957- )
    Adrienne Rich (1929-2012)
    Sandy Stone (1937- )
    Lilian Faderman (1940- )
    Gloria Anzaldúa (1942-2004)
    Barbara Smith (1946- )
    Bonnie Zimmerman (1947- )
    Eve Kosofsky Sedgwick (1950-2009)
    Judith Butler (1956- )
    Michael Warner (1958- )
IMPORTANT PREDECESSORS:
    Simone de Beauvoir (1908-86)
    Del Martin (1921-2008)
    Frank Kameny (1925-2011)
    Luce Irigaray (1930- )
    Barbara Gittings (1932-2007)
    Hélène Cixous (1937- )
    Harry Hay (1912-2002)
    Phyllis Ann Lyon (1924- )
    Jacques Derrida (1930-2004)
    Kay Tobin Lahusen (1930- )
    Kate Millet (1934- )
    Craig Rodwell (1940-93)
ADVANTAGES: exposes and challenges our ingrained cultural assumptions about what is "normal," particularly with regard to sexual orientation.
DISADVANTAGES: in a reading that focuses on issues of sexuality, other literary aspects of the text can be overlooked or ignored.

DEFINITION: the practice of interpreting a literary work from an LGBTQ perspective, characterized by its rejection of traditional categories of gender and sexuality.

---

Following a pattern similar to many other critical approaches, queer theory developed as scholars recognized a need to understand literature—and the world—from the perspective of lesbian, gay, bisexual, transgender and questioning people and cultures.

The Western world has a long history of discrimination against the LGBTQ community. For centuries, non-heterosexual activity was seen as a "crime against nature." Those caught engaging in same-sex behavior could be imprisoned, disfigured or even put to death. While the legal consequences for same-sex activity had eased by the twentieth century, intolerance was still the norm. Those arrested for "homosexual acts" had their names and pictures published in the local newspaper and soon after were fired from their jobs, evicted from their apartments, and lost any chance of getting a bank loan for a car or a home.

Such discrimination became particularly virulent during the Cold War. By the mid-1950s, the U.S. was immersed in McCarthyism. Often forgotten from this era is that the prejudice against the LGBTQ community equaled or surpassed that perpetrated against alleged communists. The U.S. State Department asserted that gays and lesbians were high-level threats to national security because they were often blackmailed to keep their sexual orientation secret. Consequently, thousands of people lost their military or government jobs—or were denied employment altogether—when they were thought to be gay, lesbian, bisexual or transgender. Even more troubling, the FBI maintained lists of people they believed to be gay or lesbian; the U.S. Postal Service kept a record of addresses where any "questionable" material was mailed; and state and local governments passed laws outlawing activities that they associated with non-heterosexual behavior. Police departments throughout the country had the authority to detain, arrest and harass any same-sex couples they caught kissing, dancing together or even holding hands.

In an effort to end such institutionalized discrimination, Harry Hay formed a gay rights organization, the Mattachine Society, in 1950. Five years later, Del Martin and Phyllis Lyon founded the Daughters of Bilitis to support lesbian civil and political rights. One goal of both organizations was to show that the only inherent difference between heterosexuals and non-heterosexuals was their sexual orientation. The Mattachine Society and the DOB brought together likeminded people in major cities throughout the U.S. While their efforts may have seemed to result in little perceptible progress for the LGBTQ community, their work provided the foundation upon which later change would be built.

Observable change came in 1969. That summer, on June 28, New York police raided the Stonewall Inn, a Greenwich Village bar catering to the non-heterosexual community. At the time, the Stonewall Inn was the largest LGBTQ establishment in the country. While police raids at such bars had become common, people responded to this particular raid with a series of violent demonstrations that lasted several days. These mass protests, now known as the Stonewall riots, are considered the beginning of the Gay Rights Movement in America.

Following the Stonewall riots, gay and lesbian leaders felt empowered to stand up to the individual and institutional bigotry that had plagued the LGBTQ community for centuries. The Gay Liberation Front, formed shortly after the Stonewall riots, advocated an aggressive stance against oppression. The Gay Activists Alliance was founded in December of that year. By 1971 most major cities in North America and Europe were served by one or another gay rights group and one of several LGBTQ newspapers, such as *Gay*, *Gay Power* and *Come Out!*.

In 1970, the first LGBTQ studies course was developed at UC Berkeley. However, acceptance of such courses hasn't come easily. It wasn't until 1986 that the first program in gay and lesbian studies was formed, and 1989 when the first department of Gay and Lesbian Studies was established. Other universities have slowly—sometimes grudgingly—followed suit. As recently as 1997, for example, Yale University refused a four million-dollar endowment because it stipulated that Yale establish a professorship in gay studies. Even today, a number of colleges refuse to offer even one course in LGBTQ studies.

## The History of Sexuality

Though colleges have been slow to embrace LGBTQ topics on an institutional level, individual scholars have undertaken serious LGBTQ research since the 1970s. Much of this early work was inspired by the writings of Michel Foucault, particularly volume 1 of his three-volume work, *The History of Sexuality* (1976; trans. 1980).

Foucault examines sexual behavior from the seventeenth to the twentieth century, highlighting the attitudes toward gay men throughout this time. For Foucault, homosexuality was born when Carl Westphal first categorized it in 1870. Westphal referred to same-sex relations between men as "contrary sexual sensations" in the medical journal, *Archiv für Psychiatrie und Nervenkrankheiten* (*Archives of Psychiatry and Nervous Diseases*). Richard von Krafft-Ebing coined the term, "homosexual," within two decades. In *Psychopathia Sexualis* (1886; trans. *The Sexual Psychopath*, 1892), Krafft-Ebing worked extensively to categorize what he saw as sexual abnormalities. He and his contemporaries identified and named those who engaged in numerous other "psychosexual perversions" as well: "zoophiles," "zooerasts," and "auto-monosexualists," among others.

Prior to this time, according to Foucault, these various sexual acts were labeled simply "sodomy," a term that encompassed nearly everything other than the procreative relations between a husband and wife. Depending upon the type of "sodomy" one engaged in, if the person was caught, he could be tortured or executed. Foucault argues though, based on judicial records, that such punishments were relatively rare, leading him to conclude that the Victorian era was ambivalent about same-sex activity.

In Foucault's view, identifying and naming "homosexuality" initiated a chain of events that led to widespread repression and discrimination that continued for well over a century. He notes that,

> Homosexuality appeared as one of the forms of sexuality when it was transposed from the practice of sodomy [. . .]. The sodomite had been a temporary aberration; the homosexual now was a species.

As Foucault sees it, the social condemnation of "homosexuality" emanates from the propagation of power. Not institutional power passed down by "law, prohibition, liberty, and sovereignty," but the power of "knowledge" disseminated through discourse. For Foucault, the history of sexuality—indeed, the history of the world—has been shaped by this "power-knowledge."

"Knowledge," to Foucault, isn't necessarily factually accurate. Foucault's "knowledge" refers to accepted "truths" (whether they are true or not) that the dominant ideology treats as fact. When homosexuality was identified and categorized, the prevailing wisdom changed regarding this type of sodomy. The dominant discourse told us that this was "abnormal" and "perverse" behavior performed by psychological "degenerates." As one might imagine, then, if a culture's dominant ideology sees heterosexuality as normal and all other expressions of sexuality as abhorrent, then homosexuality becomes a societal problem that must be stopped. Consequently, the Western world's approach toward homosexuality changed.

As Foucault notes, classifying "homosexuality" as a psychological disorder may have abolished torture and execution for those few who were convicted of same-sex offenses, but it also put everyone suspected of such behavior under closer scrutiny. While the executions may have ended, suspected "homosexuals" were locked away in asylums and subjected to countless texts, experiments and "corrective" medical procedures. This new approach impelled every gay man to conceal his sexual orientation from all but his most trusted companions. The seemingly simple act of labeling homosexuality, then, had lasting repercussions for the entire LGBTQ community.

## Compulsory Heterosexuality

Many female LGBTQ scholars identified with the early years of feminism's second wave. By the mid-1970s, however, this began to change. During this time, opponents of the feminist movement often characterized feminists as simply "disgruntled lesbians." To fend off such misperceptions, some feminists began to distance themselves from non-heterosexual women. This left lesbian feminists such as Gloria Anzaldúa, Bonnie Zimmerman and Adrienne Rich feeling increasingly excluded from the feminist movement. Rich responded to these developments with her provocative essay, "Compulsory Heterosexuality and Lesbian Existence" (1980).

The history of women, according to Rich, is fraught with subjugation. Central to this subjugation is a compulsory heterosexuality forced upon women by a patriarchal ideology. Drawing on the work of Kathleen Gough, Catharine A. MacKinnon, Kathleen Barry and others, Rich argues that a woman's heterosexual preference isn't a natural aspect of biological evolution. Instead, it is a "lie" imposed upon women in order to reinforce the male dominated society.

Rather than seeing women as either heterosexual or lesbian, Rich sees women's sexuality operating on a varying "lesbian continuum." One woman's lesbian existence might seek out female companionship while another's might look for something more intimate. If all women were to recognize this aspect of themselves, according to Rich, it would end women's subservience to men. It is in men's best interest, then, to ensure that women stay committed to their heterosexual lifestyles. Rich demonstrates how heterosexuality is enforced by expanding on Kathleen Gough's eight characteristics of male power. For Rich, each of these characteristics stems from a form of compulsory heterosexuality:

1. denial of women's sexuality (with such things as chastity belts, clitoridectomies, and harsh punishments for adultery)
2. forced sex (through rape; prostitution and idealization of heterosexual romance)
3. exploitation of their labor (the free labor expected of wives and mothers)
4. control of their parental rights ("legal kidnapping," forced sterilization)
5. physical confinement (foot binding, "feminine" dress codes, enforced economic dependence)
6. use of women as objects of exchange (pimping, arranged marriages, "giving away" the bride in a traditional marriage)

7. suppression of creativity (the persecution of midwives and healers through witch trials, the economic exclusion of women in creative endeavors)
8. withholding of knowledge (limiting access to education and careers in the sciences, destroying evidence of lesbian contributions to history and culture)

While compulsory heterosexuality is often implemented through force, it is also—perhaps more insidiously—imposed through a patriarchal ideology. This ideology teaches women from a young age to idealize a life that conforms to "traditional" gender roles. Romantic fairy tales, examples of ideal beauty, fantasies of perfect weddings and expectations of motherhood all work to indoctrinate girls and young women to become ideal servants in a patriarchal society. Rich argues that change can only come when women realize that heterosexuality has been unnaturally foisted upon them.

## The Homosocial Continuum

Eve Kosofsky Sedgwick examined the effects of compulsory heterosexuality on men. While enforced heterosexuality suppresses women in a patriarchal society, Sedgwick sees it operating in equally pervasive ways on men. When heterosexuality becomes obligatory, men are forced to redirect any non-heterosexual feelings through socially acceptable channels. For Sedgwick, this is illustrated in literature when two male characters compete for the attention of the same woman.

Sedgwick sees desire between males, or "male homosocial desire," couched in literary allusions to the love triangle. In one of her earlier works of queer theory, "Homophobia, Misogyny, and Capital: The Example of *Our Mutual Friend*" (1983), Sedgwick uncovers within Dickens' novel the homoerotic tension between Bradley and Eugene as they both vie for Lizzie's love. Sedgwick expands upon these ideas in her book, *Between Men: English Literature and Male Homosocial Desire* (1985), identifying similar examples in works by Shakespeare, Wycherley, Tennyson and others. The love triangle, for Sedgwick, is an avenue through which men's unconscious desire for each other can be fulfilled. Expanding upon René Girard's belief that the bond between the competing men in a love triangle is actually stronger than the bond either of the men share with the woman—the supposed object of their affection—Sedgwick concludes that the woman is the conduit through which the men are able to connect. In other words, an elemental aspect of any love triangle is a homosocial desire shared by the two rivals.

Sedgwick describes "male homosocial desire" as the entire continuum between homosexuality and heterosexual "male bonding" exercises. She argues that the "heavily freighted bonds between men" in the form of homosocial desire work to maintain the "exchange-of-women framework" inherent in any patriarchal society. Such bonds appear throughout Shakespeare's sonnets, for example, in varying groupings of the speaker, the Fair Youth, the Rival Poet, and the Dark Lady. We see it again in Wycherley's *The Country Wife* with Sparkish and Pinchwife, in Tennyson's *Princess*, in Eliot's *Adam Bede*, and Thackeray's *Henry Esmond*. Indeed, Sedgwick suggests that any such grouping should be viewed with scrutiny.

Sedgwick expands upon these ideas in *Epistemology of the Closet* (1990). She begins by offering seven "axioms" to clarify the genesis and nature of queer theory:

1. People are different from each other.
2. The study of sexuality is not coextensive with the study of gender; correspondingly, antihomophobic inquiry is not coextensive with feminist inquiry. But we can't know in advance how they will be different.
3. There can't be an a priori decision about how far it will make sense to conceptualize lesbian and gay male identities together. Or separately.
4. The immemorial, seemingly ritualized debates on nature versus nurture take place against a very unstable background of tacit assumptions and fantasies about both nature and nurture.
5. The historical search for a Great Paradigm Shift may obscure the present conditions of sexual identity.
6. The relation of gay studies to debates on the literary canon is, and had best be, tortuous.
7. The paths of allo-identification are likely to be strange and recalcitrant. So are the paths of auto-identification.

Sedgwick then provides extended readings of Melville, Wilde, Nietzsche, Henry James and Proust from the perspective of queer theory. She finds evidence of recurring homoerotic undertones throughout these works. Claggart from Melville's *Billy Budd*, for example, acts out of jealousy and unrequited homosexual desire. The tragedy for James' character, John Marcher, is that he is a gay man living a doomed existence as a heterosexual. Indeed, for Sedgwick, a persistent suggestion of homoerotic desire and homosexual panic is entwined in all manner of literary texts. One goal of the queer theorist, then, is to uncover these hidden subtexts in order to understand how they are defined by a culture. For many scholars, Sedgwick is considered the founder of queer theory because she charted the path that would guide queer theory for the next two decades.

## Sexual Identity as a Performative Act

Contemporary queer theory has also been shaped significantly by the work of Judith Butler, particularly her ideas on the nature of gender and sexual identity. She believes that our understanding of sexual identity, as well as our understanding of gender, has been flawed for centuries. In her essay, "Performative Acts and Gender Constitution: An Essay in Phenomenology and Feminist Theory" (1988), Butler introduces her concept of gender performativity. She expands upon this in her books, *Gender Trouble* (1990) and *Bodies that Matter* (1993).

Before Butler, theorists—notably feminist theorists—often drew a clear distinction between sex and gender. For them, sex was defined by biological differences while gender was a socially constructed creation shaped by one's cultural environment. In other words, our sex is a natural identity while our gender is a constructed one. Butler disagreed. She believes that our categories of sexual identity—male and female—are also socially constructed. Indeed, Butler argues that any identity categories tend to function as "instruments of regulatory regimes, whether as the normalizing categories of oppressive structures or as the rallying points for a liberatory contestation of that very oppression."

Butler draws her theory of sex and gender from Jacques Derrida's understanding of citation and repetition in performative speech acts. In his essay, "Signature, Event, Context" (1972), Derrida argues that, when we communicate, we are *performing* language. The meaning of the words we use is based upon the previous uses (or citations) of those words. For Butler, sex and gender operate in the same way, as performative acts. In other words, according to Butler, we act the role of a male or female just as we act the role in a play.

In a play, we have the stage, the setting and the audience to remind us that we are performing a role. In our performance of sex and gender, however, everything in our world constantly reinforces the belief that our role is real. Every day, we are inundated with "ideal" and "typical" men and women. We see them in movies, television and on the news. They are in advertisements for beauty products, automobiles, toys and food: this is what a man is; this is how a woman looks and behaves. Even when men and women are presented in "nontraditional" roles—the man as homemaker, the woman as business leader, construction worker, or even professional fighter—they will (almost without exception) still conform to our patriarchal standards of masculinity and femininity.

As we perform the role of a sexual identity—male or female—throughout our lives, this constant repetition reinforces the illusion that these binary sexual categories are real. Seeing it again and again, in other words, convinces all of us that there are only two distinct sexes, male and female, with their corresponding genders. Even feminist efforts to define and unite women result in reinforcing these binary sexual categories. Eventually, these categories become for us an unquestioned "reality."

The result, as we are shown these representations of "man" and "woman" every day of our lives, is to guide us into predetermined categories of sex and gender. In other words, children grow up thinking, "since these people have the same biological construction as I do, then this is my sex and this is how I should look and act." Thus, we aren't able to choose the sex and gender roles we perform. They have already been chosen for us by the dominant ideology of our culture. This becomes problematic for those who don't identify with either of these two predetermined categories. Our constructed "reality" of only two sexual categories is accompanied by the belief that heterosexuality is a natural function of biological necessity. Everything else, then, is seen as "deviant" and "perverse."

For Butler, the solution begins by understanding that sex and gender are unstable and "free floating." She therefore supports gender parody such as cross-dressing and drag performances. Such activities, Butler notes, undermine our socially constructed categories of identity by highlighting "the imitative structure of gender itself." Only after we have abolished identity categories will we be able to move beyond a repressive patriarchal ideology that sees any non-heterosexual activity as abnormal.

## Implementation

One of the earliest queer readings of a text—still considered a quintessential example of a queer interpretation—is Eve Kosofsky Sedgwick's "The Beast in the Closet: James and the Writing of Homosexual Panic." In it, Sedgwick examines Henry James' short story, "The Beast in the Jungle," from the perspective of queer theory.

As Sedgwick sees it, James' protagonist, John Marcher, is an "irredeemably self-ignorant man" who doesn't realize he is gay. In this interpretation, the "secret" that is alluded to throughout the story is Marcher's unrecognized sexual orientation. For Sedgwick, the story's tragedy isn't that Marcher has wasted his life, but that society's compulsory heterosexuality has denied him his sexual identity.

To prove her argument, Sedgwick begins by examining the history of male homosexual panic. According to Sedgwick, this panic reveals itself in the unmarried Gothic fictional hero and again in the Victorian era bachelor character. Sedgwick sees the bachelor as a manifestation of the homosexual panic that arises from the fear of being outed as a gay man. Contrary to the common view of the bachelor as a serial Lothario, Sedgwick argues that the bachelor lifestyle was more often adopted to conceal one's true sexual orientation. Sedgwick points to James as an example. She sees James' own commitment to bachelorhood as a means to disguise the "inobliterable" fact of his own homosexuality.

For Sedgwick, such biographical details suggest parallels between James' personal life and the life of his bachelor character, John Marcher. She focuses particular attention on James' relationship with Constance Fenimore Woolson, a "deaf, intelligent American woman author, who clearly loved [James]." Drawing on Leon Edel's biography of James, Sedgwick concludes that James' intimate encounters with Woolson were James' attempts at "heterosexual self-probation." He used Woolson, in other words, to experiment with a heterosexual identity. When James' attempts to identify as a heterosexual had failed, according to Sedgwick, Woolson's unrequited love drove her to suicide.

Sedgwick believes that James often translated his homosexual desires into written heterosexual ones. In doing so, however, he "reliably left a residue" of material that he either didn't bother to translate or that translated poorly. In "The Beast in the Jungle," this residue has the form of a barely perceptible theme of male homosexuality that exists as a "thematics of absence." The story, of course, revolves around absence: John Marcher's absence of heterosexual desire for May Bartram, the woman "he should have desired."

For Sedgwick, though, the "absence of speech" is more significant. This type of absence is obvious in allusions to Marcher's "secret" that is never uncovered. Sedgwick argues that Marcher's "secret" is rooted in male homosexual panic. As she puts it, "Marcher's secret has *a* content, that content is homosexual." Sedgwick points out that, when James wrote "The Beast in the Jungle" (1903), same-sex male sexuality was considered:

> Unspeakable, Unmentionable, *nefandam libidinem*, "that sin which should be neither named nor committed," the "detestable and abominable sin, amongst Christians not to be named," [and] "the love that dare not speak its name."

In the years following Oscar Wilde's 1895 trial on sodomy and indecency charges, talk of same-sex desire was suppressed like never before. As Sedgwick notes, descriptions of Marcher's secret ("his singularity," "'the real truth' about him," "the secret of the gods," etc.) were equally apt to describe homosexuality during this period.

Sedgwick implies, too, that James was aware of this double meaning when he wrote the story. Sedgwick quotes an excerpt from James' personal notebooks which suggests that James had considered other names for Marcher's character, including, "Assingham," "Coxster," "Dickwinter" and "Didcock." Considering the name he finally chose—Marcher (one who marches, conforming to the footsteps of those around him)—we could conclude that he understood the various implications of that choice. In other words, James knew that his character, John Marcher, was imprisoned by his society's compulsory heterosexuality. Any thorough analysis of the story, according to Sedgwick, must at least consider that possibility.

As Sedgwick illustrates, a queer reading can incorporate elements of other theoretical approaches (such as psychoanalysis and new historicism) into its analysis. The queer theorist can use these tools to examine a story from a queer perspective and gain new insight into the work.

## Important Moments in Queer Theory

- **1950:** Mattachine Society formed
- **1951:** Donald Webster Cory (Edward Sagarin) publishes *The Homosexual in America*
- **1955:** Daughters of Bilitis founded
- **1957:** Evelyn Hooker's "The Adjustment of the Male Overt Homosexual"
- **1965:** first Annual Reminder demonstration at Philadelphia's Independence Hall
- **1966:** Compton's Cafeteria riot in San Francisco
- **1969:** Stonewall riots in New York's Greenwich Village
- **1969:** Gay Liberation Front founded
- **1969:** Gay Activists Alliance founded
- **1970:** first LGBTQ studies course offered at UC Berkeley
- **1972:** Guy Hocquenghem's *Homosexual Desire*
- **1972:** Karla Jay and Allen Young edit *Out of the Closets*
- **1973:** American Psychiatric Association discontinues its classification of homosexuality as a mental disorder
- **1976:** the first volume of Foucault's *The History of Sexuality*
- **1980:** Adrienne Rich's "Compulsory Heterosexuality and Lesbian Existence"
- **1984:** volumes 2 and 3 of Foucault's *The History of Sexuality*
- **1985:** Eve Kosofsky Sedgwick's *Between Men*
- **1990:** Judith Butler's *Gender Trouble*
- **1990:** Sedgwick's *Epistemology of the Closet*
- **1990:** formation of the International Gay and Lesbian Human Rights Commission
- **1990:** David Halperin's *One Hundred Years of Homosexuality*
- **1990:** Paula Bennett's *Emily Dickinson: Woman Poet*
- **1993:** Michael Warner's *Fear of a Queer Planet*
- **1993:** Butler's *Bodies that Matter*
- **1994:** Teresa de Lauretis' *The Practice of Love*
- **1994:** LGBT History Month established in U.S.
- **2004:** Butler's *Undoing Gender*
- **2010:** publication of the "Activist's Guide" by Yogyakarta Principles in Action

## Important Terms

compulsory heterosexuality
gender identity
lesbian continuum
homosocial desire
marginalization
sexual identity

essentialism
gender performativity
lesbian existence
homosocial continuum
power-knowledge
social construction

## Study Questions

1. Analyze a story of your choice from the perspective of queer theory and one other theoretical approach of your choice. How do the two readings compare? Which theory do you think provides the most rewarding analysis, and why? Use specific examples from the story as you develop your response.
2. Read Poe's "The Cask of Amontillado" from the perspective of queer theory. Formulate an argument that either proves or disproves that the insult mentioned in the first sentence has its origins in an intimate same-sex interaction. Whatever your initial opinion, you should thoughtfully consider your opposing point of view. If you want to argue, for example, that the insult is not sexual in nature, you'll want to read the story as if it is, finding whatever textual proof you can to support that view, before rebutting it with your own conclusions.
3. Perform a queer reading of Conrad's "The Secret Sharer." Pay particular attention to the narrator's interactions with Leggatt and the descriptions and images that accompany those interactions. How do they first meet? Where does Leggatt hide? What does he wear? How is he described? etc. Include in your interpretation a discussion of the homosocial continuum with regard to the bond between Leggatt and the narrator. (Keep in mind, too, that all descriptions and actions come to us filtered through the perspective of Conrad's first-person narrator.)
4. After reading either Lawrence's "The Prussian Officer" or Barnes' "A Night Among the Horses," undertake some preliminary research on the story and the author to determine in which direction you would take a queer analysis of the piece. Would you focus primarily on the covert text of the story itself? On the author? On his or her body of work? Or would you pursue another avenue of interest? Explain the reasons for your decision.
5. From a queer theoretical perspective, write a brief essay about a story of your choice that uncovers some truth about the story that isn't explicitly stated in the text. Examine all aspects of the story to find at least one significant truth that is implied but not actually written in

the text. Perhaps you'd like to focus on the story's plot or its theme. Maybe a character's motivations become clear when viewed through the lens of queer theory. Or maybe you'd like to study the author's biography or his or her body of work and develop an argument based upon your findings. Whatever topic you choose, you should focus on developing an insightful conclusion.

## Selected Bibliography

Bennett, Paula. *Emily Dickinson: Woman Poet.* Iowa City: Iowa UP, 1991.
—. *My Life a Loaded Gun: Dickinson, Plath, Rich, and Female Creativity.* Champaign: Illinois UP, 1990.
Butler, Judith. *Bodies that Matter: On the Discursive Limits of "Sex."* New York: Routledge, 2011.
—. *Gender Trouble: Feminism and the Subversion of Identity.* New York: Routledge, 2006.
Butler, Judith, and Athena Athanasiou. *Dispossession: The Performative in the Political.* Cambridge, UK: Polity, 2013.
de Lauretis, Teresa. *Alice Doesn't: Feminism, Semiotics, Cinema.* Bloomington: Indiana UP, 1994.
—. ed. *The Practice of Love: Lesbian Sexualities and Perverse Desire.* Bloomington: Indiana UP, 1994.
Derrida, Jacques. "Signature, Event, Context." *Limited Inc.* Trans. Jeffrey Mehlman and Samuel Weber. Evanston: Northwestern UP, 1988.
Faderman, Lillian. *Odd Girls and Twilight Lovers: A History of Lesbian Life in Twentieth-Century America.* New York: Columbia UP, 1991.
Foucault, Michel. *The History of Sexuality, Volume I: An Introduction.* Trans. Robert Hurley. New York: Vintage, 1990.
Fuss, Diana, ed. *Inside Out: Lesbian Theories, Gay Theories.* New York: Routledge, 1991.
Halperin, David. *One Hundred Years of Homosexuality and Other Essays on Greek Love.* New York: Routledge, 1990.
—. *Saint Foucault: Towards a Gay Hagiography.* Oxford: Oxford UP, 1995.
Hocquenghem, Guy. *Homosexual Desire.* Trans. Michael Moon. Durham: Duke UP, 1993.
Jay, Karla, and Allen Young, eds. *Out of the Closets: Voices of Gay Liberation.* New York: New York UP, 1992.
Krafft-Ebing, Richard. *Psychopathia Sexualis.* New York: Arcade, 1998.
Narayan, Uma. *Dislocating Cultures: Identities, Traditions, and Third World Feminism.* New York: Routledge, 1997.

Rich, Adrienne. "Compulsory Heterosexuality and Lesbian Existence." *Signs* 5.4 (Summer 1980): 631-60.
Sedgwick, Eve Kosofsky. *Between Men: English Literature and Male Homosexual Desire*. New York: Columbia UP, 1985.
—. *Epistemology of the Closet*. Berkeley: California UP, 1990.
Sinfield, Alan. *Cultural Politics—Queer Reading*. New York: Routledge, 2005.
Stimpson, Catharine, and Ethel Spector Person, eds. *Women: Sex and Sexuality*. Chicago: Chicago UP, 1980.
Warner, Michael. *Fear of a Queer Planet: Queer Politics and Social Theory*. Minneapolis: Minnesota UP, 1993.
Wittig, Monique. *The Straight Mind*. Boston: Beacon, 1991.

# 13

# Ecocriticism

**FOCUSES ON:** the overt and covert text, paying particular attention to the text's stated and unstated stance on ecological issues.

**BECAUSE:** ecocriticism is guided by an undisguised political agenda, the goal of which is to reverse the disastrous impact that humans have had on our environment; ecocritics are interested, then, in humans' relationship with nature and the ways in which literature shapes this relationship.

**DEVELOPED IN:** 1990s.

**NOTABLE PRACTITIONERS:**

Michael P. Branch
SueEllen Campbell
Harold Fromm
Terry Gifford
William Howarth
Glen A. Love
Timothy Morton
Vandana Shiva
Kate Soper
Lawrence Buell
Christopher Cokinos
Greg Garrard
Cheryll Glotfelty
Joel Kovel
Michael Löwy
Dana Phillips
Scott Slovic
Karen J. Warren

**IMPORTANT PREDECESSORS:**

Ralph Waldo Emerson (1803-82)   Margaret Fuller (1810-50)
Henry David Thoreau (1817-62)   J. Sterling Morton (1832-1902)
John Muir (1838-1914)   Rachel Carson (1907-64)
Arne Næss (1912-2009)   Murray Bookchin (1921-2006)
Raymond Williams (1921-88)   Edward Abbey (1927-89)

**ADVANTAGES:** exposes the deep-seated anthropocentric belief system at work within texts while highlighting the role that nature plays in shaping literary works and the role that literary works play in shaping the natural world; the merger of ecology and literary analysis also facilitates a more reasoned argument for environmental sustainability.

**DISADVANTAGES:** since ecocritics focus on environmental issues within a text, other literary elements of that work can be overlooked or ignored.

**DEFINITION:** a method of literary analysis that examines the interrelationship between texts, individuals, their culture and their environment.

---

In his address to the Western Literature Association titled "Revaluing Nature: Toward an Ecological Criticism" (1989), Glen A. Love enumerated the "actual and potential horrors" threatening our existence:

> the threats of nuclear holocaust, or of slower radiation poisoning, of chemical or germ warfare, the alarming growth of the world's population (standing room only in a few centuries at the present rate of growth), mounting evidence of global warming, destruction of the planet's protective ozone layer, the increasingly harmful effects of acid rain, overcutting of the world's last remaining great forests, the critical loss of topsoil and groundwater, overfishing and toxic poisoning of the oceans, inundation in our own garbage, an increasing rate of extinction of plant and animal species.

Today, decades later, students recognize the profound importance of these "doomsday potentialities" more than any other generation in history. Still, not all students understand how ecological concerns mesh with the seemingly incongruous field of literary analysis. They frequently ask, "How is ecocriticism considered a *literary* theory?" or, "What does ecology have to do with literature?"

Ecocritics want to change this perception. They believe that literature and ecology naturally complement each other. Indeed, they argue that environmental concerns are interwoven into every aspect of human existence and therefore should be incorporated into every academic discipline. Considering the pressing nature of these concerns, ecocritics believe that it's not only possible, but essential, to read a text from an ecocritical perspective.

## The Beginnings of Ecocriticism

William Rueckert defines ecocriticism as "the application of ecology and ecological concepts to the study of literature." Christopher Cokinos describes it as "the critical and pedagogical broadening of literary studies to include texts that deal with the nonhuman world and our relationship to it." For Cheryll Glotfelty, ecocriticism is "the study of the relationship between literature and the physical environment." Lawrence Buell calls it the "study of the relation between literature and the environment conducted in a spirit of commitment to environmentalist praxis." Chad Weidner sees it as "an academic response to the economic, political, and social disorder caused by environmental upheaval."

However we define ecocriticism, the goal of all ecocritics is to facilitate responsible stewardship of our planet. According to Greg Garrard, the principles of ecocriticism date back at least as far as the late dialogues of Plato, who noted in *Critias* the degradation of Attica's hillsides. Today's ecocriticism developed as scholars gained an increased awareness of humans' impact on the natural world. This awareness grew in the wake of several disasters that highlighted the consequences of environmental negligence. In the 1980s alone, we saw images of the Bhopal disaster in India, the Chernobyl disaster in Ukraine and the Exxon Valdez oil spill in Alaska, as well as the discovery of the ozone hole above Antarctica.

Still, even though literary theory had expanded to represent all manner of contemporary issues (race, class, gender, etc.), an ecological approach to literature was conspicuously absent. As Glotfelty notes, there were "no journals, no jargon, no jobs, no professional societies or discussion groups, and no conferences on literature and the environment." This was particularly noteworthy, according to Glotfelty, since other fields in the humanities such as philosophy, religion and sociology had "been 'greening' since the 1970s."

There were individual scholars, however, who integrated ecological issues into their literary studies. By the early 1990s, these individuals had finally begun to come together. In 1991, the Modern Language Association recognized ecocriticism with a special session titled, "Ecocriticism: The Greening of Literary Studies." In 1992, ecocritics had their own group, the Association for the Study of Literature and Environment (ASLE) and, by 1993, there were two literary journals devoted to ecocriticism. When Glotfelty and Harold Fromm edited *The Ecocriticism Reader* in 1996, ecocriticism had gained acceptance as a relevant approach to literature.

## The Problem of Anthropocentrism

While ecocriticism may seem different to some students, it is similar to many other theoretical approaches. Just as queer theory, postcolonialism, Marxism, feminism, and others all examine texts from their particular points of view, ecocriticism takes what Glotfelty calls an "earth-centered approach" to literary texts. Ecocriticism is unique, however, in its worldview. As Glotfelty notes, most critical approaches examine "the relations between writers, texts, and the world," but they see "'the world' [as] synonymous with society." Ecocriticism, on the other hand, "expands the notion of 'the world' to include the entire ecosphere."

In many ways, Ecocriticism is a response to the anthropocentric nature of most Western thought. Anthropocentrism is the belief that the human being is the ultimate entity on our planet. Often accompanying this belief is the presumption that all non-human life and the Earth's natural resources exist solely to serve human needs. In other words, when we place ourselves at the center of the world, everything else becomes a commodity that we can use however we choose.

Ecocritics see anthropocentrism as a leading cause of our careless treatment of the environment. This is particularly troublesome because anthropocentrism is entrenched within numerous aspects of human behavior. It informs political policy, guides personal conduct, and is a fundamental assumption in many religions. It also shapes many of our popular modes of literary analysis. As Glen A. Love notes, other critical approaches tend to "regard *ego*-consciousness as the supreme evidence of literary and critical achievement." Ecologically conscious thought, on the other hand, is ignored because it doesn't "respond to anthropocentric—let alone modernist and post-modernist—assumptions and methodologies." An essential goal of ecocriticism, then, is to change this anthropocentric worldview.

Ecocritics believe this change begins with awareness. An anthropocentric worldview might be difficult at first to identify in a text simply because it exists as an underlying belief in so many of the stories we read, the movies we watch and the media we are exposed to. We see it in a literary work where the natural world—or a character sympathetic to it—is structured as the story's antagonist. It is also present in texts that treat nature dismissively, or texts that are overtly hostile to the environment. We see it as well when elements of the natural world—animals, plants, insects, etc.—are given human characteristics. While such anthropomorphic representations may be created innocently, they nevertheless reinforce the belief that the human animal is the pinnacle of evolution and thus the supreme living being in our world.

## Ecofeminism

In *The Comedy of Survival: Studies in Literary Ecology* (1974), Joseph Meeker argues that,

> If the creation of literature is an important characteristic of the human species, it should be examined carefully and honestly to discover its influence upon human behavior and the natural environment—to determine what role, if any, it plays in the welfare and survival of mankind and what insight it offers into human relationships with other species and with the world around us.

Ecocritics, according to Ursula K. Heise, are interested in how we relate to nature and what roles "language, literature, and art play in this relation." This perspective, Heise says, leads ecocriticism to align itself with "the scientific study of nature, the scholarly analysis of critical representations, and the political struggle for more sustainable ways of inhabiting the natural world."

Because of its wide-ranging appeal to scholars in all academic disciplines, ecocriticism has branched out to incorporate other schools of theoretical thought. One such approach is ecofeminism, which examines the issues of ecocriticism from a feminist perspective.

Feminist thinkers have long recognized an inherent connection between the values of ecocriticism and those of feminism. In *The Second Sex* (1949), Simone de Beauvoir saw similarities between the patriarchy's marginalization of women and its marginalization of the natural world. Other theorists have correlated fictional women with the fictional depictions of nature. Both are often represented as the dark, mysterious domain of evil.

Françoise d'Eaubonne coined the term *écoféminisme* in her book *Le féminisme ou la mort* (*Feminism or Death*, 1974). d'Eaubonne argues that the biggest threat to our environment is the patriarchal system. The patriarchy, she says, with its criminal and warlike logic ("*logique criminelle et guerrière*"), has led us toward ecological disaster ("*catastrophe écologique*") by depleting our resources and encouraging overpopulation ("*épuisement des ressources et inflation démographique globale*"). Furthermore, by taking over the job of agriculture that was once performed by women, men have turned agriculture into agro-industry. In so doing, d'Eaubonne believes that they have appropriated women's fertility ("*l'appropriation de la fécondité et de la fertilité*"), throwing the natural balance into chaos.

Vandana Shiva agrees. In her native India, she has witnessed the ecological problems that stem from patriarchal domination. Shiva argues that the displacement of women from significant roles in agriculture has led to the loss of biodiversity. This, in turn, has brought about desertification, poverty, underdevelopment and the devaluation of women. When such devaluation coincides with patriarchal values, Shiva believes, women become expendable. This has led to another troubling trend: female feticide. In India, there has been a significant increase in the abortion of female fetuses, causing a noticeable disparity between the birthrates of girls and the birthrates of boys. The fate of women, according to Shiva, is inextricably linked to the fate of the natural world.

Thus, for ecofeminists, the critical reading of a text has implications far beyond the world of literature. A text's handling of issues concerning a feminized nature (Mother Earth, virgin forest, etc.) suggests similar views with regard to women. Ecofeminists argue that it's essential to respect both.

## Ecosocialism

Another branch of ecocriticism is ecosocialism. Ecosocialism is an interdisciplinary study integrated in several fields of the sciences and humanities. As such, ecosocialists see literary critique as only one aspect of their agenda. Ecosocialism merges ecological concerns with the concerns of Marxism and socialism. An ecosocialist reading, then, will incorporate Marxist and socialist ideology into an ecocritical reading of a text.

From an ecosocialist point of view, our environmental problems are caused by the capitalist economic system that dominates today's world. Not only does capitalism exacerbate economic inequality, ecosocialists believe, but it also leads inevitably to ecological devastation.

The fundamental concepts of ecosocialism are articulated in "The Belem Ecosocialist Declaration" (2008), written by Joel Kovel, Michael Löwy, Ian Angus and Danielle Follett, and distributed at the World Social Forum in Belem, Brazil. According to the Belem declaration, capitalism is driven by "the imperative toward profit and thus the need for constant growth." Capitalism's "grow or die" mantra forces the creation of unneeded products, resulting in the squandering of our natural resources and the introduction of new pollutants to our environment. With capitalism, Kovel et al argue, "the only measure of success is how much more is sold every day, every week, every year."

Ecosocialists, then, see capitalism as a parasitic system that only survives through the exploitation of human labor and natural resources. Since capitalism has only made our ecological problems worse, ecosocialists believe that we need to fundamentally change our economic structure. As such, the goal of ecosocialism is to "construct a radical and practical alternative to the capitalist system." Replacing capitalism, ecosocialists believe, is the only way to stop catastrophic climate change and the "capitalist ecocide" of our planet. Only then will we be able to implement earth-friendly options to replace our outdated energy systems; transportation systems; and modes of production, distribution and consumption.

For ecosocialists, capitalist-driven ecological devastation is the most urgent problem facing our world today. This urgency is reflected in ecosocialism's activist tone. As noted in the Belem declaration, "humanity today faces a stark choice: ecosocialism or barbarism."

## Deep Ecology

Not everyone, however, agrees that ecosocialism is the answer to ecological degradation. Deep ecologists, for example, feel that ecosocialism doesn't go far enough to solve the environmental problems we face today.

Arne Næss and George Sessions developed an eight-point "Deep Ecology Platform" (1984) based on the fundamental belief that all living things have an equal intrinsic value. In *Ecology, Community and Lifestyle* (1989), Næss expands on this idea, arguing that "no single species of living being has more of [the] right to live and unfold than any other species." This view guides the deep ecology philosophy. Consequently, deep ecologists oppose any human effort at development or expansion that infringes upon the lives and well being of other living things.

David Orton outlines two significant differences between ecosocialism and deep ecology. First, Orton notes, deep ecologists believe that industrialism, not capitalism, is the root cause of environmental destruction. Deep ecologists also see overpopulation as one of the most critical problems facing our world today. According to Orton,

> This should be a priority for an ecocentric socially-just society. It is not only wrong from a human-welfare perspective—there are far too many of us—but it shows that the habitat needs of other life forms are not considered important.

Most ecosocialists, on the other hand, don't see population as an urgent issue. Ecosocialists, in fact, see deep ecology's commitment to population reduction as "anti-human." In an exchange between Ian Angus, an ecosocialist, and Saral Sarkar, representing deep ecology, Angus asserts that "people are not the problem, and reducing the number of people is not a solution." Not only that, but efforts to control population, Angus argues, will lead to "horrifying consequences" such as the one-child policy in China or the expulsion of indigenous peoples from the world's forests. Sarkar counters that today's India illustrates the devastating effects of overpopulation. Furthermore, we could reduce population gradually by implementing voluntary incentives, thereby avoiding the concerns that Angus identifies.

Despite these differences, deep ecologists and ecosocialists agree that fundamental and significant change is necessary to prevent ecological catastrophe.

## Social Ecology

Social ecologists believe that the causes of environmental degradation are more deep-seated than either ecosocialists or deep ecologists realize. To social ecologists, capitalism, industrialism and overpopulation are merely symptoms of a much more fundamental disease.

Social ecology is the study of human populations' interactions with their environments. It became known primarily through the theoretical work of Murray Bookchin, often regarded as the father of social ecology.

Probably because of its similar name, social ecology is often confused and conflated with ecosocialism. The two, however, have distinct focuses. Whereas ecosocialism critiques capitalism and examines it from a range of scientific, political and artistic perspectives, social ecology is interested in the way social problems give rise to ecological concerns.

Ecosocialism and social ecology do agree that the ecological problems we face result from inequitable hierarchical structures. They have a different conception, though, regarding the nature of these hierarchical structures. For ecosocialists, the hierarchies are generated by capitalism. For social ecologists, the hierarchies might involve ethnicity, culture, gender, economic status, or any other social relationship based upon dominance or oppression.

In other words, social ecologists believe that the root cause of ecological devastation is the hierarchical ideology common in every modern society. For social ecologists, the solution isn't to replace a capitalist economy, end industrialization or reduce our population. That would be akin to focusing "on the symptoms of a grim social pathology rather than on the pathology itself." What we must do instead, according to Bookchin, is create a new society that is completely free of hierarchical structures, whether those structures exist in the home, the workplace, politics or popular culture.

## Implementation

While ecocriticism can be applied to any literary work, Lawrence Buell believes that some texts are more conducive to an ecocritical reading than others. Such texts are characterized by four unique features:

1) a "nonhuman environment" that suggests natural history has been shaped by human history
2) the understanding that "the human interest is not [. . .] the only legitimate interest"
3) the ethical view that humans are accountable to the environment
4) the conviction that the environment is "a process rather than [. . .] a constant"

Other theorists are more receptive to applying ecocriticism to a wider range of texts. According to Cheryll Glotfelty, an ecocritic might focus on any number of aspects within a literary work. She suggests we begin by approaching a text with several questions in mind, such as:

> How is nature represented in this sonnet? What role does physical setting play in the plot of this novel? How do our metaphors of the land influence the way we treat it? How can we characterize nature writing as a genre? In addition to race, class, and gender, should *place* become a new critical category? Do men write about nature differently than wom-

en do? In what ways has literacy itself affected humankind's relationship to the natural world? How has the concept of wilderness changed over time? In what ways and to what effect is the environmental crisis seeping into contemporary literature and popular culture? What view of nature informs U.S. Government reports, corporate advertising, and televised nature documentaries, and to what rhetorical effect? What bearing might the science of ecology have on literary studies? How is science itself open to literary analysis? What cross-fertilization is possible between literary studies and environmental discourse in related disciplines such as history, philosophy, psychology, art history and ethics?

As Glotfelty's questions suggest, ecocritical readings can be diverse, but they all share the common aim of uncovering the ecological underpinnings operating within a literary work.

If we were to apply Glotfelty's process to a story like Jack London's "To Build a Fire," for example, we might find it worthwhile to examine the protagonist's clumsy and ill-fated interactions with nature. Other ecocritics may prefer to focus on London's anthropomorphization of the dog. They could argue that, by relating the dog's thoughts and giving the dog human characteristics, London's narrator contributes to the anthropocentric worldview that remains prevalent today. Still others might see the protagonist's attempts to sacrifice the dog as an illustration of humankind's belief in his favored status among Earth's living things. We could also juxtapose the protagonist's arrogance toward nature with the similar arrogance exhibited by modern industrialized societies. Or we could argue that structuring nature as the story's antagonist leads Western readers to test their own resilience by seeking out similar challenging habitats, thereby facilitate the destruction of our planet's undeveloped ecosystems.

In other words, an ecocritical reading is limited only by the theorist's imagination. All ecocritical readings are similar, though, in that they examine a text with ecological concerns always in mind, and are driven by the unbending understanding that we have an urgent need to protect our environment and everything in it.

## Important Moments in Ecocriticism

**1836:** Ralph Waldo Emerson's "Nature" published anonymously
**1844:** Margaret Fuller's *Summer on the Lakes*
**1854:** Henry David Thoreau's *Walden*
**1864:** Yosemite Grant created
**1864:** George Perkins Marsh's *Man and Nature*
**1866:** the term ecology first used by Ernst Haeckel
**1872:** first Arbor Day observed
**1872:** Yellowstone National Park established

1892: Sierra club founded
1919: construction of O'Shaughnessy Dam begins in California
1925: Alice Hamilton's *Industrial Poisons in the United States*
1949: Aldo Leopold's *A Sand Country Almanac*
1962: Rachel Carson's *Silent Spring*
1965: Western Literature Association founded
1967: Environmental Defense Fund established
1968: Edward Abbey's *Desert Solitaire*
1968: Earthrise photograph taken by astronaut William Anders
1970: first annual Earth Day celebration
1972: the Clean Water Act enacted
1972: Joseph W. Meeker's *The Comedy of Survival*
1973: Congress passes Endangered Species Act
1973: Raymond Williams' *The Country and the City*
1974: Françoise d'Eaubonne's *Le Féminisme ou la Mort*
1974: Annie Dillard's *Pilgrim at Tinker Creek*
1979: partial nuclear meltdown at Three Mile Island in Pennsylvania
1984: Bhopal disaster in India
1985: hole in the ozone discovered
1986: Chernobyl disaster in Ukraine
1989: first issue of *The American Nature Writing Newsletter*
1989: Exxon Valdez oil spill in Prince William Sound, Alaska
1991: special session of MLA: "Ecocriticism: The Greening of Literary Studies"
1991: Jonathan Bate's *Romantic Ecology*
1991: first mission of Biosphere 2 begins
1992: The Association for the Study of Literature and Environment (ASLE) founded
1993: founding of *ISLE: Interdisciplinary Studies in Literature and Environment* (literary journal)
1994: Karl Kroeber's *Ecological Literary Criticism*
1995: Lawrence Buell's *The Environmental Imagination*
1995: Kate Soper's *What is Nature?*
1995: Simon Schama's *Landscape and Memory*
1996: Cheryll Glotfelty and Harold Fromm publish *The Ecocriticism Reader*
1997: Kyoto Protocol signed
2000: Bate's *The Song of the Earth*
2001: Joel Kovel and Michael Löwy publish "The Ecosocialist Manifesto"
2001: Buell's *Writing for an Endangered World*
2003: Glen A. Love's *Practical Ecology*
2004: Greg Garrard's *Ecocriticism*
2005: Buell's *The Future of Environmental Criticism*

2006: Gabriel Egan's *Green Shakespeare*
2006: Davis Guggenheim's *An Inconvenient Truth*
2006: Robert N. Watson's *Back to Nature*
2007: Timothy Morton's *Ecology without Nature*
2009: "The Belem Ecosocialist Declaration" is distributed
2011: Fukushima Daiichi nuclear disaster
2012: Morton's *The Ecological Thought*
2013: Morton's *Hyperobjects*

## Important Terms

androcentrism
anthropomorphism
ecocide
ecology
environmentalism
social ecology

anthropocentrism
deep ecology
ecofeminism
ecosocialism
personification

## Study Questions

1. Consider five of your favorite stories. Which one is most appropriate for an ecocritical reading according to the four criteria that Buell outlines? How? Does the story seem to make an obvious attempt to raise environmental awareness, a subtle attempt, or does any such attempt seem inadvertent? What makes you reach your conclusion?
2. Compare the representations of nature in Nathaniel Hawthorne's "Young Goodman Brown" and Sarah Orne Jewett's "A White Heron." How do these representations differ? How do we account for these differences? From an ecocritical perspective, what is the significance of these representations?
3. Analyze a story of your choice from the perspective of ecocriticism and one other theoretical approach of your choice. How do the two readings compare? Which theory do you think provides the most rewarding analysis, and why? Use specific examples from the story as you develop your response.
4. The natural world plays a significant part in a number of literary texts. If we were to read Henry David Thoreau's *Walden*, John G. Neihardt's *Black Elk Speaks*, Rachel Carson's *Silent Spring*, Edward Abbey's *Desert Solitaire*, and Annie Dillard's *Pilgrim at Tinker Creek*, we would see that nature's role is at least slightly different in each of these works. We might find a number of reasons to explain this: the text's place in history; the political climate in which it was written; the text's geographical setting; the gender, ethnicity or socioeconomic status of the author; etc. With these and other texts in mind, ex-

plore how nature's role in literature has changed since Thoreau and formulate your own conclusions to explain this change.
5. Using a story of your choice, write a brief essay that examines some truth about the piece that you could only uncover from the perspective of ecocriticism. Perhaps you'd like to discuss the setting or the narrative situation. Maybe you'd like to focus on the story's plot or its theme. Or maybe you'd prefer to study the author's history of interaction with the natural world. Whatever your topic, your conclusion should be something that could not be gleaned from a simple overt reading of the text.

## Selected Bibliography

Abbey, Edward. *Desert Solitaire: A Season in the Wilderness*. New York: Ballentine, 1985.
Bate, Jonathan. *Romantic Ecology: Wordsworth and the Environmental Tradition*. New York: Routledge, 2013.
—. *The Song of the Earth*. Cambridge: Harvard UP, 2002.
Bender, Frederic L. *The Culture of Extinction: Toward a Philosophy of Deep Ecology*. Amherst, NY: Humanity Books, 2003.
Biehl, Janet. *Rethinking Ecofeminist Politics*. Brooklyn: South End, 1999.
Bookchin, Murray. *The Ecology of Freedom: The Emergence and Dissolution of Hierarchy*. Oakland: AK Press, 2005.
—. *The Politics of Social Ecology*. Montreal: Black Rose, 1997.
—. *Post-Scarcity Anarchism*. Oakland: AK Press, 2004.
—. *Social Ecology and Communalism*. Oakland: AK Press, 2007.
Buell, Lawrence. *The Environmental Imagination: Thoreau, Nature Writing, and the Formation of American Culture*. Cambridge: Harvard UP, 1995.
—. *The Future of Environmental Criticism: Environmental Crisis and Literary Imagination*. New York: Wiley, 2005.
—. *Writing for an Endangered World: Literature, Culture and Environment in the U.S. and Beyond*. Cambridge: Harvard UP, 2001.
Burkett, Paul. *Marxism and Ecological Economics: Toward a Red and Green Political Economy*. Chicago: Haymarket, 2009.
Carson, Rachel. *Silent Spring*. New York: Houghton Mifflin, 2002.
Egan, Gabriel. *Green Shakespeare: From Ecopolitics to Ecocriticism*. New York: Routledge, 2006.
Emerson, Ralph Waldo. *Nature and Selected Essays*. New York: Penguin, 2003.
Fuller, Margaret. *Summer on the Lakes, in 1843*. Urbana-Champaign: Illinois UP, 1990.
Gaard, Greta Claire, and Patrick D. Murphy, Eds. *Ecofeminist Literary Criticism: Theory, Interpretation, Pedagogy*. Urbana: Illinois UP, 1998.

Garrard, Glen. *Ecocriticism*. New York: Routledge, 2011.
Glotfelty, Cheryll, and Harold Fromm, eds. *The Ecocriticism Reader: Landmarks in Literary Ecology*. Athens: Georgia UP, 1996.
Hamilton, Alice. *Industrial Poisons in the United States*. New York: Macmillan, 1929.
Heise, Ursula K. "The Hitchhiker's Guide to Ecocriticism." *PMLA* 121.2 (March 2006). 503-16.
Heidl, Carl G. and Stuart C. Brown. *Green Culture: Environmental Rhetoric in Contemporary America*. Madison: Wisconsin UP, 1996.
Kroeber, Karl. *Ecological Literary Criticism: Romantic Imagining and the Biology of Mind*. New York: Columbia UP, 1994.
Leopold, Aldo. *A Sand Country Almanac*. New York: Ballantine, 1986.
Love, Glen A. *Practical Ecology: Literature, Biology, and the Environment*. Charlottesville: Virginia UP, 2003.
Marsh, George Perkins. *Man and Nature: Or, Physical Geography as Modified by Human Action*. Seattle: Washington UP, 2003.
Meeker, Joseph W. *The Comedy of Survival: Studies in Literary Ecology*. New York: Scribner, 1972.
—. *The Comedy of Survival: In Search of an Environmental Ethic*. Los Angeles: Guild of Tutors, 1980.
Mies, Maria, and Vandana Shiva. *Ecofeminism*. London: Zed, 1993.
Morton, Timothy. *The Ecological Thought*. Cambridge: Harvard UP, 2012.
—. *Ecology without Nature: Rethinking Environmental Aesthetics*. Cambridge: Harvard UP, 2009.
—. *Hyperobjects: Philosophy and Ecology after the End of the World*. Minneapolis: Minnesota UP, 2013.
Næss, Arne. *Ecology, Community and Lifestyle: Outline of an Ecosophy*. Trans. David Rothenberg. Cambridge, U.K.: Cambridge UP, 1993.
—. *The Ecology of Wisdom*. Berkeley: Counterpoint, 2010.
O'Connor, James. *Natural Causes: Essays in Ecological Marxism*. New York: Guilford, 1997.
Pepper, David. *Eco-Socialism: From Deep Ecology to Social Justice*. New York: Routledge, 1993.
Phillips, Dana. *The Truth of Ecology: Nature, Culture, and Literature in America*. Oxford: Oxford UP, 2003.
Sarkar, Saral. *Eco-Socialism or Eco-Capitalism?: A Critical Analysis of Humanity's Fundamental Choices*. London: Zed, 1999.
Schama, Simon. *Landscape and Memory*. New York: Vintage, 1996.
Sessions, George. *Deep Ecology for the Twenty-First Century*. Boston: Shambala, 1995.
Shiva, Vandana. *Biopiracy: The Plunder of Nature and Knowledge*. Brooklyn: South End, 1999.
—. *Soil Not Oil: Environmental Justice in an Age of Climate Crisis*. Brooklyn: South End, 2010.

—. *Staying Alive: Women, Ecology, and Development.* Brooklyn: South End, 2010.
Soper, Kate. *What is Nature? Culture, Politics, and the Non-Human.* New York: Wiley, 1995.
Thoreau, Henry David. *Walden.* New York: Dover, 1995.
Warren, Karen J., Ed. *Ecofeminism: Women, Culture, Nature.* Bloomington: Indiana UP, 1997.
Watson, Robert N. *Back to Nature: The Green and the Real in the Late Renaissance.* Philadelphia: Pennsylvania UP, 2007.
Williams, Chris. *Ecology and Socialism: Solutions to Capitalist Ecological Crisis.* Chicago: Haymarket, 2010.

# Stories

## Gooseberries
Anton Chekhov

translated by
Constance Garnett

The whole sky had been overcast with rain-clouds from early morning; it was a still day, not hot, but heavy, as it is in grey dull weather when the clouds have been hanging over the country for a long while, when one expects rain and it does not come. Ivan Ivanovitch, the veterinary surgeon, and Burkin, the high-school teacher, were already tired from walking, and the fields seemed to them endless. Far ahead of them they could just see the windmills of the village of Mironositskoe; on the right stretched a row of hillocks which disappeared in the distance behind the village, and they both knew that this was the bank of the river, that there were meadows, green willows, homesteads there, and that if one stood on one of the hillocks one could see from it the same vast plain, telegraph-wires, and a train which in the distance looked like a crawling caterpillar, and that in clear weather one could even see the town. Now, in still weather, when all nature seemed mild and dreamy, Ivan Ivanovitch and Burkin were filled with love of that countryside, and both thought how great, how beautiful a land it was.

"Last time we were in Prokofy's barn," said Burkin, "you were about to tell me a story."

"Yes; I meant to tell you about my brother."

Ivan Ivanovitch heaved a deep sigh and lighted a pipe to begin to tell his story, but just at that moment the rain began. And five minutes later heavy rain came down, covering the sky, and it was hard to tell when it would be over. Ivan Ivanovitch and Burkin stopped in hesitation; the dogs, already drenched, stood with their tails between their legs gazing at them feelingly.

"We must take shelter somewhere," said Burkin. "Let us go to Alehin's; it's close by."

"Come along."

They turned aside and walked through mown fields, sometimes going straight forward, sometimes turning to the right, till they came out on the road. Soon they saw poplars, a garden, then the red roofs of barns; there was a gleam of the river, and the view opened on to a broad expanse of water with a windmill and a white bath-house: this was Sofino, where Alehin lived.

The watermill was at work, drowning the sound of the rain; the dam was shaking. Here wet horses with drooping heads were standing near their carts, and men were walking about covered with sacks. It was damp, muddy, and desolate; the water looked cold and malignant. Ivan Ivanovitch and Burkin were already conscious of a feeling of wetness, messiness, and discomfort all over; their feet were heavy with mud, and when, crossing the dam, they went up to the barns, they were silent, as though they were angry with one another.

In one of the barns there was the sound of a winnowing machine, the door was open, and clouds of dust were coming from it. In the doorway was standing Alehin himself, a man of forty, tall and stout, with long hair, more like a professor or an artist than a landowner. He had on a white shirt that badly needed washing, a rope for a belt, drawers instead of trousers, and his boots, too, were plastered up with mud and straw. His eyes and nose were black with dust. He recognized Ivan Ivanovitch and Burkin, and was apparently much delighted to see them.

"Go into the house, gentlemen," he said, smiling; "I'll come directly, this minute."

It was a big two-storeyed house. Alehin lived in the lower storey, with arched ceilings and little windows, where the bailiffs had once lived; here everything was plain, and there was a smell of rye bread, cheap vodka, and harness. He went upstairs into the best rooms only on rare occasions, when visitors came. Ivan Ivanovitch and Burkin were met in the house by a maid-servant, a young woman so beautiful that they both stood still and looked at one another.

"You can't imagine how delighted I am to see you, my friends," said Alehin, going into the hall with them. "It is a surprise! Pelagea," he said, addressing the girl, "give our visitors something to change into. And, by the way, I will change too. Only I must first go and wash, for I almost think I have not washed since spring. Wouldn't you like to come into the bath-house? and meanwhile they will get things ready here."

Beautiful Pelagea, looking so refined and soft, brought them towels and soap, and Alehin went to the bath-house with his guests.

"It's a long time since I had a wash," he said, undressing. "I have got a nice bath-house, as you see—my father built it—but I somehow never have time to wash."

He sat down on the steps and soaped his long hair and his neck, and the water round him turned brown.

"Yes, I must say," said Ivan Ivanovitch meaningly, looking at his head.

"It's a long time since I washed . . ." said Alehin with embarrassment, giving himself a second soaping, and the water near him turned dark blue, like ink.

Ivan Ivanovitch went outside, plunged into the water with a loud splash, and swam in the rain, flinging his arms out wide. He stirred the water into waves which set the white lilies bobbing up and down; he swam to the very middle of the millpond and dived, and came up a minute later in another place, and swam on, and kept on diving, trying to touch the bottom.

"Oh, my goodness!" he repeated continually, enjoying himself thoroughly. "Oh, my goodness!" He swam to the mill, talked to the peasants there, then returned and lay on his back in the middle of the pond, turning his face to the rain. Burkin and Alehin were dressed and ready to go, but he still went on swimming and diving. "Oh, my goodness!" he said. "Oh, Lord, have mercy on me! . . ."

"That's enough!" Burkin shouted to him.

They went back to the house. And only when the lamp was lighted in the big drawing-room upstairs, and Burkin and Ivan Ivanovitch, attired in silk dressing-gowns and warm slippers, were sitting in armchairs; and Alehin, washed and combed, in a new coat, was walking about the drawing-room, evidently enjoying the feeling of warmth, cleanliness, dry clothes, and light shoes; and when lovely Pelagea, stepping noiselessly on the carpet and smiling softly, handed tea and jam on a tray—only then Ivan Ivanovitch began on his story, and it seemed as though not only Burkin and Alehin were listening, but also the ladies, young and old, and the officers who looked down upon them sternly and calmly from their gold frames.

"There are two of us brothers," he began—"I, Ivan Ivanovitch, and my brother, Nikolay Ivanovitch, two years younger. I went in for a learned profession and became a veterinary surgeon, while Nikolay sat in a government office from the time he was nineteen. Our father, Tchimsha-Himalaisky, was a kantonist, but he rose to be an officer and left us a little estate and the rank of nobility. After his death the little estate went in debts and legal expenses; but, anyway, we had spent our childhood running wild in the country. Like peasant children, we passed our days and nights in the fields and the woods, looked after horses, stripped the bark off the trees, fished, and so on. . . . And, you know, whoever has once in his life caught perch or has seen the migrating of the thrushes in autumn, watched how they float in flocks over the village on bright, cool days, he will never be a real townsman, and will have a yearning for freedom to the day of his death. My brother was miserable in the government office. Years passed by, and he went on sitting in the same place, went on writing the same papers and thinking of one and the same thing—how to get into the country. And this yearning by degrees passed into a definite desire, into a dream of buying himself a little farm somewhere on the banks of a river or a lake.

"He was a gentle, good-natured fellow, and I was fond of him, but I never sympathized with this desire to shut himself up for the rest of his life in a little farm of his own. It's the correct thing to say that a man needs no more than six feet of earth. But six feet is what a corpse needs, not a man. And they say, too, now, that if our intellectual classes are attracted to the land and yearn for a farm, it's a good thing. But these farms are just the same as six feet of earth. To retreat from town, from the struggle, from the bustle of life, to retreat and bury oneself in one's farm—it's not life, it's egoism, laziness, it's monasticism of a sort, but monasticism without good works. A man does not need six feet of earth or a farm, but the whole globe, all nature, where he can have room to display all the qualities and peculiarities of his free spirit.

"My brother Nikolay, sitting in his government office, dreamed of how he would eat his own cabbages, which would fill the whole yard with such a savoury smell, take his meals on the green grass, sleep in the sun, sit for whole hours on the seat by the gate gazing at the fields and the forest. Gardening books and the agricultural hints in calendars were his delight, his favourite spiritual sustenance; he enjoyed reading newspapers, too, but the only things he read in them were the advertisements of so many acres of arable land and a grass meadow with farmhouses and buildings, a river, a garden, a mill and millponds, for sale. And his imagination pictured the garden-paths, flowers and fruit, starling cotes, the carp in the pond, and all that sort of thing, you know. These imaginary pictures were of different kinds according to the advertisements which he came across, but for some reason in every one of them he had always to have gooseberries. He could not imagine a homestead, he could not picture an idyllic nook, without gooseberries.

"'Country life has its conveniences,' he would sometimes say. 'You sit on the verandah and you drink tea, while your ducks swim on the pond, there is a delicious smell everywhere, and . . . and the gooseberries are growing.'

"He used to draw a map of his property, and in every map there were the same things—(a) house for the family, (b) servants' quarters, (c) kitchen-garden, (d) gooseberry-bushes. He lived parsimoniously, was frugal in food and drink, his clothes were beyond description; he looked like a beggar, but kept on saving and putting money in the bank. He grew fearfully avaricious. I did not like to look at him, and I used to give him something and send him presents for Christmas and Easter, but he used to save that too. Once a man is absorbed by an idea, there is no doing anything with him.

"Years passed: he was transferred to another province. He was over forty, and he was still reading the advertisements in the papers and saving up. Then I heard he was married. Still with the same object of buying a farm and having gooseberries, he married an elderly and ugly widow without a trace of feeling for her, simply because she had filthy lucre. He went on living frugally after marrying her, and kept her short of food, while he put her money in the bank in his name.

"Her first husband had been a postmaster, and with him she was accustomed to pies and home-made wines, while with her second husband she did not get enough black bread; she began to pine away with this sort of life, and three years later she gave up her soul to God. And I need hardly say that my brother never for one moment imagined that he was responsible for her death. Money, like vodka, makes a man queer. In our town there was a merchant who, before he died, ordered a plateful of honey and ate up all his money and lottery tickets with the honey, so that no one might get the benefit of it. While I was inspecting cattle at a railway-station, a cattle-dealer fell under an engine and had his leg cut off. We carried him into the waiting-room, the blood was flowing—it was a horrible thing—and he kept asking them to look for his leg and was very much worried about it; there were twenty roubles in the boot on the leg that had been cut off, and he was afraid they would be lost."

"That's a story from a different opera," said Burkin.

"After his wife's death," Ivan Ivanovitch went on, after thinking for half a minute, "my brother began looking out for an estate for himself. Of course, you may look about for five years and yet end by making a mistake, and buying something quite different from what you have dreamed of. My brother Nikolay bought through an agent a mortgaged estate of three hundred and thirty acres, with a house for the family, with servants' quarters, with a park, but with no orchard, no gooseberry-bushes, and no duck-pond; there was a river, but the water in it was the colour of coffee, because on one side of the estate there was a brickyard and on the other a factory for burning bones. But Nikolay Ivanovitch did not grieve much; he ordered twenty gooseberry-bushes, planted them, and began living as a country gentleman.

"Last year I went to pay him a visit. I thought I would go and see what it was like. In his letters my brother called his estate 'Tchumbaroklov Waste, alias Himalaiskoe.' I reached 'alias Himalaiskoe' in the afternoon. It was hot. Everywhere there were ditches, fences, hedges, fir-trees planted in rows, and there was no knowing how to get to the yard, where to put one's horse. I went up to the house, and was met by a fat red dog that looked like a pig. It wanted to bark, but it was too lazy. The cook, a fat, barefooted woman, came out of the kitchen, and she, too, looked like a pig, and said that her master was resting after dinner. I went in to see my brother. He was sitting up in bed with a quilt over his legs; he had grown older, fatter, wrinkled; his cheeks, his nose, and his mouth all stuck out—he looked as though he might begin grunting into the quilt at any moment.

"We embraced each other, and shed tears of joy and of sadness at the thought that we had once been young and now were both grey-headed and near the grave. He dressed, and led me out to show me the estate.

"'Well, how are you getting on here?' I asked.

"'Oh, all right, thank God; I am getting on very well.'

"He was no more a poor timid clerk, but a real landowner, a gentleman. He was already accustomed to it, had grown used to it, and liked it. He ate a great deal, went to the bath-house, was growing stout, was already at law with the village commune and both factories, and was very much offended when the peasants did not call him 'Your Honour.' And he concerned himself with the salvation of his soul in a substantial, gentlemanly manner, and performed deeds of charity, not simply, but with an air of consequence. And what deeds of charity! He treated the peasants for every sort of disease with soda and castor oil, and on his name-day had a thanksgiving service in the middle of the village, and then treated the peasants to a gallon of vodka—he thought that was the thing to do. Oh, those horrible gallons of vodka! One day the fat landowner hauls the peasants up before the district captain for trespass, and next day, in honour of a holiday, treats them to a gallon of vodka, and they drink and shout 'Hurrah!' and when they are drunk bow down to his feet. A change of life for the better, and being well-fed and idle develop in a Russian the most insolent self-conceit. Nikolay Ivanovitch, who at one time in the government office was afraid to have any views of his own, now could say nothing that was not gospel truth, and uttered such truths in the tone of a prime minister. 'Education is essential, but for the peasants it is premature.' 'Corporal punishment is harmful as a rule, but in some cases it is necessary and there is nothing to take its place.'

"'I know the peasants and understand how to treat them,' he would say. 'The peasants like me. I need only to hold up my little finger and the peasants will do anything I like.'

"And all this, observe, was uttered with a wise, benevolent smile. He repeated twenty times over 'We noblemen,' 'I as a noble'; obviously he did not remember that our grandfather was a peasant, and our father a soldier. Even our surname Tchimsha-Himalaisky, in reality so incongruous, seemed to him now melodious, distinguished, and very agreeable.

"But the point just now is not he, but myself. I want to tell you about the change that took place in me during the brief hours I spent at his country place. In the evening, when we were drinking tea, the cook put on the table a plateful of gooseberries. They were not bought, but his own gooseberries, gathered for the first time since the bushes were planted. Nikolay Ivanovitch laughed and looked for a minute in silence at the gooseberries, with tears in his eyes; he could not speak for excitement. Then he put one gooseberry in his mouth, looked at me with the triumph of a child who has at last received his favourite toy, and said:

"'How delicious!'

"And he ate them greedily, continually repeating, 'Ah, how delicious! Do taste them!'

"They were sour and unripe, but, as Pushkin says:
> Dearer to us the falsehood that exalts
> Than hosts of baser truths.

"I saw a happy man whose cherished dream was so obviously fulfilled, who had attained his object in life, who had gained what he wanted, who was satisfied with his fate and himself. There is always, for some reason, an element of sadness mingled with my thoughts of human happiness, and, on this occasion, at the sight of a happy man I was overcome by an oppressive feeling that was close upon despair. It was particularly oppressive at night. A bed was made up for me in the room next to my brother's bedroom, and I could hear that he was awake, and that he kept getting up and going to the plate of gooseberries and taking one. I reflected how many satisfied, happy people there really are! 'What a suffocating force it is! You look at life: the insolence and idleness of the strong, the ignorance and brutishness of the weak, incredible poverty all about us, overcrowding, degeneration, drunkenness, hypocrisy, lying. . . . Yet all is calm and stillness in the houses and in the streets; of the fifty thousand living in a town, there is not one who would cry out, who would give vent to his indignation aloud. We see the people going to market for provisions, eating by day, sleeping by night, talking their silly nonsense, getting married, growing old, serenely escorting their dead to the cemetery; but we do not see and we do not hear those who suffer, and what is terrible in life goes on somewhere behind the scenes. . . . Everything is quiet and peaceful, and nothing protests but mute statistics: so many people gone out of their minds, so many gallons of vodka drunk, so many children dead from malnutrition. . . . And this order of things is evidently necessary; evidently the happy man only feels at ease because the unhappy bear their burdens in silence, and without that silence happiness would be impossible. It's a case of general hypnotism. There ought to be behind the door of every happy, contented man some one standing with a hammer continually reminding him with a tap that there are unhappy people; that however happy he may be, life will show him her laws sooner or later, trouble will come for him—disease, poverty, losses, and no one will see or hear, just as now he neither sees nor hears others. But there is no man with a hammer; the happy man lives at his ease, and trivial daily cares faintly agitate him like the wind in the aspen-tree—and all goes well.

"That night I realized that I, too, was happy and contented," Ivan Ivanovitch went on, getting up. "I, too, at dinner and at the hunt liked to lay down the law on life and religion, and the way to manage the peasantry. I, too, used to say that science was light, that culture was essential, but for the simple people reading and writing was enough for the time. Freedom is a blessing, I used to say; we can no more do without it than without air, but we must wait a little. Yes, I used to talk like that, and now I ask, 'For what reason are we to wait?'" asked Ivan Ivanovitch, looking angrily at Burkin. "Why wait, I ask you? What grounds have we for waiting? I shall be told, it can't be done all at once; every idea takes shape in life gradually, in its due time. But who is it says that? Where is the proof that it's right? You will fall back upon the natural order of things, the uniformity of phenomena; but is there order and uniformity in the fact that I, a living, thinking man, stand over a chasm and wait for it to close of itself, or to fill up with mud at the very time when perhaps I might leap over it or build a bridge across it? And again, wait for the sake of what? Wait till there's no strength to live? And meanwhile one must live, and one wants to live!

"I went away from my brother's early in the morning, and ever since then it has been unbearable for me to be in town. I am oppressed by its peace and quiet; I am afraid to look at the windows, for there is no spectacle more painful to me now than the sight of a happy family sitting round the table drinking tea. I am old and am not fit for the struggle; I am not even capable of hatred; I can only grieve inwardly, feel irritated and vexed; but at night my head is hot from the rush of ideas, and I cannot sleep. . . . Ah, if I were young!"

Ivan Ivanovitch walked backwards and forwards in excitement, and repeated: "If I were young!"

He suddenly went up to Alehin and began pressing first one of his hands and then the other.

"Pavel Konstantinovitch," he said in an imploring voice, "don't be calm and contented, don't let yourself be put to sleep! While you are young, strong, confident, be not weary in well-doing! There is no happiness, and there ought not to be; but if there is a meaning and an object in life, that meaning and object is not our happiness, but something greater and more rational. Do good!"

And all this Ivan Ivanovitch said with a pitiful, imploring smile, as though he were asking him a personal favour.

Then all three sat in arm-chairs at different ends of the drawing-room and were silent. Ivan Ivanovitch's story had not satisfied either Burkin or Alehin. When the generals and ladies gazed down from their gilt frames, looking in the dusk as though they were alive, it was dreary to listen to the story of the poor clerk who ate gooseberries. They felt inclined, for some reason, to talk about elegant people, about women. And their sitting in the drawing-room where everything—the chandeliers in their covers, the arm-chairs, and the carpet under their feet—reminded them that those very people who were now looking down from their frames had once moved about, sat, drunk tea in this room, and the fact that lovely Pelagea was moving noiselessly about was better than any story.

Alehin was fearfully sleepy; he had got up early, before three o'clock in the morning, to look after his work, and now his eyes were closing; but he was afraid his visitors might tell some interesting story after he had gone, and he lingered on. He did not go into the question whether what Ivan Ivanovitch had just said was right and true. His visitors did not talk of groats, nor of hay, nor of tar, but of something that had no direct bearing on his life, and he was glad and wanted them to go on.

"It's bed-time, though," said Burkin, getting up. "Allow me to wish you good-night."

Alehin said good-night and went downstairs to his own domain, while the visitors remained upstairs. They were both taken for the night to a big room where there stood two old wooden beds decorated with carvings, and in the corner was an ivory crucifix. The big cool beds, which had been made by the lovely Pelagea, smelt agreeably of clean linen.

Ivan Ivanovitch undressed in silence and got into bed.

"Lord forgive us sinners!" he said, and put his head under the quilt.

His pipe lying on the table smelt strongly of stale tobacco, and Burkin could not sleep for a long while, and kept wondering where the oppressive smell came from.

The rain was pattering on the window-panes all night.

—1898

# The Story of an Hour
## Kate Chopin

Knowing that Mrs. Mallard was afflicted with a heart trouble, great care was taken to break to her as gently as possible the news of her husband's death.

It was her sister Josephine who told her, in broken sentences; veiled hints that revealed in half concealing. Her husband's friend Richards was there, too, near her. It was he who had been in the newspaper office when intelligence of the railroad disaster was received, with Brently Mallard's name leading the list of "killed." He had only taken the time to assure himself of its truth by a second telegram, and had hastened to forestall any less careful, less tender friend in bearing the sad message.

She did not hear the story as many women have heard the same, with a paralyzed inability to accept its significance. She wept at once, with sudden, wild abandonment, in her sister's arms. When the storm of grief had spent itself she went away to her room alone. She would have no one follow her.

There stood, facing the open window, a comfortable, roomy armchair. Into this she sank, pressed down by a physical exhaustion that haunted her body and seemed to reach into her soul.

She could see in the open square before her house the tops of trees that were all aquiver with the new spring life. The delicious breath of rain was in the air. In the street below a peddler was crying his wares. The notes of a distant song which some one was singing reached her faintly, and countless sparrows were twittering in the eaves.

There were patches of blue sky showing here and there through the clouds that had met and piled one above the other in the west facing her window.

She sat with her head thrown back upon the cushion of the chair, quite motionless, except when a sob came up into her throat and shook her, as a child who has cried itself to sleep continues to sob in its dreams.

She was young, with a fair, calm face, whose lines bespoke repression and even a certain strength. But now there was a dull stare in her eyes, whose gaze was fixed away off yonder on one of those patches of blue sky. It was not a glance of reflection, but rather indicated a suspension of intelligent thought.

There was something coming to her and she was waiting for it, fearfully. What was it? She did not know; it was too subtle and elusive to name. But she felt it, creeping out of the sky, reaching toward her through the sounds, the scents, the color that filled the air.

Now her bosom rose and fell tumultuously. She was beginning to recognize this thing that was approaching to possess her, and she was striving to beat it back with her will—as powerless as her two white slender hands would have been.

When she abandoned herself a little whispered word escaped her slightly parted lips. She said it over and over under her breath: "free, free, free!" The vacant stare and the look of terror that had followed it went from her eyes. They stayed keen and bright. Her pulses beat fast, and the coursing blood warmed and relaxed every inch of her body.

She did not stop to ask if it were or were not a monstrous joy that held her. A clear and exalted perception enabled her to dismiss the suggestion as trivial.

She knew that she would weep again when she saw the kind, tender hands folded in death; the face that had never looked save with love upon her, fixed and gray and dead. But she saw beyond that bitter moment a long procession of years to come that would belong to her absolutely. And she opened and spread her arms out to them in welcome.

There would be no one to live for during those coming years; she would live for herself. There would be no powerful will bending hers in that blind persistence with which men and women believe they have a right to impose a private will upon a fellow-creature. A kind intention or a cruel intention made the act seem no less a crime as she looked upon it in that brief moment of illumination.

And yet she had loved him—sometimes. Often she had not. What did it matter! What could love, the unsolved mystery, count for in the face of this possession of self-assertion which she suddenly recognized as the strongest impulse of her being!

"Free! Body and soul free!" she kept whispering.

Josephine was kneeling before the closed door with her lips to the keyhold, imploring for admission. "Louise, open the door! I beg; open the door—you will make yourself ill. What are you doing, Louise? For heaven's sake open the door."

"Go away. I am not making myself ill." No; she was drinking in a very elixir of life through that open window.

Her fancy was running riot along those days ahead of her. Spring days, and summer days, and all sorts of days that would be her own. She breathed a quick prayer that life might be long. It was only yesterday she had thought with a shudder that life might be long.

She arose at length and opened the door to her sister's importunities. There was a feverish triumph in her eyes, and she carried herself unwittingly like a goddess of Victory. She clasped her sister's waist, and together they descended the stairs. Richards stood waiting for them at the bottom.

Some one was opening the front door with a latchkey. It was Brently Mallard who entered, a little travel-stained, composedly carrying his grip-sack and umbrella. He had been far from the scene of the accident, and did not even know there had been one. He stood amazed at Josephine's piercing cry; at Richards' quick motion to screen him from the view of his wife.

But Richards was too late.

When the doctors came they said she had died of heart disease—of joy that kills.

—1894

# The Cask of Amontillado
## Edgar Allan Poe

The thousand injuries of Fortunato I had borne as I best could, but when he ventured upon insult, I vowed revenge. You, who so well know the nature of my soul, will not suppose, however, that I gave utterance to a threat. *At length* I would be avenged; this was a point definitively settled—but the very definitiveness with which it was resolved precluded the idea of risk. I must not only punish, but punish with impunity. A wrong is unredressed when retribution overtakes its redresser. It is equally unredressed when the avenger fails to make himself felt as such to him who has done the wrong.

It must be understood that neither by word nor deed had I given Fortunato cause to doubt my good will. I continued as was my wont, to smile in his face, and he did not perceive that my smile *now* was at the thought of his immolation.

He had a weak point—this Fortunato—although in other regards he was a man to be respected and even feared. He prided himself on his connoisseurship in wine. Few Italians have the true virtuoso spirit. For the most part their enthusiasm is adopted to suit the time and opportunity to practise imposture upon the British and Austrian *millionaires*. In painting and gemmary, Fortunato, like his countrymen, was a quack, but in the matter of old wines he was sincere. In this respect I did not differ from him materially; I was skillful in the Italian vintages myself, and bought largely whenever I could.

It was about dusk, one evening during the supreme madness of the carnival season, that I encountered my friend. He accosted me with excessive warmth, for he had been drinking much. The man wore motley. He had on a tight-fitting parti-striped dress and his head was surmounted by the conical cap and bells. I was so pleased to see him, that I thought I should never have done wringing his hand.

I said to him—"My dear Fortunato, you are luckily met. How remarkably well you are looking to-day! But I have received a pipe of what passes for Amontillado, and I have my doubts."

"How?" said he, "Amontillado? A pipe? Impossible ? And in the middle of the carnival?"

"I have my doubts," I replied; "and I was silly enough to pay the full Amontillado price without consulting you in the matter. You were not to be found, and I was fearful of losing a bargain."

"Amontillado!"

"I have my doubts."

"Amontillado!"

"And I must satisfy them."

"Amontillado!"

"As you are engaged, I am on my way to Luchesi. If any one has a critical turn, it is he. He will tell me—"

"Luchesi cannot tell Amontillado from Sherry."

"And yet some fools will have it that his taste is a match for your own."

"Come let us go."

"Whither?"

"To your vaults."

"My friend, no; I will not impose upon your good nature. I perceive you have an engagement Luchesi—"

"I have no engagement; come."

"My friend, no. It is not the engagement, but the severe cold with which I perceive you are afflicted. The vaults are insufferably damp. They are encrusted with nitre."

"Let us go, nevertheless. The cold is merely nothing. Amontillado! You have been imposed upon; and as for Luchesi, he cannot distinguish Sherry from Amontillado."

Thus speaking, Fortunato possessed himself of my arm. Putting on a mask of black silk and drawing a *roquelaire* closely about my person, I suffered him to hurry me to my palazzo.

There were no attendants at home; they had absconded to make merry in honour of the time. I had told them that I should not return until the morning and had given them explicit orders not to stir from the house. These orders were sufficient, I well knew, to insure their immediate disappearance, one and all, as soon as my back was turned.

I took from their sconces two flambeaux, and giving one to Fortunato bowed him through several suites of rooms to the archway that led into the vaults. I passed down a long and winding staircase, requesting him to be cautious as he followed. We came at length to the foot of the descent, and stood together on the damp ground of the catacombs of the Montresors.

The gait of my friend was unsteady, and the bells upon his cap jingled as he strode.

"The pipe," said he.

"It is farther on," said I; "but observe the white webwork which gleams from these cavern walls."

He turned towards me and looked into my eyes with two filmy orbs that distilled the rheum of intoxication.

"Nitre?" he asked, at length

"Nitre," I replied. "How long have you had that cough!"

"Ugh! ugh! ugh!—ugh! ugh! ugh!—ugh! ugh! ugh!—ugh! ugh! ugh!—ugh! ugh! ugh!

My poor friend found it impossible to reply for many minutes.

"It is nothing," he said, at last.

"Come," I said, with decision. "We will go back; your health is precious. You are rich, respected, admired, beloved; you are happy as once I was. You are a man to be missed. For me it is no matter. We will go back; you will be ill and I cannot be responsible. Besides, there is Luchesi—"

"Enough," he said; "the cough is a mere nothing; it will not kill me. I shall not die of a cough."

"True—true," I replied; "and, indeed, I had no intention of alarming you unnecessarily—but you should use all proper caution. A draught of this Medoc will defend us from the damps."

Here I knocked off the neck of a bottle which I drew from a long row of its fellows that lay upon the mould.

"Drink," I said, presenting him the wine.

He raised it to his lips with a leer. He paused and nodded to me familiarly, while his bells jingled.

"I drink," he said, "to the buried that repose around us."

"And I to your long life."

He again took my arm and we proceeded.

"These vaults," he said, are extensive."

"The Montresors," I replied, "were a great numerous family."

"I forget your arms."

"A huge human foot d'or, in a field azure; the foot crushes a serpent rampant whose fangs are imbedded in the heel."

"And the motto?"

"*Nemo me impune lacessit.*"

"Good!" he said.

The wine sparkled in his eyes and the bells jingled. My own fancy grew warm with the Medoc. We had passed through walls of piled bones, with casks and puncheons intermingling, into the inmost recesses of the catacombs. I paused again, and this time I made bold to seize Fortunato by an arm above the elbow.

"The nitre!" I said; "see it increases. It hangs like moss upon the vaults. We are below the river's bed. The drops of moisture trickle among the bones. Come, we will go back ere it is too late. Your cough—"

"It is nothing" he said; "let us go on. But first, another draught of the Medoc."

I broke and reached him a flagon of De Grave. He emptied it at a breath. His eyes flashed with a fierce light. He laughed and threw the bottle upwards with a gesticulation I did not understand.

I looked at him in surprise. He repeated the movement—a grotesque one.

"You do not comprehend?" he said.

"Not I," I replied.

"Then you are not of the brotherhood."

"How?"
"You are not of the masons."
"Yes, yes," I said "yes! yes."
"You? Impossible! A mason?"
"A mason," I replied.
"A sign," he said.
"It is this," I answered, producing a trowel from beneath the folds of my *roquelaire*.

"You jest," he exclaimed, recoiling a few paces. "But let us proceed to the Amontillado."

"Be it so," I said, replacing the tool beneath the cloak, and again offering him my arm. He leaned upon it heavily. We continued our route in search of the Amontillado. We passed through a range of low arches, descended, passed on, and descending again, arrived at a deep crypt, in which the foulness of the air caused our flambeaux rather to glow than flame.

At the most remote end of the crypt there appeared another less spacious. Its walls had been lined with human remains piled to the vault overhead, in the fashion of the great catacombs of Paris. Three sides of this interior crypt were still ornamented in this manner. From the fourth the bones had been thrown down, and lay promiscuously upon the earth, forming at one point a mound of some size. Within the wall thus exposed by the displacing of the bones, we perceived a still interior recess, in depth about four feet, in width three, in height six or seven. It seemed to have been constructed for no especial use in itself, but formed merely the interval between two of the colossal supports of the roof of the catacombs, and was backed by one of their circumscribing walls of solid granite.

It was in vain that Fortunato, uplifting his dull torch, endeavoured to pry into the depths of the recess. Its termination the feeble light did not enable us to see.

"Proceed," I said; "herein is the Amontillado. As for Luchesi—"

"He is an ignoramus," interrupted my friend, as he stepped unsteadily forward, while I followed immediately at his heels. In an instant he had reached the extremity of the niche, and finding his progress arrested by the rock, stood stupidly bewildered. A moment more and I had fettered him to the granite. In its surface were two iron staples, distant from each other about two feet, horizontally. From one of these depended a short chain, from the other a padlock. Throwing the links about his waist, it was but the work of a few seconds to secure it. He was too much astounded to resist. Withdrawing the key I stepped back from the recess.

"Pass your hand," I said, "over the wall; you cannot help feeling the nitre. Indeed it is *very* damp. Once more let me *implore* you to return.

No? Then I must positively leave you. But I must first render you all the little attentions in my power."

"The Amontillado!" ejaculated my friend, not yet recovered from his astonishment.

"True," I replied; "the Amontillado."

As I said these words I busied myself among the pile of bones of which I have before spoken. Throwing them aside, I soon uncovered a quantity of building stone and mortar. With these materials and with the aid of my trowel, I began vigorously to wall up the entrance of the niche.

I had scarcely laid the first tier of my masonry when I discovered that the intoxication of Fortunato had in a great measure worn off. The earliest indication I had of this was a low moaning cry from the depth of the recess. It was *not* the cry of a drunken man. There was then a long and obstinate silence. I laid the second tier, and the third, and the fourth; and then I heard the furious vibrations of the chain. The noise lasted for several minutes, during which, that I might hearken to it with the more satisfaction, I ceased my labours and sat down upon the bones. When at last the clanking subsided, I resumed the trowel, and finished without interruption the fifth, the sixth, and the seventh tier. The wall was now nearly upon a level with my breast. I again paused, and holding the flambeaux over the mason-work, threw a few feeble rays upon the figure within.

A succession of loud and shrill screams, bursting suddenly from the throat of the chained form, seemed to thrust me violently back. For a brief moment I hesitated—I trembled. Unsheathing my rapier, I began to grope with it about the recess; but the thought of an instant reassured me. I placed my hand upon the solid fabric of the catacombs, and felt satisfied. I reapproached the wall. I replied to the yells of him who clamoured. I reechoed—I aided—I surpassed them in volume and in strength. I did this, and the clamourer grew still.

It was now midnight, and my task was drawing to a close. I had completed the eighth, the ninth, and the tenth tier. I had finished a portion of the last and the eleventh; there remained but a single stone to be fitted and plastered in. I struggled with its weight; I placed it partially in its destined position. But now there came from out the niche a low laugh that erected the hairs upon my head. It was succeeded by a sad voice, which I had difficulty in recognizing as that of the noble Fortunato. The voice said—

"Ha! ha! ha!—he! he!—a very good joke indeed—an excellent jest. We will have many a rich laugh about it at the palazzo—he! he! he!—over our wine—he! he! he!"

"The Amontillado!" I said.

"He! he! he!—he! he! he!—yes, the Amontillado. But is it not getting late? Will not they be awaiting us at the palazzo, the Lady Fortunato and the rest? Let us be gone."

"Yes," I said "let us be gone."

"*For the love of god, Montresor!*"

"Yes," I said, "for the love of God!"

But to these words I hearkened in vain for a reply. I grew impatient. I called aloud—

"Fortunato!"

No answer. I called again—

"Fortunato!"

No answer still. I thrust a torch through the remaining aperture and let it fall within. There came forth in return only a jingling of the bells. My heart grew sick—it was the dampness of the catacombs that made it so. I hastened to make an end of my labour. I forced the last stone into its position; I plastered it up. Against the new masonry I re-erected the old rampart of bones. For the half of a century no mortal has disturbed them. *In pace requiescat*!

—1846

# Glossary

**Actual audience:** According to Rabinowitz, it is the "flesh-and-blood people" who read a text (compare *narrative audience* and *authorial audience*).

**Aesthetic distance:** The measure of difference between the horizon of expectations and what actually happens in a story.

**Affective fallacy:** According to Wimsatt and Beardsley, it is the incorrect method of analyzing a literary work based upon how it affects the reader (compare *intentional fallacy*).

**Alienation:** In Marxist theory, this is what workers in a capitalist system feel because they have no connection to or identity with the products they helped create.

**Androcentrism:** Giving precedence to the human male point of view.

**Antagonist:** Character who opposes the protagonist (could also be an object, feeling, etc.).

**Anterior narration:** A narrative position which precedes in time the situations and events being narrated (such as "You will kill your father and marry your mother"). This is the most rare type of narration (compare *intercalated narration*, *posterior narration* and *simultaneous narration*).

**Anthropocentrism:** The belief that the human being is the ultimate entity on our planet.

**Anthropomorphism:** Attributing human characteristics to nonhuman beings and things.

**Archetype:** Recurring myths, symbols, settings or characters that are based upon universal patterns of thought.

**Authorial audience:** The (hypothetical) readers that a writer imagines will read his or her text (compare *actual audience* and *narrative audience*).

**Authorial reading:** Reading a text as if we are members of the authorial audience that Rabinowitz describes.

**Base:** According to Marxist theory, it is the part of a society that includes the means and the relations of production (compare *superstructure*).
**Binary opposition:** A related pair of linguistic terms that are opposite in meaning.
**Bourgeoisie:** The wealthy owners and "ruling" class of a capitalist society (compare *proletariat*).
**Burkean parlor:** A theoretical room used as a metaphor to describe the unending nature of academic, philosophical and theoretical discourse. Just as conversation begins before you enter a never-ending party, and continues long after you leave, so too has intellectual dialogue begun before you entered the world and will continue long after you are gone.
**Capitalism:** An economic system in which the means of production are privately owned (compare *communism* and *socialism*).
**Center:** An underlying guiding principle—to a text, a philosophy, a belief system, etc.
**Central consciousness (central intelligence):** The consciousness through which a story is narrated.
**Characters:** The people in a story. One of three essential elements in a story (*setting* and *conflict* are the other two).
**Chinese Exclusion Act:** An 1882 U.S. law that prohibited the immigration of Chinese laborers.
**Climax:** In a fictional work, the final turning point and the point of highest interest, evoking the greatest emotional response in the reader.
**Coloniality of power:** Anibal Quijano's term to describe the social hierarchal structures that result from colonialism and continue long after colonization has officially ended.
**Colonialism:** The establishment of a colony or colonies in one territory by settlers from another territory, most often resulting in the exploitation of the colony's people and natural resources.
**Commodity:** A product or service that is produced by human labor and offered for sale.
**Commodity fetishism:** The process through which a commodity's value becomes disconnected from the amount of labor exerted to create that commodity, thus obscuring the exploitation inherent in a capitalist economy.
**Communism:** An economic system based upon the common ownership of the means of production (compare *capitalism* and *socialism*).
**Complication:** An entanglement that arises during the conflict of opposing forces.
**Compulsory heterosexuality:** The idea that societal mores and expectations make heterosexuality mandatory for persons of all sexual orientations.

**Conflict:** The primary struggle between two or more opposing forces. One of three essential elements in a story (*character* and *setting* are the other two).

**Conscious:** In Freudian terms, it refers to everything within our sphere of awareness (compare *unconscious*).

**Covert text:** The unwritten "text" that is suggested by a careful reading of the overt (written) text (compare *overt text*).

**Crisis:** The point when the opposing forces in a conflict clash in the decisive action on which the plot will turn.

**The Dawes Act:** An 1887 U.S. law that divided Native American reservation land into allotments given to individual Native Americans. Much of the remaining land was sold to white settlers.

**Decenter:** A method of textual analysis that disregards any preconceptions about the text's central idea, theme or "moral."

**Decolonization:** The undoing of all facets of colonialism.

**Deconstruction:** Derrida's method of textual analysis, based upon the belief that most of the facts we "know" are constructed rather than based on reality.

**Defamiliarization:** According to Viktor Shklovsky, it is the process of taking something familiar and "making it strange" through the use of poetic devices. By doing this, we are impelled to pay attention.

**Depthlessness:** According to Fredric Jameson, the loss of a deeper context within a work of art; this leads to a waning of affect.

**Desiring-machine:** Part of Deleuze and Guattari's reconception of the unconscious to represent desire as a natural, productive force rather than a lack to be suppressed.

**Dialectical materialism:** In Marxism theory, the belief that progress arises from a struggle between opposites.

**Dialogism:** Mikhail Bakhtin argues that all language is dialogic, or part of a dialogue between the speaker and the receiver, making the context of any utterance a necessary factor in determining its meaning.

*Différance*: A term coined by Jacques Derrida to illustrate that speech should not be considered better than written text at communicating through language.

**Discourse:** The presentation of the story events in a narrative.

**Discourse time:** The time it takes to narrate a fictional piece (compare *story time*).

**Double consciousness:** W.E.B. Du Bois' term to describe how African Americans navigate through white America behind a veil that hides their true selves.

**Dynamic character:** A character who changes throughout the course of the story (compare *static character*).

**Ecocide:** Destruction of the natural world.

**Ellipsis:** A narrative tempo in which story time corresponds to no discourse time, as in "five years later" or "we saw him again the next summer" (compare *summary*, *scene*, *exposition* and *stretch*).

**Emotional distance:** How far removed, emotionally, the narrator is from the events of a story. *Catcher in the Rye*: the narrator is currently institutionalized as he tells his story; *The Outsiders*: narrator is telling of a past traumatic event; *Diary of a Madman*: narrator telling the story as he's going insane (compare *physical distance* and *temporal distance*).

**Epiphany:** A quick flash of recognition in which the fundamental nature of something (often commonplace) is suddenly perceived.

**Essentialism:** the ascribing of multiple innate similarities to people based upon one shared trait (often race or ethnicity).

**Exposition (diegesis, carry, pause):** A narrative tempo in which discourse time corresponds to no forward movement of the story; common types of exposition are descriptions or narrative asides (compare *scene*, *summary*, *stretch* and *ellipsis*).

*Fabula:* all of the events that constitute a story (compare *syuzhet*).

**First-person narrator:** The narrator (I/we) is a character in the narrative he or she recounts.

**First-person observer narrator:** The first-person narrator is not an active participant in the narrative he or she recounts.

**First-person participant narrator:** The first-person narrator is an active participant in the narrative he or she recounts.

**Flashback:** When the narrator interrupts the narration to detail (usually in scene) events that happened in the past (compare *flash forward*).

**Flash forward:** When the narrator interrupts the narration to detail events that will happen in the future (compare *flashback*).

**Gaps:** Actions or descriptions of characters and settings that are not included in the written text and are therefore filled in through the reading experience.

**Gender performativity:** Judith Butler's term to illustrate that gender identity is a performative act rather than an inherent biological trait.

**Gynocriticism:** The study of women's literature from a female perspective, untainted by the traditional patriarchal perspective.

**Heteroglossia:** According to Mikhail Bakhtin, it is the simultaneous existence of many layers of language.

**Homosocial continuum:** A continuum between homosexuality and social relationships between persons of the same sex.

**Horizon of expectations:** What a reader expects to happen in a story, based upon the reader's understanding of genre and literary conventions and shaped by everything in the reader's world (compare *aesthetic distance*).

**Hybridity:** The blend of contradictory consciences existing within a person simultaneously. Homi Bhabha sees this as an inevitable consequence of colonization.

**Hyperreality:** Baudrillard's conception of our modern world where we are surrounded everywhere by simulated reality to conceal the true nature of our existence.

**Ideal reader:** That one hypothetical (and nonexistent) reader who would notice and understand everything (symbols, puns, hidden meanings, etc.) that an author puts into a text (compare *real reader* and *implied reader*).

**Ideological State Apparatus:** Institutions that covertly maintain and perpetuate the ideology of the privileged class (compare *Repressive State Apparatus*).

**Ideology:** A society's system of beliefs and mores that often guide economic and political policy.

**Imperialism:** One government's control over another area through force or economic, ideological or political influence.

**Implied author:** The (unreal) author suggested by a text. For example, the implied author of an adventure novel might be a rugged, outdoorsy type of person, while the person actually writing the text could be a shy, unassuming person living in his mother's basement (compare *real author* and *narrator*).

**Implied reader:** A hypothetical reader suggested by a text. For example, the implied reader of Stephanie Meyer's *Twilight* series would be young teen girls, while the person actually reading the text might be someone else entirely (compare *real reader* and *ideal reader*).

**Indian Removal Act:** An 1830 U.S. law authorizing the removal of Native American peoples from the South to land west of the Mississippi River. Its enactment led to the ethnic cleansing of the "Five Civilized Tribes" (Cherokee, Chickasaw, Choctaw, Muscogee-Creek and Seminole) and the resultant "Trail of Tears."

**Intercalated narration:** A type of narration whereby a narrating instance is temporally situated between two moments of the action, as in an epistolary or diary narrative ("The Yellow Wallpaper," *Diary of a Madman*, etc.). (Compare *anterior narration*, *posterior narration* and *simultaneous narration*.)

**Intentional fallacy:** According to Wimsatt and Beardsley, it is the incorrect method of analyzing a literary work based upon what the author intended the work to say or do (compare *affective fallacy*).

**Interpretive community:** A loosely formed group that shares similar strategies for interpreting a text.

**Langue:** According to Saussure, an overarching structural system (such as a language, or a genre of literature) (compare *parole*).

**Literariness:** According to Roman Jakobson, it is a text's form, style, and use of literary devices that "makes a given work a literary work."

**Logocentrism:** A term Derrida uses to highlight Western society's privileging of spoken language (logos) over written language (compare *phallocentrism*).

**Marginalization:** The social process of becoming or being made marginal (to relegate or confine to a lower social standing or outer limit or edge, as of social standing)

**Means of production:** The raw materials and non-human assets used in the manufacture of products (compare *mode of production* and *relations of production*).

**Metafiction:** Fiction that overtly addresses the act of fiction writing

**Metaphor:** A figurative comparison wherein a word or phrase is used in place of the actual thing it describes, as a means of suggesting a similarity between the two (compare *simile*).

**Metanarrative:** A grand narrative that explains and charts the history of an entity, an idea, a belief system, etc.

**Mode of production:** The means and the relations of production; in other words, it is everything that is used in the creation of a product—people, factories, tools, etc. (compare *means of production* and *relations of production*).

**Model minority:** A stereotype that views all Asian Americans as hardworking, passive, studious, etc. Such stereotypes find opposition because they lead to the inaccurate belief that all Americans of Asian descent are identical.

**Monologic narrator:** A narrator represented by a single voice or consciousness; it is the most common type of narrator (compare *polyphonic narrator*).

**Narratee:** The person to whom the narrator is telling his or her story; sometimes this is obvious, but often it is not.

**Narrative audience:** Those readers who are willing and able to accept the narrative situation presented in the story (compare *actual audience* and *authorial audience*).

**Narrative distance:** How far removed the telling of the story is from the events of the story (compare *emotional distance*, *physical distance* and *temporal distance*).

**Narrative tempo:** The speed at which a narrative is related (compare *pause*, *stretch*, *scene*, *summary* and *ellipsis*).

**Narrator:** The (fictional) person who tells the story; not the same as the *real author* or the *implied author*.

**Objectification:** An attitude that regards a person as a commodity or as an object for use, with insufficient regard for a person's personality.

**Overt text:** The written text as it appears on the page (compare *covert text*).

*Parole*: According to Saussure, a constituent part of a structural system, or *langue* (such as an individual word or sentence spoken within a system of language, or an individual short story within the entire genre classification—or system—of short stories or fiction) (compare *langue*).

**Pastiche:** An imitation of another's style without the mocking that is inherent in satire.

**Patriarchy:** Male dominated society (male-dominated in every way—politically, economically, socially and, especially, covertly through ideologies and societal beliefs, customs and mores).

**Pause:** see *exposition*.

**Perpetual foreigner:** The perception that Americans of Asian descent—regardless of their ancestry—are inherently foreign and thus unable to grow into "real" U.S. citizens.

**Phallocentrism (phallogocentrism):** Jacques Derrida's term used to suggest that Western language (and therefore Western thought) is dominated by the male perspective in its privileging of speech of writing (compare logocentrism).

**Physical distance:** How far removed the narrator is from the physical setting of the story events being recounted (compare *emotional distance* and *temporal distance*).

**Play:** According to Derrida, it is the step in a deconstructive reading results after we accept as equally valid all hierarchal possibilities within a text's binary oppositions.

**Plot:** A *causally-linked* chain of events.

**Point of view (perspective, focalization):** The perspective from which the story (discourse) is narrated.

**Polyphonic narrator:** A narrator represented by the interaction of several voices, consciousnesses, or world views, none of which has more authority than the others ("A Rose for Emily").

**Posterior narration:** A narrative position in which all of the story events have already taken place before the recounting of the story. This is, by far, the most common type of narration (compare *anterior narration*, *intercalated narration* and *simultaneous narration*).

**Postulated reader:** Another name for the implied reader.

**Proletariat:** The lower class workers exploited by the bourgeoisie in a capitalist society (compare *bourgeoisie*).

**Protagonist / Hero:** Main character who changes through the course of the story.

**Real author:** The person actually writing a text; should be distinguished from the *implied author* and, especially, the *narrator*.

**Real reader:** The person actually reading a text (compare *implied reader* and *ideal reader*).

**Reflection theory:** Theory based upon the belief that a society's superstructure reflects its economic base.

**Reification:** The process through which a human worker is viewed as a mere part of a larger factory machine.

**Relations of production:** The relationship between the workers and the factory or business owner (compare *means of production* and *mode of production*).

**Repressive State Apparatus:** Institutions that overtly maintain ideological control through force or through the implied threat of force (compare *Ideological State Apparatus*).

**Resolution (falling action):** The events following the climax.

**Rhizome:** Deleuze and Guattari's model of human thought based upon the botanical rhizome.

**Second-person narrator:** The narrator uses the second-person pronoun *you* to relate the events of the narrative.

**Scene (mimesis):** A narrative tempo in which story time is equal to discourse time (compare *summary, exposition, stretch* and *ellipsis*).

**Setting:** Where (and when) a story takes place. One of three essential elements in a story (*character* and *conflict* are the other two).

**Sign:** In structuralist theory, it is an individual word in a sentence; it is the combination of a word in a sentence (the signifier) and the understanding of what that word means (the signified) (compare *signified* and *signifier*).

**Signified:** In structuralist theory, it is the concept of what a word describes; together with the signifier, it makes up a sign (compare *sign* and *signifier*).

**Signifier:** In structuralist theory, it is a group of letters that comprises a word; it works together with the signified to make a sign (compare *sign* and *signified*).

**Signifyin(g):** A language performance in which what is said (or written) expresses a meaning other than its literal connotation.

**Simile:** A comparison in which two dissimilar things are juxtaposed to suggest a similarity between the two, usually introduced with a word such a "like" or "as" (compare *metaphor*).

**Simulacrum:** A representation that has no underlying reality (compare *simulation*).

**Simulation:** A representation or imitation of a real thing (compare *simulacrum*).

**Simultaneous narration:** A narration in which the discourse takes place at the same time as the story events being related in the discourse. (Moments of simultaneous can sometimes be found in intercalated narratives—"The Yellow Wallpaper," for example.) (Compare *anterior narration, intercalated narration* and *posterior narration*.)

**Social construction:** The concept that many of the things that people "know" or take to be "reality" are actually learned from a society's ideology. In other words, do we see and understand gender differences the way we do because these are real, biological differences, or because society, over time, has taught us that these gender differences exist?

**Socialism:** An economic system in which the means of production are owned or regulated by the community as a whole (compare *capitalism* and *communism*).

**Static character:** A character who remains the same throughout the course of the story.

**Story:** The actual events within the diegesis (fictional world/universe) of the story.

**Story time:** The (fictional) period of time in which the narrated events occur (compare *discourse time*).

**Stretch:** A narrative tempo in which discourse time is greater than the story time (compare *scene, exposition, summary* and *ellipsis*).

**Subaltern:** For Antonio Gramsci the subaltern are the disenfranchised proletariat; for Gayatri Spivak, they are the forgotten masses of the colonized lower class who have "limited or no access to cultural imperialism."

**Summary:** A narrative tempo in which story time is greater than the discourse time, as in "He sprinted to Donut World, bought a dozen bear claws, and scarfed them down before he had to go back to class." (compare *scene, exposition, stretch* and *ellipsis*).

**Superstructure:** According to Marxist theory, it is the part of a society that includes its culture, government, laws and rituals (compare *base*).

**Sympathetic character:** A character with whom the reader sympathizes.

**Syuzhet:** How the events of a story are arranged and presented in a literary work (compare *fabula*).

**Temporal distance:** The length of time between the story events and the recounting of those events (compare *emotional distance* and *physical distance*).

**Theme:** What the story is about, in a figurative sense.

**Thick description:** A detailed recounting that puts into context the recounted action or event.

**Third-person narrator:** The narrator is not a character in the events he or she recounts.

**Third-person limited (over the shoulder) narrator:** The third-person narrative is told from the perspective of one character.

**Third-person objective narrator:** A narrator who has access to all of the story's events, but does not know the thoughts of any character.

**Third-person omniscient narrator:** A narrator who has access to every character's thoughts and every action in the story's world.

**Transcendental signified:** Derrida's formal term for the center.

**Unhomeliness:** Homi Bhabha's term for a colonized subject's separation from both his or her original culture and the culture of the colonizing nation.

**Unreliable narrator:** A narrator who may in error in his or her understanding or report of events being recounted, either through naiveté, derangement or dishonesty, etc.

**Unsympathetic character:** A character with whom the reader actively doesn't sympathize.

**Waning of affect:** According to Jameson, the inability of an artwork (particularly from the postmodern period) to incite our emotions (compare *depthlessness*).

**Yellow peril:** A racist idea perpetuated in the late-nineteenth century (and continued well into the twentieth century) that suggested horrifying consequences of continued Asian immigration.

**Yellowface:** The portrayal of an Asian stage or movie character by a white actor wearing makeup and prosthetics in order to appear "Asian." While most people consider it to be extremely offensive, the practice has continued in the twenty-first century.

# Index

Abbey, Edward, 256, 265, 267
Achebe, Chinua, 182, 183-186, 193, 195, 196, 202, 208, 210, 230, 232
Acosta, Oscar Zeta, 217
actual audience, 159-160, 165, 301
Adachi, Jeff, 233
Adams, Abigail, 70, 72
Adorno, Theodor, 47, 54-56, 61, 66, 67
aesthetic distance, 156-157, 165, 301
affective fallacy, 13-14, 27, 150-152, 301
Africanism, 231
Afrocentricity, 207-208, 231
Alatas, Syed Hussein, 195, 197
alienation, 51, 55, 66, 301
Alighieri, Dante, 3, 5, 6, 62
allotment, 231, 303
Althusser, Louis, 47, 58-60, 66, 67, 171
anagnorisis, 97
androcentrism, 266, 301
anecdote, 177, 178
Angelou, Maya, 87, 201, 232
antagonist, 27, 157, 259, 264, 301
anterior narration, 102, 104, 106, 301
anthropocentrism, 258-259, 266, 301
anthropomorphism, 258-259, 266, 301

Anzaldúa, Gloria E., 81, 87, 217, 222, 235, 237, 242, 246
Aparicio, Frances, 217, 236
Apess, William, 223, 225, 228, 238
Appiah, Kwame Anthony, 202, 232
archetype, 25, 38-39, 44, 302
Aristotle, 2, 4, 6, 39, 55, 96, 97, 99-100
Arnold, Matthew, 3, 5, 6, 8
Asante, Molefi Kete, 207-208, 232
Ashcroft, Bill, 182, 188, 197
assimilation, 224, 231
authorial audience, 159-163, 165, 301
authorial intent, 10, 27, 159
authorial reading, 159-161, 163, 165, 302

Bacon, Francis, 3
Baker, Jr., Houston A., 202, 208, 210, 232
Bakhtin, Mikhail, 15, 16, 21-24, 27, 54, 61, 90, 126, 190, 303
Bal, Mieke, 96, 100, 101, 106, 108
Baraka, Amiri, 201
Barth, John, 128, 130, 142
Barthes, Roland, 40, 90, 91, 94-96, 105, 108, 111, 112, 115-116, 124, 128, 146
base, 53-54, 56-58, 66, 302
Bate, Jonathan, 265, 267

Baudrillard, Jean, 128, 136-137, 142-143, 144, 305
Baym, Nina, 87
Beardsley, Monroe, 8, 10-14, 27, 150-151, 159-160
Beauvoir, Simone de, 34, 70, 74, 75-78, 85, 87
Beckett, Samuel, 129, 141, 144
Bender, Frederic L., 267
Benjamin, Walter, 47, 54-56, 61, 66, 67
Bennett, Paula, 242, 252, 254
Bhabha, Homi K., 182, 190-191, 195, 197, 203, 305, 309
Biehl, Janet, 267
Bierce, Ambrose, 95-96, 103-104
binary opposition, 83, 93, 106, 116, 119, 122, 123, 124, 190, 302
Black Hawk, 223, 225, 228, 238
Bleich, David, 147, 157-159, 161, 164, 165
Bloom, Harold, 30, 126
Boal, Augusto, 47, 66, 67
Boccaccio, Giovanni, 5, 6, 99
Bodkin, Maud, 30, 39, 44, 45
Bookchin, Murray, 256, 262, 263, 267
Booth, Wayne C., 147, 149, 164, 166
Bourdieu, Pierre, 167, 173, 179
bourgeoisie, 50-51, 54, 56-58, 66, 302
Branch, Michael P., 256
Brecht, Bertolt, 47, 55, 65, 67
Brooks, Cleanth, 8, 28
Brown, Sterling Allen, 201
Buell, Lawrence, 256, 257, 263, 265, 269
Bulosan, Carlos, 210, 216, 234
Burkett, Paul, 267
Butler, Judith, 70, 242, 248-250, 252, 254, 304

Calderón, Héctor, 222, 236
Campbell, Joseph, 108
Campbell, SueEllen, 256
capitalism, 50-51, 62-65, 66, 131, 138-140, 184, 261-263, 302
Carby, Hazel V., 202, 232
Callahan, S. Alice, 223, 238

Carson, Rachel, 256, 265, 266, 267
de las Casas, Bartolomé, 223, 238
catharsis, 55, 97
center, 121, 124, 302
central consciousness, 27,32
de Certeau, Michel, 167, 173
Césaire, Aimé, 182, 184, 195, 197
Chan, Jeffery P., 210, 216
Chan, Sucheng, 217, 234
character, 2, 23-24, 27, 97, 98-99, 101-103
characterization, 2, 15, 27, 101-103, 157, 194-195
Chatman, Seymour, 96, 106, 108
Chávez, César, 217, 221
Chekhov, Anton, 10, 25-26, 83-84, 95-96, 175-177, 270-278
Cheung, King-Kok, 210, 217, 234
Chi, Lu (Lu Ji), 2, 4, 6
Chin, Frank, 210, 215, 216-217, 234
Chinese Exclusion Act, 212-213, 216, 231, 302
Chomsky, Noam, 31, 36, 91, 108, 117
Chopin, Kate, 74, 78-79, 83, 84, 161, 279-282
Chow, Rey, 210, 217, 232
Christian, Barbara, 202, 208-209, 210, 232
Chu, Louis, 211, 216, 236
Churchill, Ward, 223, 229
Cixous, Hélène, 70, 80, 85, 87, 242
climax, 27, 302
Cohn, Dorrit, 96
Coke, Allison Hedge, 223
Cokinos, Christopher, 256, 257
Coleridge, Samuel Taylor, 3, 5, 8, 32
colonialism, 183-186, 191, 192-193, 302
coloniality of power, 192-193, 196, 302
commodity, 56, 62, 64, 66, 259, 302, 306
commodity fetishism, 66, 138, 143, 302
communism, 48, 50, 59, 61, 63, 66

complication, 27, 302
compulsory heterosexuality, 246-247, 250, 251-252, 253, 302
condensation, 44
conflict, 27, 121-122, 303
conscious, 30-35
context, 10-13, 22-24, 149-152, 168-171,
Cook-Lynn, Elizabeth, 223, 226-228, 230, 238, 239
Cooke, Michael G., 201, 204-205, 210, 232
Copway, George, 223, 225, 228, 239
Coronado, Raúl, 222, 236
Cortázar, Julio, 130, 142, 144
covert text, 34, 42, 44, 79, 123, 230, 303
crisis, 27, 303
Culler, Jonathan, 100, 105, 109, 126

Dávila, Arlene, 217, 236
Dawes Act, 224, 231, 303
decenter, 121-122, 124, 135, 303
decolonization, 184, 192-193, 196, 303
deconstruction, 117-124, 140, 187, 189, 303
deep ecology, 261-262, 266
De la Campa, Román, 222, 236
defamiliarization, 18-21, 28, 155, 303
Deleuze, Gilles, 129, 134-136, 142, 144, 189, 303, 308
Deloria Jr., Vine, 223, 228-229, 239
depthlessness, 138-140, 141, 143, 303
Derrida, Jacques, 80, 111, 112, 117-124, 126, 129, 173, 189, 190, 208, 220, 242, 249, 254, 303, 306, 307, 309
desiring-machine, 135, 143, 303
deterritorialization, 135, 143
dialectical materialism, 50, 66, 303
dialogism, 22-23, 28, 303
diction, 15, 97
diegesis, 102-103, 106, 304
*différance*, 120-121, 124, 303

discourse: colonialist, 184, 185-186, 188, 193, 208; Foucault, 171-173, 177, 178, 188, 245; narratology, 19, 102-105, 106, 303
discourse time, 102-103, 106, 303
displacement, 33, 44
double consciousness, 196, 203, 205, 231, 303
dream work, 32, 44
Dryden, John, 3, 5, 6
Du Bois, W.E.B., 202, 203-204, 205, 232, 303
dynamic character, 27, 176, 303

Eagleton, Terry, 6, 47, 50, 61, 62-63, 66, 67, 130, 144, 159
Eastman, Charles A., 223, 225, 228, 239
Eco, Umberto, 93, 106, 109, 112, 124, 127, 128, 142, 144, 164, 165
ecocide, 261, 266, 303
ecofeminism, 259-260, 266
ecology, 256, 257, 259, 261-262, 265
ecosocialism, 261, 266
Egan, Gabriel, 266, 267
ego, 33, 41, 44
Ehrenreich, Barbara, 82, 87
Eikhenbaum, Boris, 15, 17-18, 21, 27, 52
Eliot, Thomas Stearnes, 8, 9, 27, 28
ellipsis, 102-103, 106, 304
Emerson, Ralph Waldo, 3, 256, 264, 267
emotional distance, 103, 106, 108, 304
Empson, Sir William, 8, 9-10, 12, 27, 28
Engels, Friedrich, 5, 47, 48-52, 54, 65, 68
Ensler, Eve, 70, 81, 85, 87
environmentalism, 266
epiphany, 27, 304
essentialism, 189-190, 196, 207-208, 211, 231, 253, 304
exposition, 102-103, 106, 304

*fabula*, 19-20, 28, 304
Faderman, Lillian, 242, 254
falling action, 27, 308
Faludi, Susan, 70, 82, 85, 87
Fanon, Frantz, 182, 184, 195, 197, 202, 233
first-person narrator, 27, 101-103, 106, 304
first-person observer, 101-103, 106, 304
first-person participant, 101-103, 106, 304
first wave (feminism), 74-76
Fish, Stanley, 147, 149-153, 155, 161, 164, 165
Flaccus, Quintus Horatius (Horace), 2, 4, 6, 97
flashback, 102, 106, 304
flash forward, 102, 106, 304
Flores, Juan, 217, 236
Flores, William V., 236
focalization, 101-103, 106, 307
Foucault, Michel, 111, 116-117, 124, 127, 128, 129, 144, 167, 171-173, 174, 177, 179, 182, 188-189, 190, 198, 220-221, 242, 244-245, 252, 254
Frankfurt School, 54-56, 65
free indirect discourse, 102
Freeman, Jo (Joreen), 70, 87
Freud, Sigmund, 30, 31-36, 41, 43-44, 45, 303
Freund, Elizabeth, 166
Friedan, Betty, 34, 70, 76-77, 85, 87
Fromm, Harold, 256, 258, 265, 268
Frye, Northrup, 28, 30, 39-41, 44, 45, 90, 127, 242
Fuller, Margaret, 256, 264, 267

Gadamer, Hans-Georg, 147, 153, 164
Gage, Matilda Joslyn, 70, 74, 84, 87
Gandhi, Leela, 197
Gallagher, Catherine, 167, 169, 173-174, 178, 179
gaps, 153-155, 161, 165, 304
Garrard, Glen, 256, 258, 265, 268
Gass, William H., 6, 144

Gates, Henry Louis, Jr., 202, 205-208, 210, 230, 233
Geertz, Clifford, 167, 173-174, 180
gender identity, 242, 249-250, 253
gender performativity, 248-250, 253, 304
Genette, Gérard, 96, 100-103, 105-106, 109
Gifford, Terry, 256
Gilbert, Sandra M., 85, 87
Gilman, Charlotte Perkins, 63-65, 74, 78, 83-84, 101, 105, 124
Gittings, Barbara, 242
Glotfelty, Cheryll, 256, 257-258, 263-264, 266, 268
Gouges, Olympe de, 5, 6, 70, 73-74, 84, 87
Gramsci, Antonio, 47, 56-58, 63, 65, 68, 182, 189, 309
Greenblatt, Stephen, 167, 168-171, 173, 177-178, 180
Greer, Germaine, 70, 87
Guattari, Félix, 128, 134-136, 142, 144, 303, 308
Gubar, Susan, 85, 87
Guevara, Ernesto, 197
Guillory, John, 167
Gukovsky, Grigory, 15
Gutenberg, Johannes, 5
gynocriticism, 78-80, 82, 86, 304

Habermas, Jürgen, 68, 128, 145
Halperin, David, 242, 252, 254
hamartia, 97
Harjo, Joy, 226, 239
Hassan, Ihab, 128, 129, 140-141, 142, 145
Hawkes, Terrence, 105, 109
Hawthorne, Nathaniel, 80, 96, 122-124, 162
Hay, Harry, 242, 243-244
Heidegger, Martin, 128, 153
Heise, Ursula K., 260, 268
hero (protagonist), 27, 40, 97, 111, 301, 307
heteroglossia, 23-24, 28, 304
Hocquenghem, Guy, 242, 252, 254

Holland, Norman Norwood, 45, 91, 109, 127, 147, 157-159, 161, 165, 166
Holub, Robert C., 164, 166
homosocial continuum, 247-248, 253, 304
homosocial desire, 247-248
hooks, bell, 70, 88, 202, 233
Hopkins, Sarah Winnemucca, 223, 228, 239
Horace, 2, 4, 6, 97
horizon of expectations, 155-157, 165, 301, 304
Horkheimer, Max, 47, 54-56, 66, 67
Howarth, William, 256
Hsieh, Liu (Liu Xie), 2, 4, 6
Husserl, Edmund, 15, 17, 117, 153
Huyssen, Andreas, 145
Hwang, David Henry, 210, 215, 216, 230, 234
hybridity, 190-191, 196, 203, 305
hyperreality, 130, 136-137, 143, 305

id, 33, 41, 44
ideal reader, 159, 165, 305
Ideological State Apparatus, 58-60, 66, 305
ideology, 52, 56-63, 65, 66, 116, 137, 138-140, 159-161, 172-173, 244-248, 250, 258-261, 305
imperialism, 184, 188-193 195, 196, 198, 305
implied author, 141, 149, 159-161, 165, 305
implied reader, 101, 153-155, 164, 165, 166, 305
in-betweenness, 190-191, 196
Indian Removal Act, 224, 228, 231, 305
indigenousness, 192-193, 226-227, 231
intentional fallacy, 10-13, 15, 27, 150, 160, 305
intercalated narration, 102, 104, 106, 305

interpretive community, 152-153, 155, 165, 305
Irigaray, Luce, 35, 70, 80-81, 85, 88, 242
Iser, Wolfgang, 147, 153-155, 161, 164, 166

Jakobson, Roman, 90, 91, 94-96, 305
James, Henry, 3, 4-5, 10
Jameson, Fredric, 47, 61-64, 66, 68, 128, 130, 138-140, 142-143, 145, 303, 310
Jauss, Hans-Robert, 147, 153, 155-157, 161, 164, 166
Jencks, Charles, 128, 129-130, 140
Ji, Lu, 2, 4, 6
Johnson, B.S., 145
Johnson, Samuel, 5
Jong, Erica, 88
Jung, Carl Gustav, 30, 35, 38-39, 43-44, 45
Justice, Daniel Heath, 223, 229, 240

Kameny, Frank, 242
Kelsey, Penelope Myrtle, 227, 229, 240
Kiberd, Declan, 182, 191, 195, 198
Kingston, Maxine Hong, 210, 215, 216, 230, 234
Kolodny, Annette, 80, 85, 88
Koshy, Susan, 210, 217, 234, 235
Krafft-Ebing, Richard, 244, 254
Kristeva, Julia, 30, 35, 44, 70, 80, 88, 106, 109
Kroeber, Karl, 224, 240, 265, 268
Krupat, Arnold, 223, 226, 229, 240

Lacan, Jacques, 30, 35, 36-38, 44, 45, 190
*langue*, 92, 96, 305
Laó-Montes, Augustín, 236
de las Casas, Bartolomé, 223, 238
late capitalism, 66, 138-140, 143
de Lauretis, Teresa, 242, 252, 256
Leavis, Frank Raymond, 8, 29

Lenin, Vladimir Ilyich, 21, 52, 58, 184, 195, 198
Lentricchia, Frank, 29
lesbian continuum, 246, 253
lesbian existence, 246, 252, 253, 255
Lévi-Strauss, Claude, 38, 40, 61, 91, 94-96, 105, 106, 124, 224, 240
Lewis, C. S., 29, 147
Li, David Leiwei, 210, 217
Limón, José, 236
Lincoln, Kenneth, 226, 240
Linderman, Frank B., 228, 240
literariness, 19-21, 28, 305
logocentrism, 120, 124, 306, 307
London, Jack, 264, 268
Longinus, Dionysius Cassius, 2, 4, 6
Lothe, Jakob, 96, 106, 109
Love, Glen A., 256, 257, 259, 265, 268
Löwy, Michael, 256, 261, 265
Lukács, György, 47, 53-54, 57, 61, 65, 68
Lundquist, Suzanne Evertsen, 226, 240
Lyotard, Jean-François, 128, 130-134, 136, 142, 145

Macaulay, Catharine, 5, 6, 70, 72, 74, 84, 88
Mailloux, Steven J., 147, 166
de Man, Paul, 126
Mannoni, Octave, 198
Marcuse, Herbert, 35, 47, 54, 61, 66, 68
marginalization, 75-76, 82-83, 85, 139, 178, 183, 196, 207, 208, 218, 242, 253, 260, 306
Martin, Del, 242, 243
Marx, Karl, 47-52, 65, 68
Matthews, John Joseph, 225, 226, 228, 240
Mauron, Charles, 30, 35-36, 43, 44
Mayakovsky, Vladimir, 15, 17-18, 21, 27
Mbembe, Achille, 198
McDowell, Deborah E., 202, 208, 233

McGann, Jerome, 167, 178, 180
McHale, Brian, 128, 130, 145
means of production, 50, 66, 302, 306, 308, 309
Medvedev, Pavel, 15, 21-22, 27
Meeker, Joseph W., 259, 265, 268
Memmi, Albert, 184, 195, 198
melody, 97
metafiction, 141-142, 143, 306
metanarrative, 130-134, 143, 306
Mignolo, Walter D., 182, 192, 193, 195, 198, 222, 237
Miller, J. Hillis, 126, 127
Millet, Kate, 70, 79, 82, 85, 88, 242
mimesis, 41, 106, 308
mirror stage, 37, 44
mode of production, 50, 53, 62, 64, 66, 306, 308
model minority, 214-215, 231, 306
modern period, 56, 129-130, 139, 206
Momaday, N. Scott, 226, 228, 240
monologic narrator, 101, 107, 306
Montaigne, Michel de, 3, 5, 7
Montrose, Louis A., 167, 178, 180
Morrison, Toni, 201, 208-209, 210, 230, 233
Morton, J. Sterling, 256
Morton, Timothy, 256, 266, 268
Muir, John, 256
Muni, Bharata, 3, 5, 7

Næss, Arne, 256, 262, 268
narratee, 43, 101, 105, 126, 164, 165, 307
narrator, 24, 27, 101-103, 104-106, 141-142, 149, 185, 304, 305, 307, 308, 309
narrative audience, 159, 165, 301, 307
narrative distance, 41, 106, 306
narrative tempo, 102-103, 306
Neihardt, John G., 223, 228, 240, 266
Nelson, Robert M., 224, 229, 240
neocolonialism, 196
narrative tempo, 102-103, 106, 304, 306, 308, 309

Ng, Fae Myenne, 235
Nietzsche, Friedrich, 128, 248

objectification, 7, 85, 306
Oboler, Suzanne, 217, 222, 237
O'Connor, James, 268
Occom, Samson, 225, 228
Okada, John, 211, 216, 235
Omi, Michael, 235, 237
Ong, Walter, 166
Orientalism, 186-188, 196
Othering, 75-77, 196, 230
overt text, 44, 79, 123, 303

Paglia, Camille, 70, 88
*parole*, 92, 305, 306
pastiche, 138-140, 142, 143, 307
patriarchy, 79, 84, 85, 260, 307
pause, 102-103, 106, 309
Pavić, Milorad, 143, 145
Paz, Octavio, 217, 221, 237
Pérez Firmat, Gustavo, 217, 224, 237
peripeteia, 97
perspective, 27, 101, 307
perpetual foreigner, 211-212, 215, 231, 307
phallocentrism, 85, 120, 126, 306, 307
Phelan, James, 147, 164, 166
Phillips, Dana, 256, 268
physical distance, 106, 304, 306, 307, 309
pioneers (feminism), 70, 71-74
Pizan, Christine de, 70, 71, 84, 88
Plato, 2, 4, 7, 9, 120
plot, 27, 39, 63, 97-100, 106
Poe, Edgar Allan, 44, 101, 161-163, 283-287
point of view, 27, 101, 307
Pokagon, Simon, 228, 241
polyphonic narrator, 101, 106, 306, 307
Pope, Alexander, 3, 5, 7
posterior narration, 102, 104, 106, 303, 305, 307, 308
postmodern period, 129-130
postulated reader, 165, 307
Poulet, Georges, 147, 166

power, Foucault and, 171-172, 176, 177, 178, 182, 189, 145
coloniality of, 192-193, 195, 196
power-knowledge, 245, 253
Prashar, Sadhana, 7
proletariat, 50, 54, 56-57, 67, 189, 302, 307
Pulitano, Elvira, 227, 229, 241
Prince, Gerald, 96, 100, 101, 106, 109, 147, 164
projection, 33, 44
Propp, Vladimir, 96, 96-99, 100, 105-106, 109
protagonist, 27, 40, 97, 111, 301, 307
Pruitt-Igoe housing project, 129, 142
Pynchon, Thomas, 129, 130, 142

Quijano, Anibal, 182, 192-193, 195, 198, 237, 302

Rabasa, José, 224, 237
Rabinowitz, Peter, 47, 159-164
Rajashekhara, 5
Ransom, John Crowe, 8, 9, 27, 29
real author, 307
real reader, 102, 148, 159, 165, 307
reflection theory, 53-54, 66, 307
reification, 51, 59, 62, 65, 66, 307
relations of production, 50, 53, 66, 302, 308
Repressive State Apparatus, 60, 66, 308
resolution, 27, 122, 308
rhizome, 135-136, 140, 143, 308
Rich, Adrienne, 242, 246-247
Richards, Ivor Armstrong, 8, 9-10, 14, 27, 29, 147, 149-150
Ridge, John Rollin, 223, 228, 241
Riffaterre, Michael, 147
Rimmon-Kenan, Shlomith, 102, 106, 109
Robbe-Grillet, Alain, 142, 145
Rorty, Richard, 128, 145
Rosenblatt, Louise, 147, 149-150, 151, 164, 166
Rowlandson, Mary, 71, 84, 88

Said, Edward Wadie, 182, 186-188, 190-192, 195, 196, 198, 216, 235
Saldívar, José David, 222
Saldivar, Ramón, 222, 238
Sánchez, George I., 217, 221, 238
Sandoval, Anna Marie, 238
Saporta, Marc, 130, 142, 145
Sarkar, Saral, 262, 268
Sartre, Jean-Paul, 58, 61, 66, 68, 75
de Saussure, Ferdinand, 90, 91-95, 97, 105, 109, 112, 124, 305, 306
scene, 102-102, 106, 309
Scholes, Robert, 109
second wave (feminism), 71, 76-81
Sedgwick, Eve Kosofsky, 242, 247-252, 255
Septo, Robert B., 210, 253
setting, 263, 266-267, 302, 303, 304, 308
sexual identity, 248-251, 253
Shakespeare's sister, 74-76
Sheng, Bi, 5
Shiva, Vandana, 256, 260, 268
Shklovsky, Viktor, 15, 17-20, 27, 52, 105, 109, 302
Shor, Ira, 64
Showalter, Elaine, 70, 78-79, 82, 85, 98
Sidney, Sir Philip, 3, 5, 7, 8
sign, 92-93, 106, 120, 206, 306
signified, 92-93, 106, 120, 140, 206, 306
signifier, 92-93, 106, 120, 140, 206, 306
signifyin(g), 205-206, 230, 231, 232, 309
Silko, Leslie Marmon, 226, 229, 241
simulacrum, 130, 137, 142, 143, 144, 309
simulation, 136-137, 142, 143, 309
simultaneous narration, 102, 104, 106, 302, 305, 307, 309
Slovic, Scott, 256
social construction, 76, 80, 85, 253, 308
socialism, 50, 55, 261

social ecology, 262-263
Sollors, Werner, 202, 222, 238
Soper, Kate, 256, 265, 269
Spivak, Gayatri Chakravorty, 184, 188-190, 195, 199, 207, 211, 309
static character, 27, 176, 232, 303. 309
Stavans, Ilan, 217, 222, 238
Steinem, Gloria, 70, 88
story, 102-103, 106, 309
story time, 102-103, 106, 308, 309
stretch, 102-103, 106, 309
subaltern, 188-190, 195, 196, 198, 199, 201, 207, 237, 309
sublimation, 36, 44
Sui Sin Far, 210, 216, 235
summary, 102-103, 106, 309
superego, 33, 41, 44
superstructure, 53-54, 56-58, 66, 309
sympathetic character, 27, 309
Syphers, Judy, 70, 88
*syuzhet*, 19-20, 28, 309

Tan, Amy, 210, 215, 216, 230
Tarrant, Shira, 71, 88
Tausk, Viktor, 30
temporal distance, 102, 103, 106, 108, 126, 309
Theophrastus, 4
Thion'o, Ngũgĩ wa, 195, 199
thick description, 174, 177, 178, 309
third-person narrator, 101-104, 106-107, 309
third wave (feminism), 71, 81-82, 85, 89
Thoreau, Henry David, 256, 264, 266, 267, 269
Tobin Lahusen, Kay, 242
Todorov, Tzvetan, 96, 99-100, 105, 109
Tomashevsky, Boris, 15, 18
Tompkins, Jane P., 164, 166
Tong, Rosemarie, 89
transcendental signified, 121, 124, 309
transference, 45

Trotsky, Leon, 20, 21, 22, 53, 66, 68
Tynyanov, Yury, 15

unconscious, 30, 31-34, 35-38, 43-44, 46, 56, 60, 61-63, 66, 76, 112, 115, 154, 171, 247
unhomeliness, 191, 196, 310
unreliable narrator, 104-105, 106, 132, 149, 309
unsympathetic character, 27, 310

Vattimo, Gianni, 68, 145
Veeser, Harold Aram, 169, 178, 180
Vizenor, Gerald, 223, 226, 229, 241
Voloshinov, Valentin, 15, 21-22, 27
Vonnegut, Kurt, 142

Walker, Rebecca, 70, 80, 85, 89
Wand, David Hsin-fu, 210, 216, 235
waning of affect, 138-139, 143, 303, 310
Warner, Michael, 242, 252, 255
Warren, Robert Penn, 8, 28
Warrior, Robert Allen, 223, 229, 241
Weaver, Jace, 223, 229, 241
*Wenfu* 2, 4, 6
West, Cornel, 202, 233

White, Hayden, 167, 173, 180
Wilde, Oscar, 3, 8, 248, 251
Williams, Raymond, 167, 183, 256, 265
Wimsatt, Jr., W.K., 8, 10-14, 27, 29, 150, 160, 301, 305
Wittgenstein, Ludwig, 129, 143
Wittig, Monique, 242, 255
Wolf, Naomi, 70, 81, 85, 89
Wollstonecraft, Mary, 5, 7, 73-74, 76, 84, 89
Womack, Craig S., 223, 229, 241
Wong, Sau-ling Cynthia, 210, 217, 235
Woolf, Virginia, 11, 68, 70, 74-75, 78, 80, 85, 89
Wordsworth, William, 4, 6, 7, 267
Wright, Will, 105, 110
Wright, Richard, 68, 202, 204-206, 209
Wurtzel, Elizabeth, 89

Yamamoto, Hisaye, 211
Yamanaka, Lois-Ann, 210
yellow peril, 213, 231, 310
yellowface, 214, 231, 310
Young Man, Alfred, 233

Zimmerman, Bonnie, 242, 246
Zitkala-Ša, 223, 225, 228, 241
Žižek, Slavoj, 30, 68-69, 127, 129, 146
Zunshine, Lisa, 147

www.ingramcontent.com/pod-product-compliance
Lightning Source LLC
Chambersburg PA
CBHW020331240426
43665CB00043B/219